45.00

D0221040

1996

Dante's
Political Purgatory

John A. Scott

Colorado Christian University
Library
180 S Garrison
Lakewood, Colorado 80226

University of Pennsylvania Press

Philadelphia

Copyright © 1996 by the University of Pennsylvania Press
All rights reserved
Printed in the United States of America

Library of Congress Cataloging-in-Publication Data

Scott, John A. (John Alfred), 1932–
    Dante's political Purgatory / John A. Scott.
        p.   cm. — (Middle Ages series)
Includes bibliographical references and index.
ISBN 0-8122-3346-8 (alk. paper)
1. Dante Alighieri, 1265–1321.   Purgatorio.   2. Dante Alighieri, 1265–1321—Political and
social views.   3. Politics in literature.   I. Title.   II. Series.
PQ4448.S28   1996
851'.1—dc20   95-43007
                                                                                    CIP

Contents

Abbreviations   vii

Preface   ix

Part One: Dante's Politics   I

Chapter 1: Dante's Political Experience (1265–1302)   3

Chapter 2: Dante's Political Experience: Exile and Conversion (1302–1305)   21

Chapter 3: *Exul Inmeritus* (1305–1321)   36

Part Two: Dante's *Purgatorio*   61

Introduction to Part Two   63

Chapter 4: Cato: A Pagan Suicide in Purgatory   69

Chapter 5: Manfred and Bonconte   85

Chapter 6: The Sordello Episode (*Purgatorio* VI–VIII)   96

Chapter 7: The Dream and the Entrance to Purgatory (*Purgatorio* IX–X)   128

Chapter 8: The Poem's Center (*Purgatorio* XII–XVIII)   144

Chapter 9: The She-Wolf and the Shepherds (*Purgatorio* XIX–XX)   158

Chapter 10: The Apocalypse (*Purgatorio* XXIX–XXXIII)   179

Conclusion   212

Notes   215

Bibliography   269

Index   285

Abbreviations

Aen.	Virgil. *Aeneid*. H. Rushton Fairclough, ed. Cambridge, Mass.-London: Harvard University Press and William Heinemann, 2 vols., 1953.
Benvenuto	Benvenuti de Rambaldis de Imola. *Comentum super Dantis Aldagherij Comoediam*. G. F. Lacaita, ed. Florence: Barbèra, 5 vols., 1887.
Bosco-Reggio	Dante. *La Divina Commedia*. U. Bosco and G. Reggio, eds. Florence: Le Monnier, 3 vols., 1979.
Buti	*Commento di Francesco da Buti sopra la Divina Commedia*. C. Giannini, ed. Pisa: Nistri, 3 vols., 1858–1862.
Compagni, *Cronica*	Dino Compagni. *Cronica*. G. Luzzatto, ed. Turin: Einaudi, 1968.
CDD	*Codice diplomatico dantesco*. R. Piattoli, ed. Florence: Gonnelli, 1950.
City of God	Augustine of Hippo. *The City of God Against the Pagans*. G. E. McCracken et al., eds. and trans. Cambridge, Mass.-London: Harvard University Press and William Heinemann, 1972.
Conv.	Dante. *Convivio*. In *Opere minori*, vol. 1: Part 2, 3-885. C. Vasoli, ed. Milan-Naples: Ricciardi, 1988.
DVE	Dante. *De Vulgari Eloquentia*. In *Opere minori*, vol. 2, 26–237. P. V. Mengaldo, ed. Milan-Naples: Ricciardi, 1979.
Ecl.	Dante and Giovanni del Virgilio *Egloghe*. In *Opere minori*, vol. 2, 645–89. E. Cecchini, ed. Milan-Naples: Ricciardi, 1979.
ED	*Enciclopedia Dantesca*. U. Bosco et al., eds. Rome: Istituto dell'Enciclopedia Italiana, 6 vols., 1970–1978.
Ep.	Dante. *Epistole*. In *Opere minori*, vol. 2, 505–643. A. Frugoni and G. Brugnoli, eds. Milan-Naples: Ricciardi, 1979.

Giacalone	Dante. *La Divina Commedia*. G. Giacalone, ed. Rome: Signorelli, 3 vols., 1968–69.
Inf.	Dante. *Inferno*. G. Petrocchi, ed. Milan: Mondadori, 1966.
MGH	Monumenta Germaniae historica.
Mon.	Dante. *Monarchia*. In *Opere minori*, vol. 2, 280–503. B. Nardi, ed. Milan-Naples: Ricciardi, 1979.
Ottimo	*L'Ottimo commento della Divina Commedia: testo inedito d'un contemporaneo di Dante* [Andrea Lancia]. A. Torri, ed. 3 vols. Pisa: Capurro, 1827–1829.
Par.	Dante. *Paradiso*. G. Petrocchi, ed. Milan: Mondadori, 1967.
Pézard	Dante Alighieri. *Oeuvres complètes. Traduction et commentaires par André Pézard*. Paris: Gallimard, 1965.
Phar.	Lucan. *The Civil War ("Pharsalia")*. J. D. Duff, ed. Cambridge, Mass.-London: Harvard University Press and William Heinemann, 1977.
PL	*Patrologiae cursus completus. Series Latina*. J.-P. Migne, ed. 221 vols. Paris: Garnier, 1844–1864.
Purg.	Dante. *Purgatorio*. G. Petrocchi, ed. Milan: Mondadori, 1967.
Rime	Dante. *Rime*. In *Opere minori*, vol. 1: Part 2, 249–552. G. Contini, ed. Milan-Naples: Ricciardi. 1984.
Sapegno	Dante. *La Divina Commedia*. N. Sapegno, ed. Milan-Naples: Ricciardi, 1957.
S. Th.	Aquinas, *Summa Theologica*. De Rubeis, Billuart et al., eds. Turin: Marinetti, 6 vols., 1932.
Villani, *Cronica*	Giovanni Villani, *Nuova Cronica*. G. Porta, ed. Parma: Ugo Guanda, 3 vols., 1990.
VN	Dante. *Vita Nuova*. In *Opere minori*, vol. 1: Part 1, 3–247. D. De Robertis, ed. Milan-Naples: Ricciardi, 1984.

Preface

Dante's Political Purgatory was conceived as a whole in two parts: a political biography of Dante Alighieri followed by a detailed analysis of the political thread that runs throughout his *Purgatorio*. The first part offers something otherwise unavailable in English: a sketch of the poet's experience of politics from his birth in a Guelf commune to his death after twenty years of exile and the way this experience is inextricably bound up with his writings. The latter were for the most part composed during that exile, when Dante virtually never ceased proclaiming the need to accept the divine ordering of the world under God's two representatives on earth, the Pope supreme in the spiritual sphere and the Emperor supreme in the political realm.

The second, major section leads to the inescapable conclusion that the *Purgatorio* was inspired in large measure by the lesson drawn by the poet from Henry VII's attempts (1310–1313) to restore imperial power and authority in Italy. The lesson of those four years does not imply merely a denunciation of the causes for the failure of Henry's enterprise: it includes the immense hopes aroused in the poet's breast by that same enterprise, which appeared to him as proof that his political ideal was no utopian vision but a para-edenic state that could be realized on earth. Henry's failure stood as a supreme warning to contemporary humanity and its leaders, but it could also be seen as an incitement to abandon the Dark Wood of spiritual and political anarchy and to achieve God's purpose for humanity on earth.

Our understanding of the second *cantica* of Dante's masterpiece is partial and fragmentary without this historical-political approach. When critics have spoken of Dante's *Purgatorio* as representing a mood of melancholy and nostalgia (e.g., *Purg.* VIII. 1–6), they have tended to stress the traditional view that the second *cantica* is the most "human" section of the *Comedy*, where artists and poets come to the fore. While not denying the element of truth contained in such an appraisal, the present study wishes to redress the critical balance by highlighting the *Purgatorio*'s lifeblood, which is to be found in the desperate desire for purification felt by the poet—not only as a vital moment in his personal experience of the afterlife but also as a necessary and urgent reformation for the whole of humanity *on earth*.

It is undoubtedly possible to read the *Inferno* without giving too much thought to Dante's political worldview. The main political message concerns the poet's own exile and, more particularly, Florence's suicidal state, although at the very beginning the coupling of Aeneas with St. Paul (*Inf.* II. 13–30) and at the end the infernal trinity of Judas, Brutus, and Cassius should make the reader reflect on the poet's belief in the divinely-willed establishment of the Roman Empire and the Christian Church. This belief was accompanied by his passionate conviction that humanity's well-being could only be assured through total collaboration between those two supreme authorities.

As I shall try to demonstrate, however, such a reading ignores a major thread in the basic allegory of the poem: namely, Virgil's role, which is to lead the pilgrim through not only Hell but also Purgatory—a pagan guide in this most Christian realm!—to the Earthly Paradise, which represents the happiness attainable by humanity in this life. In the *Comedy*, there are in fact *two*—not three—guides for the pilgrim's conquest of both earthly and eternal happiness: Virgil, who in this respect mirrors the Emperor's role in the world, and Beatrice, whose function in the poem reflects that of the ideal spiritual guide on earth—the Church, led by the Supreme Pontiff (*Mon.* III. xv. 7–10).

That limited approach is, moreover, impossible when we arrive at the *Purgatorio*, where the whole *cantica* is shot through with the vital message found at the heart of the poem and stated most explicitly at its very center, in the fiftieth canto (*Purg.* XVI. 106–8): that God has given humanity two luminaries to light up its dual path to salvation, the true way to happiness in this world (the Emperor) and the way to blessedness in the next life (the Pope). While the political focus highlights the weakness of the Empire in the *Purgatorio* and the corruption of the Church in the *Paradiso*, that same central section in the second *cantica* gives us the definitive diagnosis reaffirmed at the end of Dante's poem (*Par.* XXVII. 139–41). There, Beatrice tells Dante that, since the Emperor is not allowed to govern the world as God wills, humanity—like the pilgrim—is now lost in the dark wood of error and destruction. The tragic state of the world has been wrought by greed, the she-wolf that has turned even the shepherds into wolves (ll. 55–57).

From the very first canto of *Purgatorio*, with the astonishing pagan presence of Republican Rome in the figure of Cato of Utica, to the end of the poem, with its equally astonishing absence of contemporary church-men, the political thread is an essential element in the understanding of the overall message that awakened Dante's sense of mission and inspired the writing of the greatest poem of the Christian Middle Ages. As its title implies, the present study focuses on the *Comedy*'s central section in the conviction that its political/religious discourse echoes and reverberates throughout the poem, and that a better understanding of its message will lead to a deeper appreciation of the whole.

It remains for me to express my profound gratitude for the invaluable help and support I have received from Charles Till Davis, my wife, and Lorenzo Polizzotto, whose critique and cogent suggestions made this book less defective than it would otherwise have been. To Anna Laura and Giulio Lepschy I owe an immense debt of gratitude, for without their generous hospitality I should not have been able to carry out much essential research.

Note

Quotations from Dante's *Comedy* are taken from *La commedia secondo l'antica vulgata*, edited by Giorgio Petrocchi, 4 vols. (Milan: Mondadori, 1966–1967). Editions used of Dante's other writings are found under the appropriate heading (*Conv.*, *DVE*, *Ecl.*, *Ep.*, *Mon.*, *Rime*, *VN*) in the list of abbreviations. Translations of all texts quoted are my own unless otherwise indicated.

JOHN A. SCOTT
University of Western Australia

PART ONE

——————

DANTE'S POLITICS

I

Dante's Political Experience
(1265–1302)

TO UNDERSTAND DANTE'S POLITICAL THOUGHT, it is essential to remember that the Florentine poet gave his full allegiance to a creed that claimed to govern the totality of human experience. The Christian Church to which he belonged attempted to exercise control over every facet of the lives of the men and women entrusted to its care.[1] So, to reach even a partial understanding of Dante's thought, we must jettison our own experience of politics in modern democracies, where the "art of government" is too often deemed an abstruse science, and everyday political affairs are regarded with disfavor as something largely devoid of justice and morality. Nothing could be further removed from Dante's all-embracing faith than the post-medieval tendency to divorce the various spheres of human activity, a result of the increasing fragmentation of knowledge and the way men and women interpret their beliefs and experiences.

Dante Alighieri was born in May 1265, during a virtual state of civil war in Italy. This offshoot of the tragic struggle waged between the Empire and the Papacy in Western Europe reached its climax in the thirteenth century and fueled the rivalries and dissensions endemic to the Italian peninsula.[2] Historians employ useful shorthand to describe a highly complex situation when they refer to this struggle as the conflict between Guelfs and Ghibellines. The term "Guelfs" denotes supporters of the Papacy, as opposed to the Ghibellines, who championed the Empire. Such clear-cut distinctions, however, cannot be applied to the realities of thirteenth-century Italian politics without gross oversimplification.

The terms "Guelf" and "Ghibelline" originated at the time of the rebellion of the Welf, Henry, duke of Bavaria after the election of Conrad to the imperial throne in 1138. Eventually exported to Italy, they were italianized as *guelfo* and *ghibellino*. According to Machiavelli, writing in the sixteenth century (*Istorie fiorentine* I. 21), this split first took place in 1167 during Frederick Barbarossa's campaign in Tuscany. The fourteenth-century chronicler Giovanni Villani, however, ascribes their adoption to the year 1215 (*Cronica* VI. 38) and points out that the factions were already in existence. According to both Villani and Dante (*Inf.* XXVIII. 106–8; *Par.* XVI. 136–47), the murder of Buondelmonte de' Buondelmonti on Easter Sunday 1215 by members of the Amidei clan brought matters to a head in Florence.

Since the government of the Florentine Commune at the time supported the Emperor Otto IV Welf, the Amidei with other enemies of the Buondelmonti formed the "Party of the Ghibelline or Swabian," thus indicating their support for Otto's rival, Frederick II Hohenstaufen. The choice of this vendetta episode by Villani, Dante, and Dino Compagni as "the cause and beginning of the accursed Guelf and Ghibelline parties in Florence" is significant (Villani, ibid.; cf. Compagni, *Cronica* I. 2). Acted out at the base of the statue of Mars, the murder exemplified a curse laid on the city by its former patron, the pagan god of war (*Inf.* XIII. 147–50), minimizing any ideological element in the conflict.

It is, however, at a moment when the struggle between Empire and Papacy was at its height that we find the first documented use of the terms "Guelf" and "Ghibelline" (*Annales Florentini* II, for the year 1242). And as the Guelf faction triumphed in Florence, so Siena and Pisa, its traditional rivals, remained staunchly Ghibelline. At first the conflict seemed to involve chiefly the "noble" families of the Florentine Commune. A new and decisive element was introduced in 1244, when the Ghibellines made overtures to win the support of the *popolo* by inviting the leaders of the seven major guilds to join the city councils. The experiment was soon abandoned. Six years later, however, the *popolo* seized control of the city, while the nobles were engaged in their customary feuds, at the battle of Figline in September 1250. That same year saw the death of the formidable emperor Frederick II, *stupor mundi*, who had been solemnly deposed by Innocent IV at the Council of Lyon in 1245. The exiled Guelfs returned to Florence (*Inf.* X. 49–50), where both sides were forced to take stock of the new political situation in Florence. Alongside the Council of the Commune a new General Council (with representatives from the city's six wards or *sesti*) was established under the significantly designated "Captain of the People." As John Najemy observes: "For the first time in the history of the city, the legitimacy of communal government depended on the consent and representation of local and professional associations. For several years the *popolo* kept members of both the Guelf and Ghibelline parties out of important office."[3]

This rule of the *Primo popolo*—celebrated as a golden age by later chroniclers—lasted until the disastrous defeat suffered by the Florentine Guelfs in September 1260 at Montaperti (*Inf.* X. 83–93; XXXII. 76–111). At first the *popolo* remained neutral, seeking above all a peaceful solution to the Guelf-Ghibelline struggle. In 1258, however, the Ghibellines attempted to seize power "against the *popolo*" (Villani, *Cronica* VII. 65), and leaders like Schiattuzzo and Uberto degli Uberti were put to death, while others were forced into exile. This "plot," followed by the shame of defeat suffered at the hands of the hated Sienese, helped to deflect the sympathies of the *popolo* toward the Guelf party—and it was in fact the guilds that rose against the Ghibellines in 1266.

Dante thus came to the world in a Tuscany dominated by Ghibelline power. But before he was a year old that power was broken for good in central and southern Italy by the rout and death of Manfred at Benevento (February 1266; *Purg.* III. 103ff.). After a brief government under the direction of two Jovial Friars—one a Guelf, the other a Ghibelline, but both hypocrites according to Dante and Villani (*Inf.* XXIII. 103–8; Villani, *Cronica* VIII. 13)—Manfred's victor, Charles of Anjou, king of Sicily and Naples and from 1277 king of Jerusalem (*Purg.* VII. 113, XX. 61–69), held the reins of power in Florence with the title of Imperial Vicar in Italy, as the imperial throne was now vacant. Charles continued as *Podestà* of Florence for no less than twelve years, while the senatorship of Rome and a pattern of alliances in northern Italy extended his power throughout the Italian peninsula. During his overlordship, the *popolo* was excluded from the government, although some of the great Florentine banking families received economic privileges from Charles; they were knighted and even given political office in return for the financial support they continued to provide.

In 1280 Pope Nicholas III (*Inf.* XIX. 46–120), fearing the predominance of Angevin and French power, sent his nephew Cardinal Latino Malabranca to the city. In February of the following year, fifty Guelfs and fifty Ghibellines embraced publicly and swore to keep the peace. Ghibelline and Guelf nobles frequently broke it nevertheless. In March 1282 the rebellion against Charles known as the Sicilian Vespers and the expulsion of the French from Sicily gave new hope to the Ghibellines, who tried to find support among the lower guilds in Florence even as the Guelfs wooed the seven major guilds. The result was a triumph for the *popolo*, the creation of a system of government controlled by the guilds, which elected every two months from among their members six Priors, who ruled the Commune together with the revived General Council, Captain of the People and the *Podestà*. Although the democratic element was later strengthened by the inclusion of members of the five lesser guilds in 1287, the guilds themselves tended to be dominated by nobles or *magnati*, who managed to manipulate elections and control the Priors.

The long-drawn-out war against Arezzo (Dante took part in the Florentine victory at Campaldino in 1289: *Inf.* XXII. 4–5) and the campaign against Pisa highlighted the financial mismanagement and corruption in the Commune. Florence's difficulties offered Giano Della Bella, a wealthy merchant from a noble family (*Par.* XVI, 127–32), an opportunity to redress the situation. Siding with the *popolo*, Della Bella dominated the Commune for a brief but highly significant period of two years (1293–1295). He was the guiding spirit behind the *Ordinamenti di Giustizia*, which were approved on 17–18 January 1293. These ordinances were clearly directed against the ruling classes of the previous decade: they excluded from the Priorate anyone who did not exercise a profession or trade within a guild, while setting up a new office—that of *Gonfaloniere di Giustizia*—with special responsibility for controlling the behavior of the "magnates." Any magnate who killed a member of the *popolo* was automatically sentenced to death, his property confiscated, and his house destroyed by the *Gonfaloniere*.

Other communes passed similar legislation. But a truly revolutionary turn was taken in April 1293 (during Giano Della Bella's priorate and at his instigation), when five provisions were added that effectively deprived magnates of all their political rights. A list of 150 families was drawn up; their members were declared ipso facto to be magnates and, as such, they were excluded from holding major office in the Commune. Each magnate had to swear an oath of obedience and offer a bond of 2,000 lire that he would keep the peace. In evidence, the word of a *popolano* was to be preferred to that of a *magnate*. Not all the *magnati* were noble, while a number of noble families (including the Medici) were not included in the list of magnates. As Nicola Ottokar has shown, it is not possible to distinguish between *magnati* and *popolani* by using purely economic or social criteria. The *magnati* were not a homogeneous social class; they were citizens designated as *potentes*, *nobiles* or *magnates*, the enemies of Giano and of those who regarded themselves as *popolani*. In other words, the term "magnate" was used and exploited in much the same way as similar terms ("counter-revolutionary" or "communist") were to be in the future.

Giano Della Bella "did his utmost for the sake of justice against the guilty" (Compagni, *Cronica* I. 12), but his actions led his numerous enemies to seek all possible means to bring about his downfall. Unjustly accused of supporting one of the nobles, Corso Donati (*Purg.* XXIV. 82–90, *Par.* III. 106–7), Giano was forced into exile. Henceforth the leading offices in Florence were once again in the hands of the *Popolo Grasso*. The *Popolo Minuto* "lost all strength and vigor" (Compagni, *Cronica* I. 17). The fundamental principles of the *Ordinamenti di Giustizia* were in part annulled by amendments passed in July 1295, allowing magnates to enroll in a guild and thus to enjoy political rights and be eligible for office in the Commune.

Dante took advantage of the new situation by becoming a member of the Guild of Physicians and Apothecaries (*Arte dei medici e speziali*). The choice is perhaps not so surprising when one remembers that, in order to study medicine, it was necessary to have a grounding in philosophy. At the end of the year (14 December 1295), Dante, as the representative of the *Sesto* of St. Peter's Gate, one of the six wards into which the city of Florence was divided, took part in procedural debate concerning the election of the Priors.

Already thirty years old, Dante made his entry on the political scene relatively late (men came of age politically at the age of 25 in Florence). His progress was due to personal prestige and to his position—or lack of it—in the Guelf party. By 1295 he had shown himself to be the leading lyric poet in Italy, his originality well attested by his recent *Vita Nuova*. His poetic achievement was bolstered by the study of philosophy, which he had begun in earnest soon after Beatrice's death in June 1290. Dante now became passionately interested in ethical problems such as the true nature of nobility—a theme highly topical in Florence around 1295, as we have just seen. It sparked off a remarkable development in his writing. Only one or two years earlier, Dante had stated in the twenty-fifth chapter of his *Vita Nuova* that vernacular poetry should occupy itself exclusively with the theme of love. Suddenly, we find him deeply committed to themes of social import. The study of Aristotle's *Nicomachean Ethics*, the influence of Guinizzelli, and the social turbulence of Giano Della Bella's "reform" all led Dante to abandon the "sweet rhymes of love" for the "harsh and subtle" verses (*Rime* LXXXII. 14; *Conv.* IV) expressing philosophical, moral and social truths—although the bitter experience of exile was necessary to turn the youthful poet of love into the solitary voice of Italy's *cantor rectitudinis* or "singer of righteousness" (*DVE* II. ii. 8).

By now Dante had also had ample opportunity to witness the frequent changes in Florentine laws and governments, which he was to denounce in *Purg.* VI. 139–51. And his six years of active involvement in Florentine politics only served to drive home the lesson of the mutability of human affairs as exemplified in his native city. It is therefore not surprising that the poet of the *Comedy* chose two thirteenth-century Florentines—Farinata degli Uberti (d. 1264) and Cavalcante de' Cavalcanti (d. before 1280)—to illustrate the truth of Christ's warning that "every city or household divided against itself shall fall" (Matthew 12.5). Scholars have claimed that the author of the *Inferno*, in which the moral structure is based on Aristotle and Cicero, was at a loss to find the right location in this structure for heresy, a sin peculiar to Christianity. They have overlooked the essential link the poet wished to establish between heresy and political faction: both tear at the heart of the community, shattering the unity of man's cities even as they attempt to destroy the unity of the City of God. Hell is a true mirror of what sin and corruption have wrought on earth: hence, as the travelers pass through the gates of the devil's city, they encounter an infernal cemetery that is also a reflection of the devastation caused by political feuds on earth. Fittingly, two citizens of Florence—one the leader of the Ghibelline faction, the other a leading Guelf—exemplify the divisions and the hatred that had separated them in life and that now unite them in the tomb of eternal damnation. In *Inferno* X the Florentine poet wrote one of the most telling commentaries on the political life of the Florence he had known, loved, and hated.

The year 1294 had sown the seeds for the future. That May, the papal interregnum that had lasted since April 1292 was brought to an end in a most unexpected manner. The bitter feud between the Colonna and the Orsini parties finally made possible the election of a compromise candidate, proposed by Cardinal Latino Malabranca. The new pope, Celestine V, was Pietro da Morrone, eighty years old, "simple and unlettered" (Villani, *Cronica* IX. 5) but with a reputation for sanctity. His election gave rise to immense hopes of reform within the Church. Celestine's life as a hermit promised to serve as a model of poverty and spirituality in contrast with the worldliness of his predecessors. He even appeared to some as the longed-for *pastor angelicus*. Celestine was, however, no administrator. Overwhelmed by the enormity of the burden placed on him, he abdicated on 13 December 1294, after a reign of only seven months. We have no evidence of Dante's reaction at the time. Far more relevant to our purpose, however, is the fact that the poet, when he came to recast his experiences and to evaluate them in the *Inferno*, placed Celestine among the cowards rejected by both God and the devil.[4]

The world-judge of the *Comedy* condemned Celestine for betraying the hopes of the faithful who had looked to him for guidance. Far from purifying the Church of its subservience to worldly power and ambitions, Celestine proved to be a political disaster in his submission to Charles II of Anjou, for whom he created no fewer than seven French and three Neapolitan cardinals during his brief term of office. Celestine did not go to Rome but remained in Naples on Angevin territory; thus, instead of freeing the Church from political interference in its internal affairs, Celestine became Charles's puppet. All this underlies the word used by Dante to characterize Celestine's behavior, the hapax *rifiuto*. For the poet-judge of the *Comedy*, Celestine's abdication was not an act of humility; it was instead "il gran rifiuto" (*Inf.* III. 60), the great refusal of his age, a refusal to cooperate with God's grace, a refusal of God's choice as manifested in the papal election, a refusal to fulfill the Pope's supreme duty, to obey the divine command to feed Christ's sheep, to "lead mankind to eternal life" (*Mon.* III. xv. 11). Already in 1294, Jacopone da Todi had forecast Celestine's damnation if he proved unequal to the task of leading the Church toward salvation,[5] and the events of that year must have dissuaded Dante from looking to another *pastor angelicus* when he eventually came to share many of the ideals of the Spiritual Franciscans.[6]

Celestine's abdication was a traumatic experience for many of the faithful, especially when, only eleven days later, his antithesis, Benedetto Caetani, was elected pope as Boniface VIII. A gifted administrator and an expert in canon law, Boniface did all he could to increase the power of the Church—and of his own family. The results were catastrophic. The papacy's prestige and spiritual authority were degraded, and through its political ambitions the papacy became a pawn on the European chessboard. In spiritual matters Boniface incarnated that legalistic approach to religion often the hallmark of the Western Church—an approach condemned by Dante.[7] The judgment of a modern historian is not so very different from Dante's: "The pontificate of Boniface VIII, too often regarded as a high point of papal pretensions, had in reality been a disaster of the first magnitude for the church."[8] For the medieval poet, the Pope's terrible example was the primary cause of the universal greed and corruption that had infected the world in 1300 (*Par.* XVIII. 126). Boniface's greed, hypocrisy, and legalism made of him "the Prince of the new pharisees"—until the poet had this sea lawyer proved wrong by the devil in theological debate (*Inf.* XXVII. 85ff.). Most of this was to be revealed in the first years of Dante's political career, but already in July 1295 Boniface showed his mettle by confiscating 80,000 florins from the Guelf League on the specious grounds that, since Adolf of Nassau had not yet been crowned emperor in Rome, the Holy See was constrained to oversee Tuscany "during the vacancy of the Empire."

The year 1294 also saw the death of Brunetto Latini, notary to the Florentine Commune, politician, and writer, to whose memory Dante pays moving tribute in *Inferno* XV. 79–87: the pilgrim tells the damned soul that he will never forget the debt he owes for the way Brunetto had taught him *come l'uom s'etterna* ("how man makes himself eternal"). In his writings, Brunetto expressed great admiration—an admiration unique at the time—for Cicero the man and the politician, based on his impassioned defense of the Roman state against the treacherous aristocrat, Catiline. In this, Brunetto sowed the seeds of Florentine civic humanism and pointed out for Dante and his fellow citizens the true nature of nobility, rejecting the feudal criteria of lineage and wealth, and basing it on personal achievement and good works. Brunetto stressed the essential link that should exist between rhetoric and good government, a view fundamental to the whole movement of civic humanism. He thus foreshadowed the terrible lessons of *Inferno* X by highlighting the evils of faction that destroy the commonwealth (*Tesoretto*, 178–9), and affirmed the universality of the Empire, despite his Guelf allegiance.[9] Brunetto's example of political commitment helped to make the author of the *Vita Nuova* aware of the need to bind learning and literature to the external world. It encouraged Dante to adopt that view of the totality of politics, of politics indissolubly linked to ethics and humanity's earthly goal, which was destined to heal the divorce between the poetry of the inner world of love and the outer world of social reality that had characterized the early phases of the poet's literary output. Exile and the example of Brunetto Latini lie behind the encyclopedic vision and the political message of the *Convivio* and the *Comedy*.

If this was the lesson, then how did Brunetto teach Dante "how man makes himself eternal" (*Inf.* XV. 85)? Charles Davis and Umberto Bosco give the most convincing answer. Mortals can achieve a kind of earthly immortality through their spiritual nobility, since the fame derived from a man's good works lives on after his death: "after his death, the renown created by his good works shows that he is still alive."[10] Professor Davis observes: "Since Brunetto extended the sphere of Ciceronian rhetoric to the written as well as the spoken word, his concept may be applied appropriately to Dante as author of the *Convivio*, the *Letters*, the *Monarchia*, and the *Commedia*."[11]

This is undeniably true, as the poet's own son pointed out some twenty years after his father's death: "For among the other things which this Ser Brunetto taught the author were those which act as a spur to the acquiring of renown for virtue and knowledge, whereby one lives forever and has an imperishable name in this world."[12] Even so, we can be more specific. It is hardly possible to suppose that the poet of the *Comedy* is telling us that Brunetto had shown him how man wins the eternal glory of Paradise; on this score there must have been many other better qualified teachers in Florence during the first three decades of Dante's lifetime. Any interpretation must moreover consider that the poet always chose his words with great care. The use of the reflexive form in "come l'uom s'etterna" may well underscore that Dante's tribute is concerned not with the reward of eternal glory conferred by God (nor is it man who acquires this) but rather with the process and the institutions whereby man perpetuates the memory of his achievements and his good works on earth. Just as the memory of the saints "s'etterna" or is preserved on earth by the Church, so the memory of good citizens and their achievements on behalf of the commonwealth is preserved by the community and acquires a semblance of eternity in this world. In other words, in this view of man as a political animal we find what Ernst Kantorowicz aptly named "the fiction of a quasi-infinite continuity of public institutions." The Commune is seen as an autonomous State that never dies, an attitude that may be viewed as the secularization of a theological concept not unlike that noted by Kantorowicz with regard to the glory gained by those who fell in battle for their country, where "eternal fame or glory so conspicuously takes the place of eternal beatitude or is paired with it."[13]

The title of Kantorowicz's essay is "Pro patria mori" ("to die for one's country"). *Pro patria vivere* ("to live for one's country") would be an apt variation encapsulating Brunetto's civic message. This is already hinted at in the famous summation by Villani (*Cronica* IX. 10), in which he claims that Brunetto was "a great philosopher and a great master of rhetoric. . . . he was the first to begin to educate the Florentines and teach them the elements of oratory, and how to guide and govern our republic according to Politics." It is this *politica* or art of good government that encourages man to virtuous action as a member of a community (*polis*). It was a commonplace of medieval political thought that bad government produced evil citizens: a Dominican theologian, Remigio de' Girolami, even went so far as to claim that no one could be a good Christian if he were not a good citizen.[14] As is well known, the rediscovery of Aristotelian political thought helped to provide a theoretical justification for the existence of the state, which now came to be regarded as a product of nature. Aristotle's political animal is indeed at the root of Dante's Christian political thought. At all stages for the Florentine writer "man is by nature a social animal" in what he called "the universal community of the human race" (*Conv.* IV. iv. 1–6).

As J. P. Canning has pointed out: "The chief innovation of late medieval political thought was the development of the idea of the secular state as a product of man's political nature."[15] Essential for Dante, however, was the fundamental relationship between ethics and politics that was the burden of Brunetto Latini's message, a message to be conveyed to the citizenry through the skillful use of rhetoric, for "this art of rhetoric . . . is part of . . . the art of government" (*La rettorica*, 40). Thus the shade's final words to the pilgrim during their encounter urge the latter to turn to Brunetto Latini's *Tresor*, "in which I am still alive" (*Inf.* XV. 119–20) and in which his teaching still speaks to all men, reminding them of the primacy of politics and urging them to work together to build a true commonwealth, a political medium that will ensure the preservation and fulfillment of their good actions. There Brunetto had claimed that "the art which teaches how to govern the city is chief, sovereign and queen of all arts. . . . Hence the good that comes from this knowledge is truly human, because it forces human beings to do good and not evil" (*Tresor* II. 3 [176]).

Later, Dante would come to see in the Emperor the supreme guide to happiness in this world. The teachings of philosophy, however, must guide the Emperor (*Mon.* III. xv. 10). Brunetto's teaching helped to bolster Dante's passionate belief that politics must always be governed by ethical considerations—something Machiavelli and his heirs were to reject as impossible. The author of the *Vita Nuova* went on to study Aristotelian political thought in a number of texts. From his fellow Florentine, however, he learned "come l'uom s'etterna," how men and women live in a community that is an extension of the individual, whose mortality is salvaged by the perpetuation of a commonwealth based on justice and good works. In his *Rettorica* (II. iv. 3), Brunetto claimed that "eloquence was born for most virtuous reasons . . . namely, to love God and one's neighbor, for *without that humanity would not have endured*"—words that may be seen as a pendant to our poet's "come l'uom s'etterna."

Latini's *Tresor* also showed the importance of the dissemination of knowledge in a social context, the need for it to reach a broad-based public. It encouraged Dante to take the radical decision to break down the barriers of philosophy by inviting men and women immersed in practical affairs and deprived of a knowledge of Latin to take part in a true *Convivio* or banquet of knowledge; in other words, an aim utterly different from the young poet's intention of writing only about love for a narrow élite, the *fedeli d'amore*. The example of Latini's life and works taught Dante that he must never divorce his responsibilities as a writer from those he had as a citizen of Florence and the world. This was indeed the political lesson taught him by his "master."

In the early 1290s Dante "discovered" philosophy, which he began to study by attending "the schools of the religious" and "the disputations of the philosophers" (*Conv.* II. xii. 7). After about two years and a half, this new passion "chased away and overcame all other thoughts." It is therefore highly probable that Dante studied the writings of Aristotle in Latin translation at Santa Maria Novella, where he would have come into contact with the teachings of Remigio de' Girolami, a remarkable pupil of Aquinas who was Lector there for forty years until his death in 1319.[16] For Professor Davis, it was perhaps from Remigio (rather than from Brunetto, although the two influences may well have been complementary) that the Florentine poet "learned those two Aristotelian propositions which were fundamental to his philosophical and political thought: first, that man as a rational creature naturally desires the knowledge which is his perfection; and second, that man is naturally a citizen, a civil and political animal." As far as the latter belief is concerned, this "curious thomistic proto-Hegelian" (as Kantorowicz defined Remigio) wrote a remarkable treatise *De bono communi*, where he asserted that a citizen "should be willing to go to Hell rather than see his commune there, if this could be done without offending God." Remigio even went so far as to claim that someone who is not a citizen cannot properly be called a man.[17] We can only make conjectures about the effect such a radical proposition may have had on Dante, if indeed he came into contact with it. However, the very fact that a Dominican friar could make such statements in Florence during Dante's lifetime is significant. Certainly with regard to the later phases of Dante's political thought we find notable common ground in the two Florentines' denunciation of faction and its destruction of the commonwealth, of greed or *cupiditas* as the root of all evil, of the Donation of Constantine as a poison injected into Christ's Church, and in their immense admiration for the heroes of republican Rome.

Of equal importance was the message broadcast by certain Franciscan preachers at this time. At Santa Croce—the other great Florentine "school"—Petrus Johannis Olivi (Pierre Jean Olieu, d. 1289) and Ubertino da Casale spoke fervently of Francis's ideal of poverty, inspired as they were by Joachite yearnings for the reform of the whole Church and its liberation from temporal corruption.

Thus when Dante entered political life in earnest in 1295, a number of political lessons and experiences conditioned his outlook. His six years of practical involvement in the affairs of his native city were marked by moderation, combined with hostility toward aristocratic and papal interference in the government of Florence. His insistence on the importance of spiritual nobility according to the courtly love tradition (*Vita Nuova* XX) was given an ideological slant in his *canzone, Le dolci rime d'amor ch'i' solia* (which looks forward to the Filippo Argenti episode in *Inferno* VIII), while Dante's fateful decision to "collaborate" with the popular regime seems to have provoked Guido Cavalcanti's aristocratic indignation, expressed in the latter's sonnet *I' vegno 'l giorno a te 'nfinite volte.*

Elected to the *Trentasei del Capitano* (November 1295 to April 1296), Dante spoke on 14 December 1295 before a council of the captains of the twelve major guilds. As on future occasions, he was concerned with the method of electing the Priors: he voted with the majority to turn down a proposal that the outgoing Priors should take part in the election of their immediate successors. In May 1296 Dante was co-opted to an important body, the Council of One Hundred (which had been set up in 1289), where—on 5 June—he spoke out against granting political asylum to exiles from Pistoia and supported a proposal to give special powers to the Priors to punish anyone, "and especially magnates," guilty of using violence or other means of injury or intimidation against *popolani* holding public office. We know that he was a member of one of the councils in 1297, but the official records are missing for the next two years. We must, however, assume that Dante won the confidence and the respect of many colleagues, since he was elected to the highest office, the Priorate, only five years after his entry onto the political scene.

In the meantime, the relative calm of the two years following Giano della Bella's expulsion was shattered by the polarization of the ruling Guelf party into two factions, fueled by the hatred and rivalry that existed between the Cerchi, "men of lowly origin, but great merchants and very wealthy," and the Donati, "who were of more ancient lineage, but not so wealthy" (Compagni, *Cronica* I. xx). By the 1290s both families had reached the top of the Guelf hierarchy. Both were deprived of the possibility of holding political office by the Ordinances of Justice of 1293, although with other magnates they still controlled the *Parte Guelfa* (and it was Giano della Bella's intention of appropriating the funds of the *Parte Guelfa* on behalf of the Commune that hastened his downfall in 1295).

As Dino Compagni makes clear, however, the origins and make-up of the two clans were very different. The Cerchi were *nouveaux riches* (a group Dante was later to condemn in *Inf.* XVI. 73–75, although for the immediate future he found himself on the same side). Their wealth and ostentation became proverbial and symptomatic of Florence's economic supremacy. Conscious of their widespread business interests, the Cerchi tended to favor compromise, especially with the *popolani* in power. Social upstarts, they created resentment by such acts as the purchase of the palazzo of an ancient noble family, the Counts Guidi, in 1280. They were thus neighbors of both the Alighieri and the Donati families (Dante's wife, Gemma, was a Donati), in a district that soon became known as the "ward of scandal" because of frequent feuding (Villani, *Cronica* IX. 39).

In the year of Dante's birth, 1265, the Cerchi bank—soon to become the largest of the Florentine banking companies—lent immense sums of money to the Pope and Charles of Anjou for the latter's conquest of southern Italy and Sicily. They also gained the support of many of the leading Florentine families, including the Strozzi, Cavalcanti, and Portinari (Folco Portinari is thought to be the father of Dante's Beatrice). Business interests, however, led the Cerchi to lend money even to notoriously Ghibelline elements in Pisa, Verona, and the Romagna—a link that sparked accusations of pro-Ghibelline activities in 1301. The Donati, rivals of the Cerchi, found some of their leading supporters in papal bankers like the Spini and others who continued to finance the victorious House of Anjou. Vieri de' Cerchi had fought valiantly at Campaldino in 1289, where victory for the Florentine forces was in part due to Corso Donati's quick-thinking and characteristic insubordination. Vieri's personality was the opposite of Corso's; cautious and eager for compromise, he did not join the rebel magnates in July 1295, and in 1299 he proved incapable of seizing the opportunity offered by Corso's banishment from Florence. Vieri also refused to take a sufficiently firm stand against the Pope's political interference in Florentine affairs, adopting a legalistic attitude of non-intervention at the height of the crisis in 1301, something that proved disastrous for his whole party. Dante, who had found himself on the same side, condemned the whole family for its "felony" in *Par.* XVI. 95.

A leading figure on the stage of the Florentine power-game for some twenty years, Corso Donati was a handsome, courageous bully who despised the mercantile origins and attitudes of his hated rivals (it was even rumored that he had murdered his first wife, who was a Cerchi). Corso's numerous acts of violence and provocation against the popular regime led to his exile in 1299, when Pope Boniface had him appointed first *Podestà* at Orvieto and then governor of the Massa Trabaria. In May 1300 he was condemned to death *in absentia* by the Florentine Commune for plotting to overthrow the state; Corso had his revenge, however, some eighteen months later, when he returned to destroy his enemies and gained virtual control of Florence for the next three years. His political allegiances were largely based on personal animosity and opportunism—the latter well reflected in his third marriage to the daughter of Florence's most feared enemy, the Ghibelline leader, Uguccione della Faggiuola. Dino Compagni compared Corso to Catiline (*Cronica* II. 20), while Dante forecast his ignominious death and damnation in *Purg.* XXIV. 82–90.[18]

The feud between the Cerchi and the Donati factions was given a political label in 1300. In a vain attempt to pacify neighboring Pistoia, the Florentine authorities summoned to their city the leaders of the rival factions, the White Cancellieri and the Black Cancellieri, who all belonged to a leading family in Pistoia. Instead of achieving peace, however, the Florentines likewise split into two factions: on the one hand, the White Guelfs (headed by the Cerchi), who tended to be jealous of Florentine independence, and, on the other, the Black Guelfs and the Donati, who sought allies in Pope Boniface and the House of Anjou, while they accused the Whites of betraying Mother Church with the Ghibellines. Dante sided with the White Guelfs, although his wife was a Donati and despite his aversion for the attitudes and behavior of the *nouveaux riches*.[19]

On May Day 1300, a serious brawl occurred between the rival families and their supporters, during which Ricoverino de' Cerchi's nose was cut off:

This same blow proved to be the ruin of our city, because it greatly increased the hatred among its citizens. . . . The city was divided yet again, among the magnates, the middle and the lower classes; and even the clergy could not prevent themselves from siding with one or the other of the said factions. All the Ghibellines sided with the Cerchi, because they hoped to receive less injury from them; as well as all those who were of the opinion of Giano della Bella. . . . Guido, son of Messer Cavalcante Cavalcanti, was also of their party, because he was the enemy of Messer Corso Donati. (D. Compagni, *Cronica* I. 22)

Six days later, Dante was sent as Florentine ambassador to the nearby commune of San Gimignano in order to ensure its continued support for the Guelf League and its participation in the election of the new Captain.[20] On 10 May Corso Donati was sentenced to death *in absentia*.

A difficult situation was made even more dangerous by the events following the appointment on 23 May of Cardinal Matteo d'Acquasparta as papal legate in Tuscany and northern Italy. At the beginning of June, the cardinal hurriedly left the Romagna in order to deal with the critical situation in Florence. He immediately proposed that candidates for the Priorate be selected from a list of names publicly chosen from those of the leading citizens in each ward. However, the traditional system prevailed, and on 18 June Dante Alighieri was elected with five others to the highest political office in Florence for the traditional period of two months (15 June to 15 August).

As every reader of the *Comedy* knows, the poet later marked the Spring of 1300 the moral nadir of his life, making it the fictitious date for his vision of absolute evil and his rejection of mortal error. It was certainly an appropriate time. On the threshold of a new century, the year 1300 held out hope of universal renewal through the first Holy Year proclaimed in the history of the Christian Church. On a personal level, it marked the midpoint in the poet's theoretical life-span of seventy years. The same year saw the highwater mark of his political ambitions, but disaster and exile followed. In fact, in a letter now lost (but recorded by Leonardo Bruni) Dante later claimed that all his troubles and misfortunes could be traced back to his Priorate.[21]

On 23 June some of the magnates attacked the consuls of the guilds and leading members of the popular government as they filed past in procession with votive offerings for the feast of Florence's patron, St. John the Baptist, which was to be celebrated on the following day. The Priors acted resolutely, exiling fifteen leaders of both the Black and the White factions. Dante thus agreed to the exile of seven White Guelfs, including his friend Guido Cavalcanti, who immediately left for Sarzana. The Blacks, however, refused to leave Florence. At this point Cardinal Matteo d'Acquasparta was granted extraordinary powers to act in accord with the government to achieve peace—whereupon he called for troops from Lucca. The government was only just able to save the situation but at the cost of conflict with the Franciscan cardinal, whose policies were so unpopular that an attempt was made on his life some time in the middle of July. The results were predictable. On 22 July Pope Boniface reacted angrily, attributing the cardinal's failure to the work of devils and the wicked Priors of Florence (of whom Dante was one), and conferring authority on his legate to take adequate measures to punish the guilty officials and their city. The Priors held firm and the Black leaders went into exile, but the first papal salvo had been shot across Dante's bows. The Cardinal left the city and excommunicated the Priors (Dante's successors) toward the end of September, after the latter had revoked the sentence of exile against the White leaders.

The Whites, led by the Cerchi, were determined to protect Florentine independence, although they wished to avoid a showdown with the Pope. On the other hand, the papal legate's failure made Boniface seek a more radical solution. From the start of his pontificate, Boniface had been determined to support Charles II of Anjou's attempts to reconquer Sicily (lost in 1282 after the revolt of the Sicilian Vespers), contributing no less than 750,000 florins to the cause. In the person of Charles of Valois, brother of Philip IV of France, the Pope thought he had found the solution to both the Sicilian and the Tuscan problems.

Boniface had further occasion to deplore White supremacy in Florence. On 18 April the Commune had condemned three Florentines at the papal curia for subversive activities. They included Simone Gherardi degli Spini, of the Florentine banking house to which the Pope owed more than 57,000 florins and which held a virtual monopoly of loans to the Holy See in 1300. On 24 April Boniface sent a letter to the bishop of Florence insisting that the condemnation be revoked on pain of excommunication and summoning the accusers to appear before him within fifteen days. When this proved to be of no avail, Boniface sent another letter to the bishop and, on 15 May, he wrote to the Inquisitor, Fra Grimaldo da Prato, claiming that he was acting in the best interests of Tuscany while the Empire was vacant (thus renewing the papal claim to imperial rights during a vacancy, for it must not be forgotten that Tuscany was still officially part of the Empire). Once again, excommunication was threatened—especially against Lapo Saltarelli, who had led an embassy to Boniface in March and who had stated publicly that the Pope should not interfere in the government of Florence. Saltarelli's subsequent betrayal of his fellow Whites did not save him from being condemned to death with Dante in 1302 by the (Black) Commune for corruption while holding political office (cf. *Par.* XV. 127–29).

By the beginning of 1301 Boniface sought to preserve Guelf hegemony in central and southern Italy by ensuring that the immense resources of the Black bankers should be placed behind Charles of Valois' Italian and Sicilian campaigns. Charles arrived in Italy, met with Boniface in September and with Corso Donati in October. The situation was critical for Florence's White Guelfs.

We know something of Dante's activities in the preceding months. On 14 April the former Prior voted on the method of electing the Priors. On 28 April he was appointed for two months overseer of certain road works — possibly, but not necessarily, with military implications. The record of his intervention on 19 June, on the other hand, leaves no doubt regarding the political nature of this act. On that day, on no fewer than two occasions, Dante spoke out resolutely against a papal request (transmitted by Cardinal Matteo d'Acquasparta) that Florence should continue to support Boniface's "crusade" against Margherita Aldobrandeschi in the Marittima by maintaining an armed force in the papal camp, after the expiry of the two and a half months for which Florentine aid had been granted on 17 April. The motion to continue supporting the Pope's military action on the borders of Tuscany was carried in the Council of One Hundred with 49 votes in favor and 32 against. As George Holmes points out, "The sentence, 'Dante Alagherii consuluit quod de servitio faciendo d. pape nichil fiat' [*Dante Alighieri proposed that nothing should be done regarding the pope's request for aid*], sounds dramatic, but in the political context its implications were limited. . . . It meant that that particular contingent should be withdrawn from papal service, not that the papal alliance should be abandoned, still less that a general anti-papal stance should be adopted." Nevertheless, the consequences for Dante's political career were indeed "dramatic," for his actions were judged not with the objectivity of a twentieth-century historian but by an irascible fourteenth-century Pope and by political enemies only too ready to accuse him of opposition to the Supreme Pontiff.[22]

On 13 September Dante reaffirmed his support for the popular regime; on 30 September he voted in favor of eight proposals designed to strengthen the Priors' powers to proceed against all perpetrators of acts of violence, aggression, and false witness. At this point, Dante joined Albizzo Corbinelli in proposing an amnesty for Neri, the son of Gherardino Diodati (one of the White Priors immediately preceding Dante's priorate). The amnesty was granted. It is interesting to note that Neri had been wrongly condemned for a crime he had not committed by that same *Podestà*, Canto de' Gabrielli da Gubbio, who sentenced both Gherardino and Dante to death in March 1302.

The arrival of Charles of Valois in Italy (*Purg.* XX. 70–78), his meeting with Black envoys in Bologna and with the Pope at Anagni, and the indecision shown by the Cerchi and other leading Whites all precipitated the crisis. Shortly after 28 September the Florentine government sent a special mission to Boniface in Rome to try to save the situation; Dante was perhaps a member.[23] The mission was a failure. On 1 November Charles of Valois entered Florence. Corso Donati returned from exile and, with the help of mob law, pillaged and destroyed the houses and property of his enemies. The Priors, of whom Dino Compagni was one, were forced to resign; their successors, elected on 8 November, were all Blacks, and Canto de' Gabrielli da Gubbio was installed as *Podestà* on November 9. By June 1302 the death sentences totalled 559.

The results for Dante are well known and have already been cited. On 27 January 1302 Dante Alighieri and three others were condemned in absentia for crimes of fraud, barratry, and extortion. They were further charged with destroying the unity of Pistoia by imposing one-party government, with the consequent expulsion of the faithful Blacks, and by leading it away from union with Florence, its subjection to Holy Church and Charles of Anjou, peacemaker in Tuscany. Because they did not obey the summons, the four were condemned to death with eleven others on March 10; if they fell into the power of the Florentine Commune, they would be burned at the stake: *igne comburatur sic quod moriatur*.[24]

2

Dante's Political Experience:
Exile and Conversion (1302–1305)

RELATIVELY LITTLE IS KNOWN ABOUT Dante's movements during his twenty years of exile. In June 1302 he was in Tuscany—at San Godenzo in the Mugello—where, with sixteen other exiles (including Vieri de' Cerchi and Lapo degli Uberti, Farinata's son), he solemnly undertook to make restitution for any injury suffered by the Ubaldini, a powerful Ghibelline family in the struggle against the Black Guelfs in Florence. It is likely that in February Dante had already joined the White exiles together with the Ghibellines in the Val di Chiana. The death sentence passed on him in March was one of the obvious results of this spectacular alliance. Associating with the Ghibelline exiles turned out to be a fatal mistake for the Whites, since it alienated most of the Guelf communities in Tuscany and caused Charles of Valois to intervene yet again, while it appeared to justify the Pope's support for the Blacks and the drastic measures taken by him to punish the White "traitors" to the Guelf cause and Holy Mother Church.

From a military point of view, too, the alliance was a failure. After one or two minor successes, Castel del Piano, defended by some six hundred Whites, was lost in July through the treachery of Carlino de' Pazzi (*Inf.* XXXII. 69). That autumn, after the usual cessation of military activities owing to bad weather, Dante went to Forlí, to the court of the Ghibelline leader, Scarpetta degli Ordelaffi, who had agreed to command the White soldiers in their campaign against Florence. It was probably as Scarpetta's envoy that Dante went to Verona, where—from May/June 1303 to March 1304—he found his "first refuge" at the court of Bartolomeo della Scala.[1]

The great event of 1303 was the death on 11 October of the man Dante held to be chiefly responsible for his exile: Pope Boniface VIII. The Pope's death followed closely on his humiliation at Anagni. The event stamped the seal of failure on papal policy, which for almost a century had been based on rivalry with and hostility to the Empire, relying on French support for this opposition. Since that conflict left an indelible imprint on Dante's political and religious thought, a brief summary must now be given.

The first Pope of the thirteenth century, Innocent III (1198–1216), did his best to extend papal influence into all spheres of human activity. One of the ablest lawyers and politicians of his age, Innocent was the first pope to assume the title "Vicar of Christ" as distinct from the traditional "Vicar of Peter." Innocent declared that the Pope held the right to confirm imperial elections. He based this claim on the imperial rights supposedly conferred on the popes by Constantine the Great (Emperor from 306 to 337 A.D.), according to the notorious document known as the Donation of Constantine. The latter told how Constantine, cured of leprosy by Pope Sylvester I in the year 314, had handed over the civil government of the western half of the Empire to the Pope and his successors, declaring that the bishop of Rome had precedence and authority over every bishop and church in the world. Although it was suspect and rarely used by the Popes, with the advances made by the humanists in both history and linguistics Lorenzo Valla, in 1440, was at last able to prove the Donation a preposterous anachronism. Dante, however, had little choice but to accept the document as authentic. He nevertheless declared it invalid, both because Constantine had no authority to give away any part of the Empire and because the popes had no right to accept temporal power (*Monarchia* III. x; *Inf.* XIX. 115–17; *Purg.* XXXII. 124–29; *Par.* XX. 55–60).

In the bull *Venerabilem fratrum* (1202) Innocent gave definitive expression to the medieval concept of *translatio imperii*—namely, that the Empire had been transferred from the Greeks to the Romans to the Franks and then to the Germans. As a result, no elected pretender could have a right to the imperial throne, proclaimed to be a papal favor, granted only after the candidate had been approved, confirmed, and crowned by the Pope. In the decretal *Novit ille* (1204), Innocent seized on King John's accusation that the king of France had "sinned" against his vassal, in order to assert the Pope's right to intervene in secular affairs *ratione peccati*—where sin had been or might be committed (a formula that covered just about every possibility).

It was in fact Innocent who recognized Frederick II as Emperor, after excommunicating and deposing Otto IV, the Guelf. As a result, Frederick, who combined the claims of the Holy Roman Emperor in, for example, Lombardy, with absolute royal power in southern Italy and Sicily, became the most powerful ruler in Italy since Theodoric.[2] Excommunicated on no fewer than four occasions and by two successive popes, Frederick was formally deposed by Innocent IV at the Council of Lyon in 1245. On this occasion Innocent used the argument of the two swords (cf. *Monarchia* III. iv) against the Emperor. According to Innocent, the two swords given by Christ to St. Peter (Luke 22, 38) and his successors signified their *plenitudo potestatis*, in other words their supremacy in both temporal and spiritual affairs. A variety of interpretations abounded since Henry IV first quoted it in 1076 in an attempt to establish a total separation between royal authority and the authority of the priesthood. Moderates tended to see it either as devoid of allegorical significance (*Monarchia* III. iv. 16) or as signifying the two Testaments—also, the sword of God's Word and the sword of action (*Monarchia* III. ix. 19). Innocent, however, used it to imply that papal authority created the Emperor and that he should wield the "material sword" at the Pope's command (*ad nutum*); moreover, he could be deposed if the Pope judged him unsuitable, while the Pope was entitled to assume all imperial rights and authority whenever the Empire was vacant. Papal authority was at its zenith, when Innocent IV (1243–54) launched a war of annihilation against Frederick and gave it the legal status of a holy crusade. Dante deplored the tragedy of this internecine struggle at the very heart of his poem (*Purg.* XVI. 115–17). He dated the headlong decline of northern Italy as stemming from papal opposition to Frederick II's divinely instituted imperial authority, although he makes no specific mention of Innocent IV, Frederick's implacable enemy (cf., however, *Ep.* XI. vii. 16).

After Frederick's death in 1250, his illegitimate son Manfred (*Purg.* III. 103–45), was excommunicated in 1258, and then again in 1261 by Urban IV, a Frenchman, who offered the crown of Sicily to Charles of Anjou. The papacy's involvement in temporal affairs was now such that the Pope no longer hesitated to use the whole arsenal of weapons—both spiritual and political—at his disposal. Moreover, when Urban threatened to dispense the debtors of the Tuscan banks from their obligations, he swung the greatest economic power in Western Europe behind the Angevin claimant, making it clear that support for the last of the Hohenstaufen would mean financial ruin for all who dared to oppose the political schemes of the head of Christ's Church. Those schemes were crowned with success by the death of King Manfred and the rout of the Ghibellines at Benevento in 1266 (*Inf.* XXVIII. 15–16; *Purg.* III. 118–32), a decisive battle whose outcome installed the Angevin dynasty in southern Italy and led to the establishment of the powerful Guelf League throughout the peninsula.

Although the Empire remained vacant for almost a quarter of a century and Frederick's imperial successors never formed a dynastic threat to the papacy, Popes were seen to have debased their spiritual authority, and they were left to face the factious spirit of the Roman nobility as well as the mighty power of France, which they had reared against themselves. The proud universalism of thirteenth-century Popes was then replaced by what constituted—for Italians such as Dante, Petrarch, and St. Catherine of Siena—the "Babylonian captivity" of their successors in Avignon for over six decades of the fourteenth century. In this religious-political drama, the pontificate of Boniface VIII (1294–1303) played a crucial role.

Boniface's legitimacy was contested by the more extreme Spiritual Franciscans, who remained faithful to St Francis's example of absolute poverty and who felt they had been betrayed by the abdication of Celestine V in 1294. They rallied around Boniface's great enemy, the Colonna family, who in turn looked to the king of France, Philip the Fair, for support against the man accused of blackmailing Celestine, of rigging his own election in 1294, and of various other crimes against the Church. Dante's attitude toward Boniface was complex. In *Inferno* XIX. 52–57 the poet forecasts the Pope's damnation for simony and denounces his fraudulent election, while in *Paradiso* XXVII. 22–27, St. Peter himself, the archetypal Pope, is made to declare that his "place" (a word repeated three times), now vacant in the eyes of Christ, has been usurped by Boniface, who has not hesitated to turn Peter's burial place into a sewer. On the other hand, in *Purgatorio* II. 98–99 Boniface's proclamation of the indulgences connected with the first Holy Year (22 February 1300) is held to be valid. Even more significant are the verses in the twentieth canto (*Purg.* XX. 86–93) in which the humiliation suffered at the hands of the emissaries of the King of France is compared to Calvary, with Boniface clearly portrayed as Christ's vicar on earth. It would seem, therefore, that *sub specie aeternitatis* Boniface is a usurper in God's eyes; *sub specie mundi*, however, he is the Pope, the unworthy heir of blessed Peter (*indignus haeres beati Petri*).[3]

Faced with a clear threat to his authority and legitimacy as Pope, Boniface reacted in characteristic fashion. He not only excommunicated Cardinals Iacopo and Pietro Colonna together with Stefano, Iacopo Sciarra, and others (11 May 1297), but he even launched a crusade against them (14 December 1297). Six years after the loss of the last Christian bastion in the Holy Land, this Holy War against fellow Christians came to be regarded by the author of the *Comedy* as the ultimate debasement of the crusading ethic (*Inf.* XXVII. 85–111; *Par.* IX. 121–38, XV. 139–48). Instead of

uniting his flock as a good shepherd must do, Boniface injected civil war
into the very heart of Christendom (*Par.* XXVII. 46–51). However, his
greatest crime, in Dante's eyes, was surely his claim to political supremacy
over the Emperor.

In letters addressed to the imperial electors in Germany (13 May
1300), Boniface stated that the Holy See had transferred the Empire to the
Germans and that it now intended to take back the province of Tuscany.
When he finally confirmed Albert as Emperor (30 April 1303), Boniface
knew he was engaged in a mortal struggle with the king of France, and
did not attempt to press his claim to the overlordship of Tuscany. Instead,
he condemned France's overweening pride, *superbia Gallicana*, as exemplified in the French refusal to recognize the Emperor's universal authority:
"they lie, because by law they are—and must be—under the Roman King
and Emperor."[4] In his *Promissio* of 17 July 1303, Albert (*Purg.* VI. 97–117;
Par. XIX. 115–17) solemnly recognized the papacy's right to transfer the
Empire, and in his immediate reply (drafted by his Chancellor) Albert acknowledged the "unbounded authority" of the Holy See. The King of the
Romans even went so far as to declare himself the Pope's liegeman. Boniface could hardly have hoped for a greater victory over the Emperor—at
least in theory. In reality, the situation was very different, as events later
that year were to highlight.

In 1303 the conflict between Boniface and Philip the Fair reached its
climax. By turning chiefly to France for support in their struggle against
the Hohenstaufen, the popes created a sorcerer's apprentice they were soon
unable to control. Already in 1202, in his decretal *Per venerabilem*, Innocent III had recognized the fact that the king of France acknowledged
no superior in temporal matters. This rise of the *regnum particulare*, with
its affirmation of the autonomy of the sovereign state, is one of the most
important developments in Western Europe at this time, but the Popes
who attempted to exploit it in their determination to weaken the universal claims of the Empire did not foresee that a similar movement toward
national autonomy would eventually break the universality of the Church
in the same region. Moreover, the papal armory—with its arguments directed at proving the inferiority of imperial power—proved singularly ineffective when it came to dealing with a mere king, for here there was no
election, no confirmation, no oath of obeisance, no *translatio imperii*. As
Philip the Fair boasted, he held his kingdom by the grace of God and the
sweat of his knights.

When matters came to a head, Philip did not hesitate to launch a full-scale propaganda war against Boniface. He had the papal bull *Ausculta fili* publicly burned in February 1302, and he broadcast forged documents, including a false bull (*Deum time*) in which the Pope supposedly told the king that he was subject to papal authority "both in spiritual and temporal matters . . . we hold those who believe otherwise to be heretics."[5] Far more telling, however, was Philip's main line of defense, for he set out to persuade public opinion that the Pope was attacking and undermining the French nation. He achieved this outstanding victory by various means, including the first meeting ever of the Estates General on 10 April 1302 in the church of Notre-Dame in Paris, where the three orders (clergy, nobility, and third estate) gave their total support to the king, after being told that the Pope claimed feudal overlordship over the kingdom of France. Philip thus appealed to national pride and unity, and he won the day.

Rumors circulated in 1298 that Boniface had received ambassadors from Albert of Austria while seated on a throne, crowned with the Emperor Constantine's diadem, holding the temporal sword and keys of the kingdom of heaven in his hands, and exclaiming "I am Caesar, I am the Emperor" (*Ego sum Caesar, ego sum imperator*). Two years later, at the time of the Jubilee, Boniface had himself commemorated in a fresco at the Lateran as the true successor of Constantine, its founder. The tiara worn by Boniface at his coronation and depicted in the fresco was identical with the one attributed to Pope Sylvester, although "The secular crown which Sylvester himself . . . had preferred not to wear was now assumed by Boniface."[6] A series of setbacks followed this high-water mark. In 1301, Edward I and the English Parliament scornfully rejected Boniface's claim that Scotland was a papal fief. Denmark and Hungary proved just as hostile to papal interference in their affairs. In 1302, with the peace of Caltabellotta, Boniface was compelled to recognize the power of Frederick of Aragon in Sicily; moreover, his protégé Charles of Valois left Italy at the end of that year, a spent force.

From this position of relative weakness Boniface issued the most famous document in the annals of the medieval papacy, his bull *Unam sanctam* (18 November 1302). As the opening words imply, Boniface's whole argument rested on the fundamental principles of unity and hierarchy. He claimed that both the material and the spiritual swords were in the power of the Church: the material sword to be used for the Church "by kings and soldiers, but at the will and by permission of the priest."[7] Moreover, "One sword ought to be under the other and the temporal authority subject to the spiritual power." Following Hugh of Saint Victor (*De Sacramen-*

tis Christianae Fidei) and the coronation ceremonial, Boniface proclaimed that "the spiritual power has to institute the earthly power and to judge it if it has not been good"; anyone who rejects this divinely ordained spiritual power "resists the ordinances of God unless, like the Manicheans, he imagines that there are two beginnings." Then, the final anticlimax: "We declare, state, define and pronounce that it is altogether necessary to salvation for every human creature to be subject to the Roman Pontiff"— an anticlimax because, as Tierney points out: "The words are resounding enough, but they seem to refer quite clearly to the pope's spiritual supremacy and have no obvious relevance to the problems of church and state. They were in fact borrowed from a treatise of Thomas Aquinas called *On the Errors of the Schismatic Greeks*."[8] They were also singularly mistimed, and the dénouement was rapid.

In March 1303 Philip the Fair's chief minister, Guillaume de Nogaret (whose grandfather had been burned as an Albigensian heretic) denounced Boniface as a usurper and notorious criminal, demanding that a General Council depose him. In April Boniface declared his intention of excommunicating Philip and went on to prepare the decree *Super Petri solio* at his summer residence at Anagni. However, on the eve of its promulgation (7 September 1303) Nogaret and the Pope's mortal enemy, Sciarra Colonna, stormed the town with eight hundred soldiers and held the pontiff prisoner. Although quickly liberated by the townsfolk, Boniface did not recover from the shock and died a few weeks later (11 October). His defeat and humiliation at the hands of the Most Christian King of France made a profound impression on the future poet of the *Comedy*.

Like Calvary (to which it is expressly compared in *Purg.* XX. 85–90), the scandal of Anagni must have struck the future author of the *Comedy* as a "just vengeance" (*Par.* VII. 20): a punishment for Boniface's crimes, the hybris that devoured the Pope, his *libido dominandi* that had led him to claim a political power that God never intended to confer on His vicar in the spiritual sphere. For Dante the lesson of Boniface's pontificate—indeed, from the whole course of thirteenth-century history and before— was that God had created two great luminaries, two separate authorities for the temporal and spiritual realms, and they must not be confused in the same individual "since, when united, the one does not fear the other" (*Purg.* XVI. 112).[9] Instead, Empire and Papacy must each reign supreme, working together to safeguard their particular authority.

We may well ask ourselves: when did Dante first absorb this lesson? There is no simple answer. First, as we have already seen, Dante, as a member of the Florentine ruling class, opposed the papacy's imperialistic aims in Tuscany; and he suffered persecution and exile as a result. The need for the elimination of ecclesiastical interference in politics and affairs of state must have been obvious to Dante before his exile. He was then, however, a Guelf living and working in a Guelf city. The next stage, which led to a radical political conversion, occurred in the period 1303–1304. The poet himself singled out his stay in Verona with Bartolomeo della Scala for special mention in the central episode of *Paradiso*, where his ancestor Cacciaguida foretells his exile (*Par.* XVII. 70–75); it must be remembered that at this time Verona was the Ghibelline capital of Italy. Moreover, Dante's reason for leaving Verona was itself connected with the death of Boniface, for eleven days later Niccolò Boccasini, a Dominican, was elected Pope as Benedict XI. Renowned for his honesty (Benedict was beatified in 1738), this friend of the Cerchi family and a witness to Boniface's humiliation at Anagni inspired great hope among the White exiles through his policy of pacification and his appointment of Cardinal Niccolò da Prato as papal legate and peacemaker in Tuscany, Romagna and the Marca Trevigiana (31 January 1304). The Cardinal entered Florence and was granted special powers from the Florentine government to facilitate his mission (17 March 1304). At this critical juncture, Dante must have felt it essential to return to Tuscany—to Arezzo, where he was one of the twelve councilors of the "White Party of Florence," on whose behalf he wrote a letter to Cardinal Niccolò, declaring the White exiles' readiness to accept a truce and place themselves in his hands.

The letter (*Ep.* 1, probably written in early April) states that the Whites have only striven for "the peace and liberty of the people of Florence" (*Ep.* I. ii. 6), and that they had waged civil war with the sole purpose of restoring their country to well-being—a difficult pronouncement for the man who was later to condemn Curio to the depths of Hell.[10] That same month, representatives of the White party, accompanied by a few Ghibellines, re-entered Florence, where peace between the parties was solemnly sworn in the church of Santa Maria Novella on April 26. However, as Compagni laconically observed, "the Blacks had no desire for peace" (*Cronica* III. 7), and the situation became more and more explosive—until Cardinal Niccolò advised both Whites and Ghibellines to leave the city (June 8). Further riots and destruction of property followed their hurried departure.

On June 10 Cardinal Niccolò left Florence, placing the city under interdict. Less than a month later, the Pope died—rumor had it that he had been poisoned (Villani, *Cronica* IX. 80)—and with him disappeared a brief moment of optimism and possible reconciliation. Most scholars agree that at this point Dante broke away from the other White exiles and he refused to join in what proved to be their last attempt to return to Florence by force (20 July 1304). His final judgment of these companions is given in the *Comedy*, when Cacciaguida refers to the shame and bitterness his great-great grandson will feel at being associated with

> . . . la compagnia malvagia e scempia
> . . . che tutta ingrata, tutta matta ed empia
> si farà contr' a te . . .
>   Di sua bestialitate il suo processo
> farà la prova; sí ch'a te fia bello
> averti fatta parte per te stesso.[11]

This solitary party eventually led the author of the *Comedy* to condemn both Guelfs and Ghibellines as the source of all of Italy's woes (*Par.* VI. 97–108). For the present, however, we must concern ourselves with Dante's immediate conversion to the Ghibelline or imperial cause.

In 1952 A.P. d'Entrèves pointed to 1304–7 "as the possible years of Dante's 'conversion' to the imperialist doctrine."[12] What evidence we have certainly supports this view, and it is no less an authority than Dante himself who tells us—in a rare autobiographical excursus—that he held two radically opposed political views during his lifetime. First, he had subscribed to the Augustinian, radical Guelf view of the Roman Empire as based not on right but on violence alone (*nullo iure sed armorum tantummodo violentia*). Later, however, he had come to realize that the Ghibellines were right in their claim that the Empire was willed by God and founded on justice (*Mon.* II. i. 2). Valuable evidence may once again be gleaned from the tenth canto of *Inferno*, when the Pilgrim meets the shade of the great Florentine leader of the Ghibellines, Farinata degli Uberti. Farinata declares that Dante's family, the Alighieri, had been his enemies, but his boast that he had twice defeated and scattered them is countered by the pilgrim's passionate rejoinder that on both occasions his Guelfs had returned to Florence, while Farinata's descendants have never overcome their exile. As I have shown elsewhere, the poet portrays the pilgrim Dante as he truly was in the year 1300, a citizen and ruler of Florence, still enmeshed in the partisan conflicts at a municipal level, who had not yet risen to the universal vision that inspired the *Comedy*.[13] He learns of his impending political defeat and exile from Farinata, thus joining him as yet another victim of those fratricidal struggles (*Inf.* X. 79–81, 124–32).

The first years of exile must have witnessed Dante's conversion to the imperialist doctine. His stay in Verona, singled out at the center of *Paradiso* as a landmark in the exile's wanderings, is in fact the only one specifically mentioned, when the Florentine condemned to be burned at the stake experienced Bartolomeo's "courtesy" and liberality. Bartolomeo's generosity was most likely extended to a White Guelf not wholly unsympathetic to the Ghibelline cause (symbolized by the "holy bird" or imperial eagle in *Par.* XVII. 72), and its effects can hardly have failed to make a deep impression on Dante's proud but impoverished person.

Whatever our conjectures about the psychological impact of Dante's stay in the Ghibelline capital of northern Italy, there is decisive evidence in the *De Vulgari Eloquentia*—evidence not correctly evaluated by the few scholars who have attempted to consider it. Typical in this regard is d'Entrèves, who asserts: "it is striking that Dante makes no mention whatever of the Empire in the writings of the early years of his exile. If there is anything politically relevant to be gleaned from the *De Vulgari Eloquentia* and the first three books of the *Convivio*, it is Dante's growing sense of Italian nationality."[14] Admittedly, the author of the *DVE* was supremely conscious of "what is the greatest and strongest bond of a nation: the unity of language," as Professor d'Entrèves himself demonstrated in a fine essay entitled "*Gratiosum lumen rationis.*"[15] Nevertheless, it is essential to take into account what may be learned from a passage in that work, written before February 1305. In his search for the "vulgare illustre," the author of the *De Vulgari Eloquentia* examines the claims of the so-called Sicilian poets in the twelfth chapter of the first book. In his analysis of their achievements, he exalts the roles of both Frederick II and his son Manfred as patrons. Their noble example, we are told, inspired the most gifted poets of Italy to practice their art at the court of the Hohenstaufen:

But those illustrious heroes, Frederick Caesar and his well-born son Manfred, displaying the nobility and rectitude of their character, as long as fortune permitted, followed what is human, disdaining what is bestial. Hence, those who were of noble heart and gifted by God strove to attach themselves to the majesty of such princes; so that in their time whatever shone forth from the noblest spirits of Italy first appeared at the court of those mighty sovereigns.[16]

The tone of this panegyric goes far beyond the factual recognition of the "Sicilians" as the first Italian poets to have used the *vulgare illustre*. As far as Dante's description of Frederick and Manfred as *illustres heroes* is concerned, P. V. Mengaldo quotes Aquinas's Aristotelian opposition between the superhuman *virtus heroica*, which makes men similar to angels, and the *bestialitas* that makes them descend to the level of brutes.[17] We should also bear in mind the meaning given by Dante to the epithet "illustrious," when, in *DVE* I. xvii. 2, he claims:

when we call something illustrious, we understand by this that it shines forth illuminating and illuminated; and in this way we call men illustrious either because, illuminated by power, they illuminate others by justice and charity, or else because, having themselves received excellent instruction, they in turn—like Seneca and Numa Pompilius—give exemplary instruction to others. And the vernacular of which we speak has been exalted by both instruction and power, while at the same time it exalts its followers by conferring honour and glory on them.

Frederick and Manfred were therefore exalted by their power, their glory, and the example they set for others to follow, "disdaining all that is bestial" (*DVE* I. xii. 4). What, we may well ask, were those teachings that so impressed themselves on the mind of the newly exiled citizen of Guelf Florence?

In his circular of 1232 Frederick showed the way for the author of the *Convivio* in his conviction that learning brings true freedom. Moreover, like the *Convivio*'s ideal audience, the Emperor did his utmost to overcome the handicaps and the distractions of the active life in order to acquire knowledge "without which the lives of mortals cannot be lived in noble fashion."[18] The Emperor insists that the sharing of knowledge in no way decreases it, but on the contrary augments it and is of the greatest benefit to everyone. Some eight years earlier, in an epistle announcing the foundation of the University of Naples, Frederick had declared his intention of nourishing those starved of intellectual food, exalting the idea of intellectual nobility acquired through study and knowledge. All this is germane to the language and spirit of the *Convivio*, a truly revolutionary work intended to open up the closed shop of scholastic philosophy and make its riches available to men and women caught up in the turmoil of practical affairs. Frederick's promotion of Latin translations of Greek and Arab philosophers had made possible the great Aristotelian debates of the thirteenth century and the emergence of a secular culture.

There was a clear connection between the Ghibelline spirit and Latin Averroism.[19] Moreover, as Dante saw clearly enough, Frederick's son Manfred (who studied philosophy at Bologna) continued his father's patronage of scientific inquiry. In his translation of a Hebrew text, *De pomo sive de morte Aristotilis* (1255), Manfred stressed the benefits of philosophy as a way of understanding God.[20] Particularly relevant to our investigation is the fact that Dante's pro-Ghibelline stance is immediately evident in the description of Manfred as the noble and worthy son of the great Emperor (*DVE* I. xii. 4: "benegenitus eius"). For any contemporary, the epithet "well-born" (*benegenitus*) was a highly polemical refutation of Guelf propaganda. The latter not only exaggerated Manfred's supposed crimes (his "abominable atrocities and acts of cruelty," according to the Bull of Excommunication, 10 April 1259) but also denounced his illegitimate birth as the natural son of Frederick and Countess Bianca Lancia. Readers of the *Comedy* may further contrast the epithet "well-born" with the poet's reference to bastardy in *Purg.* XVIII. 125: Giuseppe, the illegitimate offspring of Alberto della Scala, is described as the bastard *ill-born* ("che mal nacque").

It is surely impossible to doubt Dante's vigorously Ghibelline, anti-Guelf attitude when he wrote this passage (c. 1304), with its exaltation of the Staufen rulers of Sicily, whose achievements remained to the eternal shame of the contemporary rulers of Italy (*DVE* I. xii. 3). Just as significantly, we are told that—as a result of Frederick's and Manfred's patronage—whatever has been produced by Italian poets is called "Sicilian." This surprising statement (paralleled in the *Regles de trobar* of Joifre de Foixà) is justified by the observation that, since Sicily was at that time the seat of royal power, it was also the cultural center of the whole of Italy and thus gave its name to that culture (*DVE* I. xii. 4). We recall that Dante made this claim when Sicily was still a kingdom, ruled by Frederick II of Aragon (1296–1337), but without any claims to cultural leadership. Both the context and the wording therefore suggest that the author of the *De Vulgari Eloquentia* was pointing to a unique set of historical circumstances, when Sicily was the center of the Empire under Frederick II and then retained for a short while her pre-eminent role and cultural prestige under Frederick's worthy successor, Manfred. Under both rulers, Sicily was the hub of political power and royal authority; at their courts all the greatest achievements of the noblest intellects of Italy saw the light of day (*DVE* I. xii. 4).

What has not been noticed is that under Frederick II the Magna Curia at Palermo had been the seat of imperial power—something that obviously impressed Dante in 1304. This was in the best medieval tradition, according to which the imperial court followed the Emperor's person (just as the papal curia was wherever the Pope might be)—and Dante gives not the slightest hint that it should have been otherwise. Such silence would surely have been impossible after the poet's discovery of Rome's providential mission as the unique political and religious capital of the world—a discovery first expressed in 1306 or 1307 in the fourth book of the *Convivio* with all the ardor of a neophyte. The exaltation of Rome in the fifth chapter has its *raison d'être* in Dante's vision of the Eternal City designated by God as the center of world empire. What we find expressed there is not just an abstract concept—at a time when both Pope and Emperor were guilty of abandoning Rome—but attachment to a physical city, whose very walls are worthy of reverence "beyond anything we normally deem proper for what is purely human" (*Conv.* IV. v. 20). In fact, this chapter (utterly irrelevant to the immediate problem of defining the Emperor's competence in philosophical matters) is a paean to Rome, where the name of "the holy city" returns obsessively no fewer than six times in a few lines, and its pagan "citizens who were not human but divine" are granted divine inspiration.

We must now contrast this later passage with *DVE* I. xi, where the hunt is on for Italy's illustrious vernacular. Dante begins by examining the credentials of Roman speech. He justifies this order of precedence by ironically referring to the Romans' claim to priority "over all others," and goes on to exclude them categorically from the prize, since their speech is judged to be nothing but a hideous jargon, the worst of all the Italian dialects (I. xi. 2: "tristiloquium, ytalorum vulgarium omnium . . . turpissimum"), reflecting the turpitude of their customs and behavior. We find not one word about the providential mission of Rome, no hint of the contrast between the poet's later vision of Rome and the sordid reality of the Roman jargon and customs. I do not believe that Dante's later vision of Rome's imperial destiny would in any way have lessened the harshness of his judgment. On the contrary, I imagine it would have inspired an attitude not unlike the poet's condemnation of unworthy Popes (heightened by his reverence for the papal office and by contrast with the ideal Peter)—an attitude likely to bring home the incongruity between the baseness of Roman speech and manners on the one hand and Rome's ideal destiny on the other.[21]

We should also note that, in chapter eighteen, Dante speaks of an ideal court in the Italian peninsula, which, while not physically united and located like the court of the king of Germany, nevertheless has its members "united by the gracious light of Reason" (I. xviii. 5).[22] Mengaldo, the most authoritative editor of the *De Vulgari Eloquentia*, specifies that

Rex Alamannie ("King of Germany") refers to Albert I of Habsburg, who had been elected King of the Romans in 1298. Marigo generalizes: "the German court is unified by the Emperor, who is also 'King of Germany.' Nevertheless, as both Emperor and 'King of the Romans,' he should have his seat in Rome"—which is precisely what Dante does *not* say.[23] On the contrary, it is essential to note that in the *De Vulgari Eloquentia* Dante does not state that Albert as Emperor should govern from Rome, whereas he does in fact imply this some two years later. In *Conv.* IV. iii. 6—just before the exaltation of Rome's providential origins and growth—Dante claims that Frederick II was "the last emperor of the Romans up to our own day, despite the fact that Rudolf, Adolf, and Albert have all been elected." This refers to the fact that the latter were merely elected, but they never received the imperial crown. Later, by the time Dante came to write the sixth canto of *Purgatorio*, he clearly condemned "German Albert" for his refusal to act as a true Emperor and for his desertion of Rome:

> Vieni a veder la tua Roma che piagne
> vedova e sola, e dí e notte chiama:
> "Cesare mio, perché non m'accompagne?"[24]

From this analysis, we must surely conclude that the *De Vulgari Eloquentia* does not represent a "nationalistic" phase in Dante's political thought, one situated halfway between *civitas* and *imperium*, as some scholars have argued.[25] Once more, I must insist on the absence of any mention of the essential role of Rome (which was to become a linchpin of the poet's mature political thought), despite the recognition that a political vacuum existed in Italy, "since we are without a court" (*DVE* I. xviii. 5). Instead, all the evidence points to a vigorous Ghibelline moment, corresponding to Dante's conversion to the imperial thesis, during or just after his stay in Verona and before his discovery of the providential mission of "Rome and her empire" (*Inf.* I. 20)—something that makes its first appearance (c. 1306–7) in the extraordinary digression found in *Convivio* IV. iv–v.

The fact that the White Guelf exile wrote Epistle I in the spring of 1304 (just before his definitive break with the other Whites) presents no difficulty, since the White Guelfs were then allied with the Ghibellines of Arezzo, in which Ghibelline stronghold the Epistle was written. Far more significant is Dante's break with his fellow exiles, who would later turn against him in their madness and ingratitude (*Par.* XVII. 64–66). Scholars generally agree that the cause of this shame was the Whites' third attempt to return to Florence by force, which ended in total disaster, when (20 July 1304) four hundred Whites and Ghibellines were slaughtered at the battle of La Lastra.[26] One of Dante's friends and commentators tells us that Dante was now suspected of treachery by the Whites. The *Comedy* would seem to confirm this hostility, when Brunetto Latini tells the Pilgrim:

> "La tua fortuna tanto onor ti serba,
> che l'una parte e l'altra avranno fame
> di te; ma lungi fia dal becco l'erba."[27]

3

Exul Inmeritus (1305–1321)

THE DEATH OF BENEDICT XI IN JULY 1304 found the College of Cardinals split into two hostile factions. Matteo Orsini and Francesco Caetani, who defended the policies and memory of Boniface VIII, headed one of the factions. The second was led by another member of the Orsini clan, Napoleone—his sister was married to a Colonna, the sworn enemies of Boniface—and was inspired by a spirit of compromise with French anti-Bonifacian policies and the Colonna-Spiritual Franciscan alliance. The conclave, held in Perugia, went on for some ten months. It was soon clear that an external candidate would have to be found. At long last Bertrand de Got, archbishop of Bordeaux, was elected on 15 June 1305 and became Clement V. The results are well known: the papal curia was established at Avignon (in 1309) and came to be regarded by Dante as the Babylonian exile of the Church. This, however, was not foreseen by the electors, who wrote to Bertrand from Perugia, announcing his election and exhorting him to come to Italy: "There is no doubt that in the see of Peter you will reside more strongly, you will shine more brightly. . . . Everyone is stronger in his own house and calmer in his own church." The leader of the pro-Clement party in 1305, Cardinal Napoleone Orsini, wrote to the king of France after the Pope's death in 1314, complaining bitterly that he had not spent ten long months "in prison in Perugia" in order to see "Rome . . . fallen into extreme ruin, the see of St Peter. . . . desolate, the patrimony of the church . . . despoiled by thieves . . . and the whole of Italy . . . given over to devastation."[1]

Clement stayed away for the whole of his pontificate. However, the fact that most of the papal treasure remained in Italy and that the Pope resided in modest quarters in Avignon makes it likely that the "beginning of the Great Exile was not marked by any conscious, momentous decision to move the Papacy to France."[2] An important element in Clement's decision to reside in Avignon was the choice of Vienne as seat for the Council projected originally to begin its work on All Saints' Day, 1310. The Viennois was still part of the Empire, while Avignon formed an enclave in the Comtat Venaissin, standing in territories of the Angevins of Naples (who were themselves the Pope's vassals).

Dante placed Clement among the simonists in Hell, accusing him—through the mouth of his predecessor, Nicholas III—of sins even worse than those committed by Boniface and of being a mere puppet of the French king:

> "... verrà di più laida opra,
>   di ver' ponente, un pastor sanza legge,
>   tal che convien che lui e me ricuopra.
>   Nuovo Iasón sarà, di cui si legge
>   ne' Maccabei; e come a quel fu molle
>   suo re, cosí fia lui chi Francia regge."[3]

This alludes to the (erroneous) belief that Clement owed his election to the influence of Philip IV, to whom the archbishop of Bordeaux was supposed to have made various promises: the king and his followers would be freed from the excommunications incurred under Boniface VIII, Bertrand as Pope would assign to Philip one half of all the benefices of the kingdom; and he would condemn his predecessor's actions, create cardinals friendly to France, and reinstate the Colonna cardinals. For Dante, however, Clement's gravest sin was his betrayal of Henry VII in 1312–13—a crime denounced from the very heights of paradise (*Par.* XXX. 142–48). For Christendom in general, Clement's policies had results of immense consequence: the gradual abandonment of Italy, with all the financial and political results of this move, and the transformation of the College of Cardinals into a predominantly French institution. In 1305 three-quarters of the cardinals were Italian; by 1310 the non-Italians were—for the first time—in a majority; and by 1316 Italians held hardly more than a quarter of the votes in the Sacred College.[4]

Clement's move to Avignon meant that the *Comedy* was composed at a time when both Pope and Emperor had abandoned Rome, so that she was now "bereft of both her lights" (*Ep.* XI. x. 21). These historical circumstances add particular poignancy to the pilgrim's initial meeting with Virgil in the *Comedy*, where he speaks of Aeneas as chosen by Divine Providence to be the father of Rome, center of both Church and Empire (*Inf.*

II. 20–24). Despite the uncertain chronology of Dante's writings, I believe that the *Comedy* cannot have been begun before the interruption of
the *De Vulgari Eloquentia* (c. 1305); nor does it seem likely that its overall
plan could have inspired Dante to begin work on his Christian epic before
his discovery of the central mission of Rome in God's providential plan
(1306–1307).

It is difficult to trace Dante's moves after his departure from Arezzo
in 1304. Petrocchi inclines toward the possibility of a prolonged stay in
Treviso at the court of Gherardo da Camino. Renucci and others stress the
need to insert an important sojourn in Bologna, the only place in Italy
where Dante could have found the necessary cultural resources to enable
him to write the *Convivio*.[5] It was perhaps in Bologna, the city of Giovanni,
aptly surnamed "del Virgilio" (with whom Dante exchanged a poetic correspondence at the end of his life), that Dante discovered in Virgil one
of the mainsprings of his *Comedy*. Some time about the year 1307, the
exiled poet gave up his attempts to reinstate himself in the eyes of those
who, struck by the false charges laid against him and his obvious poverty,
despised and condemned him. The *De Vulgari Eloquentia* had been interrupted in the middle of a sentence (II. xiv. 2); now, he abandoned the
fourth book of his treatise on the riches and nobility of philosophy, though
it equaled in length the other three parts of the work and contained Dante's
initial statement of Rome's divinely inspired history and universal mission
(*Conv.* IV. iv–v).

The discovery of Rome's imperial mission was most probably made
as the result of a "rediscovery" of Virgil. Among the many possible meanings hidden in the description of the shade of the Latin poet as "one who
seemed faint through long silence" (*Inf.* I. 63) is the signal that a mass of
allegorical interpretations had buried Virgil's original message, his glorifi-
cation of Rome's destiny and that of her Empire.[6] Instead, that message—
which was to become a cornerstone of both the *Comedy* and the *Monarchia*—was rediscovered and first proclaimed by Dante in the fourth book
of his *Convivio* (IV. iv. 11): "This office [the universal empire], then, was
obtained by the Roman people not principally by means of force, but by
divine providence. . . . Such is Virgil's judgment in the first book of the
Aeneid, when he portrays God as declaring: 'To their rule [the Romans] I
set no limit, whether of place or time; to them have I given empire without end.'"[7]

The final section of the *Convivio* offers valuable evidence on the
way Dante read—and was inspired by—Virgil.[8] Although the *Vita Nuova*

(c. 1293–95) reveals some acquaintance with Virgil's works (most clearly in *VN* XXV, 9), Dante himself tells us (*Conv.* II. xii. 4) that in the early 1290s his knowledge of Latin left a great deal to be desired—and, as is well known, knowledge of the classics in medieval schools was gained mostly through anthologies and collections of quotations where edification was the primary concern. It is, therefore, interesting to note that, until *Convivio* IV, Dante had quoted only from the first, second, and fourth books of Virgil's epic. In *Conv.* IV. xxvi. 8–9—only three chapters before he interrupted the work—we find for the first time a reference, and a highly significant one at that, to both the fifth and the sixth books of the *Aeneid*: "What a spurring occurred when Aeneas had the courage to go down alone with the Sybil into hell in search of his father's soul . . . as is shown in the six book of that [hi]story!" This striking example of Aeneas' *magnanimitade* (magnanimity in the sense of fortitude or courage) was of the utmost relevance for the poet-pilgrim of the *Comedy*. Dante himself was to "go down into hell," as he tells us: "and I alone was preparing to bear the strife, both of the journey and of the pity" (*Inf.* II. 3–5)—until he was shown the way out of the *selva oscura* by the shade of none other than Virgil himself, the pilgrim's magnanimous guide, endowed with exemplary fortitude (*Inf.* II. 44).

Dante's firsthand knowledge of the Latin classics, which had already surfaced in the *De Vulgari Eloquentia*, comprises another unique feature of the finale to the *Convivio*. The references to Books V and VI of the *Aeneid* are introduced by the description of Virgil as "our greatet poet" (*Conv.* IV. xxvi. 8; cf. "our greatest Muse" in *Par.* XV. 26, in which the reference to Aeneas' meeting with Anchises reminds us that Dante, too, was to "seek out his father's soul" in his meeting with Cacciaguida). This, as Leo points out, is "the first epithet of praise . . . added to Vergil's name." The German scholar thus came to the conclusion that "while writing the last chapters of the fourth book of the *Convivio* . . . [Dante] read again, or in part for the first time, classical Latin poetry and prose." This reading—especially of Book VI of the *Aeneid*—provided "the final impulse" to begin work on the *Inferno* "under the guidance of *lo maggiore nostro poeta*, who had led *Aeneas* into Hell and would, therefore, be a good *duce* on such an expedition."[9] It is also pertinent to note that at Dante refers to Virgil's poem as "la detta *istoria*" (*Conv.* IV. xxvi. 9), where the word emphasized ("story" or "history") may well point to the fact that the *Aeneid* had now become for him an essential stage in the journey toward salvation. Together with the pregnant term *scritture* ("writings/scripture"), used to designate primarily Virgil's poem in *Conv.* IV. iv. 6, this shows that the *Aeneid* was for the mature Dante not so much an allegorical treasure-house as a historical document, the "Bible of the Empire," in accordance with what Dante's contemporaries knew as the *Nova Rhetorica*, where "history" was defined "an account of exploits actually performed, but removed in time."[10] Such an interpretation represents a radical stand in an age when the practice of literature was "under continual attack from the secular and (especially) the regular clergy, and, among the last, especially from the Domincan Order . . . [for whom] poetry is at best marginally and at worst not at all true."[11] For Dante, on the other hand, Virgil's epic offered not only a true record of history but also the revelation of God's workings in pagan history. This vision of literature's essential role in life and the shaping of human destiny inspired Dante for the rest of his life.

During this period (1304–8), papal policy—largely influenced by cardinals Napoleone Orsini and Niccolò da Prato—aimed to pacify the rival parties in the Italian peninsula. The little we know about Dante's moves shows that in 1306, perhaps as a result of the hardening of Guelf attitudes in Bologna, he was in the Lunigiana. There, at Sarzana, Franceschino Malaspina, Marquis of Mulazzo, empowered Dante to negotiate with Antonio da Camilla, bishop of Luni, at Castelnuovo di Magra regarding contested rights over the castles of Sarzana, Carrara, Santo Stefano, and Bolano. The negotiations were successful, recognizing all the gains made by the Malaspina family during the thirteenth century and enhancing their prestige. In *Purg.* VIII. 122–32, in his imagined encounter with Corrado II, Dante praises this family for its chivalric virtues and the unique example it offers to a world gone astray. Dante's *Ep.* IV, of 1307–8, may well have been addressed to Moroello Malaspina, Marquis of Giovagallo, the "fiery vapor from Val di Magra" (*Inf.* XXIV. 145) who led the Black exiles to victory against the Whites of Pistoia, and whose wife Alagia Fieschi is praised in *Purg.* XIX. 142–45. If so, the exiled poet's friendship with a Black Guelf general (perhaps as a result of Cino da Pistoia's mediation) is another instance of the attempts at pacification that were a consequence of the policies practiced by the papal legates in Italy, and which may also have left their mark on the political catholicism that inspired Dante's choice of *exempla* in his *Purgatorio*.

Hopes for a general reconciliation reached a climax—followed by total failure—at the time of Emperor Henry VII's expedition to Italy (1310–1313).[12] Henry's predecessor, Albert of Austria, had been assassinated by his nephew John on 1 May 1308 (*Purg.* VI. 100–101). Philip IV of France attempted to seize this opportunity to have his brother Charles of Valois elected to the imperial throne. Some of the cardinals, however, succeeded in convincing the Pope that it would be better to have an Emperor who might serve as a counterweight against excessive pressure from France. Earlier that year, Henry's younger brother Baldwin had been appointed archbishop of Trier, becoming one of the three ecclesiastical electors of the Holy Roman Empire. He now campaigned effectively for Henry, who was unanimously elected Emperor on 27 November 1308. Henry was French-speaking; he had signed the protest of the French nobles against Boniface VIII in 1302, and whereas he held the county of Luxembourg as a fief of the Empire, he was also a vassal of the king of France. Nevertheless, after his election, he displayed great independence and unwavering devotion to the imperial myth, doing his utmost to put into practice the Emperor's role as the guardian of peace and justice at the pinnacle of the temporal hierarchy. Even his enemies recognized his nobility of character.

Henry's chief concern was to secure papal approval for his election. In June 1309 an embassy was dispatched to Avignon in order to assure the Pope that, as soon as he had been crowned "King of the Romans," the new Emperor would set out on a crusade to liberate the Holy Land (which remained one of Clement's and Christendom's most potent mirages). By the end of July, Clement had officially recognized Henry, although the date set for the imperial coronation was almost three years away (2 February 1312). Henry, who had achieved reconciliation with the Habsburgs, announced his plans to be crowned in Rome and his intention of pacifying the warring factions in Italy. The ambassadors that the Emperor-elect dispatched to the territories theoretically subject to the Empire in what was known as "The Kingdom of Italy" (*Regnum Italicum*) — Piedmont, Lombardy, Veneto, Emilia, Liguria, and Tuscany — had a mixed reception. Since the death of Frederick II, these provinces and their proud, flourishing urban centers had enjoyed over half a century of independence from imperial control and government. Many were obviously reluctant to accept any lessening, real or implied, of the powers they had acquired. Two extremes were already evident. On the one hand, the imperial embassy received a truly royal welcome on 20 June 1310, as it entered Pisa, a city where Ghibellinism and the Empire were associated with its past glories (Pisa was to remain Henry's most faithful Italian supporter until the bitter end). On the other hand, if Dino Compagni is to be believed, already in the summer of 1309 Pisa's neighbor and traditional rival, Florence, had brought diplomatic pressure to bear on Henry "not to cross [the Alps], since it was enough for him to be king of Germany" (*Cronica* III. 24). Moreover, by March 1310 Florence had succeeded in creating a military league purporting to defend the interest of the Guelf party and those of its members, as well as to honor "Christ and the Church, the Pope and the cardinals, and King Robert of Sicily." The latter had persuaded the Pope in 1309 to lift the interdict placed on Florence some five years earlier. The previous month, when Henry's ambassadors arrived in Florence and requested among other things that the Commune abandon its siege of Ghibelline Arezzo, Betto Brunelleschi, unable to contain his feelings, expressed what quickly proved to be official Florentine policy: namely, that "never had the Florentines lowered their horns for any lord," thus echoing the reply given in 1281 by the Florentines to a request that they should swear an oath of fealty to Rudolph of Habsburg.[13]

Although Tuscan Guelf policy in 1310 did not yet deny the traditional rights of the Emperor-elect in that region, it was clear that Henry desperately needed unambiguous papal support. He received it with the encyclical *Exultet in gloria* (1 September 1310), in which the pontiff ordered all Italians to accept Henry as their rightful Emperor. At Lausanne (11 October), Henry capitulated to Clement's conditions that he recognize papal rule over Perugia and the entire Romagna, as well as over the Patrimony of St. Peter in Tuscany, while he promised to protect the Guelfs from oppression and to conserve them in their rights and jurisdictions: "the list of lands claimed for the Church was . . . farther reaching than even the most extensive of the concessions made by that most generous of Roman kings, Rudolph of Habsburg. . . . Never before had an emperor bound himself in this way."[14] On 23 October Henry and his army arrived at Susa. The Emperor-elect's situation was in fact extremely weak from both a military and a financial point of view. As a result of two other contemporaneous military expeditions, Henry arrived in Italy virtually without funds of any kind and with a small contingent of about five thousand troops, a motley crew deprived of its military leaders.

Dante wrote his own circular "To all and singular the Princes of Italy, and the Senators of the Sacred City, as also the Dukes, Marquises, Counts, and Peoples" of the peninsula, greeting the dawn of a new day and comparing Henry's mission to that of Moses, who had led the Israelites from slavery to "a land flowing with milk and honey" (*Ep.* V. i. 4). The Epistle, the first of three letters inspired by Henry's coming, is unique in its optimism. It begins with the announcement of a new age promising "consolation and peace," and it ends on a note of exultation fired by Clement's public blessing: "This is he whom Peter, God's Vicar, exhorts us to honor, whom Clement, the present successor of Peter, illumines with the light of the Apostolic blessing; so that where the spiritual ray is not sufficient there the splendor of the lesser luminary may offer its light."[15] It is noteworthy that, flushed by the ideal co-operation between the spiritual and the temporal leaders of Christendom, Dante should here have accepted the traditional interpretation of the two "great lights" (Genesis 1. 16) as restated by Clement V in his *Divine sapientie*, addressed to Henry VII on 26 July 1309. The Empire was thus "the lesser luminary" (cf. *Ep.* VI. ii. 8)—a concept Dante refuted implicitly by the unscientific but potent image of the two suns at the very center of his poem (*Purg.* XVI. 106–8) and rejected explicitly for its hierarchical implications in *Monarchia* III. iv. 16. Nevertheless, and in agreement with Clement's initial moves, in Epistle V Dante asserted his cardinal belief in the mutual independence of the two supreme powers, whose authority proceeds directly from God: "from whom as from one point the powers of Peter and Caesar both derive."[16] Just as significant is the likening of Henry to the sun: the Sun of Peace that will revive justice on earth, "justice which, like the heliotrope, deprived of his light, had grown faint" (*Ep.* V. i. 3; cf. Virgil, *Eclogue* IV. 5–6, and *Ep.* VII. i. 6). Biblical tropes abound. Henry is not only compared to Moses leading his people to the promised land; he is even greeted with the messianic title "lion of the tribe of Judah" (*Ep.* V. i. 4; cf. Genesis 49. 9–10; Revelations 5. 5). He, the good shepherd, will recognize and guard his sheep (*Ep.* V. v. 17).

Two biblical quotations are of paramount significance. The first consists of the opening words: "Behold now is the acceptable time," a quotation from St. Paul (2 Corinthians 6. 2), announcing the "day of salvation." It echoes Isaiah's messianic call (Isaiah 49. 6–12) whereby the "light of the Gentiles" brings God's salvation "to the furthest corners of the earth . . . to revive a ruined country . . . restoring to freedom and to the light men bound in darkness . . . they will hunger and thirst no more . . . theirs is a merciful shepherd, that will . . . give them drink. . . . Exiles from the north and west, exiles from the south will return." These striking parallels are reinforced by the second quotation (*Ep.* V. v. 15; Luke 21. 28): "lift up your hearts, for your salvation is near." In Luke's Gospel, this is preceded by the reference to Christ's Second Coming (verse 27: "then they will see the Son of Man coming in a cloud, with His full power and majesty"). A third clue may perhaps be found in the exhortation to woeful Italy to rejoice (*Ep.* V. ii. 5): "Letare iam nunc miseranda Ytalia." It is possible here to perceive an echo of the *Regina Coeli* (cf. *Par.* XXIII. 127–28) with its triumphant call to rejoice at the Lord's resurrection: "Gaude et laetare, Virgo Maria—Alleluia!—Quia surrexit Dominus vere—Alleluia!"

For the first time, we have indisputable evidence of Dante's conception of the Emperor's function as Christological given his role as the inheritor of Christ's kingship (cf. especially *Purg.* XXIX and *Par.* VI). In other words, the Florentine exile looked to "the emperor's two natures, human and divine, or rather, in the language of that age, a ruler 'human by nature and divine by grace.'"[17] A second cardinal point is that Dante sees himself invested with a prophetic mission.[18] The figure of the Old Testament prophet upbraiding his people for their rebellion to God's Law appears most clearly in Epistle VI, addressed only a few months later (31 March 1311) to the "most iniquitous Florentines within the city" that had organized the resistance to Henry's attempts to assert his rule. It opens with the affirmation of the divine mission entrusted to the Holy Roman Empire and the warning that "when the imperial throne is vacant, the whole world goes astray . . . and unhappy Italy . . . is tossed with such buffeting of winds and waves that no words could describe."[19] The Florentines are as guilty as the builders of Babel in their attempts to set up a Florentine—as opposed to a Roman—*civilitas.*[20] Dante's role as prophet is most evident in the fourth paragraph, in which he forecasts Florence's doom, telling its wicked citizens: "To your sorrow . . . you will see your buildings . . . crash down . . . You will see your populace . . . united and crying out against you in fury . . . your churches . . . pillaged . . . and your children doomed to pay for their father's sins in wonder and ignorance." The latter phrase is an obvious echo of the Old Testament prophets' warning of God's punishment to be visited even unto the third and fourth generation (Exodus 20. 5; 34. 7; Jeremiah 32. 18; Lamentations 5. 7). In order to drive home his message, Dante refers in the next sentence to his "prophetic soul" (*presaga mens mea*; cf. *Aen.* X. 843), instructed to foretell the future "by unmistakable omens as well as by irrefutable arguments" (*Ep.* VI. iv. 17). After denouncing the Florentines as the barbaric slaves of greed, which leads them to reject the observance of the most sacred laws where is found "the essence of perfect liberty," Dante reiterates the Emperor's Christological role in that Henry shares "our pains of his own free will, as though to him—after Christ—the prophet Isaiah had pointed the finger of prophecy, when he foretold what God's Spirit revealed: 'Surely he hath himself borne our griefs, and carried our sorrows.'"[21]

On 17 April 1311, Dante addressed Henry directly. He not only compares the Emperor to Titan but refers to him unambiguously as "our sun" (*Ep.* VII. ii. 7: *sol noster*), a pointer both to the "two suns" of *Purg.* XVI. 107 and to Henry's messianic role as "God's minister, son of the Church and promoter of Rome's glory" (*Ep.* VII. i. 8). This second paragraph develops most forcefully the Christological implications. John the Baptist's words are quoted: first, his question to Jesus (ii. 7: "Art thou he that should come or must we look for anther?": Matthew 11. 3; Luke 7. 19), and second the sacred words Dante assures us sprang to his lips when he saw the Emperor in person, possibly at his coronation in Milan, in January of that same year (Luke 1. 47): "Behold the Lamb of God, behold him who taketh away the sins of the world."[22] John the Baptist was considered to be the greatest of the prophets, "who preceded the true light" (*Vita Nuova* XXIV. 5). Here, if Dante is a *figura* of John, then Henry is a *figura* of Christ. Nevertheless, like the prophets of old who upbraided the kings of Israel, Dante chides the Emperor for his neglect of Tuscany as if for him "the Imperial rights under your guardianship" were limited to northern Italy, when (as Virgil must remind him) the Empire is limited in extent only "by the Ocean, his glory by high heaven" (*Aen.* I. 287; cf. *Ep.* V. vii. 21, *Mon.* I. xi. 12). It is a rebuke not only for Henry's dallying in the north but also for the limitations placed on imperial sovereignty by the Promise of Lausanne sworn by him the previous October.

The description in the fifth paragraph of Henry's son as "a second Ascanius" implies that the Emperor must act like Aeneas, who was "chosen in the Empyrean heaven to be the father of glorious Rome and of her empire" (*Inf.* II. 20–21) — even as rebellious Florence is likened to Amata, who committed suicide in despair over her daughter's marriage to Aeneas and Turnus's supposed death (*Aen.* VII. 96–101, XII. 593–607). Florence is the viper of civil war (*Aen.* VI. 832–33), the multiheaded hydra, the Goliath that must be slain so that "the Philistines shall flee and Israel shall be liberated" — while Henry, "new son of Jesse" (viii. 29: "proles altera Isai"), is seen as the new David, the most authoritative *typus Christi* or forerunner of Christ. Dante's self-apportioned task was clear to Villani, who asserted that he wrote this letter to Henry "upbraiding him for his dilatoriness, virtually in the guise of a prophet" (*Cronica* X. 136). No one has seen this prophetic aspect of Dante's work more clearly than Bruno Nardi, who claimed that a prophet is one who passionately takes part in the sufferings, turmoil, and aspirations of his age, so that he is led to "denounce and attack the wicked, and point to the goal set by God. His language is not the clever, circumspect speech used by politicians . . . the inner heat that consumes him brings to his lips fiery words of passion, commanding and threatening."[23] In this sense at least, no one could have been more of a prophet than Dante.

What came to pass, however, belied all Dante's deepest hopes and aspirations. By mid-April 1311 both Cremona and Brescia were in open rebellion, and an important change in papal attitude and policy had begun to appear. On 30 March Clement V sent a letter to Henry regarding embassies sent to him by the Tuscan Guelf communes; here the Pope's acceptance of their claims for autonomy indicated "the Pontiff's absolute refusal to support Henry's program for imperial restoration in Italy."[24] A rapprochement between Clement and Philip the Fair was also evident, when on 27 April (in the bull *Rex gloriae*) the Pope publicly cleared the French king of all responsibility for the outrage committed against Boniface at Anagni, ordering the nullification of all acts issued by Boniface and Benedict XI against Philip. Hitherto, everyone had admitted that Henry was the legitimate lord of imperial Italy. Now, however, Florence refused to refer to him as "King of the Romans" or "Emperor," insisting on the alienating formula "King of the Germans" and rejecting the imperial titles. Then, on 1 April 1311, the Florentine Commune declared that it and its allies would no longer allow Henry or his forces to enter the territories under their control.

The perception of Florence as the heart of the rebellion against Italy's divinely appointed sovereign inspired Dante's letters of 31 March and 17 April, as he waited anxiously in the Casentino as the guest of Count Guido di Battifolle (who in fact soon joined the opposition and, after Henry's death, became Robert of Anjou's vicar in Florence). Florence's untiring manoeuvers to turn the Pope against the Emperor led her most famous son to liken her to the incestuous Myrrha, "truly passionate for her father's embraces, since she wickedly and wantonly seeks to breach the agreement between you [the Emperor] and the Supreme Pontiff, who is the father of fathers" (*Ep.* VII. vii. 26). Dante therefore urged his Emperor to turn away from his campaign in northern Italy and hasten to destroy Florence, "the root of this monstrous perversion" (vi. 22). The Florentines reacted by excluding Dante from the general amnesty proclaimed on 2 September 1311. Giovanni Villani confirms Dante's analysis, claiming that, if Henry had hastened south to Tuscany, he would have swept all before him not only in Tuscany but even in Rome and the southern kingdom.[25] Instead, the siege of Brescia dragged on for another five months and proved a Pyrrhic victory. Not only had Henry lost two-thirds of his small army, but the Emperor who had initially wished to banish the terms Guelf and Ghibelline (Compagni, *Cronica* III. 26) was now forced by the situation "to assume more and more the role in which Florence had cast him—the chief of the Ghibellines and the tyrannical oppressor of communal liberties. . . . The Emperor-elect had passed over too many Guelf lords."[26]

Henry himself does not appear to have realized the full extent of the dangers threatening him, and as late as May 1312 he continued to send copies of confidential negotiations to the French king. On 21 October 1311 the Commune of Genoa presented him with the keys to their city: "and gave him full control of the city, an event that was thought to be quite remarkable, for the liberty and power of the Genoese was such that no other Christian city could match them either on land or sea" (Villani, *Cronica* X. 24). In December, however, news came that Robert's brother, Duke John of Gravina, had arrived in Rome with a large body of troops. Henry now placed Florence under a ban, and from 24 January 1312 all Florentines—except those who, like Dante, had been exiled for partisan reasons—were declared rebels of the Empire. Eventually, the Emperor-elect reached Rome, and on 26 May 1312 there took place "one of the greatest battles fought in Rome during the Middle Ages."[27] Florence was able to parade in triumph the captured standards of the King of the Romans. The Guelf troops from Tuscany, however, soon began to drift away, as did many of the imperial soldiers. In the general confusion, Henry was crowned Emperor by Cardinal Niccolò da Prato—not in S. Peter's but in St. John Lateran.

On the day of his coronation (29 June 1312), Henry dispatched encyclicals claiming that imperial authority proceeded directly from God and declaring that all men and kingdoms ought to be subject to the Emperor, in imitation of the celestial hierarchy.[28] Philip the Fair retorted that the kings of France had never had or acknowledged any temporal superior. The Pope's reaction was less predictable and far more insidious: for more than six months after the coronation, Clement did not officially address Henry as Emperor. Ten days before that event he ordered Henry to swear an oath that he would not invade Robert of Anjou's kingdom, and commanded the Emperor to leave Rome on the very day of his coronation, prohibiting him from returning to "lands of the Church." Despite these setbacks, and although abandoned by many northern nobles, Henry was now sure of his imperial title. He therefore reacted vigorously to any attempts to lessen his authority and concluded a series of treaties with Frederick of Trinacria. In September he finally moved against Florence, attempting to besiege the city with a force that was greatly outnumbered and incapable even of encircling the city, until he fell ill with malaria and had to lift the siege on 31 October. Leonardo Bruni assures us that, despite all the hopes he placed in the successful outcome of Henry's attack on Florence, Dante's love for his native city was such that he refused to be present at the siege.[29]

The dénouement was played out over ten months. In mid-February 1313 King Robert ended three years of procrastination by accepting the captainship of the Guelf League; some two months later the Priory offered him the signory of Florence for five years: "Robert of Anjou had become the figurehead uniting all the powers in the peninsula that fought against the Luxembourg Emperor."[30] On 26 April Henry VII condemned Robert (who obviously enjoyed papal protection) to death as a rebel of the Empire. Philip the Fair publicly championed his cousin and opposed the Emperor, and Robert himself denounced Henry as an enemy of the Church and of peace. The Pope went so far as to threaten the Emperor with excommunication (12 June) if he should invade the Angevin kingdom. Much hung in the balance when Henry's moves against Robert were interrupted by the Emperor's death of malarial fever on 24 August 1313.

Despite the scepticism of modern historians, Dante's immense hopes in the successful outcome of the Emperor's mission were shared by many of his contemporaries, and even Giovanni Villani states that, if death had not intervened, Henry would have "conquered the *Regno* and taken it away from King Robert . . . and then . . . it would have been an easy thing for him to conquer the whole of Italy and many other provinces" (*Cronica* X. 53). Later Dante would condemn the Pope as the mastermind behind the betrayal of Henry's attempts to restore peace and order to Italy, as the poet directed the reader's attention to one of the few vacant seats in Heaven, one surmounted by a crown and awaiting the arrival

> "de l'alto Arrigo, ch'a drizzare Italia
> verrà in prima ch'ella sia disposta . . .
>   E fia prefetto nel foro divino
> allora tal, che palese e coverto
> non anderà con lui per un cammino."[31]

It is astonishing that, at the moment when the poet summons up all his powers to describe the reality of Heaven and the beatific vision, he should still turn back to the political tragedy so recently played out on earth—and thunder the prophetic news of Clement's damnation, whereby the Pope who betrayed the Emperor will propel Boniface ("him of Alagna") farther down into the infernal rock of the third *bolgia* of Fraud.

For our present purpose, it is also significant that the years of Henry's expedition saw the composition of at least the greater part of the second *cantica* and witnessed the motivating force behind the political element that is such an essential feature of the *Purgatorio*. Moreover, the final stages of the political tragedy undoubtedly made Dante even more aware of the dangers spread abroad by the claims for papal plenitude of power and Guelf rule.[32]

If the dating of the second *cantica* must perforce include the fateful years of Henry's attempt to restore imperial rule and bring peace and unity to Italy, then these same years of immense hopes and crisis experienced by Dante must also be judged as the motivating force behind Dante's only political treatise, the *Monarchia*. Its dating is one of the most controversial issues in Dante studies. Despite the strong arguments put forward for 1308 by Bruno Nardi (who places the Latin treatise before the *Comedy*), a consensus still exists for 1311–12. The notorious aside "as I have already stated in the *Paradiso*" of *Monarchia* I. xii. 6 would, if genuine, place the commencement of the work after the first cantos of the *Paradiso* had already been written. No one, of course, knows when Dante began the *Paradiso*, although virtually everyone agrees that the poet completed it only just before he died. The most important point in the controversy is undoubtedly the question whether or not the Latin treatise was written at some time during the composition of the poem. Most scholars would agree that the genesis of the *Monarchia* is to be found in the hopes and disillusionments occasioned by Henry VII's Italian expedition. Boniface VIII's skirmishes with Philip the Fair had also sparked off a political debate that proved to be of great importance for Dante's defense of the Empire; however, it was not before 1311–12 that the Florentine exile could have penned the opening lamentation of *Monarchia* II. i. 3: "I was struck with sorrow at the fact that kings and rulers were united in one thing alone, in opposing their Lord, their Anointed One, the Roman Emperor." Here is the core of bitter experience that produced the *Monarchia* as we know it, at some time between 1314 and 1316, or even as late as 1318.

Decisive develoments took place in 1313–14 and brought the whole problem of imperial authority to a head. Robert of Anjou at last showed his true colors when he responded to Henry's condemnation by appealing to the Pope on the grounds that the Empire (founded on violence) had been legitimately replaced by self-governing kingdoms and states as a result of the Donation of Constantine, while the Emperor's authority was subordinate to that of the Pope even in the temporal sphere.[33] Robert's second petition to the Pope (written shortly after Henry's death) was violently anti-imperial: Henry VII was listed with Nero, Domitian, Trajan, and Frederick II in an effort to demonstrate the harm inflicted by emperors on Italy and the Church. Recent experience demonstrated that such emperors were usually Germans "who adhere to barbaric ferocity rather

than to the profession of Christianity." Robert therefore requested that the
Pope should not confirm any future "King of Germany" and that he take
all steps necessary to ensure that no imperial candidate should ever again
set foot on Italian soil.[34] As W. Bowsky comments: "The course of experience and polemic at last brought Robert of Anjou to demand the destruction of the Roman Empire."[35]

Far worse for Dante were the steps actually taken by Clement. Six
months after Henry's death (14 March 1314), the Pope issued the bull
Romani principes, which claimed that the late Emperor had sworn fealty to
the papacy, declaring himself to be a vassal of the Church. Another solemn
pronouncement in the bull *Pastoralis cura* (issued the same day Clement
appointed Robert of Anjou imperial vicar in Italy) justified Robert and revoked all of Henry's judgments against the Angevin on the grounds that
the Pope was not only entitled to take over imperial authority during a vacancy, but that he was in fact superior to the Emperor as a result of "that
plenitude of power which Christ . . . conceded to us."[36]

One month later (20 April 1314) Clement, the "lawless shepherd" (*Inf.*
XIX. 83), died. Both the Empire and the Church were now without leaders.
Dante seized the opportunity to write to the cardinals assembled in conclave at Carpentras, lamenting the virtual destruction of the Church and
the abandonment of Rome, "to which . . . Christ confirmed the empire of
the world, that Rome which Peter and Paul, the Apostle to the gentiles,
consecrated as the Apostolic See by the sprinkling of their blood" (*Ep.* XI.
ii. 3). He accuses the cardinals of leading the Church astray, selling and
bartering in the Temple, espousing Greed, and eclipsing Rome's sun (cf.
Par. XXVII. 34–45). The Church Fathers, he claims, are ignored and neglected; only the decretalists are studied for "riches and benefices" (vii. 16;
cf. *Par.* IX. 133–35). Nevertheless, the Italian cardinals should realize that
Rome—whose present condition would move "even Hannibal to pity"—
is still "the country of the illustrious Scipios" (x. 21, 25; a surprising association for ecclesiastics—but one reiterated in *Par.* XXVII. 61–62, where it
is put into the mouth of St. Peter, the archetypal pope). Dante, therefore,
exhorts them to unite in order to fight the good fight for "the Spouse of
Christ, for the seat of the Spouse, which is Rome, for our Italy, and . . . for
the whole of the community now in pilgrimage on earth" (xi. 26).

The Epistle's prophetic tenor is set by the opening quotation from
Lamentations 1. 1: "How doth the city sit solitary that was full of people!"
Jeremiah's prophecy of the destruction of Jerusalem, brought about by the
leaders of the Pharisees, is used to describe the contemporary situation,

in which Christ's Bride, the Church, has been brought to such a pass that "Jews, Saracens, and Gentiles . . . cry out 'Where is their God?'" (*Ep.* XI. iii. 4).[37] While addressed to the Italian cardinals—and, in particular, Napoleone Orsini, who was largely responsible for the disastrous election of Clement V at Perugia in 1305—the letter is a passionate attack on the whole Church leadership, which "has espoused avarice . . . ever the mother of impiety and iniquity" (vii. 14: *semper impietatis et iniquitatis . . . genitrix*). Everyone is muttering what Dante alone dares to cry aloud. False prophets and astrologers claim that everything is governed by necessity, whereas in reality the cause lies in the cardinals' misuse of their free will (iii. 4). Let no one think, however, that Dante is guilty of the sin of Uzzah (2 Samuel 6. 6–7; *Purg.* X. 55–57), for he does not concern himself with the Ark of the Church but "with the unruly oxen that are dragging it away into the wilderness" (l. 12). Indeed, following the example of St. Paul, Dante declares himself to be one of the least of Christ's sheep: "By the grace, then, not of riches but of God, I am what I am, and the zeal of His house has devoured me" (*Ep.* XI. v. 9; cf. 1 Corinthians 15. 9)—where the zeal of the Old Testament prophets (Psalm 68. 10) is added to Paul's "by God's grace I am what I am." God has placed his truths even in the mouths of babes and sucklings (Psalm 8. 3). The blind man has proclaimed the truth which the Pharisees strove to conceal and pervert (John 9. 1–41). These biblical precedents, Dante declares, are his justification for speaking out; and we note the significance of the vital Pauline element, superimposed on the prophetic tradition of the Old Testament. The result is of truly biblical intensity: in the words of Raffaello Morghen "without equal in any other writer of the Middle Ages."[38]

Despite the uncertainties surrounding the precise dating of the *Monarchia*, recent scholarship has convinced me that Dante's treatise on Empire is largely the result of his witnessing Henry VII's imperial mission and its failure, but that it acquired its present form after he had begun to write the first few cantos of the *Paradiso*. Depending on the dating of this work, it will be necessary to assign the definitive version of the Latin treatise to 1314 (Cosmo, Mazzoni) or 1316–18 (Ricci, Petrocchi, Hollander-Rossi).[39] The editorial work of Ricci and Shaw has swung the critical balance. Shaw's research has clearly shown that the phrase *sicut in Paradiso iam dixi* (*Mon.* I. xii. 6: "as I have already stated in *Paradiso*," cf. *Par.* V. 19–24) is found "in all the Latin codices . . . and in all the codices of Ficino's version."[40] This later dating, among other things, rules out any fundamental opposition between the *Monarchia* and the *Comedy*. Clearly the two works are complementary products of the final stage in Dante's political and religious thought. While the Latin treatise focuses on problems concerning the concept of Empire, the *Comedy* embraces every facet of human experience and thought.

The first two books of the *Monarchia* deal with concerns already touched upon in *Convivio* IV. iv–v: the necessity for the world to be ruled by one supreme sovereign, the Emperor (Book I), and God's pivotal granting of the universal Empire to the Roman people for all time (Book II). Dante affirms his belief that the Emperor is the ultimate guarantor of peace and justice; the Roman Empire gave the world the *pax universalis* or universal peace necessary for Christ's coming into the world, just as it also provided the secular justice necessary to condemn Him to death, thereby ensuring the salvation of the human race (cf. *Par.* VI. 82–90). In Book III, Dante tackles the burning question whether the Emperor's authority proceeds directly from God or whether it descends to him through some vicar or minister. The experience of Henry VII's disastrous mission, but also the hierocratic claims of Clement V and his successor, John XXII, must have fueled this last section of Dante's treatise: the poet of the *Comedy* is bent on using every possible argument to prove the Emperor's autonomy in the secular sphere. In so doing, Dante refutes the reasoning of the hierocrats with their appeals to Holy Writ (chapters 4 to 9), to history (chapter 10: the Donation of Constantine), and finally to reason (chapters 11–12: the *reductio ad unum*, the desire to reduce everything to a singular, all-embracing unit[y], which had such a powerful attraction for the medieval mind and which underlay Boniface's *Unam sanctam*). The last four chapters of Book III are the *pars construans*, in which, having exposed the errors in the arguments of those who maintain the Emperor's dependence on the Pope, Dante sets out to prove that the Empire "does not depend upon the authority of the Church" but instead depends "immediately upon God" (III. xii. 2). The Empire "flourished in all its power" even before the Church came into existence (III. xii. 3); Christ is the exemplar for the Church and, as such, before Caesar's representative, Christ declared that His kingdom was not of this world (III. xiv. 3–5; John 18. 36).

Most important for anyone who tries to understand Dante's political (and religious) thought is the notorious last chapter, in which we are told that human beings are unique in that they constitute "a middle-term between corruptible and incorruptible things" (III. xv. 5). God has therefore set up two goals: the first, happiness in this life, typified by the earthly paradise; the second, the happiness of eternal life, signified by the heavenly paradise. We reach the first goal, thanks to the teachings of philosophy and by the exercise of our moral and intellectual virtues; we arrive at our ultimate end by means of spiritual teachings and the three theological virtues. Human greed, however, is such that these aids would be ignored if humanity were not constrained and led by two guides: the Supreme Pontiff "who is to lead humanity to eternal life in accordance with revelation; and the Emperor who, in accordance with philosophical teaching, must lead it to temporal happiness." Moreover, "God alone elects and confirms the Emperor."[41]

This constitutes what Francesco Mazzoni has rightly called the basic allegory of the *Comedy*, whereby the pilgrim's journey represents the conquest of a twofold happiness within the context of the two goals assigned by God, the first in the order of Nature, where Virgil is the guide, and then in the order of Grace, where Beatrice's supranatural guidance is necessary.[42] All too often, Dante's poem has been regarded exclusively as a spiritual ascent to God, thus ignoring the totality of the poet's message, which is bent on leading humanity to both its goals, the one set firmly in this world (Virgil / Emperor ⟶ Earthly Paradise) and the other providing salvation and eternal beatitude. The Epistle to Cangrande rightly points to the poet's primary intention: "the whole as well as the part was conceived, not for speculation, but for a practical purpose."[43]

The immediate message of the *Comedy* is that humanity *in via* has been corrupted by the evil example set by its spiritual leader (*Par.* XVIII. 126). The Church is guilty of confounding within itself the spiritual and temporal powers that God has willed to be independent though mutually supportive (*Purg.* XVI. 127–29). The divine formula of two guides and two complementary but distinct goals has been obliterated:

> "Soleva Roma, che 'l buon mondo feo,
> due soli aver, che l'una e l'altra strada
> facean vedere, e del mondo e di Deo.
>   L'un l'altro ha spento; ed è giunta la spada
> col pasturale, e l'un con l'altro insieme
> per viva forza mal convien che vada;
>   però che, giunti, l'un l'altro non teme:"[44]

The message Dante sets at the center of his *Comedy* highlights the consequences of the rejection of God's blueprint for the world, as set out in Book III of the *Monarchia*:

"Dí oggimai che la Chiesa di Roma,
per confondere in sé due reggimenti,
cade nel fango, e sé brutta e la soma."[45]

A leading authority on medieval thought has asserted that, in positing
two ends for humanity on earth in the *Monarchia* "the unity of mediaeval
Christendom, with its subservience to the Popes, has now been abruptly
and utterly shattered," while another authority has claimed "In the *Comedy*
there is no longer any trace of the two final ends found in the *Monarchia*."[46]
Francesco Mazzoni, however, has directed our attention to two passages
in the writings of St. Thomas Aquinas in which Dante could have found
humanity's two beatitudes linked, the one to the realm of Nature and the
other to that of Grace; in both "Thomas's thought is expressed in terms
very similar to those used by Dante."[47] No less an authority than Dante
himself tells us that his thesis "is not to be so narrowly interpreted as to
imply that the Roman Prince is not in some things subordinate to the Roman pontiff, since our temporal happiness is in a certain way subordinate
to our eternal happiness" (*Mon.* III. xv. 17). The latter phrase regarding
the relative subordination of temporal to eternal happiness—*cum mortalis
ista felicitas quodammodo ad inmortalem felicitatem ordinetur*—has caused
endless controversy.[48] It is, therefore, helpful to turn to a passage in the
Quaestio in utramque partem, written in 1302 at the time of the ideological
struggle between Boniface VIII and Philip the Fair, in which the Pope's
right to intervene outside the strictly spiritual domain is limited to special
cases that pertain "in some way" (*quodam modo*) to spiritual matters.[49] In
other words, there is no retraction or volte-face on Dante's part at the end
of the treatise, but rather a reaffirmation of what had been clearly stated at
the beginning of the discussion (*Mon.* III. iv. 20): namely, that "temporal
government does not owe its existence to the spiritual government, nor its
power . . . nor even its operation as such—although it certainly does receive from it the capacity to function more effectively, by the light of grace
which God confers on it in heaven and which is dispensed on earth by the
supreme pontiff's blessing." Such was Dante's dream, something that had
seemed reality for a brief moment when Henry VII had received Clement's public benediction for his imperial mission, but which for the rest of
the poet's life remained little more than a mirage, a nostalgic ideal.[50]

It seems likely that Dante's stern admonition to the imperial electors in *Monarchia* III. xv. 13, reminding them that they are not so much
"electors" as the mouthpiece of God's choice for the Empire (*denuntiatores*

divine providentie), was occasioned by the dual election that occurred in October 1314. After Henry's death the House of Luxembourg attempted to check the power of the Habsburgs by supporting Duke Lewis of Bavaria against the latter's rival, Frederick of Austria. On 19 October the archbishop of Cologne and Rudolf, Count Palatine of the Rhine, elected Frederick. The next day, a majority of electors cast their votes in favor of Lewis. Both were crowned on 25 November: Lewis in the traditional place, Aix-la-Chapelle, but by the archbishop of Mainz (to whom this prerogative did not belong), while Frederick was anointed according to tradition by the archbishop of Cologne, but at Bonn. These events probably provide the backdrop to Dante's warning in the final chapter of the *Monarchia*, when he points out: "And so it sometimes happens that discord arises among those privileged to make this proclamation, because all—or some of them—are so blinded by the mists of greed that they fail to perceive the face of the divine dispensation" (*Mon.* III. xv. 14).

On the narrower front of Tuscany, Henry VII's death did not prevent a renewed Ghibelline threat from Pisa, where Uguccione della Faggiuola had taken over command of the city with some eight hundred of Henry's German cavalry. Uguccione made peace with Lucca and Siena, and in June 1314 he established a Ghibelline regime in Lucca, with his own son as *Podestà* and the Guelfs cast into exile. Florence was thus threatened by a powerful Ghibelline alliance controlling the western valley of the Arno. As a result, and with San Miniato under siege, on 19 May 1315 Florence proclaimed a general amnesty to all exiles on condition of their paying a fine and undergoing the *oblatio* in the Baptistery of San Giovanni, which involved the wearing of sack-cloth and a miter and holding a penitential candle in one's hand. Although it is likely that the *oblatio* would have been dispensed with in 1315, Dante refused to accept any indication that he had been guilty of some transgression: "Is this then the gracious recall of Dante Alighieri to his native city, after the sufferings of almost fifteen years of exile? Is this the reward of innocence which is obvious to everyone? . . . Far be it from this preacher of justice to pay those who wronged him. . . . If some other way can be found . . . which does not lessen the reputation and honor of Dante, I will accept it without delay. But if Florence can be entered by no such way, then I will never enter Florence. What! can I not anywhere gaze upon the face of the sun and the stars? Can I not contemplate the most precious truths under any sky?"[51]

On 29 August 1315, in the fiercest battle to have been fought for many years on Tuscan soil, the Florentine Guelfs were slaughtered at Montecatini, among them a nephew of King Robert of Naples. Florentine resistance only hardened, however, as Giovanni Villani pointed out (*Cronica* X. 74). Among the exiles whose hopes were dashed was Dante Alighieri, once again (this time, together with his sons) condemned to death on 15 October and 6 November 1315.[52] The poet was now fifty years old, fated to spend a further six years in exile until his death during the night of 13–14 September 1321. In 1312 or 1313, he stayed in Verona as an honored guest at the court of Cangrande della Scala. In 1317 or 1318, he made his final move, to Ravenna. In 1316, after a two-year vacancy (and with only six Italian cardinals out of a total of twenty-three in the Sacred College), the French party once more prevailed with the election of Jacques Duèse, cardinal-bishop of Porto, as John XXII. Of this Pope Raoul Manselli writes that he was one of those chiefly responsible for the gap separating the mass of the faithful from the Church hierarchy in the fourteenth century (*ED* III, 190). And from the Heaven of Justice Dante denounced the malpractices of a Holy Father who set an evil example that corrupted the whole contemporary scene:

> Già si solea con le spade far guerra;
> ma or si fa togliendo or qui or quivi
> lo pan che 'l pïo Padre a nessun serra.
>   Ma tu che sol per cancellare scrivi,
> pensa che Pietro e Paulo, che moriro
> per la vigna che guasti, ancor son vivi.
>   Ben puoi tu dire: "I' ho fermo 'l disiro
> sí a colui che volle viver solo
> e che per salti fu tratto al martiro,
> ch'io non conosco il pescator né Polo."[53]

In this, perhaps the most scathing of Dante's diatribes against churchmen, the poet of justice accuses Pope John XXII of destroying Christ's vineyard, the Church militant, in his adoration of the image of John the Baptist found on the florin, accompanied by his vulgar dismissal of Saints Peter and Paul as "the fisherman and Old Paul" (the Pope's French pronunciation "Pol" sarcastically conveyed in the rhyme-word "Polo"). The condemnation is then repeated by none other than St Peter, in *Paradiso* XXVII. 58–60, when the archetypal Pope prophesies the damage inflicted by Clement V, the Gascon, and John XXII, a native of Cahors: "Cahorsines and Gascons prepare to drink of our blood. O good beginning, to what vile ending you must fall!"—"Cahorsine" constituting a fierce reminder that the Pope's birthplace had become a byword for usury (*Inf.* XI. 50). Although John was himself a sober, frugal person, the papacy's wealth and splendor scandalized many contemporaries, especially the Spiritual Franciscans, who advocated absolute poverty and whose views profoundly influenced the poet of the *Comedy*. Although John XXII's condemnation of the views of the Spirituals was not published until after Dante's death, the bulls *Sancta Romana* (1317) and *Gloriosam Ecclesiam* (1318), together with the persecution of radical Franciscans in Provence, pointed the way to the terrible crisis unleashed by the bull *Cum inter nonnullos* (1323) and in part foreseen by the poet of *Par.* XII. 121–26.

Even more important for our present purpose is the bull *Si fratrum* (April 1317), in which John XXII attempted to apply the theory of papal supremacy over the Empire, as expounded in his predecessor's *Romani principes* and *Pastoralis cura*. Just after his election John had received from Naples the draft of a bull that would have removed Italy totally from the Empire. The Pope, however, was not eager to increase the power of Robert of Anjou. As soon as he was crowned, he urged Lewis of Bavaria and Frederick of Austria to end their rivalry by peaceful means; and for several years he preserved an apparently neutral attitude toward both claimants to the imperial throne. Then, with *Si fratrum*, he inserted into canon law an act declaring that, whenever the Empire was vacant, its jurisdiction and administration devolved upon the Pope, since God had conferred on the latter the right to command both in heaven and on earth.[54] The supreme pontiff also expressed astonishment that those who had received vicariates or other offices from Henry VII had not sought ratification by the Holy See; they would be excommunicated if they did not resign forthwith.

On 16 July 1317 John confirmed Robert of Naples in the vicariate-general conferred on him by Clement V. His first sanctions were directed against Matteo Visconti, Cangrande della Scala, and Passarino Bonaccolsi, and on 6 April 1318 the three "tyrants" were summoned to appear before him within three months. The Pope, however, had overplayed his hand. Excommunication and other spiritual weapons had been debased by frequent use for political ends, and a Milanese chronicler objected: "Is Pope John XXII waging a just war against Milan? It seems not, for he should not intervene in wars, but only in spiritual matters." Many shared the spirit of Dante's *Monarchia* and *Comedy*. Moreover, as G. Mollat observes: "This is why the events in Lombardy and the surrounding regions have such great importance; they foreshadow the birth of what has been called the spirit of the modern world long before the days of Machiavelli."[55]

One of the trio who resisted the Pope was Dante's patron, Cangrande della Scala (*Par.* XVII. 76–93), who had been appointed Henry VII's vicar in March 1311. In March 1317 Cangrande was named vicar imperial in Verona and Vicenza by Frederick of Austria; the following year, he was elected Captain General of the Ghibelline League in Lombardy. Whether or not Dante dedicated his *Paradiso* to Cangrande della Scala, the exiled poet expressed feelings of admiration for and gratitude towards Cangrande at the heart of the third *cantica* (*Par.* XVII. 76–93). According to Giorgio Petrocchi, this remarkable excursus offers an important clue to the problem of Dante's departure from Verona, which probably took place in 1318.[56] Dante left the Ghibelline capital of northern Italy and made his way to the moderately Guelf but peaceful town of Ravenna, where Guido Novello da Polenta—the nephew of Francesca, whom the Florentine poet had placed among the lustful in his *Inferno*—was *Podestà*. There, in the company of his children (Pietro, Jacopo, and Antonia) and friends such as Dino Perini and Pietro Giardini, Dante was able to finish his *Comedy* just before his death, as well as revive the Virgilian bucolic tradition in correspondence with Giovanni del Virgilio. In this poetic exchange, which demonstrated yet again his constant need for artistic experimentation, he defended his use of the vernacular and hinted at the danger awaiting him in Bologna, should he accept the invitation to receive the poetic crown in that city. In Dante's second Eclogue, the danger is personified by Polyphemus, whose jaws are "familiar with the drip of human gore" (*Ecl.* 4, 77). This phrase most probably refers to the situation brought about by the election in 1321 of Fulcieri da Calboli to the post of Capitano del Popolo in Bologna. As *Podestà* of Florence in 1303, Fulcieri had already been condemned by the poet in *Purgatorio* XIV. 58–66, in similar terms to the ones found in the Eclogue, for his cruel persecution of Florentine exiles, whose "living flesh" he sells.

Dante—although he yearned for the public recognition afforded by the poetic laurel—remained in the relative calm of Ravenna, with its memories of the solemn artistic representation of imperial law and justice in the mosaics celebrating Justinian's supreme achievement. In the summer of 1321, he journeyed to Venice as a member of an embassy sent to the Doge by the Lord of Ravenna in an attempt to settle a long-standing feud. On his way back along the malarial seaboard, Dante contracted a fever and died after his return to Ravenna, during the night of 13–14 September. He was buried in the Church of San Pier Maggiore (later San Francesco). Only half a century later (25 August 1373), the Florentines decided to honor Florence's most famous son and exile by commissioning Giovanni Boccaccio to give public lectures on the *Comedy*; thereafter, their repeated requests to have the poet's remains returned to his native city caused the Franciscans to conceal them in a wall, until they were rediscovered in 1865 on the occasion of the sixth centenary of Dante's birth. Despite everything, Boccaccio's words remain true in his apostrophe to Florence: "He lies in Ravenna, a city far more venerable and ancient than you are . . . a city rejoicing in the fact that, together with other gifts from God, she has been chosen by Him to be the perpetual guardian of so great a treasure."[57]

DANTE'S
PURGATORIO

Introduction to Part Two

THE FIRST THREE CHAPTERS EXAMINED IN DETAIL and set in historical context Dante's experience of politics, including two decades spent in purgatorial exile. The second part of this book offers a close analysis of the political element that is such an outstanding feature of his *Purgatorio*. This second part of Dante's poem has all too often been seen as a moment of rest and nostalgia, inspired by imaginary encounters with artists and poets and reunion with friends. While recognizing the element of truth behind this view, the present study sets out to complement it by highlighting the all-important political thread that binds together the *cantica*, and gives life to the memorable figures of Cato, King Manfred, Sordello, Marco Lombardo, Pope Adrian, Hugh Capet—as well as to other essential elements in the drama such as the Angel at the Gate, the Valley of the Negligent Rulers, and the climactic scenes played out in the Earthly Paradise. Of the three states depicted in the *Comedy*, Purgatory is the only one rooted in time and, therefore, destined to pass away. As such, it mirrors most closely our transient life on earth: the souls Dante meets there are all pilgrims, destined sooner or later to be eternally united with God. In this sense at least, Purgatory reflects the ideal Christian community on earth. As always in Dante's work, however, we find a dialectic between the ideal and reality— a reality that falls far short of the state of peace, unity and justice still attainable by sinful humanity in this world. Whoever penned the Epistle to Cangrande rightly claimed that Dante's poem was written not for the sake of speculation but with the express purpose of influencing human behavior in this life (*Ep.* XIII. xvi. 40). Nowhere is this truer than in its central section, the *Purgatorio*.

As readers of the *Comedy*—a work based on *terza rima*—are aware, the author uses a typical narrative strategy, the creation of a trinitarian symmetry at certain focal points in order to drive home his fundamental message. Hence, the universal significance of the political element in Dante's "sacred poem" is underscored at three crucial points in the second *cantica* where the poet proclaims the need for a right ordering of this world, a state of balance and harmony for humanity *in via* that can be attained only when the supreme spiritual and political authorites work together in fruitful harmony according to God's providential order: first, in Antepurgatory (*Purg.* VI. 91–96); second, in Purgatory proper (*Purg.* XVI. 97–114); and a third time in the Earthly Paradise (*Purg.* XXXII. 48–60).

The poet's originality in the topography of his second realm has been well documented. What has not been assessed is the significance of the fact that Dante placed his Purgatory on the slopes of the mountain of the Earthly Paradise. The *Comedy* is the first—and *only*—work of vision literature in which the Earthly Paradise is directly linked to Purgatory.[1] That link is important for understanding the poem's overall allegorical structure and message. In the last chapter of the *Monarchia* (written most probably after his *Purgatorio*), Dante states that humanity has two goals. The first is to reach the happiness attainable in this life, prefigured in the Earthly Paradise and to which the Emperor must serve as guide in accordance with the teachings of philosophy. Three simple questions come to mind. Is there an Earthly Paradise in the *Comedy*? Where is it located? Is someone led there; and, if so, who guides that person? The answers, obvious as they are, need to be stated: yes, the Earthly Paradise is indeed to be found there, situated above Purgatory proper, and it is Virgil, the Aristotelianized poet of imperial Rome, who guides Dante there.

It is clear that Virgil is many things to the pilgrim: at times, the "voice" of reason; at others, a father- or a mother-figure; always, a pagan damned for all eternity. It would have been surprising enough for a medieval poet to choose a pagan to guide a Christian through Hell—even one who had sung of Aeneas' descent to the underworld—but to choose a pagan guide in that most recent of Christian realms, Purgatory, a region under the guardianship of another Roman who lived before Christ, the republican hero Cato who committed suicide rather than accept the rule of the first Roman Emperor! The enormity of such a decision has rarely been faced. The justification for Dante's choice of Virgil cannot be theological; it must be political. That does not exclude a religious dimension: we may even glimpse a parallel between Virgil and Moses, both belonging to a pre-

Christian past, when it was possible to find both spiritual or philosophical guidance and political leadership in the same person. One of the numerous explanations for Virgil's appearance as if "faint through long silence" (*Inf.* I. 63) is surely that the various allegorical incrustations placed on his *Aeneid* over the centuries—and still evident in the last part of Dante's unfinished *Convivio*—had virtually obliterated Virgil's imperial message. The simple fact remains that Virgil in the poem mirrors the Emperor's role and *raison d'être*, as specified in Dante's treatise on the Empire. Virgil's silence and disappearance from the Earthly Paradise thus reinforce the interpretation of the Griffin's role that sees in it a pointer to the divinely-inspired mission of the ideal Empire as the custodian of Justice.

The importance of the political element in Dante's thought has been examined in magisterial fashion by such experts as Bruno Nardi, Charles Davis and Joan Ferrante—to name but a few of the scholars to whom I owe an immense debt. It is nevertheless exciting to discover how much still remains to be done in this field of Dante studies, especially as applied to the major figures and episodes in the *Purgatorio*. The latter will form the subjectmatter of the second part of this study. To cite but one apparently minor example, however, the predominantly political aspect of Dante's religious vision is nowhere more in evidence than in the poet's choice of *exempla* for that peculiarly Christian virtue, humility. After the canonical choice of Mary, who would not expect God's scribe to have selected outstanding examples offered by the legion of Christian saints and martyrs, especially in the century and in the very land that had witnessed the extraordinary humility practiced by that *alter Christus*, the *poverello* from Assisi? Instead, however, we find an Old Testament king beside the truly astonishing choice of a Roman emperor highlighted for our edification in *Purgatorio* X. 64–93. Whatever virtues had been attributed to Roman emperors, humility was certainly not among them. Yet the poet of *Purgatorio* was determined to show a trinity of examples (Mary, David, Trajan) calculated to shock the reader into an awareness of God's providential plan, which required the Roman people to govern the world and dispense justice in the temporal sphere, while at the same time providing a lesson for errant humanity in 1300. Thus Dante uses David's removal of the Ark to the Holy City as a *figura* of the need for the head of Christ's Church to abandon Avignon and return to Rome, just as the Emperor (in 1300, imprisoned by greed on the wrong side of the Alps) must perforce follow Trajan's example in dispensing justice from the Eternal City.

The whole of Dante's Purgatory moves toward the *telos* of the Earthly

Paradise. The Pilgrim is led there by Virgil, who first saves him from the
she-wolf of Greed—as only the Emperor can do for humanity as a whole—
and who then leads him through the realization of the nature of evil and
its purification to the place where humanity can enjoy true happiness, as
Beatrice's ironic question (*Purg.* XXX. 75) reminds the Pilgrim. Virgil, like
the Roman Empire, had been born a pagan. Unlike the Roman Empire,
Virgil was not converted to Christianity. However, he is able to accomplish
his task, since, for Dante, the Empire did not depend on the Church for
its authority; indeed, it had already flourished in the fullness of its power
and authority before the Church was brought into being (*Mon.* III. xii. 3).
Who, then, could better represent the ideal Emperor's mission of leading
humanity to the happiness attainable in this life than the Aristotelianized
vates of Rome's imperial destiny?

What has not been appreciated hitherto is the extent to which Dante
politicized the Christian myth of Eden. Two basic facts characterized that
myth: first, that humanity *in via* had been expelled from the Earthly Paradise; second, that no living person could re-enter it. The first belief is well
illustrated by some lines penned by Brunetto Latini, who referred to Adam
and Eve's sin and their expulsion from Eden in his poem *Il Tesoretto*, concluding (ll. 464–67):

> e per quello peccato
> lo loco fue vietato
> mai sempre a tutta gente.[2]

The second aspect, the Earthly Paradise as the ultimate taboo for humanity,
is dramatically illustrated in the *Comedy* by the shipwreck of Ulysses and
his companions, which had been willed by God (*Inf.* XXVI. 136–42). We
are, moreover, reminded of humanity's tragic exclusion at the beginning
of the second *cantica*, when the Pilgrim and his guide gaze at the desert
waters which have never been navigated by any man capable of returning
to the land of the living (*Purg.* I. 130–32). That same perpetual exile "from
the land of delight" had been referred to in Dante's *De Vulgari Eloquentia* (I. vii. 2) and it was generally reinforced in the medieval imagination
by legends recounting attempts to storm the Earthly Paradise, which remained supremely inaccessible to humanity on earth.

No one before Dante had thought of setting up a figural link between
the happiness attainable through good government and virtuous behavior
on earth, on the one hand, and the Earthly Paradise lost through origi-

nal sin, on the other. Yet that is precisely what Dante does, both in the *Monarchia* and in the basic allegory of his Christian epic, in which he does not hesitate to subvert the myth of Eden and its primordial taboo. In the Christian view of history, time is linear: Eden was lost at the beginning and for all time. In the polysemy of Dante's poem, Eden not only harks back to the Golden Age but also represents a state of universal peace and justice, attainable *in the future* under the Emperor's guidance. The irony is total. In the Christian tradition Eden was deserted, no living person could be found there.[3] Nevertheless, in Dante's mature thought, it became the symbol of a "political" goal accessible in this life to the whole of humanity.

If, as Joan Ferrante has shown, all sins and all virtues illustrated in the *Comedy* have political overtones, it seems that we must now add the myth of Eden to the list of topics seized upon and transformed by Dante's political vision. The pilgrim's purgatorial journey begins with the astonishing discovery of a pagan suicide who acts as the custodian of Christian Purgatory, and it ends with the redisvoery of an equally astonishing Earthly Paradise, where Dante beholds first the Griffin, symbolizing ideal Rome and her Empire, and then Beatrice, representing God's ideal Church. His political purgatory—which has led him to observe the excommunicate figure of King Manfred (responsible in part for Florence's most terrible defeat at the hands of the hated Sienese Ghibellines), the repentant Sordello, the negligent rulers, God's "two suns," the crimes committed by the royal house of France, and the tragic spectacle of contemporary humanity's apocalyptic downfall—is now at an end. Dante thus begins his ascent with his beloved to that heavenly Rome "of which Christ is a Roman" (*Purg.* XXXII. 102).

Our task is to map Dante's purgatorial journey in detail and to show how it is structured by his experience of politics and his political thought. The major locations on the map have been delineated, and a thematic treatment has been discarded in favor of a seriatim approach, which charts the ideal reader's step-by-step discovery of Dante's second realm.

4

Cato: A Pagan Suicide in Purgatory

AS THEY ARRIVE AT THE SECOND *cantica*, Dante's readers have just encountered Brutus and Cassius in the pit of Hell, condemned with Judas Iscariot to being crunched in Lucifer's anti-trinitarian jaws for their treachery in murdering Julius Caesar, their lord (*Inf.* XXXIV. 61–67). It would be difficult to exaggerate the surprise in store for these same readers when, after an exordium of a mere thirty lines, they encounter the idealized figure of Caesar's great opponent, Marcus Porcius Cato (95 B.C.–46 B.C.), the Stoic defender of the Roman Republic who committed suicide at Utica.

The text (*Purgatorio* I. 37–39) tells us that the four stars representing the cardinal virtues so lit up Cato's face that the pilgrim saw him as though illuminated by the sun (an image of divine grace throughout the poem).[1] Amazingly, the pagan Stoic is not only present in this Christian realm, but he is even—if we are to believe Virgil's words in the second canto (ll. 65–66, 82)—the guardian of the seven terraces of Purgatory. Amazement is more than justified (it has worried most of Dante's interpreters over the centuries), in that Cato bore a triple handicap as a candidate for salvation in the Christian economy of the *Comedy*: he had committed suicide; he was a pagan; and he was the implacable opponent of Julius Caesar, the first Emperor *de facto* according to *Convivio* IV. v. 12.

Cato's Suicide

Dante's ideal readers have already discovered the punishment meted out for the mortal sin of suicide (in the unnatural wood of *Inf.* XIII, quickly followed by the first reference to Cato, in a canto that opens significantly with an evocation of "the love of my birthplace," *Inf.* XIV. 1–15). They

may—or may not—have read St. Augustine's attacks on the Stoic elevation of suicide, in particular, the Saint's criticism of Cato's lack of fortitude
as opposed to the exemplary courage shown by Samson and a multitude
of Christian martyrs (*City of God* I. xxii–xxvi). Admittedly Augustine preferred Cato to Caesar (*City of God*, V. xii); nevertheless, his condemnation
of Cato's suicide was total, and Aquinas, for whom suicide was a crime
worse than murder, repeats it.[2]

As Charles Davis has demonstrated, Remigio de' Girolami (a Dominican lector in Florence for many years) joined his contemporary Dante
in praising "Cincinnatus and Cato" while "taking a positive view of Cato's
suicide."[3] And Theodore Silverstein, in an article first published in 1938,
has drawn our attention to a remarkable, unpublished work by another
contemporary, Nicholas Trivet, in which we find "an account of Cato's
death which . . . corresponds remarkably with what is evidently Dante's
conception. In it the suicide is seen as an act of high virtue undertaken in
behalf of *bonum honestum*, patriotic in its gesture of opposition to the 'in-
vader of the republic.'"[4]

The passage chosen by Dante to vindicate what he called Cato's "ineffable sacrifice" (*Mon.* II. v. 15) was taken from Cicero's *De Officiis* (I. xxxi).
The Roman author claimed that what might have been interpreted as a
sin in others, whose lives were less irreprehensible, could only be attributed to Cato's refusal to accept the destruction of republican liberty: "and
yet it could have been counted a sin if they had taken their own lives, because their lives were more superficial and their conduct more easy-going;
however, since nature had conferred on Cato such an incredible gravity of
character, which he had strengthened with absolute constancy, remaining
always true to the purpose and resolve he had taken, it was more fitting for
him to die rather than that he should look upon the face of a tyrant."[5] Two
things stand out above all: on the one hand, Dante's admiration for Cato's
magnanimitas, the latter's "incredible gravity"; and, on the other, his association of Cato's suicide with freedom (*Purg.* I. 71–74). Before following
these two avenues, however, we should state that, for the world-judge of
the *Comedy*, human conduct had to be judged by the moral laws known to
the individual; suicide was not a sin for a pagan whose conscience dictated
otherwise. We thus find Dido and Cleopatra among the lustful (*Inf.* V. 61–
63), not among the suicides, and Lucretia in Limbo (*Inf.* IV. 128) despite
her condemnation by St. Augustine.

The poet's fascination with the "virtue" of *magnanimitas* or *magnitudo animi* has been well documented.[6] While the word's semantic field was

rich in possible meanings, in Dante's time it did not signify generosity or liberality (meanings gradually recaptured with Petrarch and the rise of Renaissance courts); instead—just before embarking on the *Comedy*—Dante made magnanimity synonymous with fortitude: "this spur is called fortitude or Magnanimity, the virtue that shows the place where one must stop and fight" (*Convivio*, IV. xxvi. 7). This is all the more striking because the same part of his unfinished work (IV. xvii. 4–5), Dante had first given a purely Aristotelian-Thomistic definition of magnanimity, listing it as a virtue connected with great honor and fame.

Dante's "teacher," Brunetto Latini, made the same identification between magnanimity and fortitude in his *Tresor*: "Magnanimity, which is called fortitude. . . . This term signifies great courage or prowess."[7] It is therefore hardly surprising that among the Republican heroes read to sacrifice themselves with acts of exemplary courage for the public good—and Cato's name caps the list—we should find Camillus already referred to as *magnanimus* in *Monarchia* II. v. 12. This Stoic interpretation of magnanimity had been much in evidence in the writings of Cicero and Seneca, for whom the virtue of *magnanimitas* was accompanied by an ability to despise the caprices and blows of fortune—or, as Latini puts it, "the man who is magnanimous . . . is neither puffed up by prosperity nor cast down by misfortune."[8]

As we shall see, such qualities were associated to a supreme degree with the figure of Cato in the works of Cicero, Seneca, and Lucan. Moreover, as far as I am aware, it has not been noted that the praise of Cato in *Convivio* IV. v. 16 is complemented by the reference to his Stoic *magnanimitas* in the very next chapter (IV. vi. 9–11): "There were philosophers in very ancient times . . . who believed . . . [that it was necessary] to follow truth and justice without any compromise, never for any reason to display suffering, never to display happiness, never to feel any passion at all. . . . And they and their followers were called Stoics, and one of them was that glorious Cato [*quello glorioso Catone*] about whom I dared not say anything in the passage above." The epithet *glorioso* is to be noted. In *Vita Nuova* II. 1, Beatrice is described as "the glorious lady of my mind" (*la gloriosa donna de la mia mente*)—where *gloriosa* signifies that her soul has risen to heavenly glory (*VN* XXXI. 11: "ed èssi gloriosa in loco degno"), and, as S. Aglianò observes, even when referring to a secular context of military or civic glory Dante's use of the term frequently implies veneration and even sacredness.[9]

For the moment, however, we must return to the idea of liberty, so resolutely extolled in the fifth chapter of the second book of the *Monarchia*, in which (as we have just seen) Dante's praise of Roman heroes celebrates "the ineffable sacrifice of that strictest champion of true freedom, Marcus Cato . . . [who] in order to kindle the love of freedom in the world, showed how greatly it was to be prized by choosing to die a free person rather than to live deprived of freedom."[10] Seneca, too, had coupled freedom with Cato's mortal wound, self-inflicted, "through which freedom gave up the ghost," even as he had extolled the Roman hero's sword, which gave to Cato the freedom it could not give to Rome: "Neither did Cato survive freedom, nor did freedom survive Cato."[11] It is therefore not *in spite of* but *because of* his suicide, his "ineffable sacrifice" and virtual martyrdom, that Cato is praised in both the *Monarchia* and the *Comedy*, and Virgil's words anticipate what we have just read in Dante's Latin treatise:

> "Or ti piaccia gradir la sua venuta:
> libertà va cercando, ch'è sí cara,
> come sa chi per lei vita rifiuta.
>
> Tu 'l sai, che non ti fu per lei amara
> in Utica la morte, ove lasciasti
> la vesta ch'al gran dí sarà sí chiara."[12]

It is surely significant that Cato's suicide is not mentioned in the *Convivio* (IV. v. 16), while the passage just quoted from *Purgatorio* I leads both conceptually and chronologically to its apotheosis in Book II of the *Monarchia*.[13] In both later works Cato's death—his exemplary sacrifice—is associated with freedom, an ideal that lies at the heart of Dante's conception of life in this world, one that will be celebrated both at the end of his purgatorial journey (when, in *Purg.* XXVII. 140, Virgil declares that the pilgrim's will has been made "free, upright and whole") and at the summit of his ascent through paradise, where the pilgrim recognizes the grace and power of Beatrice that have brought him to total freedom: "You have brought me from slavery to freedom" (*Par.* XXXI. 85: "Tu m'hai di servo tratto a libertate").

Such liberty is primarily a religious one, based on freedom from sin; or, as Dante states in *Monarchia* I. xii 2, liberty is based above all on freedom of the will. Free will—God's greatest gift to man (*Par.* V. 19–22; *Mon.* I. xii. 6)—lies at the heart of the *Comedy* thematically as well as structurally (*Purg.* XVI. 70–84 marks the center of the poem's central canto). In the twelfth chapter of the first book of the Latin treatise, Dante equates freedom of the will with political liberty: "humanity enjoys the greatest freedom when governed by the Emperor"—a state enabling it to achieve not only true happiness on earth but also eternal beatitude in heaven.[14] In his classic study published in 1912, Enrico Proto pointed out that, in Dante's poem, the political freedom for which Cato killed himself is transformed into the moral and spiritual freedom of Christianity.[15]

The same essential link between political and moral freedom is highlighted in Epistle VI of 31 March 1311, addressed to "the most iniquitous Florentines." In it their fellow-citizen accuses them of being slaves to "overmastering greed," which

has brought you into captivity to the law of sin [Romans 7. 23], and forbidden you to obey *the most sacred laws; those laws made in the likeness of natural justice, the observance of which . . . is not only no slavery, but for anyone who observes them freely and spontaneously is clearly for a penetrating mind the very essence of perfect liberty. . . .* Since only those who submit of their own free will to the law are free, what do you call yourselves who . . . in defiance of every law conspire against the Prince who is the very giver of the law?[16]

The absorption of political liberty into Dante's religious universe is in fact the essential theme of Auerbach's thesis: "the political and earthly freedom for which he [Cato] died was only an *umbra futurorum*: a prefiguration of the Christian freedom whose guardian he is here appointed . . . the Christian freedom from all evil impulses, which leads to true domination of self, the freedom for the acquisition of which Dante is girded with the rushes of humility. . . ."[17]

The reference to the scene at the close of the first canto (lines 130–36; 94–105) is a reminder of the amazing transformation of Cato, the "magnanimus" *par excellence*, into the patriarch who admonishes Virgil of the need to gird Dante with the reed of humility, an essential virtue in the Christian dispensation, seemingly opposed to the pagan quality of *magnanimitas* or *magnitudo animi*:

> "null'altra pianta che facesse fronda
> o indurasse, vi puote aver vita,
> però ch'a le percosse non seconda."[18]

Dante regarded, however, the suicide of the "authentic" Cato of classical antiquity as an act of supreme self-sacrifice on behalf of the *res publica*; and, as we learn at the beginning of *Monarchia* II. v: "Whoever purposes the good of the commonwealth, purposes the goal of right."[19] It is therefore interesting to discover that—as Lorenzo Minio-Paluello pointed out in 1956—we find a similar attitude in a passage of the *De Bono Communi*, written by Remigio de' Girolami: "One reads of innumerable heroic [N.B. the Latin *virtuosis*] Romans that they frequently exposed themselves to death for the state, in other words for the common good, for they cared more for the good of the commonwealth than for their own. . . . Thus Cato killed himself, as some believe, because the dominion of Rome had fallen to Julius Caesar and he believed that the state was in great peril."[20] As Ernst Kantorowicz points out in his essay "*Pro patria mori*," it was "only in the thirteenth century that the Christian virtue of *caritas* became unmistakably political . . . it was . . . activated to sanctify and justify, ethically and morally, the death for the political 'fatherland'. . . . The whole problem of *patria* . . . was more lively discussed in the age after Aquinas than ever before in the Middle Ages."[21] Of significance, too, is the fact that: " 'Fight for the fatherland,' was supposedly Cato's device, for so it was found in the *Distichs* falsely ascribed to him. Both *literati* and lawyers liked to refer to this maxim . . . and thereby ethicize the idea of *patria* after the model of the suicidal pagan"; indeed, in medieval times, the putative author of the *Disticha Catonis* was renowned and venerated for his virtue and wisdom.[22]

For Dante, then, Cato's suicide was an act both of supreme self-sacrifice, offered up for the common good, and a symbol of the true freedom promised to humanity under the Christian dispensation. The dramatic contrast already noted in the *Comedy* between the damnation of Brutus and the salvation of Cato is virtually adumbrated in the judgment passed by "moral Seneca" (*Inf.* IV. 141) on their suicides: "that same death which in Cato is a glorious thing, immediately becomes shameful and dishonorable in Brutus."[23]

Cato the Pagan

We must now turn to the portrait of Cato in the classical authors Dante knew and loved. First, we note the essential link between the Stoic hero's suicide and his love of freedom. This has already been illustrated through quotations taken from the writings of Seneca, but it is most forcefully and concisely established by Lucan in his *Pharsalia*, in which Cato swears that he will "follow to the grave the mere name and empty ghost of Freedom." At the end of his life, Cato reiterates in a rhetorical question to Labienus his determination to "fall in battle, a free man, [rather] than witness a tyranny."[24] Cato's role in Lucan's epic is, above all, to denounce the evils of civil war (cf. the title given in all manuscripts: *De Bello Civili*), a catastrophe only too well known to Dante and his contemporaries, and one most vehemently attacked in the second *cantica* (*Purg.* VI. 82–117). The importance of such testimony was bolstered by the belief that "that great poet Lucan" (*Conv.* IV. xxviii. 13) was not a writer of poetic fiction but a historian.[25] Moreover, as Ettore Paratore has observed, Lucan's poem is after the *Aeneid* the work most systematically exploited by Dante (*ED* III, 697).

In Virgil's work, Dante's "pagan Bible," the Christian poet discovered on Vulcan's shield Cato, the Elysian legislator, standing in exemplary opposition to the sinister figure of Catiline enclosed by the infernal gates of Dis: "the abodes of Hell, the high gates of Dis, the penalties of sin, and you, Catiline, hanging on a frowning cliff, and trembling at the faces of the Furies; far apart, the good, with Cato their lawgiver" (*Aeneid* VIII. 667–70). It is only possible to guess at the fascination exerted on the poet's imagination by Cato's separation from the damned and by the presence of the poet's own name in the phrase "his dantem iura Catonem." We may also note that the concept of *magnanimitas* was introduced in Roman literature during the decade 70–60 B.C., when three historical figures embodied the debate concerning the nature of true magnanimity: on the one hand, Catiline and Caesar, the villainous *factiosi*; on the other, Cato representing the republican tradition of Roman *virtus*.[26] Moreover, this seminal debate was graphically reported for Dante in Brunetto Latini's *Tresor* (III. 37): "Cato spoke of the Roman heritage which Catiline had defiled, and said that it had been gained through virtue as well as by arms, through wisdom and righteous government and integrity."[27]

For Cicero (*De Finibus* IV. 16), Cato was the "exemplar of all the virtues," a phrase echoed by Seneca in his *De Tranquillitate Animi* (XVI. i. 1) as well as by Dante in the *Convivio* (IV. xxviii. 19), when he declared that in Cato true nobility or perfection of soul demonstrated all the human virtues throughout the various stages of his life, a message reinforced by the splendor of the four Cardinal Virtues that light up Cato's face, as we have seen, in the opening scene of Dante's Purgatory.

In the *Pharsalia* Lucan portrays Cato as "the abstract idea of virtue."[28] Lucan's description of Cato's whole campaign, his guidance of his small band of faithful followers across the desert, his refusal to go beyond the limits dictated by heaven, his rejection of the idea that wisdom or truth could be "buried in the desert sands" (*Phar.* IX. 576–77) inspired Dante with one of the basic antitheses (Cato-Ulysses) in the *Comedy*—an opposition possibly sparked off by Seneca's assertion "that in Cato the immortal gods had given to us a truer exemplar of the wise man than earlier ages had in Ulysses and Hercules . . . he [Cato] came into conflict with ambition . . . with the boundless greed for power which the division of the whole world among three men could not satisfy."[29] For Dante, Lucan's account was historical proof that Cato possessed to a supreme degree the virtue of prudence, the greatest of the Cardinal Virtues (*Purg.* XXIX. 130–32), indeed the one that must govern men's *actions* and that constitutes the basis of political wisdom. Thus, even in imperial Rome—under Nero—the republican hero could be portrayed as "the true father of his country, a man most worthy to be worshipped by Romans . . . and if they ever, now or later, free their necks from the yoke and stand upright, they will make a god of Cato."[30]

Such an attitude underpins Dante's extraordinary claim in *Convivio* IV. xxviii. 15: "And what earthly man was more worthy of signifying God than Cato? None, certainly"—although it would be difficult to prove that the poet of the *Comedy* intended to establish an analogy between Cato and Christ.[31] Nevertheless, Cato's self-sacrifice as presented by Dante both in the *Monarchia* and in the *Purgatorio* evokes such a parallel. Robert Hollander even goes so far as to state that "For any Christian the phrase, 'he who for liberty gives up life' [*Purg.* I. 72], can only point to Christ's sacrifice."[32]

Certainly, as a Christian reader, Dante must have been struck by parallels with the Redeemer inherent in Lucan's references to Cato as both scapegoat and redeemer. In Cato's central speech in Book II of the *Pharsalia*, his dedication to the ideal of *libertas* as expressed in lines 302–3 (quoted above) leads to the exclamation: "Let Rome pay atonement in full to the pitiless gods . . . But would it were possible for me, condemned by the powers of heaven and hell, to be *the scapegoat for the nation!*" This in turn leads to the prayer that his supreme sacrifice may bring about the redemption of humanity: "may I stand between and intercept every blow dealt in this war! *Let my blood redeem the nations, and my death pay the whole penalty incurred by the corruption of Rome.*"[33] No less a figure than Pope [Saint] Gelasius I (492–496) interpreted these words in a Christological key, associating them with Christ's redemption of humankind.[34]

Such evidence must surely be taken into account when we recall Aquinas's statement that "many pagans received a revelation concerning Christ. . . . If, however, some were saved without such a revelation, *they were not saved without faith in the Saviour*; for, although they did not have explicit faith, *they nevertheless had implicit faith in divine providence*, believing God to be the liberator of humanity in ways He would choose according to His pleasure . . ."[35] André Pézard (in somewhat cavalier and untypical fashion) dismissed the problem by positing a parallel with the proto-baptism of Rhipeus, carried out by the three Theological Virtues, according to *Paradiso* XX. 118–26. Hence, he argued: "If the three theological Virtues made a Christian of a companion of Aeneas, the ancestor of Rome, why should not the four cardinal virtues have made a Christian of the last Republican of Ancient Rome?"[36] The upper case used by him in "theological Virtues" perhaps gives Pézard his unconscious answer; for, as Dante writes in the final chapter of the *Monarchia*, the beatitude offered to humanity in this life is to be gained by following "the teachings of philosophy" and "by acting in accordance with the moral and intellectual virtues"; but the supernatural beatitude of Heaven may only be achieved "by spiritual teachings which transcend human reason," accompanied by "the theological virtues: namely, faith, hope, and charity."[37] Certainly, the appellation "sanctus" found in Lucan's poem (*Phar.* IX. 554: "sancto Catoni"), quickly followed by the description of the pagan hero as "full of the God whom he bore hidden in his mind" (IX. 564), would not have escaped Dante's scrutiny. More specifically, however, both Enrico Proto and Mario Sansone point to that same passage in the ninth book of the *Pharsalia* (564ff.), in which Cato refuses to enter the temple of Jupiter Ammon, as the source—or pretext—for Dante's belief in Cato's possession of implicit faith.[38]

The most important link with Cato's appearance on the shores of Dante's Purgatory has, however, received scant attention. It lies in the significance of a work already mentioned in passing, the *Disticha Catonis*, which has been well described by Richard Hazelton as that "most ubiquitous of mediaeval books."[39] In the schools of Dante's age, this text "was not only the first full-length literary piece the student read," but it also served as "a compendium of the root ideas that informed the thinking of mediaeval men," so that it was in the *Disticha Catonis* that students first absorbed *inter alia* "the idea of *contemptu mundi* . . . the sense of *mensura* . . . an idea of history," and it was through the *Disticha* that they "first became aware that Horace, Virgil, and Ovid . . . spoke with authority."[40] If we add the fact that "few books have been so attentively read by so many readers," leaving "an indelible imprint on the minds of the young," it is surely far less surprising that Cato was converted into a Christian moralist, a sage, like Solomon.[41]

More significantly, all the thirteenth- and fourteenth-century commentaries examined by Hazelton contain "a statement that the book deals with the *quatuor virtutes cardinales*."[42] As we have already noted, Dante's Cato is the embodiment of the Cardinal Virtues. Why, then, are we not told by the poet that he also possessed the Theological Virtues necessary for salvation? Why is no explanation offered, similar to those given for the salvation of those other pagans, Rhipeus and Trajan (*Par.* XX. 103ff.)?

The answer must surely lie in the fact that the author of the *Comedy* was convinced—primarily, through his reading of the *Pharsalia* and the *Disticha Catonis* (confirmed by *Aeneid* VIII. 670)—that Cato had been granted the grace of implicit faith. I thus take issue with Kenelm Foster, who stated in his authoritative analysis of Dante's attitude regarding the possible salvation of pagans: "The only alternative to pagan unbelief that we are allowed actually to see in the *Comedy* is the miraculously induced explicit faith of Trajan and Rhipeus. . . . It is as though the concept of implicit faith had no relevance at all to him [Dante]."[43] On the contrary, I would argue, the concept was so important in Dante's theology that it remained unique to Cato's case: no one else was "worthier of signifying God" (*Conv.* IV. xxviii. 15), no one else in the *Comedy* was accorded the extraordinary privilege of implicit faith. Explicit faith needed proof of its manifestations; implicit faith did not. Cato, for Dante, was truly "full of the God whom he bore hidden in his mind" (*Pharsalia* IX. 564: "Ille deo plenus, tacita quem mente gerebat").

Cato, the Opponent of Julius Caesar

For a student of Dante's political thought, Cato's opposition to Julius Caesar is the most worrying aspect of the poet's choice of Cato as the guardian of Purgatory in what has been termed "the noblest portrayal of Purgatory to have issued from the human spirit."[44] Worrying, because even when the double handicap of paganism and suicide has been eliminated, there still remains the paradox of Dante's exaltation of Cato, despite the latter's ardent republicanism and his implacable hostility to Caesar, the first Emperor (*Conv.* IV. v. 12). Already in 1977 I insisted on the apparent contradiction in Dante's choice of the Republican era as the most glorious phase in the history of Ancient Rome, highlighting the passage in *Conv.* IV. v. 12 in which it is claimed that Rome "from Brutus the first consul until Caesar the first emperor" was "raised up with citizens that were not human but divine, who were inspired to love her with a love not human but divine." The words *infino a* ("until") would seem to imply that Rome's glorious tradition of virtuous heroes came to an end with the founding of the Empire.[45] Moreover, it has frequently been remarked that Dante (who condemns no fewer than four popes to Hell) does not list even one pagan emperor among the damned, despite the fact that in medieval times Nero, for example, was a byword for wickedness.[46] Hence, "what history tends to put asunder—empire and republic—Dante would join together. . . . In brief, Dante's formulation would seem to have been as follows . . . the [ideal] emperor will work to bring about a return to what Julius Caesar, the first 'emperor' . . . himself violated, the ideal of republican civic virtue."[47] On the other hand, it is necessary to fill out the picture.

Given the fundamental role Lucan's epic played in Dante's portrayal of Cato, we should do well to look at the portrait of Caesar offered in the *Pharsalia* (something that has not to my knowledge received sufficient attention). Cato as hero is set off against Caesar as the villain of the piece. In Lucan's scheme of things, not only is Caesar guilty of the heinous crime of disobeying the Roman Senate and of causing civil war, but his savage bloodlust is highlighted, for example, in the following passage (emphases mine):

Caesar, frantic for war, rejoices to find no passage except by shedding blood; it pleases him that *the land of Italy on which he tramples* supplies him with a foe . . . [that] battle follows battle with no interval between. He would rather burst a city gate than find it open to admit him; he would rather *ravage the land with fire and sword* than overrun it without protest from the husbandman. He scorns to advance by an unguarded road, or to act like a peaceful citizen.[48]

After the apotheosis of Cato in Book Nine, there is the presentation to Caesar of Pompey the Great's severed head by Ptolemy of Egypt, on whose orders Pompey had been murdered while seeking refuge after his defeat at Pharsalus, in the name of the friendship that had bound him to Ptolemy's father.[49] The whole scene, a fierce indictment of Caesar, was already hinted at in *Phar.* IX. 276–280 ("whoever bears my head to the hated tyrant will receive no small reward for his gift"), in which Cato's description of his august opponent as "the hated tyrant" is fully borne out by the poet-narrator's judgment. When Caesar sees that Pompey is safely dead, "he shed crocodile tears and forced out groans *while his heart rejoiced*"— with the climactic epithet "traitor" in the aside: "How deep the stain cruel Fortune spared the honor of Rome when she would not suffer a traitor (*perfide*) like you to have mercy on Magnus while he yet lived" (*Phar.* IX. 1035–62; emphasis mine). "Tyrant" ("Romani . . . tyranni," *Phar.* X. 342), "traitor": such judgments of Caesar, coming from one of the greatest poets of antiquity, were not to be taken lightly, especially, when one remembers that treachery is the worst sin punished in Dante's Hell.[50]

Lucan's portrayal of Caesar ends on an undignified note. Opposed to Cato's stoic courage and self-control is Caesar's behavior when faced with a conspiracy, led by Pothinus, Pompey's assassin, to kill him. He takes refuge in "an unworthy hiding-place," overcome by fear (X. 440–44). The ignominy of Caesar's position is driven home in lines that must have struck Dante as totally at variance with Caesar's providential mission (*Par.* VI. 55–72)—not unlike the salacious jibe recorded against him in *Purg.* XXVI. 77–78, where the Italian poet follows a medieval source in recalling Caesar's homosexual relationship with the subject king of Bithynia.[51] After this unflattering portrait, Lucan's unfinished poem breaks off with a final reference to Caesar's crimes and the vengeance that will strike him down in the manner of his death (X. 528–29). His immense greed (the sin symbolized by the she-wolf in *Inf.* I. 49ff.) has already been evoked (*Phar.* X. 149–50), as Caesar learns "to squander the wealth of a plundered world" (X. 169) and encourages Rome in her newfound taste for opulence and luxury, destined to destroy her *virtus* (I. 161).

The antithesis Caesar-Cato could not be more clearly drawn than in the portrayal, on the one hand, of the latter's contempt for the law—as in his exclamation after crossing the Rubicon, "Here I leave peace behind me and *the laws which have been already been violated*" (*Phar.* I. 225; emphasis mine)—and, on the other, the insistence on Cato's cult of Law and Justice. Lucan's epic theme is "war worse than civil . . . and legality conferred on crime" (*Phar.* I. 1–2), in defiance of "the laws and ordinances of the universe" (*Phar.* II. 2), a theme embodied in the *persona* of Caesar. In radical opposition to this "bloodthirsty ogre" (Macaulay) stands Cato, "the true father of his country" (*Phar.* IX. 601: "parens verus patriae"), who "worshipped justice and practiced uncompromising virtue" (*Phar.* II. 389), and embodied all that Dante most admired in the history of the Roman Republic, so that "*Libertas* is the crucial issue in this vision of republican activity."[52] Moreover, like Dante himself, who claimed that he had risen above all parties (*Par.* XVII. 68–69), "when the citizens were leaning toward either Caesar or Pompey, *Cato alone established a definite party for the Republic* . . . on one side the people and the whole proletariat eager for revolution—on the other the senators and knights . . . *and there were left between them but these two—the Republic and Cato.*"[53]

As far as Dante's view of Caesar is concerned (and the role he plays in the *Comedy*), insufficient attention has been given to the brief description in *Inf.* IV. 123, in which "Caesar armed, with griffin eyes" is found beside the great Trojan hero, Hector, and Aeneas, father of Rome and her Empire (cf. *Inf.* II. 20–21)—a triad encapsulating Dante's view of the providential process whereby the Roman Empire was created. Now, after the fundamental study by Peter Armour, it is possible to appreciate the ambivalence of the Griffin as a symbol in Dante's work. The poet "selected a notoriously fierce creature . . . and made of it a symbol of that power [the Empire] which he had once considered violent but which he had since come to regard as a marvellous creation by God for the peaceful government and guidance of mankind." So Fra Giordano told the Florentines in 1305 that the griffin is "an animal which is fierce beyond measure."[54] Quoting a multitude of classical sources, as well as the Bible (Leviticus 11. 13; Deuteronomy 14. 11–12), Armour shows that "the griffin of tradition was a large, swift, and terrifying predator."[55] These characteristics parallel the picture of Caesar found in Lucan's *Pharsalia*, and one readily evoked by the pregnant sketch of Caesar the aggressive conqueror in the line already quoted (*Cesare armato con li occhi grifagni*). The epithet *armato* is particularly significant, in view of Caesar's decision to initiate civil war by crossing the Rubicon with his armies in defiance of the Roman Senate and the whole republican tradition. No less significant is the detail of his *occhi grifagni* ("griffin eyes"): the violence and aggression necessary for the foundation of the Roman Empire are implied, but with a typically dantesque verbal strategy that looks forward to the close of the *Purgatorio*. There, in that Earthly Paradise, which symbolizes the beatitude attainable under the guidance of Dante's ideal Emperor (*Mon.* III. xv. 7–10), the Griffin, tamed under the Christian dispensation, takes on its role of declaring the Empire's essential function as the supreme custodian and dispenser of justice. The Griffin's dual nature (*Purg.* XXXI. 81) represents at one level the ideal synthesis of Imperial Justice united with republican *Virtus*.[56]

We may, therefore, discover in the opposition Caesar-Cato the bipolarity of the Empire, an institution willed by God for the peace and happiness of humankind but one that—like all institutions on earth—was obliged to work through the dialectic of secular history. Even as the Griffin turns away from its violent nature in order to draw the chariot of humanity toward Justice and Peace (*Purg.* XXXII. 48), so Caesar's violence and illegality are vindicated by God's providential design. As Giuseppe Mazzotta points out: "by the strategy of contrasting Cato to the regicides [Brutus and Cassius], Dante suggests that there is a latent duality within the very

fabric of secular history, that there is a redeemed secular history that provides the moral middleness and area of choice between the antithetical
cities of the end."[57] Mazzotta also postulates an opposition between that
other *Veglio* in the *Comedy*, the Old Man of Crete, and Cato (*Inf.* XIV. 103;
Purg. I. 31, and II. 119): "The two figures . . . mark the pilgrim's own aske-
sis from the condition of old man to his redemption in a new man. By the
adoption of Cato to begin the new history, Dante figures the necessary
unity between historical process and prophecy"; Cato's journey "through
the desert of temptation", his quest for freedom and his self-sacrifice for
humankind, are "elements that make Cato's redemption the secular re-
enactment of Exodus."[58]

In all this, what has not been observed is that Dante may well have had
in mind Augustine's accusation against Cato, when the Saint declared that
Cato's suicide was due to his weakness, his inability to put up with adver-
sity. As proof Augustine played his trump card, pointing out that, if Cato
had truly believed that it was a disgrace for a free man to live under Caesar's
rule, he should have urged his son to join him in suicide.[59] In his admiration for the Stoic hero, Dante may well have decided to turn Augustine's
strictures on their head; the very fact that Cato had exhorted his son to
submit to Caesar's rule as first Emperor (*primo prencipe sommo*) could be
taken as proof that Cato ultimately accepted the legality and the necessity of the Empire in the divine plan after Christ's supreme sacrifice. This
would not have been the first occasion on which Dante crossed swords
with Augustine: as is well known, for the latter all earthly governments un-
accompanied by the true religion were merely "great robberies," whereas
for Dante the Empire—even in its pagan form—originated from God.[60]

Nevertheless, Dante did not iron out all the contradictions, for in
Conv. III. v. 12 we are told that Cato reached the southernmost parts of
the African desert "*with the people of Rome*, fleeing from Caesar's rule" (my
emphasis), while in *Par.* VI. 55–57 we are assured that Caesar seized the
imperial eagle "at Rome's bidding" (*per voler di Roma*). A possible explanation might be to see in the latter assertion the teleological truth, *sub specie
aeternitatis*, while the reality *sub specie mundi* would be expressed in the
earlier work.[61]

Finally, I would draw attention to the *Comedy*'s triad of redeemed
pagans: Rhipeus, Cato and Trajan. Two of these—Rhipeus and Trajan—
are revealed to Dante in the Heaven of Justice: Rhipeus, "foremost in justice among the Trojans" (*Aeneid* II. 426–27), received the grace of baptism
a thousand years before the institution of the sacrament, while Trajan was

saved through the intercession of St. Gregory the Great for his act of mercy and justice to a poor widow (*Purg.* X. 73–93). As far as Cato is concerned, we have already seen the celebration of his love of Justice in Lucan—an attribute that had earned him the supreme accolade in Virgil's epic of acting as lawgiver to the souls of the righteous in the Elysian fields (*Aeneid* VIII. 670).

What is no doubt crucial and what has not been noticed before is the significance of a passage in Boethius (*De Consolatione Philosophiae* IV. 6), in which a hidden reference to Rhipeus accompanies the allusion to a verse from Lucan concerning Cato's defeat. Dante's "sage" (*Conv.* IV. xiii. 12) states the impossibility of judging human actions according to God's truth; Boethius insists that even in "some few things of the divine depth, which human reason is able to attain, *he whom thou thinkest most just and most observant of equity, seemeth otherwise in the eyes of Providence* which knoweth all. And our disciple Lucan noteth that the cause of conquerors pleased the gods, and that of the conquered, Cato."[62] The words italicized are virtually a translation of Virgil's lines already quoted, filled out with the "seemeth otherwise in the eyes of Providence," corresponding to Virgil's fatalistic *dis aliter visum* (*Aeneid* II. 428: "Heaven's will was otherwise," in decreeing the death of this outstanding lover of Justice). This dramatic coupling of Rhipeus and Cato in "that little-known book by Boethius" (*Conv.* II. xii. 2), in the section in which Boethius treats of predestination and the mysteries of God's judgment, may well have been the spark that eventually led the poet of the *Comedy* to place the most obscure of the Trojans, mentioned only in five lines of Virgil's epic, in the Christian heaven, after his portrayal of Cato as the guardian of Purgatory.[63] Moreover, the fact that both Dante's "pagan Bible" and Boethius reported that heaven had not rewarded the extraordinary virtue of Rhipeus no doubt induced the world-judge to correct this view in his Christian epic, which showed that the true God of Christianity had in fact succored both victims, Rhipeus and Cato, in His act of redemption.

However that may be, we must not fail to note the chronological sequence of Dante's pagan trio who are united by their cult of Justice: Rhipeus (Troy), Cato (Republican Rome), and finally Trajan (Imperial Rome, before its conversion to Christianity). Once again, we admire Dante's vision of God's plan in setting up the world empire, whose origins lay in Troy and whose trajectory led to Rome—as can be seen most concisely expressed in Justianian's denunciation of Constantine's reversal of the imperial journey:

"Poscia che Costantin l'aquila volse
contr' al corso del ciel, ch'ella seguio
dietro a l'antico che Lavina tolse,
    cento e cent'anni e piú l'uccel di Dio
    ne lo stremo d'Europa si ritenne,
    vicino a' monti de' quai prima uscío;"[64]

All three are united in this providential process by their preeminent cult of Justice: Rhipeus as an individual (*iustissimus unus*); Cato, symbolizing the glorious tradition of the Roman *res publica*; and Trajan, representing that ideal, universal empire that never ceased to haunt and inspire Dante's imagination.

5

Manfred and Bonconte

A VOICE ISSUES FORTH FROM A CROWD of souls who have been compared by the poet to sheep (*Purg.* III. 79–87). They follow the leader and are "modest in countenance" (l. 87)—in utter contrast to their lives on earth, where they had been excommunicated precisely for their obstinacy and proud refusal to bow their heads to authority. Now, however, they are part of Christ's redeemed flock, although still meekly awaiting the moment when they will be allowed to begin their journey of purification up the Mountain to Eden (a moment that will come only after they have waited in Antepurgatory for a period thirty times as long as that spent under the ban of excommunication).

The voice is that of King Manfred, the illegitimate son of Frederick II, the Emperor Dante damned for heresy in *Inf.* X. 119. Born c. 1232, Manfred took over the reins of power in the kingdom of Sicily and Southern Italy at his father's death in 1250. When his brother Conrad IV died, Manfred seized the crown for himself in 1258. Pope Innocent IV, who was the guardian of the legitimate heir Corradino, excommunicated him—as did his successors, Alexander IV and Urban IV. Despite these sanctions, Manfred's power increased through a carefully planned system of alliances until in May 1259 Frederick's son was recognized as "lord" of Siena and his representative Giordano d'Anglona was installed as his vicar in Tuscany. Just over a year later (4 September 1260), the crushing victory over the Florentine Guelfs at Montaperti (*Inf.* X. 85–93), obtained by the Sienese with the help of other Tuscan Ghibellines and Manfred's cavalry, meant that Frederick's illegitimate son came to enjoy greater power in the Italian peninsula than his father had ever had. At the same time, his prestige was boosted by his daughter's marriage to the heir to the Aragonese throne.

This power and authority drove Urban IV (1261–64) to adopt every possible means to crush Manfred: in 1262 he commanded all Christians to renege on their debts to the Sienese bankers who supported Manfred, and the following year he ordered the confiscation of goods belonging to Florentine Ghibelline merchants throughout Europe. Finally, in June 1263, Urban (a Frenchman) urged Charles of Anjou, a brother of Louis IX of France, to seize the southern kingdom, which was to become a papal fief. Ironically, the same Pope who approved the rule of the *Cavalieri Gaudenti* [*Inf.* XXIII. 76–108], a lay order founded with the express purpose of putting an end to urban factions, aligned the Church with a faction in his attempt to destroy Manfred.[1]

Although Urban died before his plans could be put into practice, his newly created French cardinals ensured the election of Clement IV (February 1265), who had served Louis IX. Huge sums of money were raised to finance Charles's expedition. In May 1265 (about the time of Dante's birth) Charles of Anjou, count of Provence, arrived in Rome; on 28 June he was invested with the kingdom of Naples and Sicily by four cardinals. Nevertheless, his position was extremely precarious, since Genoese hostility meant that his army was prevented from following by sea, and it only reached Rome in December. Manfred committed the fatal mistake of inaction during these seven months. At the end of February, his army was routed at Benevento and he himself was killed. The Angevin dynasty founded by Manfred's enemy ruled Naples and the South until 1435. Manfred's defeat established the Guelf League, which, with the support of the Angevin kings of France and Naples, lasted until after Dante's death.[2]

Such, in brief, is the historical background. In order to appreciate the surprise intended by Manfred's salvation, however, one must also take into account the violent accusations hurled at Frederick's son by Guelf propagandists, both during his lifetime and afterward. For example, Brunetto Latini accused Manfred of having murdered his father and poisoned King Conrad and two of his nephews, although he failed in his attempt to have Conradin (the last legitimate Hohenstaufen) poisoned.[3] It must be remembered that Latini was driven into exile as a result of the rout at Montaperti and wrote his *Tresor* during his stay in France; nevertheless, his accusations reflect the vehemence of Guelf hatred in Dante's Florence.

We may now be ready to feel the shock waves of the poet's "scoop" when he announces to the world that, as a pilgrim on a journey willed by God, he has met and spoken with the spirit of the Antichrist's bastard in Purgatory—something so surprising that he too had been overwhelmed by wonder at his discovery, to such an extent that he remained oblivious of all else (*Purg.* IV. 1–16). Instead of the diabolical creature of Guelf propaganda, however, the pilgrim gazes at a royal figure, the embodiment of all the chivalric virtues: for Manfred is in the full flower of manhood, strikingly handsome, and of noble mien (*Purg.* III. 107). Even his enemy's minstrel had praised the dead king's great beauty, courage and wisdom.[4] As we have seen, Dante had already reacted against the Guelf stance in his *De Vulgari Eloquentia*. In the twelfth chapter of the first book, written about 1304—at a time when, as a White Guelf exile, he temporarily adopted a truly Ghibelline vision—he sang the praises of Frederick and Manfred. Both father and son were exalted as *illustres heroes*, while Manfred in his illegitimacy was acclaimed "benegenitus."[5] By the time he came to write the *Comedy*, however, Dante had discovered the providential mission of Rome, a discovery that led him to renounce the blinkered views of both Guelfs and Ghibellines (*Par.* VI. 31–33, 97–108).

Manfred's "salvation" is therefore not inspired by Ghibelline partisanship on the poet's part. On the other hand, it is perhaps naive to suppose that Dante's decision to reveal a truth so opposed to common opinion was utterly devoid of political intent.[6] Modern readers must not allow themselves to be misled by Dante's controversial "salvation" of souls who died under the ban of excommunication into discounting the gravity of the sanctions imposed by the greater form of excommunication, which ended with the relegation of the sinner "to the fire, with Judas the traitor and the devil."[7] We may thus identify the ideological nucleus of the episode in Manfred's affirmation that no sanction of the Church on earth, however grave, can prevent God's love from rescuing a sinner who repents before death (*Purg.* III. 133–35). The Florentine exile who had illustrated the catastrophic effects of spurious papal absolution imparted to Guido da Montefeltro in *Inf.* XXVII, now highlights the limitations of excommunication and papal anathema, especially when exploited as a political weapon. This message—surely, a political message if ever there was one—is adumbrated in the *terzina* (121–23):

> "Orribil furon li peccati miei;
> ma la bontà infinita ha sí gran braccia,
> che prende ciò che si rivolge a lei."[8]

This is a celebration of the infinite mercy of "the One who readily forgives" (*Purg.* III. 119): the greater the sins, the greater God's mercy to the prodigal son. Yet, from another point of view, Manfred's admission that his sins were sufficient to strike horror in his purgatorial conscience might in fact be taken to justify the ecclesiastical sanctions repeatedly hurled against

him. Instead, the poet touches on a theme that will accompany the reader
to the heights of Paradise: the presumption of human judgment, which is
so often at variance with God's eternal decrees. At the close of *Par.* XIII,
men and women will be warned against the folly of jumping to the conclusions of salvation and damnation from the mere evidence of seeing one
man making offerings in church or another robbing his neighbor. Closer to
Manfred's case is that of "Rifëo Troiano," an obscure character mentioned
very much in passing in four lines of Virgil's *Aeneid* (II. 339, 394, 426–27),
who is discovered in the Heaven of Justice (*Par.* XX. 67–69):

> "Chi crederebbe giú nel mondo errante
> che Rifëo Troiano in questo tondo
> fosse la quinta de le luci sante?"[9]

The judgments of this "errant world" are all too often incapable of com-
prehending God's reality with its mysteries of predestination and salvation,
which can only arouse a sense of wonder and awe when revealed. Dante's
Manfred has truly become *stupor mundi*.[10]

Contrasted with God's infinite mercy and generosity (His supernatural "cortesia": *Par.* VII. 91) is the vindictive persecution of Manfred's
corpse, carried out by Cardinal Bartolomeo Pignatelli, bishop of Cosenza,
who ordered the removal of the mound of stones that had been thrown
on the body by his French enemies in chivalrous recognition of Manfred's
valor, and who then had the king's body cast out of his kingdom to be
left to the mercy of the elements (*Purg.* III. 124–32). As many critics have
pointed out, Manfred's discourse is controlled and dignified without any
hint of rancor or violence. This makes his denunciation of the ferocious
vindictiveness of the men of God all the more effective in its restraint:
above all others those who ought to follow Christ's example have failed to
take into account God's infinite mercy, the possibility of true repentance
in extremis, even as they have abused the spiritual weapon of excommunication in their pursuit of political aims.[11]

Bruno Nardi, in 1964, emphasized the differences between Manfred
and his father: as the son of Bianca Lancia of Monferrato, he had received
an upbringing that enabled him to eschew Frederick's heretical beliefs. The
latter, as readers of the *Inferno* are well aware, were based on a fundamental
denial of the soul's immortality: Frederick is therefore found among those
"che l'anima col corpo morta fanno" (*Inf.* X. 15). Proof of Manfred's fervent
belief in life after death may be found in a translation he made of the *Liber*

de pomo sive de morte Aristotilis in 1255, when he found himself at death's door some eleven years before his death in battle. The original Arabic text (written in either the ninth or tenth century) had been translated into Persian and Hebrew; Manfred based his Latin version on the Hebrew text.

It is impossible to ascertain whether Dante knew Manfred's *Liber de pomo*, although it was well known among philosophers in Dante's times.[12] Certainly, as a devoted lover of wisdom (*vir phylosophie domesticus: Ep.* XII. iii. 6), Dante would have been attracted by the passionate praise of philosophy, which—Manfred claimed—leads to an understanding of the *summum bonum* and, therefore, life in both this world and the next: "There is no science like that of philosophy: it enlightens the soul and makes it delight in perfection and rectitude in this world, which is at the very basis of its well-being; and it grants knowledge and understanding of the good of the world beyond, and the one who acquires it acquires life in both worlds."[13] Moreover, in a truly Christian perspective, Manfred's text emphasizes the limitations of human knowledge and goes so far as to welcome death as a means of attaining the soul's perfection, although he stresses the fact that such perfection (signifying heavenly beatitude in perpetual union with God) does not depend in any way on our own merits but purely on God's mercy.[14] That is the lesson of the poet's "scandalous" discovery of Manfred in Antepurgatory. Nardi rightly concludes that the news of Manfred's eternal salvation was far more effective in restoring his political prestige than any attempt to excuse his struggles with the papacy might have been.[15]

Finally, we must return to the element of surprise in Dante's revelation, following a hint found in the writings of both John Freccero and Giorgio Bàrberi Squarotti. The former draws the reader's attention to "what is probably the most famous and most solemn of recognition scenes. The newly risen Christ shows his wounds to Thomas so that he may believe what he has seen . . . Christ's wounds, made manifest to Thomas, bear witness to the Resurrection. The solemnity of that moment lends to the representation of Manfred a theological force that serves to underscore the strength of Dante's imperial faith."[16] Freccero goes on to develop other points. For my present purpose, however, I would add that the way the poet structures the recognition scene is charged not only with the biblical reminiscence of the doubting Thomas but also with the pictorial representation of the *Noli me tangere* theme in medieval iconography—as can be seen in the climactic moment of his words to the pilgrim: " 'Or vedi'; / e mostrommi una piaga a sommo 'l petto" (ll. 109–10).[17] Just as Christ's resurrection was something beyond the ken of the multitude (according to whom He had been killed on the cross), so Manfred's salvation goes against the general belief that he was damned as a necessary consequence of his death while still excommunicate. In both cases, the scars on the body are testimony to the manner of death, but they also bear witness to God's eternal Truth, a reality much at variance with the fallibility of human judgment.

After the shock of finding King Manfred among the saved, the pilgrim is reassured to find an old friend, Belacqua, among the negligent; but then, in Canto V, he encounters another Ghibelline leader who had suffered a violent death in battle, as he turned to God *in extremis*. This is Bonconte, born c. 1250–1255, a member of the ruling house of Montefeltro, as he reminds the pilgrim in line 88. Whereas Manfred had died when the poet was about nine months old and was thus a figure of legendary stature and a leading protagonist in the titanic struggle between the papacy and the Hohenstaufen, Bonconte was in a sense Dante's personal enemy, since he had led the Ghibelline forces from Arezzo against the Florentine Guelfs at Campaldino in 1289. Some scholars have even suggested that it may have been Dante Alighieri himself who fatally wounded the Ghibelline general during the battle, although there is no evidence for such a hypothesis, apart from Dante's presence on the battlefield (*Inf.* XXII. 4–5).

Nevertheless, the fact that he had fought on the Guelf side at Campaldino adds a certain piquancy to the pilgrim's question regarding the disappearance of Bonconte's body:

> E io a lui: "Qual forza o qual ventura
> ti traviò sí fuor di Campaldino,
> che non si seppe mai tua sepultura?" [18]

The narrator-pilgrim is led not so much by his surprise at finding an excommunicated enemy of the Church in Purgatory as by sheer curiosity to ask a question that allows the author to invent a story once again and emphasize the essential truth that nothing can interfere with the individual's direct relationship with God. Thus Bonconte tells how he fled from the rout "on foot and bloodying the plain" (*Purg.* V. 99), until he lost both his speech and vision; he died, however, with the name of Mary on his lips—whereupon an angel seized his soul, and a devil rebelled against this act of mercy "for a little tear that takes him from me" (107), swearing vengeance against Bonconte's corpse. A tempest was thus created through the devil's powers, which hurled the frozen, lifeless body down the River Archiano and into the Arno, undoing the arms folded in the shape of a cross. [19] As Gianluigi

Toja notes: "Bonconte also dies, as do the heroes of the ancient *chansons de geste*, with the Christian's sacred seal [on his breast]."[20] The author of the *Comedy* as world-judge proves yet again his objectivity, his detachment from party bias, by announcing the salvation of one of Florence's enemies, a famous Ghibelline leader who had driven the Guelfs from Arezzo in 1287.

Further proof of Dante's impartiality may be found in the fact that Bonconte's even more famous father, Guido, was on the way to salvation according to the author of the *Convivio* (IV. xxviii. 8), although he is damned according to the author of the *Comedy* (*Inf.* XXVII). In the closing sections of his unfinished work (c. 1307), Dante had held up Guido da Montefeltro's conversion as an exemplary case of conversion in old age, when in 1296 the Ghibelline leader—"our most noble fellow Italian, Guido of Montefeltro"—had joined the Franciscan order after a lifetime of sin and opposition to the Church, "putting behind him all worldly pleasure and acts." Only three or four years later, however, the poet of the *Comedy* chose to place Guido in the eighth *bolgia* of Lower Hell. In a scene foreshadowing Dante's account of Bonconte's death, at Guido's demise St. Francis came to take up his soul to Heaven, but was prevented from doing so by a devil, who turned out to be a better logician than Francis by pointing out that it is impossible to receive absolution *before* committing a sin, since the essential act of repentance can logically take place only *after* the act of sinning (*Inf.* XXVII. 112–23). The struggle between a saint (or an angel) and a devil for possession of an individual's soul is part of medieval folklore, and most accounts take as their archetypal model the contest between the Archangel Michael and the devil over the dead body of Moses, as related in verse 9 of the Epistle of Jude: "the Archangel Michael, when contending with the devil in their dispute over the body of Moses, did not venture to accuse him insultingly; instead, he said: 'May the Lord rebuke thee.'"[21] As usual, Dante reinvigorates a medieval topos by emphasizing the subjective human element and inserting it in a broader context.

Since both father and son are subjected to the same type of altercation after their death, and since the Ghibelline father is consigned to Hell and the Ghibelline son to Purgatory, it might be argued that Dante is making a nonpolitical judgment. Although his stance is neither Guelf nor Ghibelline (and we may note that Manfred's archenemy, the Guelf king Charles of Anjou, is also to be found in Antepurgatory: *Purg.* VII. 124), it was surely not a desire to apportion equal shares to families in the after-life that led him to save the son after damning the father (Frederick-Manfred; Guido-Bonconte). Instead, in the first pair, it is the son who provides the

sensational element in the discovery of his redemption, whereas it is Bonconte's father who is damned notwithstanding his conversion and entry
into the Franciscan Order. Moreover, Guido's damnation has a political
dimension which reverberates throughout the *Comedy* and throws into relief the all-too-temporal ambitions and machinations of the spiritual head
of Christ's Church on earth. It is therefore worthwhile to cast a backward
glance at both the tenth and the twenty-seventh cantos of the *Inferno*.

As far as Frederick II was concerned, it is ironic to note that, although
accused of being a free thinker, the Emperor was—at least in his public
role—bitterly intolerant of heresy, insisting that heretics should be put to
death at the stake. On the other hand, even if the picture of Frederick as
Antichrist was discounted by the poet, it was difficult to ignore the numerous reports of his deviation from orthodoxy.[22] Furthermore, his location
in Hell—at the entrance to the Devil's City, according to the fiction of
Dante's poem—was intended to highlight the essential analogy between
heresy in the religious sphere and civil faction in the secular world, as well
as their catastrophic consequences. The essential unity of the City of Man
is destroyed by faction in the same way that heresy attempts to destroy the
unity of the City of God: as he enters the infernal city, the poet damns
both an Emperor and a prince of the Church in one pregnant announcement (*Inf.* X. 119–20). In Manfred's case (possibly encouraged by the profession of faith in God's mercy in the *Liber de Pomo*), the poet felt free to
stress the son's innate nobility of features and manners and to combat the
common belief that excommunication inevitably led to eternal damnation.
However legitimate the sentence of excommunication (and Manfred himself admits that his sins were horrendous in line 121), it can never prevent
the human soul from enjoying the fruits of God's infinite mercy through
an act of sincere repentance.

As for Guido and Bonconte, the reasons for Guido's "damnation" by
the poet are even more evident. Guido's conversion and entry into the
Franciscan order in 1296 created a sensation not unlike the one that would
no doubt have erupted had Garibaldi become a friar in the nineteenth century. It so impressed the author of the *Convivio* that he hailed it as one
of the two most memorable conversions in old age—an example radically
negated by the twenty-seventh canto of the *Inferno*. What is particularly
striking about Dante's volte-face is the chronological proximity of the two
texts: Guido's praises are sung at the end of the *Convivio*, a work interrupted in order to write the *Inferno*—in which we find the news of Guido's
consignment to Hell. As readers of the poem, we may well ask ourselves
what the reason can have been for such a dramatic change of heart.

The most likely explanation is that Dante came to learn (after writing *Convivio* IV. xxviii, and possibly through Riccobaldo da Ferrara's *Historiae*) that Guido had told Pope Boniface how the latter could defeat his rivals, the Colonna family, and trick them into defeat. This is at the heart of Guido's long, painful speech to Dante (*Inf.* XXVII. 61–129). Unlike his son Bonconte in Purgatory (who desires that his condition be known among the living), Guido does not want his infernal location to be known (ll. 61–63); his revelation to the pilgrim is thus based on the conviction that no soul has ever returned from Hell to the land of the living (ll. 64–66). In this, of course, he is utterly wrong—just as he was tragically wrong to believe in Boniface's promise of absolution (ll. 101–5). The notorious trickster is thus twice hoist with his own petard.

The Pope had bolstered that promise by his claim to possess *plenitudo potestatis*, symbolized by the two keys mentioned in line 104. Such a claim is reminiscent of the bull *Unam sanctam*, which claimed that Peter's successor possessed both the spiritual and the material "swords" or symbols of authority.[23] It was precisely to refute this claim that Dante wrote the third book of the *Monarchia*, in which he vigorously asserted the need for a Church devoted to poverty and total collaboration with an imperial power supreme in its own temporal sphere. In *Inferno* XXVII Dante wished to proclaim two things: first, the terrible consequences for humanity of the Pope's *libido dominandi*; second, the fact that even in the spiritual sphere the Pope's authority was not limitless (even he—even God—could not grant absolution before a sin was committed, because of the logical contradiction gleefully seized upon by the devil who snatches Guido's soul away from St Francis). The former led to the debasement of all religious ideals, including the launching of a private vendetta by the "prince of the new Pharisees" against the Colonna family under the banner of a crusade (ll. 85–90).[24]

Scholars who believe that Dante's interlocutors in the *Inferno* cannot be trusted, that lies are placed in their mouth by the poet, naturally refuse to believe Guido's claim that his conversion was sincere, and that he would have been saved, if he had not been tricked by Boniface:

> "e pentuto e confesso mi rendei;
> ahi miser lasso! e giovato sarebbe."[25]

But that approach is invalidated by Dante's burning desire to deliver a message "in pro del mondo che mal vive" as resolutely and as unambiguously as possible. There are, of course, difficulties (especially for the modern reader) in interpreting sections of the text, chiefly owing to lexical or allegorical uncertainties. Nevertheless, I can find no evidence in the *Inferno* to suggest that the author wishes us to understand the opposite of what the sinner-narrator states: each has passed before Minos, each has made a full confession and has been judged accordingly (*Inf.* V. 7–12).[26]

We must therefore accept the truth of Guido's statement that his conversion would have been acceptable to God if Boniface had not first threatened and then tricked him into giving fraudulent counsel: this interpretation is necessary, not only as the only logical inference from Dante's text but also as an essential clue to why the poet decided to devote such a long episode to Guido's fate. The reason is the poet's need to highlight a particular example of the disastrous effects of papal corruption not only on humanity as a whole but also on the individual. Already in the nineteenth canto of the *Inferno*, Dante had vehemently denounced papal avarice as a poison infecting the whole world:

> ". . . la vostra avarizia il mondo attrista,
> calcando i buoni e sollevando i pravi."[27]

This message will be repeated throughout the poem: the terrible example set by Christ's spiritual vicar leads the whole world astray (*Par.* XVIII. 126). Yet, even that universal poison cannot prevent an excommunicate like Manfred or an enemy of Dante's Florence like Bonconte from turning to God *in extremis*.

The salvation of both Manfred and Bonconte is essentially linked on the allegorical level to the theme of the limitations of man's intellect, a theme orchestrated throughout the *Purgatorio* and *Paradiso*—and first developed in *Purgatorio* III with Virgil's poignant words:

> "Matto è chi spera che nostra ragione
> possa trascorrer la infinita via
> che tiene una sustanza in tre persone.
>   State contenti, umana gente, al *quia*;
> ché, se potuto aveste veder tutto,
> mestier non era parturir Maria;
>   e disïar vedeste sanza frutto
> tai che sarebbe lor disio quetato,
> ch'etternalmente è dato lor per lutto:
>   io dico d'Aristotile e di Plato

e di molt' altri"; e qui chinò la fronte,
e piú non disse, e rimase turbato.[28]

On the theological-anagogical level, the episode's message is clearly stated in lines 133–35:

"Per lor maledizion sí non si perde,
che non possa tornar, l'etterno amore,
mentre che la speranza ha fior del verde."[29]

On a political level, it should be noted that Manfred does not inveigh against the French usurpers who robbed him of his kingdom nor against those who betrayed him and brought about his downfall (cf. *Inf.* XXVIII. 16–17). Instead, his words focus on the "political" persecution of his lifeless body, recalling the venomous words of Clement IV, Christ's vicar, inveighing against "the putrid corpse of that pestilential man," and highlighting the terrible contrast between the role of the Good Shepherd who goes out to save the one lost sheep (Luke 15. 4–7) and the malevolent behavior of the French Pope and his tool, the "shepherd of Cosenza" (*Purg.* III. 124–26)—a contrast reinforced by the fact that, rejected by the earthly shepherds, the excommunicate souls are now truly *pecorelle* (l. 79) of Christ's flock. As such, they suffer the terrible handicap of having to wait outside Purgatory for a period thirty times as long as their contumacy on earth. Nevertheless, Manfred's request for help through the prayers of his "good Costanza" (ll. 140–45) is a forceful affirmation of the poet's belief in the doctrine of the communion of saints, and, at the same time, a polemical statement—"qui per quei di là molto s'avanza"—directed against both heresy and abuses in the sale of indulgences.[30]

Finally, on the tropological/political level, Manfred's salvation refutes one of the fundamental premises of the hierocrats: the belief that God inevitably ratified ecclesiastical judgments—a claim enshrined in Boniface's bull, *Unam sanctam* with its customary appeal to Matthew 16. 19 ("Whatsoever thou shalt bind on earth shall be bound in heaven, and whatsoever thou shalt loose on earth shall be loosed in heaven"). Such a claim is flatly contradicted both by Manfred's presence in Purgatory, despite papal persecution, and the drama of Guido's damnation—a drama in which Pope Boniface acted as an instrument of the devil, evoked in Purgatory by both Manfred's act of humility and Bonconte's salvation *in extremis*, thanks to the salvific power of Christ's passion and Mary's intercession.[31]

The Sordello Episode
(*Purgatorio* VI–VIII)

THE THIRTEENTH-CENTURY TROUBADOUR Sordello plays a major role in the last section of Antepurgatory (Cantos VI–VIII). He first appears in striking isolation in Canto VI, when his sudden embrace of Virgil at the mere name of Mantua, their common birthplace, leads Dante as narrator to contrast such affection shown toward an apparent stranger with the internecine hatred and rivalries that destroy the cities of Italy and devastate the most beautiful part of the Empire. In Canto VII Sordello, after discovering Virgil's identity and paying tribute to his genius, leads Virgil and Dante to a beautiful valley where he points out a group of rulers, consisting of the Emperor Rudolph of Habsburg, various kings, and the Marquis of Monferrato. In Canto VIII the three poets observe the pageant played out in the valley: two angels descend from on high, with fiery but blunt swords; the poets go down into the valley and mingle with the "great souls" (1.44), among whom Dante is overjoyed to find Nino Visconti; then, all watch the spectacle as a serpent moves stealthily forward, only to be repulsed by the angels. The canto ends with an encounter between the pilgrim and Currado Malaspina. The happy discovery of Nino, a member of the powerful Guelf Visconti family, closely followed by the pilgrim's exchange of courtesies with the Ghibelline Malaspina, is yet further proof that, when he came to write the *Purgatorio*, Dante had risen beyond both his Florentine Guelf antagonisms and the vigorously Ghibelline stance evident in 1304–5.

Sordello's role is at an end, since Canto IX will describe the pilgrim's dream and ascent to the gate of Purgatory. As Professor Barolini points out in a fine study of the episode, in order to fulfill that role, Sordello is granted certain privileges by Dante: he is allowed to move and also to guide Virgil and his charge to the valley of the rulers "although as a rule only epic poets move in the *Comedy*." Thus "he enjoys quasi-epic status, a status underscored by the similarity between the valley of the princes and

Limbo, the home of the classical poets."[1] Before examining more closely
the role played by Sordello and the reasons why the author of the *Comedy* selected for this outstanding part a moderately gifted Italian poet who
chose to write in Provençal—an Italian, moreover, who resolutely aided
Charles of Anjou in the latter's invasion of Italy and crusade against the
last of the Staufen line—let us first glance at the opening of Canto VI.

The first twenty lines of the canto reflect the poet's preoccupation
with the tragic and often violent deaths of individuals caught up in the
political anarchy prevalent on earth. Indeed, of the various groups of sinners found in Antepurgatory only one—the negligent guilty of sloth, like
Belacqua (*Purg.* IV. 109–35)—is unmarked by violence. In "the Aretine" of
Purg. VI. 13, we recognize Benincasa da Laterina, a judge who condemned
to death a relative of Ghino di Tacco and was murdered in Rome by Ghino.
Another native of Arezzo is found in line 15, identified by Benvenuto and
others as Guccio dei Tarlati, a member of the Ghibelline family victorious in Arezzo between 1287 and 1289, who was likewise murdered by his
enemies, the Guelf Bostoli family. The latter also killed Federico Novello,
introduced in the very next line, the son of Count Guido Novello di
Bagno, who had been Manfred's vicar in Florence. We thus have two Ghibelline noblemen killed by the Bostoli, their Guelf opponents—in other
words, victims offered as *exempla* before we encounter the tragic spectacle
of whole families or parties destroyed by the political divisions ravaging
Italy (ll. 106–15).

Federico Novello, portrayed as praying "with hands outstretched"
(l. 16) in an act of supplication imploring forgiveness and an end to the
fratricidal struggles, is a striking maquette created by Dante, the master
sculptor. Next to him is Gano or Farinata degli Scornigiani, put to death
in 1287 by Count Ugolino (who was himself murdered with his family:
Inferno XXXII. 124–XXXIII. 90). Gano was the son of "the good Marzucco" (l. 18), a nobleman who joined the Franciscan Order in 1286 and
whom Dante may have met in Florence at Santa Croce. Like Manzoni's
Fra Cristoforo, Marzucco showed his fortitude by persuading his family
not to seek vengeance for his son's death. As Barolini points out: "Dante
places here a soul whose personal situation is an emblem of Italy's problems: this man, deliberately named only by city and family connections, is
a Pisan killed at the behest of another Pisan, Ugolino, on account of his
loyalty to yet a third Pisan, Nino Visconti"—whom the pilgrim will meet
soon enough in Canto VIII.[2]

Up to this point, Italy's woes have been highlighted. Now, however,
and in preparation for the guilt shared by the negligent princes found in

Cantos VII and VIII, the net is cast wider with the coupling of "Count Orso" and "Pierre de la Brosse" (ll. 19–24). The former (murdered by his cousin) belonged to the infamous Alberti di Mangona family (already denounced for fratricide in *Inferno* XXXII. 40–60). The latter, although possibly of humble birth, rose to be Grand Chamberlain to Philip III of France. In 1278, at the moment of Philip's disastrous war with Aragon (*Purg.* VII. 103–6), Pierre was accused of high treason and executed. From lines 22–24, it is clear that Dante regarded Philip's second wife, Mary of Brabant, as responsible for Pierre's downfall, although it is impossible to ascertain the precise reason for her vendetta. There are at least two possibilities. The first is that on the death of Philip's eldest son in 1276, Pierre accused Mary of having poisoned the heir to the throne, in order to ensure the royal succession for her own son, Philip the Fair. This would fit in with the Italian poet's fiercely anti-French attitudes and his personal attacks on Philip IV (*Purg.* XX. 85–93, XXXII. 148–60, *Par.* XIX. 118–20). Mary would thus have done her best to rid herself of such a powerful adversary by having some letters forged, which purported to show that Pierre had been in secret correspondence with the king of Aragon and thus betrayed his master. The second hypothesis is that Mary played the role of Potiphar's wife in falsely accusing Pierre of having attempted to seduce her. However this may be, the Provençal form *inveggia* (l. 20: "envy") sends us back to the corruption so typical of court life that had led to the death of another innocent man (*Inferno* XIII. 64–69), while the general poison of corruption and homicidal envy is here seen to have in its power no less a figure than the Queen of France.

After this dense prelude, Dante creates in Canto VI a dramatic contrast between the two halves of the canto. In the first 27 lines, a throng of souls implore the pilgrim's help in obtaining the prayers of their relatives on earth; so much so that he has difficulty in satisfying their requests. Like the winner of "the game of hazard" (l. 1), who "does not stay, and listens to this one and that one . . . and so defends himself from the pressing throng," he attempts to stave them off. Theological doubt follows (ll. 28–48). Then, with a dramatist's feeling for the *coup de théâtre*, the poet makes Virgil turn toward "a soul who, all alone, is looking toward us" (ll. 58–59). After the encounter with the jostling crowd, the contrast could not be greater: the soul's isolation—emphasized by the alliteration and repetition of *sola soletta* ("all alone")—is accompanied by a description of the silent, proud shade as a magnanimous man of Aristotelian stamp, identified as the troubadour Sordello in line 74. Sordello's statuesque mien, his haughty contempt, his silence and strong, piercing gaze—all these are hallmarks of the spirited *magnanimus*, as we discover in Aquinas's commentary to Aristotle's *Ethics*: "And [the Philosopher] says that the magnanimous man's movements are measured, his voice is measured, and his speech is firm and slow" (*In decem libros Ethicorum Expositio* IV, lect. X). In a few verses, Dante's verbal concision has created yet another unforgettable portrait of a proud, self-sufficient human being, reminiscent of Farinata degli Uberti, as Croce was the first to observe and as the poet himself perhaps hinted at in Virgil's indication *Ma vedi là* (58: "But see there"), echoing his *Vedi là Farinata* of *Inferno* X. 32 ("See there Farinata"). It is interesting to note that the fourteenth-century commentator Benvenuto da Imola pointed to the similarity with the solitary figure of Saladin among the "great spirits" (*spiriti magni*) of Dante's Limbo, since both men had distinguished themselves by their "singular virtue" in the world.[3] The portrait of Sordello is intensified by the following *terzina*:

> Ella non ci dicëa alcuna cosa
> ma lasciavane gir, solo sguardando
> a guisa di leon quando si posa.[4]
>   (*Purg.* VI. 64–66)

Virgil goes up to the motionless shade and inquires about the quickest way up the mountain. Sordello ignores the question; "but asked us about our country and way of life" (ll. 69–70). Virgil is only able to get out the name of his birthplace Mantua (in its Latin form, line 72, and, as Benvenuto grasped, the beginning of the celebrated epitaph attributed to the Latin poet, "Mantua bore me"), when Sordello leaps forward to embrace his still unknown fellow countryman, crying out "O Mantuan, I am Sordello from your native city!" (ll. 74–75) in utter contrast to his former silence and immobility.

As a result, the poet-narrator breaks into what he refers to as a "digression" (l. 128) but which is technically an example of *amplificatio* according to the rules of medieval rhetoric.[5] It is in fact an integral part of the sixth canto: a passionate invective against the present state of Italy (ll. 76–78):

> . . . serva Italia, di dolore ostello,
> nave sanza nocchiere in gran tempesta,
> non donna di provincie, ma bordello![6]

The image of a ship without a steersman recalls *Convivio* IV. iv. 5–6, in which the Emperor is described as the helmsman or captain of a ship (an

image going back to Aristotle's *Politics*, III. iv. 1276b, 20–27), as well as
the Epistle to the Florentines of 1311 (possibly contemporaneous with *Purgatorio* VI), in which Dante claims that "when the throne of Augustus is
vacant, the whole world goes off course . . . and unhappy Italy . . . deprived
of all public guidance, is tossed with such buffeting of winds and waves as
no words can describe."[7]

The outraged cry in line 78 that Italy is no longer the ruler of provinces but a brothel or whorehouse is yet further proof that Dante chose the
Comedy's title to indicate the whole mixture or gamut of styles employed
in the poem, ranging from the noblest or "tragic" forms of expression to
the humblest or "elegiac," according to the stylistic hierarchy first put forward in *De Vulgari Eloquentia* II. iv. 5–6 and then adapted on the basis
of the Bible's "humble style" for the "sacred poem" to which both heaven
and earth have contributed (*Par.* XXV. 1–2). The use of a word like *bordello* ("brothel") would later be regarded in the Renaissance as violating
the all-important sense of decorum, but it was deemed necessary by Dante
(as was, e.g., the word *cloaca*, "sewer", placed in the mouth of St. Peter
to describe the corruption of the Vatican in *Par.* XXVII. 25) in the poet's
titanic attempt to describe the whole range of human experience from the
ineffably sublime to the limits of grotesque obscenity and absolute evil.[8]
The phrase "*non* donna di provincie" (*Purg.* VI. 78; my emphasis) reflects
Italy's fallen state, set off against the phrase found in the gloss to Justinian's codex and repeated in medieval legal texts, whereby Italy was "not
a province, but the ruler of provinces" (*non est provincia, sed domina provinciarum*). Together with the description of Rome as a "widow" in line 113
("vedova e sola"), it also echoes the famous opening of *Lamentations*: "she
that was a queen among nations is now a virtual widow: the princess of
provinces is become a tributary!"[9]

Italy is a slave (l. 76) because she is in the grip of anarchy instead of
being governed by the Emperor, who alone can offer good government,
coupled with perfect freedom (*Mon.* I. xii. 8–9). She is told to search for
any part of the peninsula that enjoys peace, and the poet-narrator contrasts
the way Sordello's noble soul had been so eager to embrace his fellow
countryman—line 81: *quivi* is stressed, "here" in Purgatory—with the constant warring between the inhabitants of contemporary Italy: lines 83–4,
"e l'un l'altro *si rode* / di quei ch'un muro e una fossa serra" ("and the one
gnaws at the other, even when enclosed by one wall or one ditch"). The
verb "rodere" brings to mind the infernal vision of the two neighbors,
Ugolino and Archbishop Roger, locked in eternal cannibalism in *Inferno*

XXXII–XXXIII). Indeed, the flashback to this infamous pair from Pisa must give added weight to Professor Barolini's parallel with Guittone's poem, *Magni baroni certo e regi quasi*—addressed to none other than Ugolino and Nino Visconti. Pisa's downfall is personified in "la migliore / donna de la provincia e regin' anco . . . quasi adoventata ancella," and Ugolino and Nino are exhorted to follow the examples of the "Roman boni, in cui ver valor foe."[10]

For Dante, the absence of an Emperor in 1300 removes the only guarantor for peace. In the *Monarchia*, Dante was able to claim that if one were to search through the whole course of history since the Fall, one would find the world at peace only under the reign of Augustus, since under that ruler "a perfect Empire was in existence."[11] Taking up the image of the Emperor as horseman (cf. *Conv.* IV. ix. 10), Dante comments on the tragic irony implicit in the fact that Emperor Justinian (482–536) had fitted out the perfect bridle, and yet in 1300 there is no rider in the saddle to guide humanity to its terrestrial goal. The Emperor's role is to act as the supreme guardian and dispenser of Justice, thus ensuring peace and happiness for humanity. The shame and responsibility for the present tragedy are all the greater in that Justinian's codification of Roman law had created this instrument of justice and civilization, and placed it in the Emperor's hands to enable him to carry out his God-given mission on earth. The Emperor must, therefore, apply the bridle of the laws—but he is opposed in this providential task by those who ought to be devout and allow Caesar to sit in the saddle, if only they would accept God's command (ll. 91–93).

Who are these persons and what is God's message to them? The common interpretation is that they are churchmen, possibly the decretalists and hierocrats attacked by Dante in *Monarchia* III. iii. 8–10; and that God admonishes them to "give unto Caesar the things that are Caesar's, and unto God the things that are God's" (Luke 20. 25; Matthew 22. 21). On the other hand, the word "devout" in l. 91 ("Ahi gente che dovresti esser devota") does not necessarily indicate only ecclesiastics: the broader semantic field includes the idea of obedience and submission to the will of God, as in the reference to Eve's disobedience in *Purgatorio* XXIX. 25–30 ("where both heaven and earth were obedient . . . if [only] she had been devout"), while the pairing of "subject and devout" in *Paradiso* XXXI. 117 is yet further proof of the meaning of obeisance to God's will and laws. The "people who ought to be devout" are all those who disobey God by rejecting the Emperor's temporal supremacy and who arouse the poet's wrath and contempt at the beginning of the Second Book of the *Monarchia*: "on seeing . . . the peoples meditating vain things . . . and the grievous sight of kings and rulers all united in only one thing, their opposition to their Lord and to the anointed one, the Roman Emperor."[12]

This audience must take to heart the lesson of how vicious the horse has become since the usurpers have dared to place their hands on the bridle (above all, since the papacy had begun to exert power and undue interference in the temporal sphere: *Purg.* XVI. 106–14; *Par.* XXVII. 139–41). And God's lesson to them? Certainly, Christ's words quoted above concerning the need to give unto the Emperor his rightful due is one; but another is the fundamental medieval concept of a hierarchy extending throughout the universe, governed by one divine authority that apportions the temporal and spiritual spheres each to one supreme guide on earth while it offers a model for ideal government.[13] The next three *terzine* of Canto VI (ll. 97–105) are at the very heart of the poet's *J'accuse*: above all, it is greed—the most formidable sin of the she-wolf—that has seized Albert and Rudolph of Habsburg in its clutches and made them neglect their duties as elected emperors to such an extent that they have allowed "the garden of the Empire" to be turned into a desert of anarchy and injustice. Such an accusation is all the more damning in view of what Dante went on to state in *Mon.* I. xi. 12, when he claimed that the Emperor was the only person immune from greed.

In *Purg.* XX. 7–12, the she-wolf is identified with avarice, denounced by St Augustine as the sin most opposed to charity. It is coupled with greed to create a semantic range equal to that of the Freudian libido (the image of the wolf returns in *Paradiso* IX. 130–32, in which the coinage of Florence has transformed the shepherd into a wolf). As St. Bernard wrote, greed and avarice are sisters, born of pride, while Vincent of Beauvais defined avarice as "the insatiable and wicked desire for any earthly things" (*Speculum doctrinale* IV. 144).

Why, however, did the poet choose a *lupa* to represent this mortal threat to human happiness, rather than the biblical *lupo*, man's traditional enemy and the form used in the line just evoked (*Par.* IX. 132: "has turned the shepherd into a wolf [*lupo*]")? One possible reason is that evil is, above all, an inversion of the Good: the *lupa* thus appears as the infernal antithesis or devilish caricature of the she-wolf, the venerated symbol of Rome and of Rome's mission to impart justice to the world. Certainly, Dante could not have gone to greater lengths in Book I of the *Monarchia* to stress the radical opposition between Greed and Justice. In the eleventh chapter, he quotes Aristotle to the effect that Greed (*cupiditas*) is the sin most opposed to Justice, so that when all cause for Greed has been removed, nothing remains contrary to Justice. Moreover, Greed cannot exist where there is nothing to desire; hence the Emperor, whose jurisdiction is limited only by the ends of the earth, cannot desire anything that is not his. Among mortal men, he is the one most immune to Greed.[14]

How, then, could Dante accuse Emperor Albert of being a prey to Greed in 1300? The answer lies partly in the fact that the Emperor can err like any other man, but more especially it is to be found in the force of the poet's conviction (already expressed, as we have seen, in the Fourth Book of the *Convivio*) that neither Albert nor his father Rudolph had ever been consecrated as emperor, the true *Rex Romanorum*. And thus we come to understand the full significance of the epithet "tedesco" as applied to Albert in line 97 ("O Alberto tedesco ch'abbandoni"): instead of acting as Roman Emperor, chosen by God to heal Italy's wounds, to administer justice, and to foster peace and unity from Rome, Albert acts as a German princeling, kept prisoner by *cupidigia* on the wrong side of the Alps (l. 104). If he had assumed his duties and rights as Emperor, he would have been truly God's vicar in the temporal sphere on earth, with nothing to desire and hence immune to greed; instead, as "German Albert," he is nothing more than one ruler among many, and like them a victim of the she-wolf. The "just judgment" called for by the poet in line 100 was most probably a reference *post eventum* to the premature death of his son and heir in 1307, followed by Albert's murder by his nephew in June 1308.

The weakness of the Empire in the second half of the thirteenth century was well known to contemporaries; compromise candidates were sought and elected; the imperial treasury was virtually empty. All this led Humbert of Romans to note—a year after Rudolph of Habsburg's election in 1273—that the Empire had been reduced almost to nothing.[15] At the time of his election, Rudolph held lands in Alsace, the upper Rhine, and what is now Switzerland. He went on to acquire Austria and Styria for his sons; his policies so frightened the imperial electors that on his death in 1291, they turned away from his eldest son, choosing the weaker Adolf of Nassau. Dante bitterly resented Rudolph's neglect of Italy and his aggrandizement of the papal dominions in the peninsula at the expense of the Empire. The poet's verdict is therefore very different from that of modern historians. The latter point out, for example, that Rudolph "was naturally forced to concentrate his attention on his own domain and the advancement of his family; his policy could not be an imperial one in the wider sense, but within its limits it was successful."[16] Or, according to another historian: "In their differing ways nearly all the German kings from Rudolf of Habsburg to Maximilian were able, Rudolf and Charles IV outstandingly so . . ."[17] Dante, however, was not aiming at the objective appraisal of a modern historian; his one concern was the Empire, its universality, and Italy, its center.

On these grounds the poet condemned Albert of Habsburg and his father, Rudolf. Albert's position was so weak that, after the defeat of his rival and his unanimous election in July 1298, he had to wait five long years before receiving papal recognition as Emperor. Then, in the last year of his life, Boniface VIII attempted to check the threat from France by reversing papal policy, which had held—since the decretal *Per venerabilem* of 1202—that the king of France acknowledged "no superior in temporal affairs." This radical shift in papal policy was embodied in the Pope's *Allegacio* of 30 April 1303, which confirmed the elction of Albert as Emperor and King of the Romans, asserting that the Emperor was superior to all earthly kings and princes, despite the ravings of the kings of France who refused to recognize this imperial supremacy: "They lie, for by law they are and must be under the Emperor and King of the Romans."[18] In the preamble, after restating the claim that the sun of Genesis stood for the power of the Church, the moon for the temporal or imperial power, so that together they should rule over the earth, Boniface even went so far as to accept the idea that the Emperor could be thought of as a sun "in so far as he is Emperor, who must illumine everyone and defend the spiritual power." This desperate volte-face, however, could not save either Boniface or Albert in Dante's judgment, for the Pope also claimed that he had received from Christ Himself the power to create the Emperor and to transfer the Empire according to his personal will. Moreover, there was a veiled threat that, even as the popes had transferred the Empire to the Germans, so the Pope, as Christ's vicar, could remove and transfer it to anyone he chose—without in any way offending justice.

It was in order to reject the whole idea of *translatio imperii*, evolved in the late twelfth century (that the Empire had been donated to the Popes by Constantine, so that they had the power to bestow it on Charlemagne or the Franks and then on those elected by the Germans), that Dante wrote Book II of the *Monarchia*. There he repeatedly declared that God had given universal empire to the Roman people as an inalienable right for all time—just as, in *Convivio* IV. iv. 11, he had already quoted Virgil as incontrovertible proof of this eternal truth: "when he says [*Aen*. I. 278–79], speaking in God's person: 'To them—the Roman people—I place no limit in possessions or in time; to them have I given Empire without end.' "

In his *Promissio* of 17 July 1303, Albert had gone so far as to recognize the Pope's power to transfer the Empire and to grant supreme temporal authority or the temporal sword to be used by the Emperor *ad nutum*, at the behest of the Church, even as he swore on the Bible to obey the Pope and his successors while acting as defender of the Church.[19] It was precisely against such a conception of the Emperor's office as owing obeisance in the temporal sphere that Dante wrote the tenth chapter of Book III of his *Monarchia*, where after asserting that the Emperor has no power to alter his jurisdiction, the office assigned to him by God, he argues:

They further say that Pope Adrian summoned Charlemagne to his and the Church's aid . . . and that Charlemagne received the imperial office from the pope. . . . Wherefore they say that all who have been Emperors of the Romans after him are likewise defenders of the Church, and must be called to that office by the Church; and from this too that dependence which they seek to prove would follow. And to destroy this argument, I say that it is null and void; for the usurpation of a right does not constitute a right.[20]

It is not merely the absence of Albert and Rudolph that is condemned in Canto VI, but their whole policy of self-aggrandizement at the expense of the Empire and its heart or "garden," where anarchy reigns and papal claims to absolute supremacy are encouraged.

Four *terzine* now hammer home the indictment, each beginning with the apostrophe *Vieni* ("Come"), an example of anaphora typical of medieval *amplificatio*. "German" Albert is called upon to come and see the tragic results of his neglect. The roll call of victims begins with a Ghibelline family from Verona, the Montecchi, and a Guelph clan from Cremona, the Cappelletti. Readers of Shakespeare will immediately think of the Montagues and Capulets as rival families in Verona, vowed to mutual destruction, according to the interpretation handed down to the English dramatist by Da Porto from the earliest Dante commentators. Only Dante's son, Pietro, points to the historical reality, that the names signify two clans or factions (the one from Ghibelline Verona, the other from Guelph Cremona) whose feuding embroiled the whole of Lombardy, while the Monaldi and Filippeschi were two families from Orvieto (the former, Guelph; the latter, Ghibelline), who likewise typified the internecine rivalry and warfare prevalent in central Italy. By 1300 the Montecchi and Cappelletti had been virtually destroyed and the Monaldi and Filippeschi were close to self-destruction. The second *terzina* calls on the Emperor to come to cure the troubles of his vassals in Italy; he is urged to consider the fate of the dominions of the Aldobrandeschi, near Siena, as an *exemplum* of the decadence of the great noble families whose power has been eroded by the conquest of the *contado* on the part of the Communes (a phenomenon decried in *Par.* XVI. 49–72). The heart of the lament is found in lines 112–14. The Emperor is told to come to see *his* Rome and listen to her lament: "O my Caesar, why are you not here with me?"; with the final crescendo in line 115: "Come and see how much the people love one another!"

Behind Dante's vigorous lament and indictment is the tone of a biblical prophet, that of a voice crying in the desert created by the Emperor's absence and the Babylonian exile of the papacy in Avignon. The same ideas and images recur in Epistle XI of 1314, addressed to the Italian cardinals in conclave at Carpentras: once more, the poet turns to the opening verse of *Lamentations* to describe Rome's state; greed is again the culprit; Rome is "widowed and abandoned" (*Ep.* XI. ii. 3: *viduam et desertam*). She, to whom Christ confirmed the gift of world-empire by both word and deed (*verbo et opere Christus orbis confirmavit imperium*), is now devoid of both her "lights" (XI. x. 21 "nunc utroque lumine destitutam"), so that for the third time she is described as a widow in her solitude (*solam sedentem et viduam*); indeed, her condition is such that it would move even Rome's greatest enemy, Hannibal, to feel pity for her desolation. So, in *Purg.* VI. 116–17, Albert, the elected Emperor, is told that if he is not moved to pity even by the state of the Italians (N.B. the *noi* of l. 116) then let him at least feel shame for the ill-fame he has acquired, notorious as he is for the neglect of his imperial duties.[21]

Then comes the most astonishing example of Dante's syncretism, as he asks God whether He has in fact turned His gaze away from the world (cf. Psalm 43. 25: "How can you turn away your face, forgetful of our need and our affliction?")—or is He preparing some mysterious, hidden way to rescue humanity? In these verses (118–23) we are reminded that it was not unknown for Christian poets in the Middle Ages to refer to God under the veil of pagan myth; but nowhere, as far as I know, do we find the paradoxical example of "Jupiter crucified" explicitly stated.[22] The epithet "just" applied to Jove's eyes in line 120 points to the role of the Heaven of Jupiter in Dante's poem. As we discover in *Paradiso* XVIII–XX, Jupiter is the Heaven of Justice, even as the eagle, symbol of the Empire and its earthly justice, is "God's bird" in *Purgatorio* XXXII. 112. This reference to *sommo Giove* (l. 118: "highest Jove") points both to God the supreme Emperor as well as to the Emperor's primary duty on earth, which is to guard and dispense Justice on earth.

Dante sums up Italy's tragic state in lines 124–26:

> Ché le citta d'Italia tutte piene
> son di tiranni, e un Marcel diventa
> ogne villan che parteggiando viene.[23]

Tyranny is evidently based on injustice and violence (cf. *Inf.* XII. 104–5). Commentators, however, are divided in their attempts to identify the Marcellus of line 125. Some believe that Dante was referring to M. Claudius Marcellus who conquered the Gauls and Syracuse and was a hero of the Second Punic War (*Aen.* VI. 854–83): the poet would be saying that every village idiot who plays partisan politics immediately becomes a national hero. Many scholars, however, prefer to identify Dante's Marcellus with Marcus Claudius Marcellus, Consul in 51 B.C., a fierce opponent of Caesar (*Phar.* I. 313: *Marcellus loquax*), who would thus be taken by the poet as the symbol of opposition to the Emperor's authority. On the whole, I would opt for the first solution, because of the pervasive use of irony in this section of the canto. The reference to Marcellus the national hero can thus serve as a bridge, linking the references to the ideal Rome of Jove, Caesar, and Marcellus with the infernal reality of contemporary Florence.[24]

A bitterly sarcastic invective against the poet's native city, "Fiorenza *mia*," brings the canto to a close. The Florentines may well rejoice, since the "digression" (l. 128) describing and bewailing the misfortunes of Italy obviously does not concern them. Others harbor justice in their hearts, but the Florentines have it constantly on their lips. Others are reluctant to take on offices of great civic responsibility, but the Florentines rush in where others fear to tread. Then comes the crowning apostrophe (ll. 136–38):

> Or ti fa lieta, che tu hai ben onde:
> tu ricca, tu con pace e tu con senno!
> S'io dico 'l ver, l'effetto nol nasconde.[25]

Regarding line 137, it is obvious that, rent by faction and political upheavals, Florence was anything but at peace or well governed; the line evokes the famous invective at the beginning of *Inferno* XXVI where the poet calls upon Florence to rejoice because not only do her wings ply across both land and sea but her name is also broadcast throughout Hell.[26] However, the trenchant irony of "tu ricca, tu con pace e tu con senno!" cannot mask the fact that Florence was enjoying a period of unprecedented wealth—as attested by the building programmes of Dante's times and the financial hegemony enjoyed by Florentine bankers.

By any standards, Florence was one of the wealthiest cities in Europe. As Jacques Bernard observes, "it was the textile industry and banking . . . which gave the Florentine economy its special character. . . . At the beginning of the fourteenth century the production of woollen cloth at Florence had reached 100,000 *pezze*, worth 1,200,000 *fiorini di auro*. . . . When the Bardi and the Peruzzi went bankrupt the king of England owed them almost 1,400,000 florins."[27] When we learn that the entire yearly revenues of the French Crown were about 2,500,000 florins, we gain some idea of the Rothschildian wealth of the leading Florentine banking houses.[28] We also come to realize one of the reasons why, during his Jubilee Year of 1300, Pope Boniface VIII reportly said: "There are four elements which rule the whole world; earth, water, air and fire. But I add the fifth element, namely the Florentines, who seem to rule the world."[29] The Dominican preacher, Remigio de' Girolami claimed that God had given Florence "seven singular gifts: abundance of money, a noble coinage, abundance of population, a civilized way of life, the wool industry, skill in the production of armaments, and a vigorous activity in the *contado*."[30] As is well known, far from extolling Florence's economic supremacy, Dante deplored its boom economy, with its "upstarts and easy money" (*Inf.* XVI. 73; cf. *Par.* XVI. 49–66).

The lash of the poet's tongue continues to strike at his beloved Florence in the following verses (139–44), and early commentators emphasize the irony in the comparison made with Athens and Sparta as the founders of law and civilization (cf. Justinian's *Institutiones*, I. xii. 10). Florence far surpasses both in her contribution to the Good Life (l. 141), a contribution based on such fine provisions (l. 142: *sottili* can mean both subtle and fragile) that what is spun in October does not last until mid-November. This example of Florence's extreme mutability (cf. *Par.* XVI. 82–84, in which blind Fortune governs Florence, like the seashore under the tidal moon) was inspired by the *coup d'état* of 1301, when the last of the White Priors, who had taken office on October 15, were forced to resign only three weeks later, on November 7. Dino Compagni was one of these, and his *Cronica* II. 5 he speaks trenchantly of their mistakes in believing that the Blacks were in good faith: "We told them we wanted to discuss peace, when instead it was time to sharpen our swords." After graphic descriptions of the extorsions, destruction of property, arson and other violence carried out by the Blacks, the Priors, we are told, abandoned by their powerful supporters, left Florence to its fate (II. 19).[31]

Florence is now commanded to reflect on the manifold changes that have occurred within living memory in the laws, currency, civic and political offices and customs, as well as the *rinovate membre* (l. 147: "renewed members"), resulting from the frequent banishment and recall of its leading citizens. The maze of Florentine political and social history, especially in the period after 1250, is conjured up; if Florence looks at herself in the cold light of truth, she will see that she is in fact like a sick woman, incapable of finding peace even as she attempts to lessen her agony by tossing and turning on the bed she has made for herself (ll. 145–51). Not content with the internal divisions caused by the Guelf-Ghibelline struggle, the Florentines added to this ideological conflict: "The *magnati-popolo* division, which approximates to a 'class' division, cut across and complicated the traditional conflicts between Guelfs and Ghibellines and between families."[32] Behind Dante's vision of Florence and his condemnation of her suicidal policies—his choice of his native-city as "the most suitable model for Hell"[33]—lies the poet's conviction that "every kingdom divided against itself shall be brought to ruin" (Luke 11. 17). Sordello's embrace of Virgil in the *Comedy* appears as the antidote to the poison of discord and hatred that has infected not only Florence but the whole of Italy.[34]

Sordello in History and in the *Comedy*

As noted in the first section of this chapter, one of the striking features of Dante's portrayal of Sordello is the latter's *magnanimitas*. In line 66, he is compared to a lion—an image that may well bring to mind the *lion couchant* of medieval heraldry. Benvenuto da Imola points to the essential theme of Sordello's magnanimity, when he observes that: "in this [simile] the author shows him to be magnanimous. For the magnanimous lion does not move or take any notice of anyone who does not molest him."[35] For the poet of the *Comedy*, the historical Sordello's magnanimity was attested by his poetical output, in which he did not fear to criticize and blame the great ones of this world for their failings and pernicious influence on contemporary society. That this is characteristic of the medieval concept of magnanimity is clear from Brunetto Latini's *Tresor*. There, we are told that

the true *magnanimus* "loves and dislikes openly, not covertly; for it seems
to him to be dishonorable to hide his feelings" (II. 23 [194]). After casti-
gating no less than eight contemporary rulers in his most famous poem,
the *planh* for Blacatz, Sordello ends on a courageous, defiant note:

> Li baro·m volran mal de so que ieu dic be,
> mas ben sapchan qu'ie·ls pretz aitan pauc quon ilh me.[36]

Since Sordello's role in the narrative of the *Comedy* is to guide the pilgrim and Virgil to the Valley of the Princes, his courage in denouncing the
failures of contemporary rulers is something that evidently struck Dante's
creative imagination.

Two points, however, must be made. The first is that, as Teodolinda
Barolini has rightly stressed, "a poem of Guittone's, who is a more significant political poet than Sordello as well as being one who wrote in Italian, is in fact the vernacular force behind *Purgatorio* VI through VIII."[37]
Dante's resentment against Guittone d'Arezzo is well documented (e.g.,
DVE I. xiii. 1, II. vi. 8; *Purg.* XXVI. 119–26). In the *Vita Nuova* (XXV. 6),
the young poet (who had been dazzled earlier by Guittone's technical vir-
tuosity) went so far as to attack those who wrote poetry in the vernacular
on any subject other than love. It is hardly surprising, then, that when the
author of the *Comedy* came to search for a "political" poet, he should have
ignored the man who came nearest to his own mastery of political invective and irony (e.g., Guittone's great canzone *Ahi lasso, or è stagion de doler
tanto*), in favor of someone who shared the same birthplace with Dante's
guide and supreme poet, Virgil. The word *Mantua* on Virgil's lips sparks
off the electrifying change in Sordello's behavior, making him abandon his
proud immobility and rush forward to embrace his as yet anonymous fellow countryman—and the sibilant-explosive force of the verbal *surse* (l. 72:
"sprang up") is redolent of the sudden impulsive embrace imagined by
the poet.

The second point forgotten by many readers is that it is not Sordello
who launches into the fierce denunciation of the anarchy oppressing Italy
in 1300. The second half of the canto (ll. 76–151) constitutes its central message, creating one of those triads so dear to the author of the *Comedy*: in this
case, the sixth canto of each *cantica* deals with a political theme in ascending
order from the municipal level of Florentine political discord in *Inferno* VI,
through the "national" level of Italy's lawlessness in *Purgatorio* VI, and
ascending to the universal plane of the Empire's providential history and

mission in *Paradiso* VI. All too often, critics have analyzed the reasons for Sordello's role in the *Comedy*, as if it were Sordello who denounced Italian disunity in what (as we have already seen) the poet himself refers to as a digression. On the other hand, Sordello's embrace of Virgil in Antepurgatory sparks off that violent outburst of hurt, scorn, and anger, on the part of the author-narrator. This basic distinction must be borne in mind.

Let us now examine some of the known facts about the historical Sordello. The dates of his birth and death are not known, but it is generally accepted that he was born near Mantua, at Goito, about the year 1200, and that he died during Dante's lifetime, in or after 1269. After spending some time at Verona in the entourage of Count Rizzardo di San Bonifacio, Sordello achieved considerable notoriety when, in 1266, he led back Rizzardo's wife Cunizza to her brothers' stronghold at Treviso. Although this medieval hijacking may have been planned by Cunizza's brothers, Ezzelino III and Alberico da Romano, it appears likely that Sordello's attachment to her was less than platonic—as Uc de Saint Circ asserted: "I know for certain that Lady Cunizza has . . . this year lost eternal life."[38] After a secret marriage with Otta di Strasso, Sordello's insecurity was such that he left Treviso in 1268–69 and journeyed to Provence, and thence to the courts of Roussillon, Castile, and Toulouse. Some time before June 1233, he took up residence at the court of Raymond Berenger, Count of Provence, where his signature is found as that of a witness on various important documents (often next to that of Romée de Villeneuve; cf. *Par.* VI. 127–42). During this period Sordello wrote his most important poetical works, including twelve *cansos*, seven *sirventes*, the celebrated *planh* for Blacatz, and the long didactic poem known as the *Ensenhamen d'onor*.

After the Count's death in 1245 Sordello stayed on at the Provençal court under the protection of Raymond's daughter Beatrice. She married Charles I of Anjou in that year (cf. *Purg.* XX. 61), and Sordello—now ennobled with the titles of *miles* and *dominus*—followed Charles on his fateful Italian expedition in the year of Dante's birth. In 1266, Sordello was languishing as a prisoner at Novara, and Pope Clement IV was moved to write to the Angevin ruler on 22 September to reproach him for his ungenerous treatment of Sordello as well as of other faithful followers. That Sordello's status was of considerable importance would seem to be evident from the mention of "My Lord Sordello" in a poem by Peire de Castelnau celebrating Charles's defeat of King Manfred at Benevento, as well as by the fiefs in Piedmont and the Abruzzi granted to Sordello by Charles, who refers to him as "our beloved companion and faithful follower" (*dilec-*

tus familiaris et fidelis noster: the appellation *familiaris* was reserved for the faithful élite of noble birth).

It is initially surprising that Dante should have given an outstanding role to an Italian who had proved himself such a staunch supporter of Charles of Anjou, a sovereign accused in *Purg.* XX. 67–69 of murdering St. Thomas Aquinas after having the last of the Staufen heirs decapitated. As ruler of southern Italy and Sicily (as well as virtual *Signore* of Florence and Lucca for the first eight years of Dante's life), Charles was the architect of a peninsula-wide Guelf policy that brought about the virtual eclipse of imperial power in Italy—leading to precisely that state of division and anarchy so vehemently condemned in the sixth canto of *Purgatorio*. It is therefore necessary to look beyond Sordello's actions to discover the reasons why Dante decided to focus his poetic spotlight on him.

Among Sordello's poems, two have received the attention of Dante scholars. One is the lament for the death of the noble Blacatz, in which the poet upbraids the leaders of contemporary Europe: they are, it is claimed, so devoid of virtue and so *descorat* or lacking in courage that they need to eat of the dead nobleman's heart in order to be fit to rule. Even St. Louis of France is told that he must eat of Blacatz's heart in order to recover Castile, which he has lost "through his own stupidity"—although the poet knows well enough that, if Louis's mother disapproves, he will not eat at all, since the king of France does nothing that might in any way annoy his mother.

The other poem is the *Ensehamen d'onor*, which C. M. Bowra claimed was so well known to Dante that he "saw in it sufficient justification for making the meeting with Sordello the occasion for a denunciation of Italy and its rulers."[39] This is to inflate the political element in Sordello's poetry (which is so different from Dante's). Nevertheless, there are some interesting points of contact between the two writers. For example, we note in lines 107–74 of the *Ensenhamen d'onor* that Sordello laments the world's decadence through sin; in lines 265–80, he tells us not only to praise our friends but also to condemn them when they are in the wrong (cf. *Convivio* IV. viii. 15). Then come the principal similarities between the two poets' views of life. In lines 507–18, we are told that wealth can only be justified through liberality toward God and our neighbor; otherwise, wealth is nothing but *pecatz e paubresa* (l. 450: "sin and poverty"). Finally (ll. 613–40), we note the theme that figures so prominently in Book IV of the *Convivio*: namely, that true nobility comes not through one's ancestry but through noble actions, "since an aristocrat is often wicked, and a bourgeois worthy of esteem . . . a truly noble heart excels on account of its noble deeds" (ll. 637–40).

At least one important similarity may be noted in the rest of Sordello's work. The theme of the *sirventes, Qui be·is membra del segle qu'es passatz*, is praise of the past, contrasted with the corruption of the present—a theme dear to the heart of the *laudator temporis acti* who wrote the central episode of his *Paradiso* in praise of the myth of Florence's virtuous past (*Par.* XV. 97–148 and XVI). Echoing Giraut de Bornelh's *Si per mo Sobre-Toz no fos* (praised by Dante in *DVE* II. vi. 6), Sordello stresses (ll. 29–31) the desperate need for virtue in a world that has gone astray: "wickedness springs from the most eminent and then, step by step, reaches down to the lowest members of society." But it is in the fourth stanza (ll. 22–24) that Dante's predecessor comes perhaps closest to him, when he breaks out with the impassioned question: "Ah! How can any man of noble birth be so devoid of all sense of honor as to bastardize his lineage for gold or silver?"[40] This is a question repeated, perhaps by chance, but clearly put by Dante in *Purgatorio* XX, where Hugh Capet is made to cry out against Charles II of Anjou's "sale" of his daughter to Azzo VIII of Este (ll. 79–81):

> "O avarizia, che puoi tu piú farne,
> poscia c'ha' il mio sangue a te sí tratto,
> che non si cura de la propria carne?"[41]

All in all, we find a considerable number of parallels or similarities in outlook, although it would be difficult to claim—as Bowra did—that "each point made by Dante [in the second half of *Purgatorio* VI] can be paralleled by something said by Sordello [in the *Ensenhamen d'onor*]."[42]

Clearly Dante had good reason to choose his Lombard predecessor as the guide to the Valley of the Princes in *Purgatorio* VII and VIII. That still, however, does not justify Sordello's role in the preceding canto. There, his birthplace gave him the necessary credentials as a candidate to illustrate the bond that should unite compatriots (what Dante called "la carità del natio loco," which survives even in the infernal situation of *Inf.* XIV. 1–3).

Teodolinda Barolini claims that Dante "singles out Sordello for praise" because, although he did not help to create the Italian *vulgare illustre*, "he did the next best thing: he turned to a *vulgare* that was already *illustre*, namely Provençal."[43] It is, however, difficult to reconcile such a point of view with Dante's ardent championing of the Italian vernacular in the *Convivio*, or with his celebration in the *De Vulgari Eloquentia* of those "Sicilian" poets who had discovered the Italian *vulgare illustre* and thus set an example to be followed by all Italian poets (*DVE* I. xii. 6; xix. 1). Moreover, Professor Barolini's penetrating study points to a clear anomaly; while Dante's Sordello is the "purgatorial corrective to Farinata . . . the lens through which the theme of love of one's native land reappears on the slopes of Mount Purgatory," his role in the *Comedy* is strangely at odds with the historical fact that this "emblem of unity" wrote the *planh* for Blacatz, "a bitter and savage poem (which, *had it been acted on, would have resulted in fighting in every corner of Europe*)."[44] For the rest, Barolini admirably sums up the reasons for Dante's choice of Sordello: first, Sordello was "a poet concerned about the behavior of rulers in his day" (hence his role in *Purgatorio* VII–VIII); second, "his embrace of Vergil, exemplifying political unity" triggers the invective "in which Dante deplores the lack of unity in Italy"; third, Sordello is a purgatorial refinement of Farinata (acting as an antithesis to Bertran de Born, the poet of schism in *Inferno* XXVIII).[45] Such is indeed Sordello's role in the narrative structure of Dante's poem. But is there not more to it than this?

According to Maurizio Perugi, Sordello is in fact the most "scandalous" representative of an Italy that is linguistically and politically a "harlot."[46] Perugi's exhaustive analysis is detailed and illuminating, although perhaps overstated. The truth may well lie somewhere in between Barolini's vision of the historical Sordello as embodying (in life) linguistic and political unity and Perugi's "noble spirit *manqué*."[47]

Before pursuing our quest, we would do well to recall Étienne Gilson's golden rule that a character in Dante's *Comedy* only retains of his historical reality whatever the poet felt he needed for the immediate purposes of the poem's universal message.[48] Let us examine the only other reference to Sordello in Dante's works, found in the *De Vulgari Eloquentia* (I. xv. 2):

We say then that those persons may well be right who claim that the speech of the people of Bologna is the most beautiful, since in their dialect they borrow various elements from their neighbors in Imola, Ferrara and Modena—just as we suppose everyone borrows in this way from their neighbors, as Sordello showed for his own city of Mantua, which is adjacent to Cremona, Brescia and Verona. He, a man of such great eloquence, abandoned his native tongue not only in poetry but in every other form of discourse.[49]

For the time being, we shall note only two things: the emphasis in the phrase "Sordellus de Mantua *sua*" and Mengaldo's observation that the

Latin verb used by Dante for "abandoned," "*deseruit* is stronger than the usual *divertere*."[50]

We now turn to that part of the *Convivio* written in either 1303 or 1304, certainly just before Book I of the *De Vulgari Eloquentia*, which must itself have been composed some time before the beginning of 1305.[51] In a passionate defense of his unorthodox use of the vernacular for his Banquet of Wisdom or Philosophy, Dante attacks not only those who would preserve all such knowledge as the monopoly of Latin, but also those who despise their own vernacular "and praise the others, *especially that of Provence*" (*Conv.* I. x. 11; my emphasis). The whole of the eleventh chapter of the first book of the *Convivio* is directed against these "wicked Italians," whose betrayal of their native language is attributed to five defects (I. xi. 1–2). Once more, those who prefer Provençal are singled out in I. xi. 14:

Cicero attacks such people at the beginning of one of his works, entitled *On the End of Goods*, because in his day they denigrated the Latin of Rome and praised the Greek language for reasons similar to those put forward by these people, who judge Italian to be base and Provençal precious.

Such are "the loathsome and evil [Italians] who consider this precious vernacular to be base, which, if it is in any way base, is so only in the fact that it issues from the harlot mouth of these adulterers" (*Conv.* I. xi. 21). In other words, Dante claims that to espouse someone else's vernacular is tantamount to (linguistic) adultery. It is one of the cardinal tenets of Dante scholarship that the poet of the *Comedy* used words with great care and precision, and we have no cause to suppose that the author of the *Convivio* was any less accurate in his choice of words. In his note to this passage in his magisterial edition of the *Convivio*, Cesare Vasoli glosses: "those who prefer a foreign vernacular to their own are guilty of adultery toward their language and, therefore, 'traitors'; and their mouth is that of a harlot because it is servile and despicable, since it basely praises a foreign language to which they are not bound by 'the natural love for one's native tongue' (X. 5)."[52]

Nowhere does Dante use the term "traitor" with regard to these linguistic adulters; anyone who has read the last section of the *Inferno* knows that treachery was for Dante the worst possible sin. We may therefore be reluctant to place an unrepentant Sordello among the blackest souls condemned to hell. On the other hand, there is no getting away from the fact that Dante refers to those who reject their mother tongue as "adulterers":

they are guilty of being unfaithful to their native language, to which they would seem to be wedded by birth and instinctive love (*lo naturale amore de la propria loquela: Conv.* I. x. 5). The word "naturale" may well bring to mind André Pézard's thesis, according to which Brunetto Latini was condemned to Hell by Dante (*Inferno* XV), because he was guilty of a kind of linguistic blasphemy in despising God's gift, his native language. Pézard himself saw the parallel with Sordello, but stressed that the latter did not despise his native language.[53] While admiring the French critic's erudition, few scholars have accepted his thesis where Brunetto Latini is concerned. Nevertheless, Pézard was surely right to stress the significance of Dante's passionate defence and exaltation of his native tongue in the *Convivio*.

The vexed question remains: why is Sordello placed by the poet in his Antepurgatory? A few believe it was because Dante numbered him among the negligent rulers. But the common rejoinder to this is the obvious historical fact that the Florentine exile could hardly have imagined that Sordello was in any sense called to govern a country, like the other negligent princes in Antepurgatory. Bowra, rejecting this view, believes that "Sordello's place indicates that he is one of the late repentant who have died violent deaths"—a view held by a number of other scholars, who thus place him with the throng of souls in *Purgatorio* V and those mentioned at the beginning of Canto VI. Bowra bolsters this hypothesis with yet another: "Apparently Dante knew something about him which is not mentioned by the brief Provençal biographies," which "are very feeble affairs and draw most of their information from the poems."[54] It is perhaps surprising that, in making this claim, the English critic did not refer to the possibility that Sordello's lover, Cunizza da Romano, who spent her last years in Florence (where she drew up her will in 1279 and where she was well acquainted with the Cavalcanti family), might have been a source of first-hand information for Dante. However attractive this conjecture, I find it difficult to believe that Sordello's isolation, which is such an outstanding feature of Dante's *mise en scène*, combined with his role linking two distinct groups (the late-repentant and the negligent rulers), does not imply an isolated category of guilt for the Italian troubadour. We must therefore ask what is the common denominator for the souls who are waiting in Antepurgatory, temporarily excluded from the essential process of purification, according to the fiction of the *Comedy*.

The answer is that they are all guilty, in various ways, of the sin of negligence. The souls divide into four groups: those who died excommunicate; those who failed to practise virtue through sloth and left repentance until the last moment; those who died a violent death and repented *in extremis*; rulers who neglected their duty but repented at the end of their lives. This still leaves us with the problem of Sordello's particular form of negligence. In order to discover this, we need to examine the concept of *negligentia* in medieval theology. As so often, our best source is the work of St. Thomas Aquinas, who gives a whole *quaestio* to the problem in his *Summa Theologica*, stating that "Negligence implies a lack of rightful solicitude"; it is in fact directly opposed to solicitude.[55] The *De Vulgari Eloquentia* is nothing if not an impassioned plea to Italian writers to contribute to the task of realizing the full potential of their native tongue by contributing to the development of "the most noble and illustrious language of Italy" (*DVE* I. xi. 1; cf. I. xvii). In Dante's judgment, few Italian writers have achieved this goal, which is based on the conviction that the vernacular language is in fact nobler than Latin (I. i. 4), while those who have failed to reach the required standards of excellence are condemned outright (e.g., *DVE* I. xiii. 1 and II. vi. 8).[56]

This process of refinement and expansion of the possibilities inherent in the Italian *vulgare* must therefore be set in the context of the quasi-contemporaneous *Convivio* I, where Dante expresses "most perfect love" of his native language with such biting force and conviction, culminating in the biblical tones of the concluding passage: "This will be a new light, a new sun, which shall rise up as the old one sets, and shall give light to those who are in darkness and obscurity, because the old sun does not shine upon them."[57] If we now re-examine the passage in *DVE* I. xv. 2 quoted above, we surely realize that the phrase "he [Sordello] abandoned his native vernacular" (*patrium vulgare deseruit*) can hardly—in the context of Dante's thought on language in 1303–1305—be interpreted as praise for his predecessor's supposed crossing of national linguistic boundaries. Especially when we recall that Sordello is described in that same passage as "a man of such great eloquence" (*tantus eloquentie vir*), we understand that, for the author of the *De Vulgari Eloquentia*, a poet of Sordello's fame and ability had a clear duty to place both at the service of the Italian *vulgare illustre*. Sordello's failure to foster the cause of his native language is all the more blameworthy in that *corruptio optimi pessima est* (cf. *Purg.* XXX. 115–20). We may now ask ourselves whether it is mere coincidence that the last poet encountered by Dante in Purgatory should be Arnaut Daniel, who is specifically praised as the "better craftsman of his mother tongue" (*Purg.* XXVI. 117: "miglior fabbro del parlar materno"), whereas the first poet found in the second *cantica* is the Italian poet who had deserted his native tongue and is still "in exile" among the Negligent in Antepurgatory. Negligence, according to Aquinas, is due to a lack of committed, fervent love.[58] This, I would submit, is exactly what was wrong with the historical Sordello: his lack of love for his native land ("la carità del natio loco"), which led him to abandon his *patrium vulgare* and, although a gifted Italian poet, to *neglect*—in the word's strongest, theological meaning—the creation of Italy's *vulgare illustre*.

This is why the poet of the *Comedy*—an ardent champion of the vernacular, which he was bent on elevating to new heights and conquests—decided to place Sordello quite apart from the other Negligent souls in Antepurgatory. Like the Emperor Rudolph, Sordello was guilty "of having neglected what he should have done" (*Purg.* VII. 92); and he is on his own because he is the only example seized upon by Dante of a truly gifted writer who failed to show due love and solicitude for his native language.[59]

As Pasquazi observes, all the negligent souls are guilty of sins based on omission rather than on positive action (*ED* I, 305: cf. *Purg.* VII. 25). In Sordello's case, it is *not* because he wrote in another tongue but because *he did not write in his native language* in an endeavor to make it *illustre* when he had the ability to do so that Dante excludes him from Purgatory proper. For, as he had already stated in his *Convivio* (IV. vii. 3): "it is a most dangerous form of negligence to allow a false opinion to take root; for, just as in a field that is not tilled, grass spreads and grows tall . . . so a false opinion . . . grows and multiplies in such a way that . . . the truth is hidden and lies virtually buried and lost."

The historical Sordello, therefore, underlies Dante's Sordello as a warning, an example to be shunned. At the end of Purgatory proper, on the terrace of the lustful, we learn of another poet, Arnaut Daniel, who was truly the "better craftsman of his mother tongue"; so that we look back along the path of discovery, which leads us from the first poet, who had deserted his native tongue and is still in exile among the Negligent in Antepurgatory, to the last poet encountered on the Mountain, who was truly the "miglior fabbro del parlar materno."[60] Thus we see that the role of Sordello as a character in Dante's poem is in large part opposed to his historical reality, as this was known and judged by the author of the *Comedy*. Just as the excommunicated souls of Manfred and his companions appear like sheep in Antepurgatory, "mandra fortunata" (*Purg.* III. 86), in utter contrast to their proud obduracy on earth which had led to their exclusion from Christ's flock, so now Sordello is transformed into a model of patriotic fervor quite alien to his historical championing of a foreign cause.

Since the sixth canto of each *cantica* was to have a political theme, an important factor in the choice of Sordello as the pilgrim's guide to the Valley of the Princes was his birthplace—and as we have seen, already in 1304, Sordello was indelibly linked with "his Mantua" (*DVE* I. xv. 2). His courage in criticizing the great and powerful of his day suggested his role as a guide. His function in the sixth canto of *Purgatorio*, however, was planned to appear in utter contrast to his actions on earth. The man who had abandoned his native tongue and neglected his duty toward the creation of a *vulgare illustre* in Italy, the Italian who had joined the French invasion and helped to extinguish Staufen and imperial power in Italy, the *familiaris* of Charles I of Anjou (the latter guilty of the murder of the greatest contemporary Italian theologian)—Sordello is nevertheless transformed by the author of the *Comedy* into a symbol of burning love, *fervor caritatis*, of his native city. At the mere sound of the name "Mantua" he abandons his proud isolation and leaps forward to embrace an unknown shade, thus giving Dante the poet the cue for his vehement denunciation of Italy's ills. Sordello thus becomes "an emblem of political and linguistic unity in the *Comedy*"[61]—something (we must add) that he was NOT in real life.

Barolini is of course correct in claiming that Bertran de Born (*Inf.* XXVIII. 118–42) and Sordello are *exempla* of the uses to which a poet can put his poetry in the service of the state: Bertran, *in malo*, guilty of turning a son against his father (and king), of fostering civil war; Sordello, *in bono*, with courageous criticism and advice to princes. Certainly, Dante's lofty ideas on the duties of a ruler (*Par.* XIII. 94–108; XVIII–XX) were very different from Sordello's feudal conception of the ruler's personal honor; nevertheless, the latter's courage or magnanimity in attacking contemporary sovereigns for their failures in carrying out their duty Dante regarded as a powerful countercheck to his pusillanimity or "viltà d'animo" in despising "his own language" (*Conv.* I. xi. 18–21).

Sordello and the Valley of the Princes

Dante's Sordello, after praising Virgil as the "glory of the Latins" (*Purg.* VII. 16), offers to guide Virgil and his charge on their way to Purgatory proper "as far as I can go" (l. 42). Night, however, is already falling and during the absence of the sun (a symbol of God's grace) the souls are unable to ascend; Sordello therefore suggests that they go to join some souls far-off to their right—a meeting he claims will be a source of pleasure. The trinity of "political" poets thus enters the valley, described by Dante according to the *topos* of the *locus amoenus* (*Purg.* VII. 73–81; cf. *Aen.* VI. 637ff.), a *figura* or foreshadowing of the Earthly Paradise situated at the top of the mountain.

Before the pageant described in *Purg.* VIII. 22–108 is played out for a special audience—the negligent princes—the poet exhorts the reader to search for an allegorical message or hidden meaning:

> Aguzza qui, lettor, ben li occhi al vero,
> ché 'l velo è ora ben tanto sottile,
> certo che 'l trapassar dentro è leggero.[62]

Dante's son Pietro (followed by Forti and others) offers the most cogent explanation of this warning: namely, that the *velo* or literal sense is so transparent that it is all too easy to *trapassar dentro* ("pass within") without arriving at the allegorical truth intended by the poet[63]—and we may add that the variety of interpretations put forward by scholars certainly bears witness to this ability to misunderstand Dante's intentions. Two angels come down from on high; dressed in green, the color of Hope, they bear "two flaming swords, broken short and deprived of their points" (ll. 26–27). When the serpent comes—perhaps the very one who tempted and corrupted Eve (l. 99)—the angels put him to flight (ll. 97–108).

The obvious association with the temptation in Eden and the Fall has tended to distract scholars from Dante's overall message. What the three poets witness is not a scene of temptation: that would be theologically absurd, since the souls in the valley are saved (as are all the souls found both in Antepurgatory and Purgatory proper; cf. *Purg.* XI. 19–24). We must, therefore, look for a meaning appropriate to these particular souls who make up the audience for the pageant. They form a comprehensive gallery of the recent political leaders of Europe, eight in number, all guilty of neglecting their moral duty, their failure to heal the political anarchy and divisions that afflicted Europe in their lifetime. In other words, "they are constantly reminded of their unfulfilled purpose . . . [they are now] at peace as they ought to have been in life but were not"—like Sordello, we may add, "They now represent the ideal they did *not* achieve."[64] By chanting St. Bernard's *Salve, Regina* (*Purg.* VII. 82), they are constantly reminded of the fact that—as true sons of Eve (*exsules filii Evae*)—they are in this valley (*in hac lacrimarum valle*), exiled both from Purgatory proper and from their true *patria*, Heaven, even as they implore the Virgin for the grace to see God after this exile (*et Jesum . . . nobis post hoc exilium ostende*).

An important clue for the proper interpretation of the scene lies in the fact that each of the angels bears a sword (*Purg.* VIII. 26). Both swords are deprived of their points (l. 27), showing that they are weapons or symbols intended for defense and protection. They are "flaming" (*affocate*), a flashback to the Cherubim's sword (*flammeum gladium*) mentioned in Genesis 3, 24 and another pointer to the Fall, although the color implied (red) may also be taken to indicate the charitable role assigned to these angels, who also appear as representatives of the two earthly guides who must lead humanity to earthly beatitude and eternal salvation (cf. *Purg.* XVI. 106–8).

In *Monarchia* III. ix. 17–19, Dante went on to deny that the mention of the two swords mentioned in Luke 22. 38 could signify the temporal and the spiritual powers. Nevertheless, in the context of the Valley of the Princes, the poet uses the swords as symbols of precisely that long-established tradition, whereby the two swords represented both the supreme spiritual authority vested in the Church, and the temporal authority granted to the Empire and other civil authority. It was in fact the Emperor Henry IV who introduced this theme in a letter of 1076, when he summoned the bishops of Germany to a Diet at Worms. The Emperor decided to check the temporal claims of the papacy by a strict dualism, which not only announced the end of the concept of the *rex-sacerdos*, but which was soon in its turn to be exploited by the papalists. In the coronation of an Emperor, the Pope or his representative gave the sword signifying temporal authority to the Emperor, "who was then said to wield the sword at the bidding of the Pope (*ad nutum*)."[65] This was a significant development in what is termed the Gelasian principle or distinction between the temporal and the spiritual powers.[66] By the time of Dante's birth the image of the two swords had become both commonplace and abused, so much so that even the leading decretalist Cardinal Hostiensis, while upholding the absolute supremacy of the spiritual power, could bewail the fact that "the spiritual sword has become a military one, stirring up and prolonging wars for trivial reasons. . . . This pestilential situation will not end until each power stays content within its own limits."[67] During the poet's own lifetime, a notorious example of hierocratic abuse of the symbol was found in Boniface VIII's ull *Unam sanctam* of 1302, in which—as we have already seen—the Pope claimed: "We are taught by the words of the Gospel that in this church and in her power there are two swords, a spiritual one and a temporal one. . . . One sword ought to be under the other and the temporal authority subject to the spiritual power."

Fiorenzo Forti correctly states that this imagery was part of "a language well known to the princes," a semiotic code they would have had no difficulty in interpreting precisely.[68] In other words, in characteristic fashion, the Dante of the *Purgatorio* had no compunction in using the imagery he later dismissed in the *Monarchia*, when (and as) it suited his purpose. The whole purpose of the third book of the *Monarchia* is to prove that temporal authority is *not* subject to the Pope's spiritual authority. We must be clear, however, about what Dante rejects in the *Monarchia*: it is not so much the imagery of the two swords as their allegorical interpretation. As we shall see, a not dissimilar case is found at the center of the poem (the "two suns" of *Purg.* XVI. 106–8). For the present, however, even if readers prefer to interpret the angels as representing only the spiritual plane, their blunt swords must indicate the spiritual guardianship granted to temporal rulers on earth in order that they may govern effectively.

The pageant of temptation reminds the princes watching that it was precisely because of the Fall and the expulsion from Eden that humanity needed to be guided by two supreme authorities. As Dante wrote in *Monarchia* III. iv. 14, they were established by God "in order to lead humanity toward certain ends . . . if man had remained in the state of innocence in which he was created by God, he would have had no need of such guides: they are remedies against the infirmity of sin."[69] In the spectacle re-enacting the tragedy of original sin, played out in a *locus amoenus* reminiscent of Eden, the former rulers of Europe observe what should have been their supreme duty, the need to achieve total, harmonious collaboration with the spiritual power in order to bring humanity to a state of peace, justice, and happiness. Their greatest impediment had been Greed, for, as we are told in the *Monarchia*, it is the greatest obstacle to Justice, charity, and peace, just as their greatest enemy during their lives on earth had been the serpent ("our adversary": *Purg.* VIII. 95). Forti has drawn our attention to a significant passage in Dante's Fifth Epistle (written most probably in October 1310), which shares a number of images with the antepurgatorial Valley:

may you conceive *like a fertile valley*, and put forth *green*, the green, that is, which shall bear the fruit of *true peace*. . . . Wherefore if you throw off that *inveterate sin*, which often *like a serpent* is cast on its back and is turned against itself. . . . Awake, therefore, all of you, and rise up to meet your King . . .[70]

What Forti does not point out (and what is crucial to our parallel) is that Dante wrote this Epistle at a time when Clement V's support and benediction had just been given publicly to Henry VII's Italian venture in the bull *Exultet in gloria* (1 September 1310)—a unique moment in Dante's lifetime of apparently total co-operation between the two supreme authorities, so that the Fifth Epistle in fact ends with the astronomical imagery rejected in *Monarchia* III. iv. 15–16: "that where the spiritual ray is not sufficient, there the splendor of the lesser luminary may lend its light."[71]

It is a commonplace of Dante scholarship that the *Comedy*'s second *cantica* is the one nearest to this world. This is in many ways true, since Purgatory is *inter alia* rooted in time: it therefore reflects God's truths as seen from the standpoint of this world, and indicates the way these truths should be applied on earth, according to the poet's ideal vision. Thus in the Valley of the Princes, the pageant brings home to the former rulers of Europe (and, of course, to Dante's readers) the necessity of achieving a proper balance between the material and the spiritual orders, based on total co-operation between the political and ecclesiastical authorities on earth. The serpent is humanity's inveterate enemy; and, in the form of *cupiditas* on earth, it must be kept in check by the two supreme authorities— as Dante spelled out in the last chapter of his *Monarchia*.

As in his *planh* for Blacatz, Dante's Sordello identifies eight "great shades" (*Purg.* VII. 91–136). The first, seated "highest . . . and does not move his lips with the others' songs" (ll. 91–93), is the Emperor Rudolph of Habsburg, born in 1218 and crowned at Aix-la-Chapelle in 1273. At an encounter with the Pope in Lausanne (October 1275), Rudolph recognized the separation of Sicily from the imperial domains; in 1278, the Pope accepted from Rudolph the formal cession of Ferrara, Bologna, and the towns of Romagna, to the papal state. In 1280, Rudolph put forward a proposal to give the kingdom of Arles in fief to Charles of Anjou. Moreover, "Rudolf of Habsburg in the first opportunist step of the most successful dynasty in European history accepted with his electors in 1279 the papal theory of the imperial constitution."[72] We may deduce what Dante thought of such a betrayal of Rudolph's imperial mission from what he had to say in *Monarchia* III. x about the supposed Donation of Constantine: namely, that the Empire does not belong to the Emperor, it is not his to give away. He is the vicar, the custodian, who must jealously guard and protect it: "Since, then, to rend the Empire would mean destroying it (inasmuch as the Empire consists in the unity of a universal monarchy), it is manifest that he who wields the authority of the Empire may not rend the Empire."[73] This is, however, coincidental to the reason for Rudolph's stay in exile in the Valley of the Princes. The specific reason is given in Sordello's description of him:

> ". . . fa sembianti
> d'aver negletto ciò che far dovea
> . . . che potea
> sanar le piaghe c'hanno Italia morta,
> sí che tardi per altri si ricrea."[74]

This recalls the accusation in *Purg.* VI. 103–105 that Rudolph and Albert of Habsburg, kept on the wrong side of the Alps through their greed (*per cupidigia di costà distretti*), had allowed Italy, the garden of the Empire, to become a wasteland of civil discord. Already in *Conv.* IV. iii. 6, Dante had claimed that the only true Emperor in the thirteenth century had been Frederick II. "although Rudolph and Adolf and Albert have since been elected," since Rudolph (1273–1291), Adolf of Nassau (1292–1298), and Albert (1298–1308) had never been crowned Emperor in Rome.[75]

Moreover, Rudolph's neglect of Italy was all the more reprehensible in that Villani assures us that Rudolph was in fact:

magnanimous, and of great prowess in arms . . . greatly feared by the Germans and Italians; *and if he had decided to come down into Italy, he would have been its master without opposition.* And he sent as his ambassador the archbishop of Trier, who came to Florence in the year 1280 to announce his coming, *whereupon the Florentines were at a loss to know what to do; and is he had crossed the Alps, they would certainly have obeyed him.*[76]

In other words, as Dante states with his usual concision, Rudolph "could have healed the wounds that have proved to be the death of Italy."

Rudolph's neighbor is Ottocar II, king of Bohemia: in life, his archenemy who had refused to recognize Rudolph's election, but who now "comforts him" (l. 97) as a token of the unity and charity that should unite Europe's rulers. Their rivalry on earth had led Rudolph to dispossess Ottocar of most of his titles and possessions (including the dukedom of Austria), and then to kill him on the field of battle in 1278 after the latter's unsuccessful rebellion. Nevertheless, the poet insists, even in the cradle Ottocar was a far better man than his son and heir Wenceslaus, king of Bohemia, who had become Rudolph's son-in-law—and who is here dismissed as wallowing in "lust and sloth" (l. 102). This theme of the degeneracy of the sons and heirs of Europe's rulers characterizes both Dante's and Sordello's poems.

Philip III of France is portrayed as deep in conversation with Henry the Fat, king of Navarre (ll. 103–11). His pusillanimity (perhaps hinted at in the metonymy "that small nose," l. 103) led Philip to a dishonorable death, while fleeing from his disastrous defeat by the king of Aragon at the battle of Las Formiguas in 1285. He strikes his breast in the familiar gesture of *mea culpa*, indicating his guilt and shame in having sired Philip IV, "the pest of France" (l. 109), and—we may add—Charles of Valois (cf. *Purg.* XX. 70–78, 85–93), although here only the former is mentioned, since it is Philip the Fair's "vicious and foul life" that causes such anguish to his father and his father-in-law Henry.

Peter III, king of Aragon, who had married King Manfred's daughter Costanza and who had seized the throne of Sicily after the revolt against the French in 1282, is described as a perfect knight, endowed with every virtue (l. 114)—an apparently incongruous description in its praise of a ruler still exiled from Purgatory. The positive element is introduced, however, to create an even greater contrast with the decadence of his heirs, James II (king of Sicily and then of Aragon) and Frederick II (king of Sicily from 1296), who have inherited none of their father's better qualities (l. 120). Frederick, indeed, will be roundly condemned for his "avarice and cowardice" at no less a judgment-seat than the Heaven of Justice (*Par.* XIX. 130–35).[77] Dante's recognition of Peter's chivalresque qualities may also have been inspired by the fact that Peter was generally thought to have set out to avenge the deaths of his father-in-law Manfred and the legitimate imperial heir Conradin. Moreover, like Manfred, Peter was excommunicated for his Sicilian expedition by the French Pope Martin IV, who invested Charles of Valois with all his titles and lands. Indeed, the Pope launched a veritable crusade against him—as a result of which, Philip III of France set out on his disastrous campaign. The Popes' tendency to debase the crusading ideal into a political weapon or even a private vendetta had already been denounced in *Inf.* XXVII. 85–90. Here, it is decried through praise of their opponent's virtues.

Sordello now refers to his erstwhile patron, Charles I of Anjou, merely as the "large-nosed one" (l. 124; cf. 113), whose heir is also far worse than his father, so that both Provence and the whole of Southern Italy have good cause to mourn their fate. It is only in *Purg.* XX. 67–69 that the poet will reveal Charles's guilt in supposedly ordering the murder of St. Thomas Aquinas. For the time being, Sordello tells us (ll. 127–29) that Charles II is as much inferior to his father as the latter is to King Peter III of Aragon. Dante's and Virgil's guide then points out Henry III of England (1216–72), whose heir (Edward I, known as the "English Justinian") is the exception to the rule that the son is always worse than the father. Finally, to complete the hierarchy, just as we found an emperor at the top, so here at the bottom is William VII, Marquis of Monferrato (c. 1240–1292), who died shut up in an iron cage at Alessandria and whose son, John I, tried to avenge him by waging a long and terrible war that made their possessions "weep" (l. 136)—yet another example of Italy's "wounds" (l. 95) the Emperor should have cured or prevented.

In the Sordello episode, no less than two negligent Emperors stand accused. Rudolph, in Canto VIII, personifies the accusations levelled against Albert and himself by the poet-narrator in Canto VI. In the three cantos that make up the episode both the anarchy prevailing in Italy and the culpable negligence of contemporary European rulers are underscored by the presence of an Italian poet guilty of negligence in that he failed to help create an illustrious literary language in Italy. The fact that Dante's text twice emphasizes that Virgil and Sordello shared the same birthplace (*Purg.* VI. 72–74; VII. 18) only serves to highlight the radical opposition set up between the two poets in the use they had made of their poetic genius on earth. Sordello recognizes Virgil's artistic achievement in *Purg.* VII. 16–19:

> "O gloria di Latin", disse, "per cui
> mostrò ciò che potea la lingua nostra,
> o pregio etterno del loco ond'io fui,
>   qual merito o qual grazia mi ti mostra?"[78]

Dante's Sordello praises Virgil "our greatest muse" (*Par.* XV. 26) for having realized the full potential of *la lingua nostra*, or Latin.[79] We must remember that, for Dante, Latin was an artificial construct (*DVE* I. i. 3), invented with strict, unchanging rules in order to remedy the curse of excessive mutability and instability afflicting natural language since God punished humanity for its hubris at Babel (cf. *DVE* I. vii–viii). The term "Latini," both in the *Comedy* and in the *De Vulgari Eloquentia*, indicates the Italians. Sordello honors Virgil as the son of Italy who displayed in and through his poetry "what our language could achieve"—most obviously, in his masterpiece, the *Aeneid*. His example is not to be surpassed but rather emulated in the sphere of vernacular poetry. As the *De Vulgari Eloquentia*'s clarion call makes clear, Italians who have taken up the recent fashion of writing in the vulgar tongue must learn to create an elevated literary language by following the examples of the classical writers (*DVE* II. vi. 7). Virgil, first in the list, who had brought the common, imperial language, Latin, to perfection, stands out as the supreme example. Sordello, "a man of such great eloquence," had failed in his duty as an Italian poet to contribute to this essential task where the Italian vernacular was concerned. Moreover, as we have seen, in his life on earth as a staunch supporter of the Angevin adventurer, Sordello had also failed to heed the message of Virgil as the herald of the Empire. In both these respects, the historical Sordello had been the antithesis of his fellow Mantuan.

Nevertheless, as we have seen, Dante transforms Sordello into a symbol of the fraternal love and solicitude that should unite not only Italians but all men and women. The author of the *Comedy* corrects the historical Sordello by making him act in Antepurgatory as a true *poeta-vate* in his spontaneous greeting of an unknown fellow countryman—an act of *caritas* out of keeping with Dante's judgment of Sordello's conduct in life, but one made possible by the courage the troubadour had in fact shown in his criticism of contemporary society and its rulers. Far from being the historical embodiment of patriotism, Dante's Sordello is in fact a palinodial figure who leads the pilgrim to a scene of edenic harmony, where the former rulers of Europe are united in their quest for peace and unity as they gaze upon a pageant symbolizing the need for fraternal collaboration between the temporal and spiritual powers on earth. After this exemplary encounter with the first of the poets found on the Mountain, the pilgrim is ready to undertake the journey through Purgatory proper. At the end of his ascent he will find another poet, one who will address him in his native Provençal, that same poetic language used by Sordello, but there (*Purg.* XXVI. 140–47) used by a poet who appears as the last penitent encountered, the paradigm of the *miglior fabbro del parlar materno* ("better craftsman of his mother tongue")—where the word *fabbro* is redolent of a gifted writer's duty to forge his *parlar materno* into an illustrious vernacular. The second *cantica*'s poetic parabola is thus complete.

7

The Dream and the Entrance to Purgatory (*Purgatorio* IX–X)

THE SECOND *cantica* IS UNIQUE IN THAT Purgatory is described only after a lengthy prelude, during which Dante encounters souls specifically (although temporarily) excluded from the realm of purgation. Ironically, Belacqua is right to point out that he is no longer a prey to his former indolence in not attempting to ascend the mountain:

> Ed elli: "O frate, andar in sú che porta?
> ché non mi lascerebbe ire a' martíri
> l'angel di Dio che siede in su la porta.
>   Prima convien che tanto il ciel m'aggiri
> di fuor da essa, quanto fece in vita,
> per ch'io 'ndugiai al fine i buon sospiri"[1]

As many commentators observe, the poem's symmetrical construction is further highlighted by the fact that the other two *cantiche* display a similar structural frontier: the first nine cantos of the *Inferno* describe the meeting with Virgil, the descent into Limbo, and the circles where the sins of incontinence are punished; nether hell is only entered at the end of the ninth canto. Dante places a clear marker to indicate the increasing gravity of the sins punished in what is truly the Devil's city. Similarly, the first nine cantos of *Paradiso* describe the Pilgrim's ascent through the first three "heavens," where, according to medieval cosmology, the earth's shadow was visible, implying a relative imperfection in the merits of the blessed who appear to Dante in the Moon, Mercury, and Venus; only in *Paradiso* X do we find the Heaven of the Sun and souls whose physical features are hidden by the light they irradiate, reflecting the ever-increasing intensity of the *lumen gloriae* and their vision of God. Nevertheless, the fact remains that Hell begins in *Inferno* IV, the blessed souls begin to appear to the Pilgrim in *Paradiso* II, whereas we have to traverse no less than nine cantos before entering the Gate of Purgatory in *Purgatorio* X.

The need to spend time in exile before the process of purification and drawing nearer to God can begin is further proof of the freedom and originality shown by the poet in his description of the other world, where the topography of Purgatory is perfectly functional, as Jacques Le Goff claims.[2] The location of the "sacred Mount" (*Purg.* XIX. 38) in the southern hemisphere at the antipodes to Jerusalem effectively highlights the opposition between the Eden of Innocence and the Calvary of Sin, between the Old and the New Adam, while the link uniting the Tiber with the shores of Purgatory (*Purg.* II. 100–105) reflects the providential role of Rome as the seat of both Papacy and Empire in the post-lapsarian world. The addition of a waiting-section, Dante's Antepurgatory, was a brilliant and original solution to the theological problem of offering salvation to men and women who had died excommunicate, or to those who had put off repentance until the very last moment. It illustrated not only God's infinite mercy but also his justice, and at the same time created an opportunity for the author of the *Comedy* to emphasize the limitations of ecclesiastical authority on earth.

Equally original was the means invented by Dante for his passage from Antepurgatory to Purgatory proper — or, more precisely, the way this passage is conveyed allegorically. Since Purgatory is the only temporal state in the other world, the *Purgatorio* is the only *cantica* where Dante's body is subjected to the temporal vicissitudes of sleep — and during the three nights the Pilgrim spends on the Mountain, he has three prophetic (hence, allegorical) dreams, described in Cantos IX, XIX, and XXVII; namely, just before entering Purgatory, halfway through, and just before leaving Purgatory to enter the Earthly Paradise, each dream strategically positioned at 9-18/19-27.[3]

The first dream occurs when the Pilgrim falls asleep in the Valley of the Princes. He takes pains to tell us that this dream revealed a truth, and that it took place just before dawn, when:

> . . . la mente nostra, peregrina
> piú da la carne e men da' pensier presa,
> a le sue visïon quasi è divina[4]

"Almost divine" (*quasi è divina*): relatively unencumbered by normal thoughts and preoccupations, our mind may then be granted a vision of the truth (cf. *Inf.* XXVI. 7). The dream is then related in lines 19–33:

in sogno mi parea veder sospesa
un'aguglia nel ciel con penne d'oro,
con l'ali aperte e a calare intesa;
   ed esser mi parea là dove fuoro
abbandonati i suoi da Ganimede,
quando fu ratto al sommo consistoro.
   Fra me pensava: 'Forse questa fiede
pur qui per uso, e forse d'altro loco
disdegna di portarne suso in piede.'
   Poi mi parea che, poi rotata un poco,
terribil come folgor discendesse,
e me rapisse suso infino al foco.
   Ivi parea che ella e io ardesse;
e sí lo 'ncendio imaginato cosse,
che convenne che 'l sonno si rompesse.[5]

Fortunately, Virgil explains what has actually happened:

"Dianzi, ne l'alba che procede al giorno,
quando l'anima tua dentro dormia,
sovra li fiori ond' è là giú addorno
   venne una donna, e disse: 'I' son Lucia;
lasciatemi pigliar costui che dorme;
sí l'agevolerò per la sua via.'
   Sordel rimase e l'altre genti forme;
ella ti tolse, e come 'l dí fu chiaro,
sen venne suso; e io per le sue orme.
   Qui ti posò, ma pria mi dimostraro
li occhi suoi belli quella intrata aperta;
poi ella e 'l sonno ad una se n'andaro."[6]

The Pilgrim is thus told that Saint Lucia, who had been sent by the Virgin Mary to intercede for Dante with Beatrice in Heaven (*Inf.* II. 97–108), has once again come to his aid by transporting him during his sleep from the Valley to the Gate of Purgatory. Dante's devotion to Lucia is proclaimed in Mary's description of him as "your faithful one" (*Inf.* II. 98; cf. *Par.* XXXI. 132); her role in the *Comedy* is generally taken to be that of symbolizing the actions of grace, *gratia illuminans*. Her very name points to Light. Recently, however, Professor Stefanini has proposed a radically different interpretation, whereby Lucia represents the Empire.[7]

Commentators tend to admire the "realistic" details of the dream; for example, the fact that the heat that shatters the dream corresponds to the warmth of the sun's rays on the Pilgrim's body (e.g., the Bosco-Reggio commentary, which warns the reader: "It would be difficult, and perhaps vain, to look for the allegorical meaning of the fire that burns Dante and the eagle in the sphere of fire").[8] However that may be, scholars rightly point to the myth of Ganymede, who was snatched up by Jove's eagle to become the immortal cupbearer to the gods (Ovid, *Metamorphoses* X. 155–61; *Aeneid* V. 252–57), as yet another indication of Dante's insistence on the unique privilege granted him by God to undertake his journey through the three realms of the other world; for, if the Pilgrim is neither Aeneas nor St. Paul (*Inf.* II. 34), it is nevertheless true that Aeneas did not rise up to the Christian Heaven and Paul did not visit the infernal regions. Moreover, as Robert Hollander points out, there are no less than three references to

classical rapes . . . one at the beginning, one during, and one at the conclusion of the dream. . . . Since the dream occurs in the canto before the arrival of Dante and Virgil on the Terrace of Pride, it is particularly fitting because it is the dream of a mortal who is singled out from his fellows and carried up to heaven to be among the immortals . . . For the other three there was no efficient grace. The pagan tales . . . are played against the Christian *figura* of the eagle as the bird of God's empire.[9]

Hollander goes on to cite Erich Auerbach, who regarded the eagle solely as "a symbol of God's Grace," quoting in particular Exodus 19. 4: "You have seen what I did unto the Egyptians, and how I bare you on eagles' wings, and brought you unto myself."[10] I use the word "solely" not because I reject this interpretation, but because it touches on only one of the three possible allegorical levels of meaning in Dante's poem, the anagogical.

The polysemy or various levels of meaning of the *Comedy* surely requires us to search for another meaning: the second or tropological meaning, according to both the *Convivio* and the Epistle to Cangrande. Despite doubts about the latter's authenticity, the Epistle remains (as Gilson pointed out in 1965) a precious document for a proper understanding of the poem's purpose: we read, for example, in paragraph 16 that "the whole as well as the part was conceived, *not for speculation, but for action*."[11] The tropological sense was epigrammatically summed up as indicating *quid agas* ("what you must do") or what Dante calls the "moral" sense in *Convivio* II. i. 5.[12] The basic distinction is clear: the anagogical sense is concerned with humanity's ultimate goal situated in the other world, while the tropological meaning has to do with human conduct on earth.

It is, therefore, in keeping with Charles Singleton's insistence on the anagogical sense of Dante's masterpiece that, in his classic essay "*In Exitu Israel de Aegypto*," the late master should have stressed the fact that "The eagle, in the realization, is Lucia, and the fire that had seemed to burn the dreamer was Purgatory proper. . . . By Lucia's coming the reader is returned to the prologue (which means a return to the Exodus figure) and invited to consider the difference between . . . 'Exodus' then and 'Exodus' now." For Singleton, the all-pervasive message of Dante's poem was one of conversion, and "Exodus is simply *the* figure of conversion."[13]

Nevertheless, Singleton focuses on only one of the two chief strands in the *Comedy*: the need for conversion, leaving behind the Egypt of Sin and the journey to the Promised Land. The other essential message of the poem—what Francesco Mazzoni calls the poem's fundamental allegory— is the need for co-operation between the two supreme powers on earth, the Empire and the Papacy, a message reiterated until the very end of the poem (*Par.* XXVII. 139–41; XXX. 142–44). Dante delivered that same message at the end of a work written during—or after—the composition of the *Purgatorio*. In the last chapter of his *Monarchia* (III. xv. 7–10), he set out what he considered to be the divine blueprint for the world and the happiness of mankind. God instituted two ends for humanity, with two supreme authorities to guide them to those ends. The first is the happiness attainable in this life (*beatitudo huius vite*); the second, the happiness attainable only in eternity (*beatitudo vite ecterne*). The first is symbolized by Eden or the Earthly Paradise, to which the Emperor must lead men and women— aided in his task by the teachings of philosophy. The second is found in Heaven and must be reached under the guidance of the Pope, with the help of revelation. This all-embracing formula must constantly be kept in mind by readers of the *Comedy*.

The poet warns his readers that he is rising to new levels of complexity:

> Lettor, tu vedi ben com' io innalzo
> la mia matera, e però con piú arte
> non ti maravigliar s'io la rincalzo.[14]

This refers most obviously to the second half of the canto; however, the *matera* is his whole journey of purification on the Mountain of Purgatory —and this is foreshadowed in the dream. It is therefore possible to heed the poet's warning and realize that the prophetic message of the dream described in the first half of the canto must be interpreted on more than one level. Scholars such as Singleton and Hollander have indicated the first level. Singleton, however, considers the fire to be merely the generic fire of Purgatory, while Hollander takes the eagle to be a symbol of God's empire in the sense of Divine Grace. That is undoubtedly the meaning of what we are told has just happened, namely Lucy's transportation of the sleeping Pilgrim. In the dream, however, as in the overall context of the poem, the eagle possesses other connotations essential to the poet's purpose in describing this oneiric vision before he begins his ascent of the Mountain.

We should do well to recall that a symbol, like a word, has no inherent meaning; it takes on meaning in a given context. Let us therefore examine the reference to eagles in the *Comedy*. There are twelve occurrences in all (*aquila/aguglia*): two to the eagle's ability to look directly at the sun (*Par.* I. 48; XX. 31–32), one to the heraldic eagle of the Polenta family (*Inf.* XXVII. 41), one as a simile indicating Homer's poetic supremacy (*Inf.* IV. 96), one to St. John as Christ's eagle (*Par.* XXVI. 53), and one to the eagles on the standards of the Roman legions (*Purg.* X. 80–81). In no fewer than five instances, the eagle clearly stands for the Roman Empire (*Purg.* XXXII. 125; XXXIII. 38; *Par.* VI. 1) and its ideal of Justice (*Par.* XVIII. 107; XX. 26). To the six cases in which the eagle is associated with Rome and the Empire must be added the periphrasis "Jove's bird" (*Purg.* XXXII. 112) the "holy bird" of *Par.* XVII. 72, and the even bolder "God's bird" (*l'uccel di Dio*) of *Par.* VI. 4. Outside the *Comedy*, the eagle symbolizes the universal Empire of Rome in *Monarchia* II. ix. 15, xi. 6, and in Epistles V. iv. 11 (*sublimis aquila*), VI. iii. 12 (*aquila in auro terribilis*), VII. i. 5 (*signa Tarpeia*—the imperial eagle is associated with the very heart of Rome, the Capitol's *Tarpeius mons* mentioned just after Dante's dream, *Purg.* IX. 136–38). Beside these five instances, we must add the highly significant allusion to Emperor Henry VII as *Iovis armiger* ("Jove's armiger") in Giovanni del Virgilio's First Eclogue to Dante (I. 26). This is the term used to designate the eagle in Virgil's reference to the rape of Ganymede (*Aen.* V. 252–55): "inwoven thereon the royal boy [Ganymede], with javelin and speedy foot, on leafy Ida tires fleet stags, eager, and like to one who pants; him Jove's swift armor-bearer [*Iovis armiger*] has caught up aloft from Ida in his talons." Giovanni del Virgilio evidently took it for granted that Dante would grasp the equation *Iovis armiger* = Eagle ⟶ the Emperor.

Moreover, two of the contexts outside the *Comedy* are of particular importance. The first has been noted by a number of scholars. It is the passage already indicated in *Ep.* V. iv. 11, in which Dante speaks of the Emperor's arrival in Italy as that of an "eagle from on high, swooping down like a thunderbolt" (*sublimis aquila fulguris instar descendens*). The image of the thunderbolt is repeated in the Pilgrim's dream: "mi parea che . . . terribil come folgor discendesse" (*Purg.* IX. 28–29). The second passage is found in *Ep.* VI. iii. 12, when Dante warns the most wicked Florentines who have rebelled against Henry that the Emperor will arrive and "terrible in gold, the eagle shall swoop down" (*cum advolaverit aquila in auro terribilis*). Here, two details are given: one is the fact that the eagle is *terribilis*, the other that it is *in auro*, in other words it is the heraldic eagle, symbol of the Empire. Both details are given in Dante's dream: "an eagle poised in the heavens *with wings of gold*" (l. 20), "*terrible* like thunder" (l. 29). Although the heraldic bird signifying the Empire was a black eagle on a gold background, we may also point to—as does Fernando Salsano (*ED* I, 339)—the golden eagle, which was repeatedly quoted by Chiaro Davanzati and others as a symbol of imperial authority.[15]

The association with the imperial eagle is made even clearer by the poet's narration of the dream: what he stresses is not so much the fact that his experience was similar to Ganymede's (that is left to the reader to deduce), but rather his belief that he found himself on Mount Ida near Troy:

> ed esser mi parea là dove fuoro
> abbandonati i suoi da Ganimede,
> quando fu ratto al sommo consistoro.[16]

Ganymede, son of the founder of Troy, is specifically associated with Mount Ida, in other words, with the mountains from which the imperial eagle issued forth, according to *Par.* VI. 6 (cf. *Par.* VI. 67–68 and *Aen.* III. 6). The poet leads us to understand that in his dream of having been borne aloft by an eagle, he felt that he was on the very spot where the Empire had been born: God's divine plan, required that Troy be destroyed and that Aeneas—the father of Rome (*Aen.* VIII. 134; *Mon.* II. iii. 11)—should bring the imperial eagle with him to Italy (*Inf.* I. 73–75). Eventually the Empire would create the *pax universalis* destined by God to prepare the world for Christ's birth. The fact that Dante dreams that he was on Mount Ida when taken aloft by the eagle is thus inextricably linked with the idea of the eagle as symbol of Rome's Empire and its divine mission. That mission is encapsulated, as we have seen, in the message delivered at the end of the *Monarchia*: humanity must be guided by the imperial authority to the temporal happiness prefigured in the Earthly Paradise.

The polysemy of Dante's poem allows us to accept the eagle as a symbol both of God's grace and of the Empire. This bifocal vision is exemplified by the fact that the eagle transports the Pilgrim "up as far as the fire" (l. 30). Commentators may admire the oneiric detail invented by the poet—the overwhelming sensation of burning—to explain the Pilgrim's sudden awakening; others, like Bosco, may claim: "I think that the precision of this detail has never been noted . . . common experience shows that certain external situations, by acting on the body, may condition images in dreams. In this case, the sun's heat on the poet's body determines in his dream 'the imagined fire' which wakens him." [17]

While arguing for a monofocal interpretation (usually Lucy and the Eagle = Grace), critics seem to have no difficulty in explaining that the eagle bears up the Pilgrim to the sphere of fire, while Lucia transports him to the Door of Purgatory. The poet merely says "as far as the fire" (l. 30). As every student of Dante knows, the sphere of fire in medieval cosmology was situated between the earth and the moon, far above the peak of Mount Purgatory—and the Pilgrim passes through that sphere only in the first canto of *Paradiso*. While the eagle as a symbol of grace may have transported the Pilgrim to the sphere of fire, nothing in the text tells us that this is the necessary or the only meaning for this "fire." In fact, when he reaches and transcends that sphere, the Pilgrim—thanks to his superhuman powers (*Par.* I. 55-57)—does not feel any sensation of burning. There is, on the other hand, a well-known incident *in Purgatory* when he is obliged to suffer the terrible effects of fire, the wall of fire that purifies all tendency to lust. It is all the more remarkable in that it is the only occasion in the poem when he is specifically ordered to take part in such an ordeal. That scene is described in *Purg.* XXVII, after the angel's warning that, although the soul is now holy, it must still be subjected to trial by fire:

> Poscia "Piú non si va, se pria non morde,
> anime sante, il foco: intrate in esso,
> e al cantar di là non siate sorde." [18]

This episode takes on a forceful dramatic impact, and the poet highlighted it through the immense fear he feels, "looking at the fire while vividly imagining human bodies I have seen burning" (ll. 17–18). Virgil enters the fray and reminds him that he protected the Pilgrim in their encounter with Geryon (*Inf.* XVI–XVII), assuring him that the fire will not harm a hair of his head, but Dante—in one of the most delightfully self-deprecating lines in the *Comedy*—will not budge: *E io pur fermo e contra coscienza* (l. 33: "But

I would not budge, despite my conscience"). Only Beatrice's name spurs him on, but as soon as he feels the intensity of that fire:

> . . . in un bogliente vetro
> gittato mi sarei per rinfrescarmi,
> tant'era ivi lo 'ncendio sanza metro.[19]

It is surprising that in their interpretations of *Purg.* IX. 30 critics have on the whole avoided the most obvious parallel: that which leads us to the only use of fire in the construction of Dante's Purgatory, especially when all are aware of the economical use made by the poet of this traditional symbol.[20]

To return to the eagle and Lucia, it must be noted that, although they accomplish similar tasks, in fact they belong to two different spheres constantly kept distinct in Dante's thought. The poet imagines that he is transported on high by human justice and grace; in order to portray this parallelism, he invents a dream in which two complementary scenes are played out. The first dream thus prefigures what will happen to the Pilgrim, who will be led by Virgil, herald and symbol of the Empire, through the wall of purgatorial fire to the Earthly Paradise. It would be hard to imagine a more elegant way to illustrate Dante's fundamental thesis: that humanity must be led by the imperial authority to the *beatitudo huius vite* symbolized by Eden. Even as the eagle, symbol of the Empire and its Justice, snatches up the Pilgrim in a dream and carries him to the fire, so Virgil will actually lead the Pilgrim to the wall of fire marking the frontier of Eden, the place where Dante's will is at last totally free and Virgil's task comes to an end:

> e disse: "Il temporal foco e l'etterno
> veduto hai, figlio; e se' venuto in parte
> dov'io per me piú oltre non discerno.
>   Tratto t'ho qui con ingegno e con arte;
> lo tuo piacere omai prendi per duce . . .
> libero, dritto e sano è tuo arbitrio,
> e fallo fora non fare a suo senno . . ."[21]

The parallelism indicated is fully borne out. In order to reach the fullest happiness attainable in this life, men and women must be guided by both the Empire (Eagle-Virgil-Justice) and the Church (Eagle-St. Lucy-Grace). It is, however, principally the Emperor's responsibility to achieve this goal;

hence, the fact that the eagle is primarily the symbol of the Empire (while St. Lucy may also point to the Emperor's essential role). Nevertheless, the Emperor needs the co-operation of the Church and grace, inasmuch as grace perfects Nature, and "mortal happiness is in a certain sense ordained with reference to [our] immortal happiness. Let Caesar, then, observe that reverence to Peter which a first-born son should observe to his father, so that illuminated by the light of paternal grace he may all the more effectively irradiate the world, over which he has been set by Him alone who is the ruler of all things spiritual and temporal."[22]

At the same time, the *Comedy*'s polysemy makes it possible for the eagle to be a symbol of regeneration—and in Brunetto Latini's *Tresor* (I. 145 [136]), Dante could read that "the eagle lives to a great age because it renews itself and casts off its old age. And most recount that it flies *so far on high toward the sun's heat that its feathers are set on fire, and it cleanses its eyes of all darkness, and then it plunges into a fountain where it bathes three times, and thus is as young as it was at its beginning*" (my emphasis). We note the parallels with the Pilgrim's sensation of burning, his immersion in Lethe and Eunoë, and his eventual state of total renewal (*Purg.* XXXIII. 14244).

The structural break between Antepurgatory and Purgatory proper is powerfully underlined by such a complex *dea ex machina* as the Lucia-Eagle, where the duality—LUCIA (Grace, but also a *figura* of the Empire) and AQUILA (symbol of the Empire, but also of grace)—is expressed through the ambiguities characteristic of dreams. The poet thus stresses the immense qualitative leap made by the Pilgrim in his journey toward earthly beatitude and toward God, as well as its dependence on divine grace. A similar structural landmark had been found in the descent on Geryon in *Inferno* XVII, which had emphasized the destruction of ordered society by fraud; here, the ascent to the gate of Purgatory is likewise found to be beyond the living Pilgrim's natural powers and may be adequately described only in a dream with its multiple levels of meaning.[23]

The Gate and the Gatekeeper

Having arrived at the Gateway, Dante sees an angel guarding it, sitting on the topmost of three steps, his appearance so bright that the Pilgrim's gaze has to be averted, while the latter's eyesight is overcome by the light reflected from the sword (*Purg.* IX. 76–84). This anti-Minos figure (cf. *Inf.* V. 4–24) has often been seen as a judge, and his sword traditionally taken to symbolize Justice. Reminiscent of the Cherubim placed by the God of Justice at the entrance to Eden and armed with a flaming sword (Genesis 3. 24), this angel cannot fail to remind us of the expulsion from Eden, the result of Original Sin and its effects (which are eliminated or purged inside the Gate). More specifically, however, if we accept Professor Armour's thesis, the Angel points to the figure and role of the ideal Pope.[24]

The single sword held before the Gate of Purgatory (which is also the entrance to Paradise, St. Peter's Gate: *Inf.* I. 134) is yet another rebuttal of the earthly Pope's damnable ambition to possess not only the spiritual sword but the temporal one as well—as Boniface VIII had claimed in *Unam Sanctam*: "We are taught by the words of the Gospel that in this church and in her power there are two swords, a spiritual one and a temporal one." The angel's robe—the color of "ashes or dry earth" (*Purg.* IX. 115)—is symbolic of the repentance and humility needed to gain access to the process of purification leading to union with God, but it also stands in diametrical contrast to the imperial regalia donned by Peter's vicar in 1300. On 22 February 1300 Boniface VIII had proclaimed the first Holy Year in a scene of imperial grandeur recorded in the loggia of benediction built by the Pope. As Charles Mitchell notes:

A singularly barbaric inscription in rhymed hexameters . . . commemorated Boniface's undertakings. The text alludes in the first part to the conversion and baptism of Constantine and to his donation of the crown to Pope Sylvester. . . . Thus, Boniface, as restorer of the Lateran, appeared firmly set in the line of Constantine, its founder, and deliberate stress was laid on the dominion which Constantine conferred on Sylvester, Boniface's predecessor in the Roman see.[25]

In fact, this theme of Boniface as the imperial heir to Constantine in Rome ran through the whole of the loggia's imagery, and Boniface's claims to plenitude of power in both spheres were reflected in the imperial insignia supposedly inherited from Constantine the Great. Just as significant for the impact such a scene may have had on Dante is the fact that a blind arch stood at the end of the papal loggia. It contained two life-size statues of Saints Peter and Paul, the two saints most closely identified with Rome and the early Church. St. Peter was represented as holding *one* key, St. Paul *one* sword, signifying the spiritual power of God's Word (Ephes. 6. 17; cf. *Purg.* XXIX. 139–41). In the loggia, the future author of the *Comedy* may well have been struck by the contrast between the ideal founders of the Church in Rome and the hubris of the *Vicarius Petri* in 1300, who was rumored to have greeted the ambassadors of Albert of Habsburg in 1298, clad in papal robes but sword in hand, with the words: "I am Caesar, I am the Emperor" (*Ego sum caesar, ego sum imperator*).[26]

We conclude, with Peter Armour, that the description of the Gate-keeper is "an implicit polemic against the worldliness of the earthly Church and Boniface VIII during the great Pilgrimage year of 1300, and specifically in the penitential season of Lent"; so that "the door which the angel opens with his perfect keys does not lead to the worldly treasure amassed by a Pope who claimed to be also Caesar, but it is built on a priceless rock and leads to a treasury greater than Caesar's, the eternal treasures of Purgatory and Paradise."[27] Or, to put it another way, the door opens the way for humanity to enjoy both the treasure of Caesar (*beatitudo huius vite*) and the treasure of Christ (*beatitudo vite ecterne*)—perhaps one of the meanings intended by Virgil's coronation and mitering of the Pilgrim at the top of the Mount (*Purg.* XXVII. 142). Moreover, the angel's report that St Peter himself had told him that he should err on the side of generosity may also be taken as an implicit criticism of the excessive use of excommunication and interdict, especially for political purposes, by the contemporary papacy:

> "Da Pier le tegno; e dissemi ch'i' erri
> anzi ad aprir ch'a tenerla serrata,
> pur che la gente a' piedi mi s'atterri."[28]

Pur che la gente a' piedi mi s'atterri: humility is essential for salvation. Indeed, it forms a *leitmotiv* in the *Purgatorio* from the very beginning when the two poets arrive on the shores of the Mount and Virgil girds Dante with the "humble plant" symbolizing this basic virtue (*Purg.* I. 133–36). Humility is the virtue most opposed to pride, the cause of both humanity's and Lucifer's fall (*Par.* XXVI. 115–17 and *Purg.* XII. 25–27). As such it is introduced on the first terrace, and its role is to offer the necessary corrective to souls who are eliminating all vestiges of the sin—according to a fixed pattern whereby each of the seven terraces offers examples of the opposite virtue, followed by *exempla* of the Capital Sin of which the souls had been guilty on earth.[29]

The first example of the virtue illustrated on each Terrace is always taken from the life of the Virgin Mary (cf. St. Bonaventure's *Speculum Beatae Mariae Virginis*). It is thus hardly surprising that the first, supreme example of humility is Mary's total acceptance of God's will at the Annunciation, when humanity's salvation was made possible through her unquestioning obedience; peace (a keyword in Dante) was made with God, and

Heaven was opened up to redeemed humanity: "the peace which for many
years had been wept for and which opened up heaven from its long ban"
(*Purg.* X. 35–36). Surprising, however, is that the other two examples of
this supreme Christian virtue are taken not from the actions or sacrifices of
holy men and women but from episodes in the lives of King David and the
Emperor Trajan. We need only recall the fact that in the thirteenth century
Francis of Assisi was often regarded as the human being who had come
closest to Christ in his insistence on the need for total humility and obedience to God's commandments, in order to appreciate the paradox that in
this Dantesque trinity two are not religious but political figures (although
David was also the inspired scribe of one of God's texts, "the singer of the
Holy Spirit," *Par.* XX. 38, and was also regarded as a *figura Christi*). Both
will in fact be revealed to Dante in the Heaven of Justice (*Par.* XX. 37ff.),
where the Pilgrim will see "how well heaven loves a just king" (ll. 64–
65). Through what Charles Singleton has called "the vistas in retrospect",
we catch glimpses of the overall masterplan that brings into yet clearer relief certain stages or episodes of the Pilgrim's journey. Accordingly, it is
only when we reach the Heaven of Justice (Jupiter) that we discover the
full extent of Dante's association of the Empire with Justice (*Par.* XVIII.
91ff.). That coupling is a far more natural association of ideas (cf. *Mon.*
I. xi) than the linking of a Roman Emperor with the peculiarly Christian
virtue of humility. Indeed, as an anachronism the attribution of humility
to an Emperor who was still a pagan when he condescended to listen to a
poor widow's complaint must surely rank with the notorious description
of Virgil's parents as "Lombards" (*Inf.* I. 68). And we may note in passing that, whereas the poet calls David "the humble psalmist" in *Purg.* X.
65, the epithet is nowhere in evidence in the description of *l'alta gloria / del
roman principato* (ll. 73–74: "the high glory of the Roman prince"). In the
Emperor's surprising humility that constitutes his *alta gloria*, it is possible
to glimpse an implied oxymoron not unlike that describing Mary as *umile
e alta più che creatura* in *Par.* XXXIII. 2 ("humble and exalted more than
any other creature"). In fact, outside its present context on the Terrace of
Pride, we should certainly be justified in interpreting Trajan's action as an
example of submission to duty ("il mio dovere"), an act of justice and *pietas*
(ll. 92–93)—and, as Benvenuto da Imola reports, "some say . . . that this
action of Trajan seems to belong to justice rather than to humility."[30]

The association of justice and pity/piety with the Emperor's office is
reiterated when the Pilgrim encounters Trajan in the eye of the heavenly
eagle because he—like David and the other spirits there—had been *giusto*

e pio ("just and merciful"), hence an example to others (*Par.* XIX. 13–18). Heaven itself is called "this most just and merciful empire" in *Par.* XXXII. 117. This pairing of two qualities seen as essential in a ruler is further emphasized by Dante's quotation in *Mon.* II. v. 5 and in *Ep.* V. vii. 3, where the Roman Empire is described as originating in God, the source of all true pity/mercy. In *Convivio* IV. xxi. 12 (following Isaiah 11. 2), Pity is identified as one of the seven gifts of the Holy Spirit, while in *Conv.* II. x. 6, we read that "pity is . . . a noble disposition of mind, receptive to love, mercy, and other charitable emotions." In other words, the Emperor's role as the dispenser of Justice must be governed by pity, as in the example of Trajan's act of humility in listening to the pleas of the *vedovella*—an act that had earned eternal salvation for the pagan Emperor, thanks to the prayers of St. Gregory the Great.[31] The metonymy whereby *del roman principato* (l. 74: literally, "of the Roman principate") signifies *del romano principe* ("of the Roman prince") confused a number of scribes, who normalized it as "del roman *principe*" while adding "gran" to the phrase "il cui valore" in order to restore the hendecasyllable.[32] Commentators, however, explain that *principato* here = *principe*, without glossing the implications. Instead, we must ask ourselves why Dante chose to place this form (a *hapax* in the *Comedy*) in a verse that could well have contained the normal form *principe*—if the latter was all that was meant. The trouble with commentaries, however, is that they tend to provide shorthand explanations: thus, the student is told that the *roman principato* of line 74 matches the *Traiano imperadore* of l. 76. In a sense, this is true. But is that all there is to it, did the poet use poetic licence to produce a *hapax* where *principato* stands for *principe*? I doubt it. Instead, I would emphasize the fact that as we enter Purgatory and find ourselves on the Terrace of Pride (where the list of examples of pride punished—*Purg.* XII. 25–63—is the longest and most complex), the very first *exempla* are a trinity comprising Mary, the mother of Christ, David, the ancestor of both Mary and Christ (*Conv.* IV. v. 5), and a Roman Emperor. It is well known that the poet's syncretism led him to illustrate the relevant virtues in the *Purgatorio* by turning to classical myth: the example following that of the Virgin on the second Terrace is the generosity shown in Orestes' refusal to allow Pylades to die in his stead (*Purg.* XIII. 31–33), while the second example of meekness on the third Terrace is likewise taken from mythology (*Purg.* XV. 94–105). This first triptych is, therefore, carefully constructed by the poet to show the glory of the Empire (ll. 73–74: *l'alta gloria / del roman principato*) in the action of an individual, Trajan (l. 76: *i' dico di Traiano imperadore*), set off beside the humility shown by

Christ's ancestor David, as well as the act whereby the Redeemer was able
to become man and thus save the world (l. 36: *ch'aperse il ciel del suo lungo
divieto*). Furthermore, the Emperor's humility whereby justice was granted
to a simple widow stands in direct opposition to the *cupidigia* (utterly opposed to both humility and charity) that makes the Emperor deaf to the
cries of Rome, his widow in 1300 (*Purg.* VI. 112–14; *Ep.* XI. x. 21).

Rome as a widow abandoned by both Pope and Emperor is found in
the opening of Dante's Epistle of 1314 to the Italian cardinals, in which
Jerusalem is called "the chosen city of David" (*Ep.* XI. i. 1: *preelecte civitati
David*). This refers to the fact that King David chose Jerusalem as the capital for his people, and that he had the Ark of the Covenant transported
there. An episode in that journey is sculpted on the first Terrace. David's
dancing before the Ark makes the "humble psalmist" appear "both more
and less than a king" and earns him the contempt of his queen (*Purg.* X.
64–69). Here, the "singer of the Holy Spirit" appears "more . . . than a
king" (l. 66) in the priestly dress put on for the occasion (*in quel caso*), while
his dancing with his robes lifted up—described as *trescando* (l. 65), a fre-
netic, popular dance (cf. *Inf.* XIV. 40)—contrasts with Dante's usual conception of noble behavior (cf. *Inf.* IV. 112–14). The scene is taken from the
Second Book of Kings (6. 22), in which David tells Micol that he is dancing for the Lord, "and I shall abase myself even further: and I will humble
myself in my own esteem; nevertheless, I shall appear far more glorious to
the servant girls you speak of." We see that the opposition *vilior/nobilior* is
inspired by the Biblical source (cf. Matthew 23. 12: "he that shall humble
himself shall be exalted"), while David's greatness ("more . . . than a king")
lies fundamentally in his readiness to abase his royal dignity before the
symbol of God's covenant and the promise of the Messiah to come.

Interestingly enough, the episode as described in *Purgatorio* X does
in fact send us back to Dante's Epistle to the Italian cardinals through the
warning contained in line 57: "which makes men fear an office not assigned
to them." This is another echo of the Second Book of Kings (6. 6–7),
this time to the moment when Uzzah put out his hand to steady the Ark
and was punished for his presumption by God's death sentence. Dante rejects that presumption in his letter to the cardinals meeting to elect a Pope
in exile:

Perhaps in indignant rebuke you will ask: "And who is this man who, not fearing
the sudden punishment of Uzzah, sets himself up to protect the Ark, tottering as
it is?" Truly I am one of the least of the sheep of the pasture of Jesus Christ; truly I

abuse no pastoral authority, since I possess no riches. By the grace, therefore, not of riches, but of God, I am what I am, and the zeal of His house has eaten me up.[33]

The Epistle is indeed concerned with "widowed" Rome and the need to return the papacy to its rightful place: "it was said: 'Peter, feed my sheep,' that is to say the sacred fold, Rome, to which, after so many triumphs and glories, Christ by word and deed confirmed the empire of the world, that Rome which the same Peter, and Paul . . . by the sprinkling of their own blood consecrated as the Apostolic See."[34] In that Epistle, the Ark is clearly *figura Ecclesie*, a prefiguration of the Church. We may therefore suppose that David's transfer of the Ark to Jerusalem—praised in *Purgatorio* X. 55ff. and *Par.* XX. 39—was for the poet of the *Comedy* a *figura* of the need to bring back the seat of the papacy from Avignon to Rome, the need to return her husand the Emperor to Rome, the widow, in an act of humility, pi[e]ty and justice. We may also assume that Trajan's great act of justice and humility was in fact carried out *in Rome*, the capital of the Empire, before the Emperor set out on one of his military campaigns. It is therefore set up as yet another reference to the "Emperor" in 1300, who remained on the wrong side of the Alps.

The three examples of humility displayed at the beginning of Purgatory not only are an obvious incentive to this essential virtue for the souls undergoing purification, but they also serve as a reminder to Dante's readers of the need to restore both the Papacy and the Empire to Rome. David, Christ's ancestor, is the *exemplum* of humility and reverence in Old Testament times, the king who brought the Ark to Jerusalem, prefiguring the Church's translation to Rome; while Mary stands at the great divide in history, the moment of the Incarnation, as the supreme example of humility seen as obedience to God's will. Finally, Trajan's act of humility in consoling a poor widow is striking proof of Dante's claim that "more than anything else, charity will reinforce justice," a combination that exists in the highest degree in the Emperor, *ut patet*.[35]

8

The Poem's Center
(*Purgatorio* XII–XVIII)

PRIDE IS AT THE ROOT OF ALL SIN (Eccles. 10. 15), and the Pilgrim will soon declare how heavily this sin weighs down his soul (*Purg.* XIII. 136–38). Once more, the number three is in evidence, when Dante encounters Omberto Aldobrandeschi, Oderisi da Gubbio, and Provenzano Salvani in Canto XI. The first is an *exemplum* of overweening pride, typical of the feudal aristocracy. Omberto belonged to the powerful Aldobrandeschi clan, Counts of Santafiora and lords of the Sienese Maremma (cf. *Purg.* VI. 111). His hubris led to his death, when he took on an invincible number of adversaries:

> "L'antico sangue e l'opere leggiadre
> d'i miei maggior mi fer sí arrogante,
> che, non pensando a la comune madre,
>   ogn' uomo ebbi in despetto tanto avante,
> ch'io ne mori', come i Sanesi sanno,
> e sallo in Campagnatico ogne fante."[1]

In fact, the same terrible sin stains the whole family and has led it to disaster (ll. 68–69)—a corollary added by the poet of the *Comedy* to his discussion of the true nature of nobility in Book IV of the *Convivio*. Pride in one's ancestral nobility (Omberto); pride in one's artistic genius (Oderisi); and pride in political success leading to humiliation and annihilation (Provenzano): such is the scope of the *exempla* chosen by the poet. Provenzano Salvani, after the Sienese victory of Montaperti (1260), had become the most powerful person in Siena: "he governed the whole city, and all the

Ghibelline party in Tuscany was under his leadership, and he was full of presumption" (Villani, *Cronica* VIII. 31). His pride and ambition made him aspire to become *Signore* or dictator of Siena (ll. 122–23):

> "ed è qui perche fu presuntüoso
> a recar Siena tutta a le sue mani."[2]

The epithet "presuntuoso" stands for an excess of *magnanimitas* or ambition that spurs men on to attempt the impossible, bringing about their fall. At the same time, the *exemplum* of Provenzano's fate—his defeat and decapitation by the Florentines at the battle of Colle Val d'Elsa in 1269—should serve as a deterrent to those who would attempt to seize dictatorial power in the Tuscan communes.[3]

The political theme returns in Cantos XIV and XVI, the center not merely of the *Purgatorio* but of the whole poem. In Canto XIV Dante comes across two spirits on the Terrace of Envy. The pilgrim introduces himself as having been born on the banks of the River Arno, but the way he appears to conceal the river's name leads one of the souls (Guido del Duca: ll. 29–66) to launch into a fierce denunciation of the corruption that has taken hold of all the inhabitants of the Arno Valley. They behave as though they had been turned into beasts by the witch Circe. This initiates what is at first a regional lament (Canto XIV), but which soon broadens into a discourse on universal corruption in the contemporary world (Canto XVI).

Circe was known to Dante especially through the lines in Virgil's epic (*Aen.* VII. 19–20), where the sorceress was credited with the power of turning her former lovers into animals. The metamorphoses of the inhabitants of the Arno Valley are certainly inspired by Dante's outburst in the *Convivio* (II. vii. 3–4), where bestiality ("the mad bestiality" of *Inf.* XI. 82–83) is denounced as the condition encompassing men and women who abandon rational living: "when it is said that a man lives, this must be understood to mean that he uses his reason, which is the life specific to him and the activity of the noblest part of his being. *Therefore, anyone who abandons reason and uses only his sensitive part, does not live as a man but as a beast*; as that most excellent Boethius says: 'He lives the life of an ass'" (my emphasis). Dante refers to a passage in Boethius' *De Consolatione Philosophiae* (IV. iii. 63–64), which contains the phrase *Asinum vivit*, applied, however, to those who are slow and stupid. In the same section (56–66), we read something close to the poet's purpose in *Purgatorio* XIV:

You cannot consider anyone transformed by vices to be a man. Does Avarice carry away the violent robber of other men's goods? You may say he is like a wolf [*Lupi similem dixeris*:: cf. *Purg*. XX. 10]. Is the angry and unquiet man [*Ferox atque inquies*] always quarrelling? You may compare him to a dog. Does the traitor rejoice at the success of his hidden intrigues? He is no better than a fox. . . . Is he immersed in filthy and unclean lusts? He is entangled in the pleasure of a stinking sow.[4]

Dante's readers must be struck by the fact that these are the beasts chosen by the poet to designate the inhabitants of the Casentino in the Upper Arno (*Purg*. XIV. 43–45: "foul swine"), Arezzo (ll. 46–48: "curs"), Florence (ll. 49–51: "wolves," cf. *Par*. XXV. 6), and Pisa (ll. 53–54: "foxes"). We may note in passing that Dante has rearranged Boethius' list—possibly in order to remind his readers of the moral order of his *Inferno* (Lust-Violence-Fraud). Even the River Arno takes on bestial characteristics in the line: "and it scornfully turns away its snout from them" (l. 48). Thus the "royal river" of *Purg*. V. 122 has been supplanted by the "accursed and ill-fated ditch" of *Purg*. XIV. 51: the heart of Tuscany has been turned into a ditch of iniquity and corruption. Its inhabitants are truly like wild beasts in their rejection of a society organized on the basis of Justice and reason. The same imagery is evident at the close of the *Monarchia* (III. xv. 9), where we are told that God has instituted two goals for the human race; nevertheless, "human greed would cast them behind, if men—like horses—*led astray by their own brutishness*, were not held to the right path by 'bit and rein.'"[5] The absence of imperial authority in Italy is alluded to yet again in the lack of all peace and Justice, which spawns the prevailing wickedness that has brought down so many Italians to a bestial level.[6]

Guido del Duca, whose eyelids are sewn up on the Terrace of Envy, now employs the prophetic "I see" (*Purg*. XIV. 58) in his foretelling of the doom that is about to strike Florence—a bitterly ironic touch underlining his claim that what he says is revealed to him by none other than God Himself (l. 57, the "true spirit" corresponds to St. John's description of the Holy Spirit as "the Spirit of truth": John 16. 13). It would be difficult to find more striking proof that the poet is concerned above all with the message he must impart "for the sake of the world that lives wickedly" (*Purg*. XXXII. 103), rather than a theological game in which his truths are reserved for Paradise. This latter view has gained ground recently especially in American Dante scholarship. Critics tend at times to turn the author of the *Comedy* into a medieval fundamentalist, such that everything placed in the mouth of a sinner in Hell (and even of the souls found in Purgatory) must be definition be erroneous. Professor Iliescu provides an example of this critical stance in claiming that all the souls in both the *Inferno* and the *Purgatorio* "reflect, in part or completely, only the worldly level of understanding. Even the answers given by Virgil are often partial *and at times completely unsatisfactory*."[7] Instead, as we have seen in line 57, the poet claims that it is the Holy Spirit, God Himself, that allows the blinded soul to see the truth of what is about to be enacted on earth.

What Guido "sees" is the actions of Fulcieri dei Calboli, who, as Podestà of Florence in 1303, persecuted the White Guelfs on behalf of the Blacks. Fulcieri is here portrayed as a ferocious hunter of the wolves inhabiting the "evil wood," reminiscent of the "savage wood" of *Inf.* I. 1–7, where the pilgrim had found himself in mortal danger, thus indicating that Florence has been transformed into an infernal city.[8] Fulcieri sells his victims' living flesh before butchering them, staining his own and his family's honor, and causing such an ecological disaster that the Florentine wood will not recover for a thousand years or more (ll. 61–66). As so often, Dante's personal experience as an exile is the basis for his proclamation of universal truths.

Guido del Duca's companion grieves at this prophecy. He is introduced in lines 88–90 as Rinieri dei Calboli, a leading Guelf from Romagna (Podestà of Faenza in 1247, of Parma in 1252, and of Ravenna in 1265), who was killed in battle in 1296. Rinieri had taken an active part in the struggles that plagued Romagna in the second half of the thirteenth century, and he had been defeated by Guido da Montefeltro in his first attempt to take possession of his native city of Forlí. Typical of the atmosphere of reconciliation in Purgatory—and the author's standpoint above both parties— is the neighborly concern shown for the sorrows afflicting Rinieri and his Guelf family by Guido, who had belonged to a noble Ghibelline family from Ravenna and who now weeps for the decadence of the "men of Romagna turned to bastards!" (l. 99). The topos *Ubi sunt?*, repeated over some twenty-seven lines, hammers home the theme that nowhere in Romagna are citizens of virtue to be found in 1300. Even a man who had opposed Frederick II's attempts to assert imperial authority over Faenza, Bernardin di Fosco, is praised as a "noble offshoot of a lowly plant" (l. 102)— although, as so often, we cannot be sure of the extent to which Dante was aware of the biographical details regarding this minor character.

On the other hand, the poet is merciless in his condemnation of the usurpation of Romagna by the Popes. Indeed, the praise of past virtue as exemplified in the lines that inspired Ariosto (ll. 109–10: "the ladies and the knight, the toils and the pastimes of old to which love and courtesy urged us") emphasizes above all the corruption of the present, "where hearts have become so evil" (l. 111), thus anticipating the denunciation of papal temporal rule in *Purgatorio* XVI. The demarcation line is clear: it is set by the cession of the imperial territories to papal claims by Rudolph of Habsburg in 1278. This marked a cataclysmic change for the poet, who found living proof of the moral degeneration of his age in the betrayal of the traditional loyalties to the Empire, a betrayal that had brought about the bastardization of the whole region. Romagna, governed by tyrants with papal support, symbolizes the corruption of the two supreme spiritual and political authorities after the Popes extended their temporal power northward to the River Po.[9]

The coupling of "love and courtesy" in the virtuous Romagna of old is to be placed alongside the "valor and courtesy" traditionally found in northern Italy before the terrible conflict between the papacy and Frederick II, "before Frederick encountered opposition" (*Purg.* XVI. 115–17). Some recent critics have questioned the value of such terms as "honor" and "courtesy" in the context of the *Comedy*. They are in fact positive criteria for the appraisal of the contemporary scene, set off against the glorious and virtuous past. In the *Vita Nuova* (XLII. 3), God is Lord of Courtesy. In the *Convivio*, the word's etymology (from the virtuous courts of former times) is exploited in order to highlight society's corruption and decadence:

Courtesy and honesty are one and the same thing; and since the virtues and fine behavior were practiced at court in former times, just as their opposites rule there nowadays, this word was derived from the courts, and courtesy signified behavior at court. *If this word were to be derived from present-day courts, especially those in Italy, it would signify nothing but baseness.*[10]

Courtesy is thus synonymous with honesty, which in its turn is defined as the pursuit of truth and justice (*Conv.* IV. vi. 9).

In the *Comedy*, the epithet *cortese* ("courteous") is applied first to God himself (*Inf.* II. 17), to Virgil and his solicitude for Dante's welfare (*Inf.* II. 134), and then, to the Angel at the Gate of Purgatory (*Purg.* IX. 92); only once is it used ironically (*Par.* IX. 58), but the last—like the first—occurrence in the poem refers to God's courtesy (*Par.* XV. 48). Just as significant is the fact that precisely in the canto under review, Heaven is alluded to as God's court:

> "E se Dio m'ha in sua grazia rinchiuso,
> tanto che vuol ch'i' veggia la sua corte
> per modo tutto fuor del moderno uso,"[11]

At the very center of Hell, the pilgrim had been asked by a Florentine:

> "*cortesia e valor* dí se dimora
> ne la nostra città sí come suole,
> o se del tutto se n'è gita fora;"[12]

Once again, we find the ascent from the particular to the universal: decadence in Florence at the center of Hell; halfway through Purgatory, decadence in central and northern Italy leading to the cause of universal corruption in 1300; and, in the middle of *Paradiso*, we find the *exemplum* of ancient Florence, the good city to whom the poet remained attached with every fiber of his being and which he held up as a glass mirroring contemporary vices and misgovernment.

In the sixteenth canto of *Purgatorio*, the two poets leave the Terrace of Envy and enter the terrace where the tendency to wrath and its effects are remedied. Unlike their discordant behavior on earth, the wrathful, although blinded by dense smog, are united and chant in total harmony the *Agnus Dei* (a symbol of Christ's mansuetude). The darkness makes it impossible for the spirits to see the pilgrim, a detail serving to emphasize the importance of speech in this whole episode: "our hearing will keep us united" (l. 36). Now, at the center of his poem, Dante meets a certain "Marco," whom the early commentators identify merely as a well-known and virtuous courtier. Benvenuto da Imola was the first to indicate his native region as Lombardy (rather than Venice, as in Lana and L'Ottimo) from the statement "I was a Lombard" in line 46. In this and the next two lines, Marco tells us all we can possibly know about his life on earth, where he combined a knowledge of practical affairs with a love of virtue which no one now strives to achieve. Nevertheless, it seems likely that he was active at the court of Gherardo da Camino, *de facto* Lord of Treviso from 1283 to 1306 — and one of the three old men in whom the virtuous past lives on as a reproof to the present (*Purg.* XVI. 121–40). In *Convivio* IV. xiv. 13 Dante had already praised Gherardo's nobility, although here the pilgrim asks who this "sage" was and thus seems almost to tempt Marco to anger.

Marco's praise of a leading Guelf, who was a colleague of the infamous Corso Donati, together with another Guelf noble, Corrado da Palazzo from Brescia (who had been Charles of Anjou's Podestà and Vicar in Florence in 1276 and Captain of the Guelf Party in 1277), should lead us to beware of attributing extreme Ghibellinism to Dante's Marco — as has been done, for example, by R. Montano, G. Giacalone, and N. Iliescu (the latter arraigning those "readers of the *Comedy* who still remain moved by the garrulity of the Ghibelline Marco Lombardo, in the *infernal darkness* of the terrace of anger").[13] For my part, I confess that I do not find Marco garrulous. On the contrary, I find his discourse extraordinarily concise and pungent, for in the space of half a canto (ll. 73–145) it deals with the most basic issues in Dante's *Comedy*: the importance of free ill; God's Justice in rewarding and punishing humanity; the creation of the human soul and its attractions to everything that reminds it of its origin in the source of all happiness and good; the consequent need for laws and a supreme temporal guide; the need for cooperation between the Empire and the Church; and the catastrophe that has ensued since "the one has extinguished the other" (l. 109) in combining temporal with spiritual power. Far from being garrulous, Marco covers an immense amount of ground in very few—about 500—words, and it would be difficult to find a better example of the poet's concision, or of his ability to combine politics (the need for humanity to be governed by the Emperor) with theology (the creation of the human soul directly by God).

Indeed, the idea that Dante in his *Purgatorio* set intellectual or doctrinal traps for his readers by creating characters who expressed falsehoods is a gross error of interpretation. Not only does it belittle the poet's purpose in writing his poem—the whole *Comedy*, not just the *Paradiso*—and his intention of opening his readers' eyes to the truth as willed by God, but it violates a fundamental law of Purgatory: namely, that souls are no longer capable of sinning (*Purg.* XXVI. 131–32; cf. XI. 19–24). The poet of the *Comedy* was above all concerned with stating the truth, a truth gradually and sequentially disclosed throughout the poem—as Virgil recognizes in *Purg.* XVIII. 46–48:

> . . . "Quanto ragion qui vede,
> dir ti poss'io; da indi in là t'aspetta
> pur a Beatrice, ch'è opra di fede."[14]

The whole truth will only be learned in Paradise, but it will include the truths enunciated along the way; Marco Lombardo's message will be reiterated by none other than Beatrice herself:

> "Tu, perché non ti facci maraviglia,
> pensa che 'n terra non è chi governi;
> onde sí svïa l'umana famiglia."[15]

Even so, as Hollander points out: "Numerically and doctrinally these three cantos [*Purg.* XVI–XVIII] are at the center of *Purgatorio* and of the entire *Commedia*." [16]

Indeed, as Marco takes over for the nonce from Virgil as Dante's mentor, his diagnosis of contemporary ills (arguably made after papal opposition to Henry VII's attempts to restore imperial authority in Italy) offers a fascinating series of flashbacks to *Convivio* IV and to the Epistles addressed by Dante to Henry and the rebellious Florentines (VI–VII). It also anticipates the doctrine to be worked out more fully in the *Monarchia*. I shall therefore examine in some detail Marco's analysis, which is prompted by the pilgrim's puzzlement at the cause of so much corruption, his doubt whether the fault lies in the evil and overwhelming influence of the stars or in a total corruption of human nature.

Marco immediately rejects the idea of astral determinism, since this would remove all justification for the punishment and reward of human behavior, and destroy the idea of God's Justice (ll. 70–72). It is true that the heavens do exert an influence on men's and women's inclinations (cf. Aquinas, *S.Th.* 2.2.95.5). Nevertheless, human beings are endowed with the light of reason and free will, which is capable of withstanding all negative circumstances, if properly encouraged and nurtured. After denying that man's will was free within Love's "arena" in his sonnet to Cino, *Io sono stato con Amore insieme*, and in Epistle IV of c. 1307, Dante set out to redress the balance first at the beginning of the *Comedy* in his condemnation of Francesca (*Inf.* V), and then by placing this essential affirmation of the freedom of human will at the heart of his poem. The strongest recantation is to be found in the development of Marco's discourse on free will by Virgil in *Purg.* XVIII. 40–74. The political consequences of this conviction are illustrated not merely throughout the *Comedy* but also in the Epistle addressed to the Italian cardinals of 1314, in which the tragedy of the contemporary Church—its exile at Avignon and its subservience to the French crown—is not ascribed to "necessity," as "certain astrologers and ignorant prophets declare," but to the "ill use of your freedom of will." [17]

Man is therefore responsible for the present state of the world gone astray; and Marco assures the pilgrim that he will be a faithful informer of the truth (l. 84). Following St. Thomas Aquinas, Dante asserts the creation of the human soul directly by God as a *tabula rasa*—except that, coming from the source of all happiness, it attempts to turn to whatever seems to offer pleasure and joy. From this theological disquisition (amplified in *Purg.* XXV. 37–78) the poet makes a surprising leap to the political consequences of the soul's instinctive attraction toward "secondary goods," where it will become entangled "unless a guide or bridle rules its love" (l. 93).

No better example of the indissoluble link between the poet's theology and his political thought could be found than this passage, in which Dante deduces the need for laws applied by a universal Emperor:

> "Esce di mano a lui che la vagheggia
> . . . l'anima semplicetta che sa nulla,
> salvo che, mossa da lieto fattore,
> volontier torna a ciò che la trastulla.
>   Di picciol bene in pria sente sapore;
> quivi s'inganna, e dietro ad esso corre,
> se guida o fren non torce suo amore.
>   Onde convenne legge per fren porre;
> convenne rege aver, che discernesse
> de la vera cittade almen la torre." [18]

The metaphor of the "bridle" standing for the laws that must be applied by the Emperor has already been encountered in *Purg.* VI. 88, and it returns (as we have already seen) at the end of the *Monarchia*, where we are told that *cupiditas*—the love of earthly things—would destroy humanity, "if men, like horses, carried away by their bestiality, were not held in check and guided 'with the bit and the reins'" (*Mon.* III. xv. 9)

As in *Purgatorio* VI, the scandalous state of anarchy on earth is declared to be all the more shameful inasmuch as God—through Justinian—has provided humanity with just laws: "The laws exist, but who applies them now?" (l. 97). No one, in fact, for the Pope—who usurps the Emperor's divinely appointed task as the executor of the Laws—is not qualified to dispense temporal justice:

> "Nullo, però che 'l pastor che procede,
> rugumar può, ma non ha l'unghie fesse;" [19]

Clearly, that we are not only at the mathematical center but also at the political heart of Dante's *Comedy*. Everyone agrees that the deep structure is clear: the poet's message is that the Pope has no right to wield power in the temporal sphere or to usurp the Emperor's role as *executor legis*, the executor of the law. In order to appreciate the centrality of the Emperor's role (and the extent of the condemnation implicit in Dante's description of Pope Clement V as "a lawless shepherd" in *Inf.* XIX. 83), we should do well to remember the essential truth that "to the medieval mind the law meant much more than to the modern world, penetrating as it did all aspects and interests of human life."[20] Moreover, the view of the Emperor as the sole *lator legis et legis executor* (*Mon.* I. xiii.7) may well be seen as Dante's response to Boniface VIII's supposed claim that he as supreme pontiff was well equipped to guard the laws of the empire.[21]

The biblical references and imagery of lines 98–99, however, are somewhat confusing. Commentators quote Leviticus 11. 3–8 and Deutoronomy 14. 7–8, referring to the law that declared that Jews were allowed to eat the flesh only of ruminants with a cloven hoof. Scholastic theologians offered allegorical interpretations of this non-Christian "law," and St. Thomas explained that the cloven hoof signified among other things the ability to distinguish between good and evil (*discretionem boni et mali*), while *ruminatio* or chewing the cud was traditionally interpreted as the meditation on and correct interpretation of Holy Scripture.[22] The former quality—to distinguish good from evil—would seem a strange omission in the qualifications for a Pope. However, Dante's son Pietro claimed that the cloven hoof (which the Pope does not possess) must be interpreted in the narrower sense of distinguishing and judging temporal as opposed to spiritual things. Benvenuto points out that the Pope in 1300, Boniface VIII, although an expert in scripture and Canon Law, confounded the spiritual and temporal realms.[23]

This is the core of Dante's rebuttal of the hierocratic case, which he later amplified in the third book of his *Monarchia*. The hierocrats' case had been built up throughout the thirteenth century, replacing the Gelasian principle of coexistence between the two powers that had dominated the political theology of the Middle Ages. That dualism had been based, as always, both on practical grounds—even at the height of its claims, the papacy could not simply ignore the realities of temporal power—and on Christ's statements that his kingdom was not of this world, so that it was the duty of a Christian to give unto Caesar the things that belonged to the Emperor and unto God the things that are God's (John 18. 36; Matthew 22. 21, Mark 12. 17). In practice, however, it was impossible to separate the things of Caesar from spiritual concerns to the satisfaction of both parties, and it has been rightly observed that "wherever the line of distinction between spiritual and temporal matters might have been drawn, for papal governmental ideology the distinction had not operational value."[24]

In the decretal *Novit* (1204), a doctrinal floodgate had been opened by Innocent III's claim that the Pope had the right to judge in temporal affairs, *ratione peccati*, whenever and wherever sin was involved. At the end of the thirteenth century, the ideological struggle between Boniface VIII and Philip the Fair inspired the hierocrats to produce a veritable phalanx of documents, all purporting to prove that (as Cardinal Matteo of Acquaparta told the ambassadors of the French king in June 1302) the Pope held "a plenitude of power" and was thus "lord of all things temporal and spiritual (cf. Psalm 2. 1) . . . the pope can judge in every temporal matter *ratione peccati*. . . . Thus temporal jurisdiction belongs of right to the pope, who is vicar of Christ and of Peter."[25] This broadside prepared the way for *Unam sanctam*, promulgated by Boniface VIII on 18 November 1302, which (ironically enough, as events were soon to demonstrate) asserted that "the temporal authority [must be] subject to the spiritual power," since "it is altogether necessary to salvation for every human creature to be subject to the Roman Pontiff." This confusion of the temporal with the spiritual authority was for the world-judge of the *Comedy* the "evil behavior . . . the cause which has made the world wicked" (*Purg.* XVI. 103–4), since Christ's flock on earth is constantly led astray by the sight of its spiritual guide wholly eaten up with desire for the false goods of this world, wealth, power, and carnal delights, "which can never fulfill their promises" (*Purg.* XXX. 132).

Instead, the dualist principle is reformulated in the strongest possible terms in Marco's harking back to the creation of a just and peaceful Christian society:

> "Soleva Roma, che 'l buon mondo feo,
> due soli aver, che l'una e l'altra strada
> facean vedere, e del mondo e di Deo."[26]

The astronomical absurdity *due soli* flies in the face of all scientific knowledge; moreover, it had been decried as an impossibility, contrary to nature, by Dante himself in his apostrophe to the rebellious Florentines: "shall there be one polity of Florence, and another of Rome? And why should not the Apostolic government be the object of a similar envy, so that, if the one twin of Delos [the moon] has her double in the heavens, the other [the sun] should have his likewise?"[27] As in 1310 (*Ep.* V. x. 30), so in 1311 Dante still accepted the traditional interpretation (which had been used by Clement V in his letter to Henry VII of 26 July 1309) whereby the sun signified spiritual authority and the moon imperial power. That allegorical interpretation of God's creation of the two *luminaria magna* (Genesis I. 16) Dante later rejected in *Mon.* III. iv. 16. By then, it had become all too obvious that such an interpretation readily lent itself to the hierocratic thesis "just as the moon . . . has no light save as she receives it from the sun, so neither has the temporal government any authority, except in so far as it receives this from the spiritual."[28]

From this evidence, it seems clear that, after 1311, Dante decided to reject the sun-moon analogy, and in *Mon.* III. i. 5 he uses the biblical term *duo luminaria magna* ("two great luminaries") when referring to the Empire and the papacy. We shall probably never know the exact moment of composition of *Purgatorio* XVI and *Monarchia* III. iv. I would, however, argue that the evidence available points to the likelihood that both passages were a reaction to the Pope's betrayal of the Emperor in 1312–1313 (*Par.* XXX. 133–44) and to such claims as those made by the Curia that the Pope, as Christ's vicar, possessed a plenitude of power to "institute, depose, correct . . . bind and suspend the imperial and royal power."[29] It is perhaps idle to speculate whether Dante was aware of the exaggerations to which the sun-moon analogy lent itself—for example, the nice calculations made by Hostiensis (Cardinal Henry of Susa) showing that "the sacerdotal dignity is seven thousand, six hundred and forty-four and a half times greater than the royal."[30] Instead, in the teeth of all scientific evidence but with forceful poetic imagery (an unusual combination in Dante), the poet claims that two suns governed Rome when the "good world" or society was created, whereas Rome is now "destitute of both lights" (*Ep.* XI. x. 21). Papal claims to absolute supremacy, renewed with catastrophic results for Henry VII's and Dante's hopes for a restoration of imperial power in Italy, in fact led the poet to return to the image he had used in regard to Henry in April 1311, when he had designated the Emperor as "our sun" (*sol noster*)— even as Manfred had referred to Frederick II as the "sun of the world" and as the Christ-like "Sun of Justice"[31]—in order, as Francesco Buti says quite simply, "not to make one inferior to the other."[32] In other words, the poet of the *Comedy* placed at the center of his poem an astronomical absurdity intended to redress the balance of power and thus eliminate the inferiority of the Empire-moon implied by the traditional equation. Even more significant is the fact (not usually emphasized) that Dante claims that the two suns must light up *two* paths for humanity, "both paths . . . the path of the world and the pathway to God," a duality foreshadowing the notorious dualism of the closing chapter of his treatise on the Empire.

We may well ask: when was this balanced society created and when did it exist for Dante? Answers have varied enormously; from before Constantine to the time of Charlemagne. The evidence of the *Comedy*, however, points to one ideal moment of collaboration that produced the most beneficial results, when the Emperor Justinian was converted to the true faith by the Pope; and only with the Pope's spiritual help was Justinian able to carry out his divinely inspired mission to prune and codify the Roman laws, thus providing the perfect instrument for humanity's temporal happiness:

> "E prima ch'io a l'ovra fossi attento,
> una natura in Cristo esser, non piúe,
> credea, e di tal fede era contento;
>   ma 'l benedetto Agapito, che fue
> sommo pastore, a la fede sincera
> mi dirizzò con le parole sue.
>   Io li credetti . . .
>   Tosto che con la Chiesa mossi i piedi,
> a Dio per grazia piacque di spirarmi
> l'alto lavoro, e tutto 'n lui mi diedi;"[33]

Admittedly, Justinian was not in Rome, as a result of Constantine's disastrous decision to move eastward "against Heaven's course" (*Par.* VI. 2), contrary to both the sun's diurnal movement westwards and to God's providential plan. Nevertheless, the just Emperor remained true to the ideal of Rome's imperial Justice.

In *Purg.* XVI. 109–14, the spiritual power has invaded the temporal realm and eclipsed the imperial sun, thus destroying the divinely instituted balance of power:

> "L'un l'altro ha spento; ed è giunta la spada
> col pasturale, e l'un con l'altro insieme
> per viva forza mal convien che vada;
>   però che, giunti, l'un l'altro non teme:
> se non mi credi, pon mente a la spiga,
> ch'ogn' erba si conosce per lo seme."[34]

"Ye shall know them by their fruits . . . a corrupt tree bringeth forth evil fruit" (Matthew 7. 16–7): northern Italy, which—before the internecine struggles of Frederick II with the papacy and the Communes—was the home of "valor and courtesy" (l. 116), has now in *Purg.* XVI. 127–29 become a den of thieves and scoundrels, an example of the universal corruption spread abroad by the Church of Rome:

> "Dí oggimai che la Chiesa di Romna,
> per confondere in sé due reggimenti,
> cade nel fango, e sé brutta e la soma."[35]

The pilgrim acknowledges the truth of what he has just heard in line 130, adding that he now understands (ll. 131–32) "why the sons of Levi were excluded from the inheritance," yet further proof of the poet's belief that the Church of Christ should be wedded to evangelical poverty. As Professor Ferrante has noted, Marco Lombardo's fundamental message of the need for co-operation between the autonomous spheres of imperial and papal jurisdiction was not only placed by Dante at the very center of his poem, but it was also located "in the section of wrath, because . . . anger properly directed towards evil and corruption is the source of all reform."[36] Moreover, as Edward Peters observes, we can now see that in the central canto of the *Purgatorio* (and of the whole poem) "The topic of earthly beatitude is . . . linked to the problem of human individuation and freedom in a remarkable discourse on political anthropology that has no equal anywhere else in medieval political thought."[37] Nowhere do we find a more forceful rebuttal of the idea that the political element is alien or hostile to Dante's poetic genius.

9

The She-Wolf and the Shepherds (*Purgatorio* XIX–XX)

As Jacques Le Goff has noted: "The rise of a monetary economy . . . provoked an explosion of hatred against money. . . . A shift in morality occurred. *Superbia*, pride, the feudal sin par excellence, until then generally considered to be the mother of all the vices, began to yield the first place to *avaritia* or desire for money."[1] Dante follows the traditional hierarchy of sins in placing pride on the lowest terrace of Purgatory as the original—and worst—sin, with the devil designated as *il primo superbo* in *Paradiso* XIX. 46 ("the first proud one," cf. *Par*. XXVI. 115–17). However, despite his acceptance of the traditional hierarchy, Dante is above all preoccupied with the sin of avarice or greed in its widest ramifications, the evil that has the whole world in its grip (*Purg*. XX. 8), symbolized by the "ancient wolf" of *Purgatorio* X. 10 and *Inferno* I. 94–99:

> "... questa bestia ...
> non lascia altrui passar per la sua via,
> ma tanto lo 'mpedisce che l'uccide;
>   e ha natura sí malvagia e ria,
> che mai non empie la bramosa voglia,
> e dopo 'l pasto ha piú fame che pria."[2]

This sin and its tentacles make the pilgrim—here, truly a representative of Everyman in 1300—lose all hope of directly ascending the mount of salvation (*Inf*. I. 54).[3]

The leading theologian of the thirteenth century, Thomas Aquinas, may well have been aware of this shift in emphasis when he devoted a section of his *Summa Theologica* to the problem "Whether pride is the beginning of all sin" (*S. Th*. 1.2.84.2), which follows immediately upon his reply in the affirmative to the question "Whether the love of money is the root of all evil" (art. 1). The latter question is of course answered in Holy Scripture (1 Timothy 6. 10). While keeping the two sins distinct, St. Thomas refers in passing to the fact that avarice is also called greed or the love of money. St. Bernard had claimed that avarice and greed are sisters born of pride, while Hugh of St. Victor had defined avarice as "the insatiable and sinful lust for glory, riches or any other thing."[4] It is, therefore, hardly surprising that St. Thomas, while forced by recent developments in the economy of western Europe to seek a middle way, followed St. Augustine in asserting that avarice is the immoderate desire for all temporal things that can be measured by money: "est immoderatus appetitus rerum temporalium . . . quaecumque pecunia aestimari possunt."[5] Purgatory's fifth terrace illustrates this dual aspect of the sin: in the second half of Canto XIX, we are shown avarice primarily as ambition in the person of Pope Adrian V, while in Canto XX, in the history of the Capetians, avarice appears as greed in its manifold guises.

According to the moral scheme set out by Virgil in *Purg.* XVII. 90–139, avarice introduces the third and last category of capital sins purged on the Mountain, where we find the results of an excessive love of secondary goods. Thus, avarice provides a necessary bridge between the spiritual sins—pride, envy, wrath, and sloth—and the purely carnal sins of gluttony and lust. Just as the Pilgrim's entrance into Purgatory proper had been heralded by a dream, so now his ascent to the final category of sin is marked by a second dream, described in Canto XIX. 9–33, Fortunately, for once the poet has given us the key to his allegorical message in XIX. 58–60, when Virgil tells the Pilgrim:

> "Vedesti . . . quell'antica strega
> che sola sovr' a noi omai si piagne;
> vedesti come l'uom da lei si slega."[6]

Quell'antica strega has been stripped of all her false allurements and her rottenness has been revealed (XIX. 31–33).

The allegorical lesson has thus been imparted. But one of the glories of Dante's poem is the fact that it brings home to us its moral message not by means of personification allegory but by its portrayal of human beings who bring with them all the complexities of human nature.[7] The pasteboard siren of the Pilgrim's dream is complemented by encounters with souls for whom we can experience true empathy. While fulfilling an exemplary purpose, they are brought to life by the poet's genius—so effectively, in fact, that we are made to feel the first part of the poet's moral lesson regarding avarice through the figure of Pope Adrian V and his *personal experience* of the vanity of all earthly riches, power, and glory.

Adrian announces his former dignity, the fact that he had reached the summit of earthly ambition, the papal throne, in Latin, the official language of the Church he had been chosen to lead: *"scias quod ego fui successor Petri"* (*Purg.* XIX. 99: "Know that I was the successor of Peter"). In utter contrast with this solemn pronouncement, however, his first words eschew the Pilgrim's euphemistic *dossi* ("backs": l. 94), choosing instead the coarsely realistic *diretri* ("backsides": l. 97) in his answer "Why heaven turns our backsides toward it, you shall now learn." In fact, in order to emphasize the lesson to be imparted, the soul tells the Pilgrim that even before he learns the reason for the method of purification or *contrapasso* undergone, he must first know that this former sinner had once been raised up to the highest dignity and surrounded with the greatest pomp on earth (cf. l. 110). Having already been described as "hidden" (l. 84) and lying face down on the ground (l. 72), the contrast with his former elevated public position on Peter's throne could not be greater.

The *contrapasso* is shared by all the souls undergoing purification on the fifth terrace. With characteristic syncretism, the poet has fused a line from Persius with the biblical chant "My soul has clung to the ground" (l. 73: *Adhaesit pavimento anima mea*).[8] In Dante's Psalm 118, King David praises God's Law, opening with the salutation: "Blessed are those who pass through life's journey unstained, those who walk according to God's law"; the Vulgate's *ambulant* ("walk") is in direct opposition with the position of the avaricious in Purgatory, where their hands and feet are immobilized by God's Justice (ll. 123–24). Scholars have long pointed out that the penitent avaricious chant the first part of the twenty-fifth verse of the psalm, without noting the direct reference to avarice in the prayer of the thirty-sixth verse: "Incline my heart toward your decrees, and not toward avarice" (*Inclina cor meum in testimonia tua, et non in avaritiam*). The fact that the souls are now prostrate (weighed down—like the proud of the first terrace—by the burden of their former sin) indicates that they had adored earthly things and serves as a reminder that their former sin of avarice had prevented their minds from reaching heavenward and had reduced them to a bestial pose in life.[9] The need for humility is rendered visually by this pose, just as the souls' humiliation is expressed by Adrian's statement in l. 117, "and the mountain has no more bitter penalty."

In ll. 99–114, the Pilgrim learns that this is the soul of Ottobono de' Fieschi, who was made a cardinal by his uncle, Innocent IV, in 1251. Elected Pope as Adrian V on 11 July 1276, he died only five weeks later on August 18. He now tells Dante that until his brief pontificate he had been guilty of the sin of avarice, primarily in the sense of ambition, the excessive desire for earthly power and splendor. With immense possessions in Liguria and the kingdom of Naples, Adrian's insatiable ambition as a young man and then as a cardinal was striking proof of what Dante wrote about riches in the *Convivio*, where they are regarded as typical of all earthly goods:

the imperfection of riches . . . can be grasped . . . also in the fact that any increase is dangerous; and since their defect is better seen in this, it is only this that is mentioned in the text, where it says that, even when amassed, not only do they not bring peace, but they increase people's thirst for them and leave their possessors even more unfulfilled . . . These lying traitors always promise to bring total satisfaction to anyone who amasses them in a certain quantity; and with this constant promise they lead the human will into the vice of avarice . . . These false traitors promise to take away every thirst and every lack, and to bring every satisfaction and fulfillment; and they do this with everyone at the outset . . . and then, when they have been amassed, instead of bringing satisfaction and appeasement, they give and bring with them an unbearable feverish thirst . . . so that truly they bring not peace but ever-increasing worry and care. (*Convivio* IV. xii. 1–5)

The contrast between the Siren's claim (l. 24: "so wholly do I satisfy him!" with its echoes of the passage just quoted) and Adrian's realization (l. 109: "I saw that there the heart could never find peace") is obvious and much to the point.

Unfortunately for critics who understand avarice in its narrowest sense, there is little evidence of a lust for money or of a conversion away from avarice at the end of Adrian's life. This led Umberto Bosco to suggest that Dante (like Petrarch, in his *Rerum Memorandarum* II. 95) mistook a passage regarding Adrian IV's disillusionment with his ascendancy as referring to Adrian V, in an unknown work derived from John of Salisbury's *Policraticus*.[10] However this may be, Manselli has in fact discovered an incident in Cardinal Fieschi's career that amounts to "a case of bribery and corruption." In April 1272, the government of Siena sent 300 gold florins to the Cardinal, in order to gain his support in its plea to have the interdict removed that had been placed on the city in 1268: "a payment which must have been accepted if a few months later it was followed by a second one of 600 pounds." [11] On its own, this would hardly have constituted an outstanding example of corruption or avarice in the curia of Dante's times. However, Manselli also points out that Ottobono Fieschi was one of those prelates who neglected the Gospels and the Church Fathers in order to concentrate on the decretals for gain—a practice vehemently denounced by our poet in various of his writings (*Par.* IX. 130–38; *Par.* XII. 82–83; *Mon.* III. iii. 9; *Ep.* XI. vii. 16). Indeed, the *Speculum* mentioned in the latter work, alongside Innocent IV and Hostiensis, would appear to be the *Speculum iudiciale* of Guillaume Durant, which its author dedicated to none other than Cardinal Fieschi in 1271. [12]

But what of Adrian's conversion? Is it to be added to the list of imagined cases of repentance *in extremis*, of which Dante's Purgatory offers some notable examples (Manfred, Bonconte)? Gioacchino Paparelli and others claim that Adrian V—who as a cardinal had given his full support to Charles of Anjou—made a complete volte-face by becoming the fiercest opponent of Charles's expansionist policy, thus reversing his predecessors' pro-French stance. Paparelli further claims that this volte-face constitutes the key motive behind this whole episode. [13] Indeed, it is possible to claim that Cantos XIX and XX of *Purgatorio* were written at a time when the See of Peter was vacant (April 1314–August 1316) and that they in fact reflect the beliefs expressed in Dante's Epistle of 1314, addressed to the cardinals in conclave at Carpentras. [14]

It is even possible that through Adrian V the poet wished to bring to mind his more famous uncle, Sinibaldo Fieschi. The latter, as Innocent IV, had been guilty (for Dante) of exceeding his powers by deposing Frederick II at the Council of Lyon in what has been described as "the papacy's most spectacular political action," of launching a crusade against the Emperor, and attempting to replace Frederick, first by Henry Raspe of Thuringia and then by William of Holland. After Frederick's death in 1250, Innocent returned to Italy, where he devoted all his energies to fighting the last of the Staufen. One of the most influential decretalists, Innocent asserted that "the pope has jurisdiction and power over all," that the supreme pontiff "consecrates and examines the emperor, and the emperor . . . holds the empire from him. . . . And so it is that, when the empire is vacant, the pope succeeds to a right which is held from the Roman church," and the pope has jurisdiction over any negligent ruler "out of the plenitude of power which he has because he is Christ's vicar." [15]

Whether or not the poet expected his readers to catch an allusion to one of the fiercest advocates of papal supremacy in the temporal sphere, he surely hoped that in reading Adrian's words (ll. 103–5):

"Un mese e poco piú prova' io come
pesa il gran manto a chi dal fango il guarda,
che piuma sembran tutte l'altre some." [16]

they would recall Marco Lombardo's earlier condemnation of papal pretensions to temporal power:

"Dí oggimai che la Chiesa di Roma,
per confondere in sé due reggimenti,
cade nel fango, e sé brutta e la soma." [17]

The *fango* in both cases is the mud of sin, but more specifically the mire of political intrigue and warfare, indicative of an exemplary opposition between temporal and spiritual concerns already hinted at in the psalmist's *Adhaesit pavimento anima mea*.

Dante had already placed a reference to the papal *gran manto* in the mouth of a Pope, in *Inferno* XIX. 69, when Nicholas III (elected a year after Adrian's death and condemned for his simony) had introduced himself with the words *Sappi ch'i' fui vestito del gran manto* ("Know that I was clothed with the great mantle"), provoking the Pilgrim's apocalyptic condemnation of humanity's corrupt spiritual leaders:

"Di voi pastor s'accorse il Vangelista,
quando colei che siede sopra l'acque
puttaneggiar coi regi a lui fu vista;" [18]

The flashback to Nicholas III is instructive, if we take into account the fact that the latter had led a virtuous life *until* his election to the See of Peter, as we read in Giovanni Villani's chronicle:

In that same year . . . they elected pope Gianni Guatani, the cardinal from the Orsini family in Rome, who led a good and most virtuous life as a young cleric and then as a cardinal . . . *but after he was called Pope Nicholas III*, he became magnanimous, and for the love of his relatives he undertook many things to make them great, and he was one of the first—or the first—pope in whose court simony was openly practiced on behalf of his relations; as a result, he greatly increased their possessions . . . beyond all other Romans in the short time he had left to live. (*Cronica*, VIII. 54; my emphasis)

For both men, possession of the *gran manto* signified the start of a new life. For Adrian, it revealed the hollow vanity of all earthly glory in words reminiscent of St. Augustine's warning that our hearts are forever restless until they come to rest in God, who made us for Himself (*Confessions*, I. 1: "inquietum est cor nostrum, donec requiescat in te"):

> "La mia conversïone, omè! fu tarda;
> ma, come fatto fui roman pastore,
> cosí scopersi la vita bugiarda.
>   Vidi che lí non s'acquetava il core,
> né piú salir potiesi in quella vita;
> per che di questa in me s'accese amore." [19]

For Nicholas, on the other hand, the *gran manto* offered endless opportunity for the worst form of avarice, simony, as well as nepotism:

> "e veramente fui figliuol de l'orsa,
> cupido sí per avanzar li orsatti,
> che sú l'avere e qui me misi in borsa." [20]

There could be no more striking example of the medieval belief that everything in this life, every facet of human experience—even election to the office of Christ's spiritual vicar—can be used *in bono* or *in malo*.

Yet it is only when we reach the nineteenth canto of *Paradiso* that we may come to appreciate the full extent of the poem's range and symmetry, for it is there that we find the opposite of avarice or greed in the Heaven of Justice. For this overview, there is no need to have recourse to the pronouncements of theologians and moralists. Dante himself tells us (*Mon.* I. xi. 11) that the greatest obstacle to Justice is cupidity or avarice: "cupidity is most opposed to justice"—while citing Aristotle, where the Greek term was translated as *avaritia* in the Latin version read by Dante.[21] Cupidity or avarice is in fact the smokescreen that pollutes the rays of the Heaven of Justice on earth, where everyone is led astray by the evil example set by the Pope:

> O dolce stella, quali e quante gemme
> mi dimostraro che nostra giustizia
> effetto sia del ciel che tu ingemme!
>   Per ch'io prego la mente in che s'inizia
> tuo moto e tua virtute, che rimiri
> ond' esce *il fummo che 'l tuo raggio vizia* . . .

O milizia del ciel cu' io contemplo,
adora per color che sono in terra
tutti svïati dietro al malo essemplo![22]

The opposition with Justice is delineated in the verbal cluster found in
Purg. XIX. 118–26 (my emphasis):

"Sí come l'occhio nostro non s'aderse
in alto, fisso a le cose terrene,
cosí *giustizia* qui a terra il merse.
     Come avarizia spense a ciascun bene
lo nostro amore, onde operar perdési,
cosí *giustizia* qui stretti ne tene,
     ne' piedi e ne le man legati e presi;
e quanto fia piacer del *giusto* Sire,
tanto staremo immobili e distesi."[23]

The description of God as "giusto Sire" may possibly bring to mind *Vita
Nuova* XXVIII. 1, where "the Lord of Justice" called Beatrice to heaven in
1290 and her lover had to learn to accept the justice of God's decree. After
that sentimental crisis, however, the traumatic experience of exile and persecution had seared the soul of a man unjustly condemned (*exul inmeritus*,
as he styles himself in Epistles V, VI, and VII), a poet who described his
nightmarish vision of Justice itself exiled from the world in his great *canzone, Tre donne intorno al cor mi son venute*, written in the early years of his
own banishment from Florence.[24] About the same time, at the beginning
of the *Convivio* (I. xii. 9), Dante did not hesitate to state that "although
every virtue is lovable in man, the most lovable one is also the most human,
namely justice . . . hence we see that its contrary, injustice, is most deeply
hated," and it was this supremely human—and divine—virtue that was to
be dissected in the fourteenth book of this unfinished work. In the *Monarchia*, Justice is synonymous with God's Will (II. ii. 5); in the *Comedy*, it is
God himself as *viva giustizia* (*Par.* VI. 88: "living Justice") who inspired
the actions of Justinian, the ideal Emperor and lawgiver. Once again, in
the canto most relevant to our purpose, God's Justice will be described as
"giustizia viva" in *Par.* XIX. 68.
     The vista that has opened up in retrospect, from *Inferno* XIX through
Purgatorio XIX to *Paradiso* XIX, shows us humanity first of all buried
upside-down in the bowels of the earth, imprisoned in the sin most op-

posed to justice, simony; then, prostrate on the ground; and finally raised up to heaven. The treatment of avarice in *Inferno* VII had been perfunctory. By the time he came to write *Inferno* XIX, however, Dante had passionately espoused the idea of Evangelical Poverty, which led him to imagine a simoniacal Pope imprisoned for all eternity in the rock of Hell (the antithesis of the Petrine rock on which Christ founded His Church), upside-down in an infernal caricature of the position chosen by Peter, the first Pope, for his crucifixion.[25] We thus find the following correlative objectives indicating the effects on the human soul of simony-avarice and then justice: the bowels of the earth, at the point farthest away from God (Hell); the ground (Purgatory); and lastly (Paradise) the eagle, the bird that soars highest and can look directly into the sun, a symbol of God's grace—itself the imperial symbol exalting Justice in the Heaven of Jupiter (*Par.* XVIII. 88–117). It would be difficult to find a more vivid indication of the diametrical opposition between avarice and justice—an opposition also expressed in the beatitude sung by the Angel of Justice on the terrace of avarice (*Purg.* XXII. 4–6): "Blessed are those who hunger and thirst after justice, for they shall be satisfied."[26] With avarice, desires can never be quenched; only the human quest for justice can truly be satisfied on earth, in the Earthly Paradise on the summit of Mount Purgatory, symbolizing the happiness attainable under the guidance of the Emperor in a perfect society on earth (*Mon.* III. xv. 7).

Having shown us the *exemplum* of a Pope, chosen by God to be the spiritual leader of humanity on earth, who until his election had been a victim of the sin destructive not only of justice but also of charity, the poet now offers us the example of a temporal leader, who had been one of its illustrious victims on earth. This leader, moreover, is not simply a king; he is the founder of the royal dynasty that—especially since the poet's birth—had formed an unholy alliance with the papacy in opposing the just claims and universal authority of the Emperor. Hugh Capet is first heard as a solitary voice, reciting three outstanding *exempla* of the opposite virtue; he later tells the Pilgrim (*Purg.* XX. 97–102) that these examples are praised by all the purgatorial victims of avarice during the day, whereas at night they recite a list of crimes committed in the lust for gold.[27]

The three positive examples are of special significance for our analysis of Dante's treatment of avarice on this terrace. The first is necessarily taken from an episode in the life of the Virgin Mary. It celebrates her acceptance of total poverty (l. 22) in giving birth in a stable to the King of Kings, the Creator of the universe and Saviour of the world. The second example is that of Gaius Fabricius Luscinus, who chose virtuous poverty instead of sinful wealth. The third praises the largesse of St. Nicholas, bishop of Myra in Asia Minor at the time of Constantine, who saved three girls from prostitution by throwing a purse of gold as a dowry for each on three successive nights.

The third example is clearly one of liberality. The second praises Fabricius' espousal of poverty, but in fact it is rather more complex. Dante praises Fabricius, who was Roman Consul twice (282 and 278 B.C.), in both the *Convivio* and the *Monarchia*. In *Convivio* IV. v. 12–13, after making the extraordinary claim that pagan, republican Rome was "exalted with citizens who were not human but divine, in whom not human but divine love inspired them to love her," Dante writes: "And who will say that it was without divine inspiration that Fabricius refused a virtually infinite sum of gold, because he would not abandon his native land?" During the invasion of Italy by Pyrrhus, who dreamed of reviving the empire of his second cousin Alexander the Great, Fabricius was sent as ambassador to Rome's mortal enemy. There, he resisted all of Pyrrhus' attempts to corrupt him, and St. Augustine cited his steadfastness as a supreme example of Roman devotion to "the earthly city," when, despite immense gifts and the offer of a quarter of the kingdom of Epirus, Fabricius could not be prized away from his country, but preferred to remain there in poverty and as a private citizen.[28] In *Monarchia* II. v. 11, Fabricius returns as "a sublime example of how to resist avarice, when—poor as he was—in his loyalty to his country he scoffed at the great pile of gold offered to him. . . . The memory of this deed has been consecrated by our Poet [Virgil] when in the sixth book he sings of 'Fabricius, mighty in his poverty.'" In both the *Convivio* and the *Monarchia*, Fabricius is praised above all as a model for resisting the lures of avarice, *exemplum avaritie resistendi*, a citizen in whom avarice was unable to overcome the love of and the loyalty to one's country. The affinity between *pietas* and *justitia* is recorded by Aquinas, in the objection (*Summa Theologica* 2.2.101.3) that, since *pietas* displays the cult of and duty toward one's country, it is one and the same thing as "legal justice" (*justitia legalis*), which is concerned with the common good. Although Aquinas concludes that the two are in fact distinct (*ad* 3), the link between the two, as well as the bond forged by the *patria*, is clearly demonstrated.

The poet has thus given us outstanding *exempla* of Aquinas's claim that avarice is opposed to both liberality and Justice (*S. Th.* 2.2.118.3.3). Both "forms" of avarice have clear political implications. Their antidotes are illustrated in the rejection of avarice by Fabricius, who remained loyal to his country despite all the enticements offered by Pyrrhus, as well as in the example of St. Nicholas, whose liberality saved three girls from prostitution, an offshoot of avarice that signifies the death of the family—and, ultimately, of the commonwealth or State. Far from being a mere picturesque detail, St. Nicholas's paternal solicitude stands in exemplary contrast to the degenerate avarice that led Charles II of Anjou to prostitute his own daughter by selling her off to Azzo VIII of Este, the parricide (*Inf.* XII. 111–12).[29]

On the other hand, Mary's example is primarily concerned with the belief that the early Church was founded in poverty. It holds up for our contemplation an antidote to the universal greed and corruption denounced by the poet in the supreme example of God's choice of a humble stable and manger for the birth of His Son. The renunciation of all worldly power and riches made by the King of Kings was one of the cornerstones of Spiritual Franciscan apologetics. Mary's acceptance of poverty highlighted on the fifth terrace of Purgatory is paralleled by the paean to St. Francis's espousal of Lady Poverty in Paradise, where the claim is made that Francis's bride had been rejected for over one thousand years since the death of her first husband, Christ:

> "Questa, privata del primo marito,
> millecent' anni e piú dispetta e scura
> fino a costui si stette sanza invito;"[30]

Above all Christ's Church must be brought back to its virtuous origins and cleansed of its omnivorous sin of avarice. For Dante, there was only one possibility—hinted at in Hugh Capet's longing for the "vengeance which, concealed, makes sweet Your anger in Your secret counsel" (*Purg.* XX. 95–96)—as well as in the poet-narrator's fulmination (ll. 10–15):

> Maladetta sie tu, antica lupa,
> che piú che tutte l'altre bestie hai preda
> per la tua fame sanza fine cupa!
> O ciel, nel cui girar par che si creda
> le condizion di qua giú trasmutarsi,
> quando verrà per cui questa disceda?[31]

The identification of the *antica lupa* ("ancient wolf") of *Inferno* I with cupidity reveals the identity of her conqueror. He is none other than the

Emperor, who—alone among mortals—is virtually immune to cupidity (*Monarchia* I. xiii. 7); since he is the sovereign ruler of the whole world, there is nothing for him to lust after, neither power nor riches (*Mon.* I. xi. 12: "the Emperor has nothing which he can desire"; cf. *Inf.* I. 103–5).[32]

The central third of Canto XX (ll. 43–93) is taken up by Hugh Capet's philippic against his degenerate and evil descendants who form "the evil plant that casts its shadow over all the Christian land" (ll. 43–44). With the image of this family tree, we recall that in Dante's times genealogical trees were drawn as real trees, growing upward. A parallel with the tree of God's Justice—found in the Earthly Paradise and intimately linked with the Empire (*Purg.* XXXII. 38–114, XXXIII. 55–72)—will be possible in retrospect, when the Capetian tree will be seen even more clearly as the evil tree of Christendom. More immediately, we note that the immense shadow cast by it over all the Christian lands is an eclipse of Justice and therefore of the "two suns" of *Purg.* XVI.106–8—an eclipse capable of turning the entire Christian world into a barren desert.[33] Like St. Peter in Paradise (*Par.* XXVII. 22–63), Hugh Capet is a spokesman for the poet's own prophetic feelings, and calls down the wrath of God on his unworthy successors— in particular, on Philip the Fair, king of France from 1285 to 1314. In lines 46–48, he evokes the revenge wreaked on France for its treachery toward Count Guy of Dampierre by the cities of Flanders in 1302, when their citizens routed the flower of French nobility at the battle of Courtrai in July 1302 and forced Philip to cede all the country north of the River Lys to Guy's son in 1305.

In three *terzine* (ll. 52–60), Hugh mixes fact and legend, stating that he was the son of a Parisian butcher and that, when the only survivor of the Carolingian dynasty became a monk, his own power was such that he succeeded in having his son crowned king, "from whom began the consecrated bones of all those kings" (the kings of France were consecrated and anointed no less than seven times with oil from the Holy Ampulla during the coronation rites at Reims). The legend that Hugh, count of Orleans, Paris, and Dreux, duke of France (at that time, the Ile-de-France), and brother to the duke of Burgundy, was the son of a wealthy cattle-dealer is mentioned, though refuted, by Giovanni Villani (*Cronica* V. 4). Whether or not Dante regarded it as legend, the idea that the French kings were descended from butchers or cattle-dealers fitted in all too well with his contempt for upstarts (*Inf.* XVI. 73; and here, ll. 56–57: "so much new-gained power") and he seized upon it in his travesty of the French royal family.[34] The last of the Carolingians did not become a monk (l. 54, as did the last of the Merovingians: G. Villani, *Cronica* III. 12); in fact, Charles, duke of Lorraine, was taken prisoner by Hugh and died in captivity in 992. Finally, it was Hugh himself who was elected king of the Franks at the Diet of Compiègne in 987, and who imposed the election of his eldest son on the nobles, thus making the crown hereditary.

The next six verses (ll. 61–66) contain further historical inaccuracies, which likewise fit in with the dramatic crescendo of crimes. In order to highlight the purple patches selected by him in contemporary French history, Dante makes Hugh assert that, until 1246 (when the County of Provence became a possession of the house of Anjou) his descendants, although of little worth, did not commit any great evil.[35] It was then that the saga of lies and territorial rape began. Unfortunately for this poetic vision, however, the historical "rape" of Normandy (listed in l. 66) had taken place half a century before, when Philip Augustus, after confiscating John Lackland's fiefs in France for felony (1202), went on to conquer Normandy, Maine, Anjou, Touraine, Poitou and Saintonge.

While Louis IX (1226–1270) is understandably excluded from the list of criminals (Louis had been canonized in 1297 by the hated Boniface VIII in an attempt to achieve reconciliation with Louis's grandson, Philip IV), the anti-Hohenstaufen Italian expedition of Charles of Anjou—which was certainly not opposed by Louis—is denounced in l. 67. With heavy sarcasm we are told that Charles went on to make amends for his act of plunder by executing Conradin, son of Emperor Conrad IV (October 1268), and then "for amends" (l. 69) he had St. Thomas Aquinas murdered in 1274 at Fossanuova, while the saint was on his way to attend the Council of Lyon.

The nine *terzine* (ll. 67–93) at the core of Dante's prosecution are marked by the use of anaphora or *replicatio*: the repetition of *per ammenda* ("for amends") in lines 65, 67, 69, and the sixfold insistence on the prophetic word *veggio* ("I see": ll. 70, 80, 86, 88, 89, 91) emphasizing the poet's resolve to hammer home the reality and urgency of his message. The fact that it is Dante's vision—and not Hugh Capet's—that lies behind this message is obvious not only from its content but also from the verbal perspective revealed in the phrase "Charles came down into Italy" (l. 67). The speaker's vantage point disclosed in the word *venne* ("came") is clearly situated not on the distant heights of the fictional Mountain of Purgatory but in Italy—as always, at the center of the poet's vision.

The "other Charles" mentioned in line 71 is Charles of Valois, brother of Philip IV. After his victorious military campaign in Flanders, he was summoned by Boniface VIII, primarily in order to assist Charles II of

Naples in his Sicilian war but also to make peace between the rival Guelf factions in Tuscany. On 28 January 1301, Charles married Catherine of Courtenay, the granddaughter and heiress of the last Latin Emperor in Constantinople. Boniface accorded him papal dispensation to marry Catherine, promising political and financial aid for the reconquest of the Eastern Empire, but on condition that Charles first pacify the papal lands (including Tuscany) and evict the Aragonese from Sicily. Charles arrived in Florence on All Saints' Day, 1301. Instead of acting as peacemaker, he persecuted the White Guelfs in a manner worthy of Totila (*DVE* II. vi. 5). Constantly in need of money, Charles of Valois "was an irresponsible adventurer who did the papal cause little good."[36] Accompanied only by a small cavalry force:

> "Sanz'arme n'esce e solo con la lancia
> con la qual giostrò Giuda, e quella ponta
> sí, ch'a Fiorenza fa scoppiar la pancia."[37]

Commentators have, I believe, missed the association of ideas behind these verses. "The lance with which Judas jousted" is clearly the weapon of treachery. However, the subsequent image evoked by Charles's aiming his lance in such a way that he rips open Florence's guts is surely not "a plebeian metaphor" (as at least one critic claims) but rather a clear visual image depicting the result of the joust, in which the evil knight slays his opponent or victim by a treacherous move (with Florence perhaps reified as the straw dummy whose innards are burst wide open).[38]

After his treacherous conduct in Florence, which left the city at the mercy of the Blacks and Dante in perpetual exile, Charles journeyed to Naples and thence to Sicily, where he waged a disastrous campaign and was obliged to make peace with Frederick III of Aragon on 31 August 1302. Even Boniface VIII was fain to recognize Manfred's grandson as king of Sicily. Charles won for himself "not land, but sin and shame" (l. 76), acquiring the nickname *Senzaterra* ("Lackland") and becoming the butt of general ridicule: "and so . . . people jeered: 'Lord Charles came to Tuscany as a peacemaker and left the country at war; and he went to Sicily to wage war, and all he brought back was a shameful peace'" (G. Villani, *Cronica* IX. 50).

The third Charles (l. 79: "the other") is Charles II the Lame, king of Naples (from 1285 to 1309) and count of Anjou and Provence. His eldest daughter was the first wife of Charles of Valois. After the Sicilian Vespers and the expulsion of the French from the island in 1282, Charles—then

Prince of Salerno—was placed in command of the Angevin fleet at Naples by his father, with strict orders not to engage the enemy. Charles, however, was lured out to sea by the Sicilian admiral, Ruggiero di Loria, who defeated him and took him prisoner (l. 79). Dante denounces his evil ways in the Heaven of Jupiter (*Par.* XIX. 127–29; XX. 62–63) and speaks of him with contempt in *Conv.* IV. vi. 20 and *DVE* I. xii. 5. In 1305, Charles "sold" his youngest daughter Beatrice in marriage to Azzo d'Este, who was supposed to have murdered his father as well as Jacopo del Cassero (*Inf.* XII. 111–12 and *Purg.* V. 77–78). We reach here the heart of the canto, in which avarice is seen by Hugh to have destroyed even fatherly love, and his descendant is so degenerate that he will sell off his daughter ("his own flesh") as pirates do their slaves:

> "O avarizia, che puoi tu piú farne,
> poscia c'ha' il mio sangue a te sí tratto,
> che non si cura de la propria carne?"[39]

The crescendo of condemnation and despair reaches its climax, sustained by the repetition of *veggio* in lines 86, 88, 89, 91, and culminating in *veder* (l. 95), the vision of the longed-for punishment that God will surely visit on the House of France. What is prophesied (ll. 86–90) is the outrage of Anagni, which took place in September 1303, and the poet claims that Christ Himself was captured in His vicar, Pope Boniface VIII.[40] There could be no more striking proof of Dante's resolve to distinguish between the individual and his office. Boniface the individual was condemned by the poet of the *Comedy* as "the prince of the new Pharisees" (*Inf.* XXVII. 85): the spiritual leader of Christianity not only wages war on members of his flock, but he even tricks one of them, Guido da Montefeltro, into eternal damnation. Dante regarded Boniface as the person chiefly responsible for his own sufferings and exile (*Par.* XVII. 46–51), and the poet has St. Peter denounce Boniface as the usurper who has turned Peter's burial place into a sewer, so that Lucifer himself rejoices at his actions (*Par.* XXVII. 22–27). And yet, this unworthy wretch destined for Hell (*Inf.* XIX. 52–4) is still *sub specie mundi* Christ's representative on earth. It is clear that Dante did not share the views of the extremist Spiritual Franciscans who claimed that Boniface was not Pope, even though he had tricked his predecessor into abdicating and then had bought his election. Already in *Purg.* II. 98–99, Boniface's Holy Year has been recognized as valid in God's eyes. Now— although the last reference to him as "him of Alagna" (in *Par.* XXX. 148) will implies that Boniface got his just deserts at Anagni (ironically, also his birthplace)—the poet sees in this evil old man Christ Himself captured, mocked, and once more put to death "among living thieves" (ll. 87–90).

This vision leads Hugh to refer to his descendant Philip the Fair, the orchestrator of the sacrilegious attack, as "the new Pilate" who hypocritically protested his innocence of any involvement with the capture of Boniface at Anagni, but who—as Pontius Pilate had done with Jesus—had delivered Christ's vicar into the hands of his enemies (ll. 91–93):

> "Veggio il novo Pilato sí crudele,
> che ciò nol sazia, ma sanza decreto
> portar nel Tempio le cupide vele."[41]

"Sanza decreto" refers primarily to the fact that on 13 October 1307, Philip the Fair's officers arrested all the Knights Templar throughout France: the action was so unexpected and so well executed that only a dozen Templars escaped. From a religious point of view, it was highly illegal, as no papal decree ("sanza decreto") had been issued—for the good reason that Clement V himself (who was at Loches, where he witnessed some arrests) had not even been informed of the king's decision to move against the Templars: "The fact that the Pope was faced with the *fait accompli* was an affront."[42] Dante's phrase "without decree" also implies that Philip's action was without divine sanction, for until that time no religious order had ever been suppressed (although Frederick II had evicted the Templars from Sicily and seized their possessions in 1229).

More puzzling, however, is the image of Philip's "greedy sails" (*cupide vele*) carried into the Temple. Bonora suggests that "the singularity [of the image]—one might almost say the Baroque liking for bold parallels—is justified by the . . . word Temple, which makes one forget how worldly was the life led by the Templars."[43] Others have convincingly posited a link with lines 80–81 (and, in particular, with the phrase "as pirates do") to evoke an act of piracy carried out by the king and his accomplices: e.g., N. Sapegno's note "*le cupide vele*: this bold, new image suggests the idea of an attack by pirates."[44]

I believe it is possible to extend our understanding of Dante's imagery and its complex ramifications, in an attempt to reveal what Leo Spitzer called "the etymology of the writing," and in so doing point to an essential link between the earthquake that shook the world at Christ's death and the quaking of the Mountain of Purgatory that brings Canto XX to a dramatic close.⁴⁵ Since the mountain, unlike the rest of the sublunary world, is "free . . . from all change" (*Purg.* XXI.43), this truly miraculous event is willed by God to signify the liberation of a soul (ll. 58–60):

> "Tremaci quando alcuna anima monda
> sentesi, sí che surga o che si mova
> per salir sú; e tal grido seconda."⁴⁶

In order to try to unravel "the etymology of the writing," we must take a circuitous route.

First, we notice that the reference in Canto XX to the annihilation of the Order of Knights Templar follows the allusion to Christ's death in lines 88–90 ("I see him once more mocked . . . and put to death between living thieves"). The Templars derived their name from the fact that they were originally lodged (c. 1120) by Baldwin II in the part of the palace of the Latin kings in Jerusalem known as the Temple of Solomon. I would suggest that the evocation of Christ's death, combined with the poet's resolve to denounce the destruction of the Order, led the poet—through the connotation inherent in the word "Temple" (the monastery of the Temple in Paris, used to designate the Order's riches in France)—to recall the rending of the veil in the temple at the moment of Christ's death (Matthew 27. 51; Mark 15. 38; Luke 23. 45). In Solomon's temple, the veil signified exclusion from the Holy of Holies; none but the High Priest could pass beyond it. The veil was thus the ultimate taboo, which no king had ever dared to challenge or disobey.⁴⁷ *Portar nel tempio le cupide vele* (l. 93: "carries his greedy sails into the temple"): although the Latin word *velum* primarily meant a sail, it could also indicate a veil or a curtain; and its plural form *vela* gave rise to the Italian word for "sail". While the phrase *cupide vele* in line 93 may also be taken to indicate the insignia of the soldiery sent to arrest the Templars, the link with piracy retained from line 81 ("come fanno i corsar") makes the conceptual leap to sails a natural one. Other connotations are evoked by the fact that the poet uses the word *vele* in association with Lucifer's infernal wings in *Inf.* XXXIV. 46–48, while Zingarelli and others record an archaic meaning of this plural form *vele* as signifying a bird's open wings; it is even possible that here *cupide vele* also contains the image of the outstretched wings of a rapacious bird of prey (*vela cupiditatis*) swooping into the temple.⁴⁸

Finally—and most significantly—St. Matthew's gospel states that the rending of the veil was accompanied by an earthquake: "And behold, the veil of the temple was rent in twain from the top to the bottom; and the earth did quake" (Matthew 27. 51). At the close of the canto (ll. 127–51), we read of another earthquake. To my knowledge, only André Pézard has pointed to the reason the poet chose this phenomenon to indicate a soul's liberation from Purgatory: "At the liberation of each soul . . . a brief tremor . . . reminds each one of Christ's ascent to heaven, when at his death the earth was shaken with a universal quake."[49] Strictly speaking, Christ's death did not mark His "ascent to heaven"; nevertheless, we can accept Pézard's theological shorthand that Christ's death made it possible for redeemed humanity to be reunited with God.

It is, however, important to be more precise. The soul's liberation from Purgatory and ascent to Paradise are in fact accompanied by two signs: the chant of praise sung by the angels at the time of the Redeemer's birth (*Purg.* XX. 136; XXI. 60; Luke 2. 14) and the earthquake that marked the moment of His death, the sacrifice that opened up Heaven once more to humankind (*Par.* VII. 47–48: "one death was pleasing to both God and the Jews, causing the earth to quake and heaven to open"). Christ's life as God incarnate and his role as Redeemer of the human race are thus evoked by these two supernatural pointers, the *Gloria* and the quake. Christ's death alone opened up Heaven for humanity (*Inf.* IV. 52–63)—just as now the completion of the purgatorial process on the Mountain, similarly marked by a miraculous earthquake, opens up Heaven for the purified soul. The redemptive milestone in Statius' supernatural life is thus marked by the same miraculous telluric phenomenon that had told the world of its redemption through suffering and love. The "etymology of the writing" would appear to be the religious and conceptual links present in the associations: Crucifixion-Temple-Veil-Earthquake-Redemption.

To return to lines 91–93, we recall that the Knights Templars were one of three great military orders founded in the twelfth century for the defense of Palestine and the protection of the pilgrim routes to the Holy Places. The Order, its rule inspired by St. Bernard, was recognized by the Council of Troyes in 1128. Very quickly it received huge gifts and endowments from various kings and Popes who wished to demonstrate their fidelity to the crusading ideal. The Order was especially numerous and influential in France, where the French king set up his treasury in the Paris temple. The fall of Acre (1291), the last Christian stronghold in the Holy Land, was the beginning of the Templars' downfall. There were accusations of treachery, of having sold out to the infidel. Their reputation plummeted, and in France drunkards were said to drink "like a Templar."[50] Nevertheless their power was such that it seemed impossible that the Order could ever be threatened, let alone suppressed. Its Grand Master, Jacques de Molay, was a cross between a prince and a cardinal, "elected like an Emperor but with absolute power like a king of France."[51] He appeared in public at the funeral of the wife of Charles de Valois on October 12, the day before the Templars were arrested, sublimely unaware of the storm cloud about to burst.

Under torture, the Templars began to confess, and on November 22 Clement reluctantly ordered the arrest of all the Templars throughout Latin Christendom. Nevertheless the sordid affair dragged on for five long years until, at the Council of Vienne on 3 April 1312, with Philip the Fair seated at his right hand, Clement promulgated the bull *Vox in excelso*, declaring the Order of Knights Templars suppressed: its property was handed over to the Hospital and—in Spain—to the military orders fighting Islam. As usual, Philip had won the day; as usual, Clement had given in, his position weakened by the memory of Boniface VIII and by the apparent threat posed by Henry VII to his temporal possessions and authority in Italy.

Historians cite Philip the Fair's undoubted piety in claiming that he must have been shocked by the reports of heresy and unnatural practices supposedly rife in the Order. They also observe that Philip did not seize most of the Templars' wealth.[52] For Dante as for so many of his contemporaries, however, the King's actions were inspired solely by avarice. Thus Giovanni Villani (*Cronica* IX. 92) claims that Philip was motivated "by greed for gain . . . the king acted through avarice . . . with numerous accusations of heresy: but it is more often said that he acted in order to rob them of their great wealth." In fact, the poet of the *Comedy*, inspired as he was by the vision of a Church devoted to the ideal of evangelical poverty, can hardly have admired a religious order whose worldly goods, in Villani's words, were "almost numberless in power and riches." Nevertheless, Philip's machinations against the Templars were grist to Dante's mill, as yet another example of Capetian greed and injustice. It is interesting to note that in this canto of avarice the poet did not include the accusation that the King had falsified the coinage of the realm (G. Villani, *Cronica* VIII. 58)—a crime he condemned instead in his heaven of Justice:

> "Lí si vedrà il duol che sovra Senna
> induce, falseggiando la moneta,
> quel che morrà di colpo di cotenna."[53]

Behind the accusation of crimes inspired by avarice lay the grand design of Dante's political blueprint for the world, his belief that peace and justice could only be assured if the imperial authority was accepted universally. The greatest blows to this authority had come from Florence's opposition to Henry VII in 1310–1313 (denounced in Epistles VI and VII), from the Capetian dynasty in France for over a century, and from the House of Anjou in Italy since Dante's birth. Already in 1202, Pope Innocent III had recognized that "the king [of France] acknowledges no superior in temporal affairs."[54] The rise of the autonomous sovereign state or *regnum particulare* was most clearly marked in France, reaching its definitive form under Philip the Fair, who was "king of all France in a way that none of his predecessors had been," and his reign "marked the point when the balance of loyalty definitely swung toward the secular sovereign state. From the political point of view, this shift marks the transition from the medieval to the modern period."[55] With his medieval vision of the political unity of Christendom, where everyone was subordinate in the temporal sphere to one imperial ruler, Dante could not but anathematize the Capetian rulers of France and their satellites.

In *Purgatorio* XIX–XX, the poet shows us how avarice—which governs the whole world (XX. 8)—holds in its clutches the pinnacles of both Church and State. Although Pope Adrian V had been converted during the few weeks of his pontificate and his confession has a personal tone, the consequences of his sin are shown to be both political and social. Like Hugh Capet, he deplores the decadence and corruption of his immensely wealthy and powerful family, excepting only his niece Alagia (XIX. 142–45)—sister of that Cardinal Luca Fieschi who gave wholehearted support to Henry VII, and wife to Moroello Malaspina, who not only befriended the poet during his exile but who was appointed imperial vicar in Brescia by Henry.[56]

In a work well known to Dante (*De Officiis* II. xxii. 77), Cicero had claimed that no vice is more hateful than avarice, especially in leaders and those called to govern the state. In another text familiar to our poet (*De Finibus* I. xiii. 43–44), Tully had pointed to the same tragic consequences as those listed in *Convivio* IV. xii. 9 ("What else, day after day, endangers and destroys cities, the countryside and individuals, so much as yet another amassing of wealth by someone?"), while specifying that greed "often destroys the very foundations of the state" (*Cupiditates . . . totam etiam labefactant saepe rem publicam*).[57]

Cicero's denunciations of the consequences of avarice form the back-cloth to *Purgatorio* XIX and XX, in which the Florentine poet in exile ar-raigned both a degenerate papal curia and the anti-imperial royal house of France before the court of Heaven for their sin of avarice, illustrating the way in which greed and avarice are—in the words of Cicero—the cause of "hatred, quarrelling and strife, of sedition and war." The figure of Dante's ideal Emperor, silhouetted as the great *Innominato* against the eschatologi-cal backdrop of this major ideological episode, adds a universal dimen-sion to its portrayal of the effects of avarice in ecclesiastical and temporal leaders. The condemnation of the history of France will find its positive pole in the history of the Roman Empire as recounted in *Paradise* VI, and the antidote to the universal poison embodied in the she-wolf of *Purgato-rio* XIX–XX will be proclaimed in the Heaven of Justice (*Paradiso* XVIII–XX), with its admonition to earthly rulers: "DILIGITE IUSTITIAM . . . QUI IUDICATIS TERRAM" (*Par.* XVIII. 91–93).

The Apocalypse
(*Purgatorio* XXIX–XXXIII)

DANTE AND VIRGIL ARE NOW JOINED BY Statius, who accompanies the two poets until the end of Purgatory. Statius, as a purified soul, stays with Dante in the Earthly Paradise, even after Virgil's departure, and drinks with him of the waters of the River Eunoë (*Purg.* XXXIII. 134–35). The most striking feature of Dante's Statius is his conversion to Christianity, for which there is no historical evidence but which he claims was due to his [mis-]reading of Virgil's Fourth Eclogue (*Purg.* XXII. 64–73). As one of the four great Latin poets designated as stylistic models in *DVE* II. vi. 7, Statius' poetry left an indelible mark on Dante's own writings (especially the *Convivio* and the *Comedy*). His place in the *Purgatorio* has been given an added dimension by Giorgio Padoan's hypothesis that Dante read Statius' *Thebaid* in the light of an allegorical interpretation attributed to Fulgentius. This may well have led the medieval poet to see in the figure of Theseus, the liberator of Thebes and the bringer of peace and justice, a covert attempt by Statius to indicate the Christ of his (supposed) new-found faith.[1] However that may be, it is clear that Statius' debt to Virgil as a poet is an original variation on the tribute paid to "my master and my author" by Dante the Pilgrim, at the very beginning of his journey (*Inf.* I. 85). Although Dante was obviously not converted to the Christian faith by his reading of Virgil, his rediscovery in the *Aeneid* of the providential mission of Rome and her Empire to some extent parallels the pagan poet's conversion.[2]

It is surely possible that for Dante the vision of the Roman Empire and its great civilizing mission as depicted in Virgil's epic found its antithesis in Statius' *Thebaid*, with its similar division into twelve books. Indeed, the condemnation of Pisa as the "new Thebes" in *Inf.* XXXIII. 89 reminds us that in medieval times Thebes was a byword for every form of crime, cruelty, incest, fratricide, violence, and anarchy. As J. Ferrante indicates, "Thebes and Troy . . . echo through Hell as emblems of self-destructiveness and pride."[3] We thus come to realize that the tragic consequences of political faction in medieval Pisa (and, by extension, throughout Dante's Italy) are already adumbrated in the reference to the nightmarish vision of Tideus, who "mad with joy and anger" seized the severed head and champed "the shattered brains" of his enemy Menalippus (*Thebaid* VIII. 751–62). The view in the pit of Hell of man reduced to the level of the beasts is introduced and then encompassed by memories of the legend of Thebes and of Statius' epic. I would therefore concur with Christopher Kleinhenz's insight that the trio of poets who travel through upper Purgatory

are all concerned with the ordering of the temporal sphere: Virgil with the establishment of Empire; Statius with the restoration of justice in the earthly city; and Dante with the *renovatio imperii*. . . . The sort of allegorization to which the *Thebaid* was subjected in the Middle Ages points to order and peace as being the desired goals of earthly society, and these can only be achieved through the advent of the peacemaker, the bringer of justice, figured by Theseus.[4]

Statius' role in the action of Dante's poem is well summed up by Ettore Paratore: "he ends up by taking on the role of mediator between Virgil and Beatrice, so much so that in *Purgatorio* XXV he is given the arduous task of instructing the Pilgrim on the problem of the soul's formation."[5] Moreover, Cantos XXI–XXVI constitute the section in *Purgatorio* in which poets and poetry are at the center of Dante's spotlight, focusing as it does first on the great achievements of Latin poetry (Statius and Virgil, in XXI–XXII, with references to Juvenal, Persius, Homer, and others in XXII) and then on no fewer than four vernacular poets: Forese Donati (XXIII–IV), Bonagiunta da Lucca (XXIV, with mention made of Jacopo da Lentini and Guittone d'Arezzo), Guido Guinizzelli and Arnaut Daniel (XXVI, with allusions to Giraut de Borneil and Guittone).[6]

Eden

In Canto XXVII, Dante passes through the wall of fire (ll. 10–54), experiences his third dream (ll. 91–113), and, standing on the threshold of the Earthly Paradise, is bidden by Virgil to enter the place that God prepared for the human race as a token of eternal peace. His guide through Hell and Purgatory now tells the Pilgrim:

"lo tuo piacer omai prendi per duce . . .
    Non aspettar mio dir piú né mio cenno;
libero, dritto e sano è tuo arbitrio,
e fallo fora non fare a suo senno:
    per ch'io te sovra te corono e mitrio."[7]

Why does Virgil "crown and miter" the Pilgrim at this juncture? The answers are many and varied. Most contemporary scholars would agree with the judgment given by Amedeo Quondam in his article in the *Enciclopedia Dantesca* ("coronare": II. 213), where he states that "Virgil does not have the possibility of conferring on Dante a spiritual authority which he himself does not possess; nor, for that matter, is Dante ready to receive it." The same point is made by Domenico Consoli, namely that Virgil has not the power to carry out "an investiture of both temporal and spiritual sovereignty."[8]

This objection overlooks an essential part of the fundamental allegory of the poem, which is highlighted in the *Monarchia*. For, while it is true that postlapsarian humanity is in need of two guides, Pope and Emperor, it is equally true, as Dante tells us in *Mon.* III. iv. 14, that if humanity had *not* sinned, it would have had no need of such guides; in other words, there was—and is—no Pope (miter) and no Emperor (crown) in the Earthly Paradise.[9] Virgil's act does not in any real sense confer imperial or papal *authority* on Dante (what Quondam and Consoli object to); instead, it is a symbolic gesture indicating that the Pilgrim—whose will is now "free, upright and whole" (l. 140)—is now his own guide in no need of the two *remedia peccati*, because he has recovered in Eden that state of innocence and justice which was humanity's birthright before original sin.[10]

My interpretation does not negate the insight provided by Joan Ferrante, when she states that Dante is prepared "for the role heaven thrusts upon him in the Earthly Paradise, when Virgil crowns him . . . when he as poet becomes the surrogate guide to the world, since the other two do not function."[11] Nor does it militate against the view put forward by Ernst Kantorowicz, that "the royal and sacerdotal dignities have been bestowed upon Dante just as on every newly baptized who through the sacrament of baptism was reborn in the original status of Adam and thereby potentially acquired immortality and eternal co-rulership with Christ in the kingdom of heaven."[12] Kantorowicz, however, does not make the necessary link between his insight ("the original status of Adam") and the Pilgrim's condition as he enters Eden.

Dante, Virgil, and Statius enter the Earthly Paradise, the state of justice and innocence symbolized by the "divine forest green and dense" (*Purg.* XXVIII. 2), utterly opposed to the *selva selvaggia*, that dark wood of error and perdition where the Pilgrim had found himself at the beginning of his journey. A beautiful lady, on the other side of a stream, who sings and plucks the flowers of God's creation, tells them that "the psalm *Delectasti*" can throw light on her role "in this place chosen for human nature to be its nest" (*Purg.* XXVIII. 76–81). There is in fact no psalm beginning with the word *Delectasti*. However, early commentators such as l'Ottimo and Francesco da Buti had no difficulty in identifying Psalm 91 of the Vulgate [92], whose fifth and six verses read: "Because Thou didst delight me [*Quia delectasti me*], Lord, in Thy work; in the works of Thy hands I will rejoice. How magnificent are Thy works, Lord, how unfathomable Thy purposes!" Dante evidently chose the passage as a hymn of praise to God's creation, here seen in all its pristine perfection. Far from being "somewhat pedantic", however, as Momigliano claimed, the biblical reference is in fact doubly appropriate, although no commentator seems to have taken up Matelda's reference to the whole Psalm, and not merely to the verses praising God's creation.[13] Psalm 91 speaks of the destruction God will visit upon His enemies, and—perhaps more relevant for the context in Eden, where the Pilgrim has finally been justified—the thirteenth verse declares: "the just man shall flourish like the palm tree and grow to great heights like the cedars of Lebanon."

Readers are kept in suspense for no fewer than five cantos before they learn the lady's name, Matelda (*Purg.* XXXIII. 119), although they may never in fact learn her true identity.[14] For our political quest, it is tantalizing to note that the early commentators either ignored the question or they had no difficulty in identifying her with the Countess Matilda of Tuscany (1046–1115).[15] Modern scholars have objected that Dante would surely not have placed in the Earthly Paradise the Countess of Tuscany who gave such powerful support to Pope Gregory VII throughout the investiture contest and whose castle at Canossa became a byword for the humiliation imposed on Emperor Henry IV. In 1110 Matelda submitted to Henry V and made him heir to the lands she had previously promised to the Holy See; however, at her death she left everything to the papacy, causing yet more antagonism between the Empire and the papacy.

Recently, Professor Ferrante (perhaps reflecting on the "coupling" of Cato and Matelda found in Buti and Benvenuto) has drawn our attention to the parallelism evident in the fact that

Cato and Matelda are counterbalancing figures. . . . Both were directly involved in the major political struggles of their time and both are surprising choices for Dante: Cato is not only a pagan and a suicide, but a defender of republican Rome against the future empire; Matelda is a Christian Countess who fought literally and figuratively to defend the church against the emperor and tried to leave her strategically located lands to the church when she died.

Ferrante goes on to suggest that the poet celebrates both historical figures for the purity of their motives and

Matelda defended the reform pope against the corruption of political power exercised within the church. Leaving her lands to the church was a mistake, but well-intentioned, like Constantine's Donation, which was far more harmful but does not deny him heaven.[16]

To this we may add that Cato is the guardian of Purgatory, Matelda the custodian of the Earthly Paradise. Between these two, from the pagan Stoic to the devout Christian, lies the whole of Dante's purgatorial experience.

As Bruno Nardi pointed out over fifty years ago, Countess Matilda was by far the best-known and the most powerful woman in the whole of Christendom, one, moreover, who exercised absolute power in Italy. Nardi quotes Cino da Pistoia's annotation to the Justinian Codex, in which Dante's friend and fellow poet singled out the great exception constituted by the Countess's jurisdiction, claiming that she was the daughter of the king of Italy, who succeeded her father and governed as king: "Comitissa Matilda . . . fuit filia regis Italiae et successit in regno et gessit omnia tamquam rex." If this was all that Dante's great jurist friend knew about the Countess, how legitimate is it to suppose that Dante knew a great deal more about her historical identity and role? It is all too easy for modern scholars to forget how difficult and how sparse precise, detailed historical information was in Dante's times. Nardi, therefore, asserts that the Matelda/Matilda of Dante's Eden, "the fearless lady . . . who 'governed everything as a king,' as Cino believed" represents the teachings of philosophy whereby humanity can arrive at the blessedness symbolized by the Earthly Paradise.[17]

Peter Armour has refined certain previous insights provided by other scholars in a convincing interpretation of Matelda's role. Dante's beautiful young woman "irresistibly recalls the Wisdom who was with God from the beginning, who was present at the Creation and rejoiced in it, who delighted to be in the company of men, but who was lost after the

Fall by the sinful descendants of Adam . . ."[18] By introducing the Pilgrim
to the triumphal procession, and to Beatrice, Matelda offers him a vision
of the right relationship between the active life and the Church on earth.
She is obviously subordinate to Beatrice, as Eden is the harbinger of the
Heavenly Paradise, whilst the relationship between the two women is illuminated by the fact that the historical Countess Matilda was the daughter
of the Countess Beatrice (who is buried with her in Pisa): "So Beatrice,
speaking to the Tuscan Dante, is using a name which, linked with her own,
conveys an unmistakable reference to the spiritual and temporal affairs of
Tuscany in the *buon tempo antico* . . . As Wisdom is to God, so is Matelda
to Beatrice . . . so is she the lover of all those who love her, the true *philoso-
phi*."[19] And, we may add, as the link between ancient wisdom and Christian
revelation, she points to the myth of humanity's golden age found in the
poets of antiquity, which was surely their glimpse of Eden, just as nectar
(and milk: Ovid, *Metamorphoses* I, 111) was in fact their imperfect vision of
the rivers in the Earthly Paradise:

> "Quelli ch'anticamente poetaro
> l'età de l'oro e suo stato felice,
> forse in Parnaso esto loco sognaro.
>   Qui fu innocente l'umana radice;
> qui primavera sempre e ogne frutto;
> nettare è questo di che ciascun dice."[20]

This is not random syncretism on Dante's part. We must constantly bear
in mind his belief that the Earthly Paradise indicates a goal, a state of justice here and now, attainable by humanity on earth under the guidance of
the Emperor (in collaboration with the spiritual guidance provided by the
Church), a goal that had in part been prepared for by the achievements of
pagan Rome. It is yet another example of the Thomistic belief that Grace
in no way eliminates nature; instead, it brings nature to perfection. And
it is interesting to note that St. Thomas refers to St. Paul's reference to
pagan poets precisely in the passage of his *Summa* (*S. Th.* 1.1.8.2) where he
discusses the relationship between grace and nature: "Since grace does not
eliminate nature but perfects it, it is therefore necessary for natural reason
to be subservient to faith . . . the authority of the philosophers may be
exploited by theology, in cases where they were able to discover natural
truths; so, Paul [Acts 17. 28] quotes the words of Aratus, when he says: 'As
some of your poets have said: *We are God's children.*'"

The Procession

Matelda tells the Pilgrim to look and listen attentively to the scene that is about to unfold on the other side of the River Lethe. This will form the subjectmatter of Canto XXIX, introduced it with the words *"Beati quorum tecta sunt peccata!"* (*Purg.* XXIX. 3: "Blessed are they whose sins are covered!"). This reference to Psalm 31 [32] alludes to the two major themes interwoven by the poet in his portrayal of the Pilgrim's experience on the summit of Mount Purgatory: that of Justice regained, on the one hand, and that of confession and judgment on the other. This penitential psalm is not merely a hint of what will happen to the Pilgrim after his passage through Lethe (when his sins will be "covered," *tecta*, and forgotten). In verse 5, it also alludes to the confession he will have to make before the heavenly court of angels (*Purg.* XXXI. 31–36): "I made known my sin to you; and I did not conceal my iniquity [*injustitiam meam*]. I said: I shall confess my iniquity [*injustitiam meam*] to the Lord: and you forgave the impiety of my sin." The psalm closes on a note of exultation for Justice regained (l. 11): "Be glad in the Lord and exult, you just ones; rejoice, all you that are upright of heart."

It has not been noticed that this psalm—quoted by Matelda in the Earthly Paradise—is precisely the source of the image found in the passage in the last chapter of the *Monarchia*, in which Dante asserts that human greed would annul and reject the guidance offered by both Emperor and Pope, "if men, like horses stampeding to satisfy their bestiality, were not held to the right path *by the bit and the rein*" (*Mon.* III. xv. 9: *in camo et freno*). To be more precise, although the quotation from Psalm 31 has been recognized by editors of Dante's Latin treatise, its implied presence in Matelda's reference has not been detected. The ninth verse of the psalm reads: "Do not be like the horse and the mule, devoid of understanding. Govern them with the bit and the rein . . ." Thus on his arrival in Eden the Pilgrim is reminded of the anarchy rampant on earth, as described in Antepurgatory, where the tragic results of the "empty saddle" and the concomitant disuse of the "bit" (*freno*) perfected by the Emperor Justinian were denounced in *Purg.* VI. 88–105, as well as the disastrous interference and hostility practiced by churchmen and other opponents of the Empire.[21]

In other words, according to the *Comedy*'s polysemy, the literal sense describes the scene in Eden; the allegorical refers to the confession and remission of sins through Christ's redemption of humanity; the tropological points to Justice and humanity's need to be held in check by the Emperor's

rule of law; and the anagogical signifies the elimination of sin and its negative content through the process of purification necessary as a prelude to
beatitude in Heaven: *Beati quorum tecta sunt peccata.*

In the prelude to Beatrice's arrival, the divine forest is lit up by what at
first seems to be lightning, but which in fact grows in intensity. The Pilgrim
is led to reproach Eve for her disobedience to God's law. Seven trees of gold
appear, which turn out to be seven candelabra—the first of many details
Dante's scene in Eden shares with St. John's Book of Revelation.[22] There,
they surround "One like to a son of man"; here, they act as "a prophetic
signal of an advent."[23] A chant of "Hosanna" is heard (l. 51), last associated
in Dante's poetic universe with the vision of Beatrice's death, as described
in *Vita Nuova* XXIII. 7, when the choir of angels had greeted Beatrice's
entry into the heavenly Jerusalem with the cry first heard at Christ's triumphal entry into the Holy City. Taken together with the biblical allusion
to Luke I. 28 and 42 underscored by the use of the Latin *Benedicta* in lines
85–87, the reader is told to expect the arrival of a female figure. That same
reader may well wonder, in the words of Solomon, "Who is this woman,
who comes like the dawn of day?" (Song of Solomon 6. 9)—especially,
when the cry is heard *"Veni, sponsa, de Libano,"* repeated three times (*Purg.*
XXX. 11–12; Song of Solomon 4. 8: "Come, o bride, from Lebanon"). One
expects the advent of Mary or the Church, the Bride of Christ. That expectation is, however, partially thrown off-balance by the masculine form in
"Benedictus qui venis!" (*Purg.* XXX. 19), and it is only when Beatrice finally
appears to the Pilgrim (ll. 31–39) that the reader begins to understand that
her role here, on Dante's personal stage, is in fact analogous to Christ's on
a universal plane.[24]

For the present, however, we must attempt to focus on the essential outlines of the procession described in Canto XXIX. The twenty-four
elders would seem to represent the books of the Old Testament.[25] The
elders march two by two, crowned with white (the symbol of their faith
in the coming of the Messiah) and chanting the words of Gabriel and
Elizabeth modified for their Edenic setting: *"Benedicta* tue / ne le figlie
d'Adamo"* (ll. 85–86: "Blessed are thou among the daughters of Adam").
We expect this greeting to be addressed to Mary, but Mary is not present—
just as the cry "Hosanna" (l. 51) implied the coming of Christ, although
Christ does not appear. The second part of the procession points to the
New Testament with the appearance of four animals symbolizing the four
Gospels (Ezek. I. 4–14; 10. 1–22; Rev. 4. 6–8). Three ladies (the theologi-
cal virtues of faith, hope, and charity) dance next to the right wheel of

a triumphal chariot, while four others (the cardinal virtues) dance by the left wheel. As the chariot reaches a point exactly opposite to the Pilgrim, a sound like thunder is heard and the procession is comes to a halt.

All too often, the pageant described in *Purgatorio* XXIX has been seen solely as a representation of Holy Writ and a static vision of the ideal Church. This ignores the idea of movement, so forcefully demonstrated at the end of the canto when the procession is brought to a sudden stop. It is therefore important for us to realize that God's Book, represented from Genesis to Revelation as a solemn procession in *Purgatorio* XXIX, is in fact a history of both the human race and of time, from the moment of creation to the end of the world. The halting of the procession thus symbolizes the end of time or temporal motion, when Christ shall come again in glory to judge humankind (Revelation 19–20). Here in Eden, a drama prefiguring the Last Judgment is played out, a personal drama where Dante the individual is judged by Beatrice (Cantos XXX–XXXI), before the poet returns to a scene of universal import (Cantos XXXII–XXXIII). Both the procession and the pageant or mystery play have a direct bearing and an urgent message for humanity on earth; they portray first the whole span of world history and the way God's providential plan has been revealed and enacted (the procession: Canto XXIX), and then the tragic spectacle of how that plan has been thwarted throughout the ages—in Dante's times, with the corruption of the Church and the papacy's Babylonian exile at Avignon (Canto XXXII).

Before proceeding to examine the last four cantos, we must return to the procession and challenge the traditional meaning attributed to the Griffin drawing the chariot, within the square formed by the four animals:

> Lo spazio dentro a lor quattro contenne
> un carro, in su due rote trïunfale,
> ch'al collo d'un grifon tirato venne.
>   Esso tendeva in sú l'una e l'altra ale
> tra la mezzana e le tre e tre liste,
> sí ch'a nulla, fendendo, facea male.
>   Tanto salivan che non eran viste;
> le membra d'oro avea quant' era uccello,
> e bianche l'altre, di vermiglio miste.[26]

The traditional identification of the Griffin with Christ is expressed succinctly by Natalino Sapegno in his commentary: "The *grifon*, a lion with the head and wings of an eagle, is certainly Christ, in whom were united two natures, human and divine (cf. Isidore of Seville, *Orig.*, XII. 2. 17)."[27] This identification is bolstered by the references to *l'animal binato* and *la biforme fera* in *Purg.* XXXII. 47 and 96 ("the two-natured animal," "the bi-formed animal"), apparently suggested by the hypostatic union of the two natures, human and divine, in Christ.

Recently, however, this interpretation has been subjected to searching analysis.[28] Perhaps the most worrying aspect is the fact that such a widely-used tool as the *Enciclopedia Dantesca* in its third volume, published in 1971 (some six years after the essay by Hardie and eight years after Francesco Mazzoni's *lectura*), still reports that "*All the commentators, both ancient and modern, are agreed in recognizing Jesus Christ in the griffin* . . . Isidore of Seville had portrayed him thus . . ."[29] Concern arises if we compare this generalization with the conclusion reached by Professor Dronke: "After long and strenuous gryphon-hunting . . . I must fully confirm the negative conclusion of Dr Colin Hardie: there is no single instance in Christian tradition of a gryphon associated with Christ before Dante—or rather, before Dante's commentators."[30] Moreover, even if such an instance were found, it would still be necessary to show that Dante had occasion to be acquainted with it and that he accepted its truly exceptional signification.

The passage from Isidore, handed down from commentator to commentator, tells us in fact that griffins are not only "violently hostile to horses," but that they also "dismember men on sight" (*equis vehementer infesti . . . et homines visos discerpunt*)—behavior difficult to reconcile with Christ's redemption of humanity and his role as Saviour of the world. Instead, the traditionally violent nature attributed to griffins surely underlies the praise directed to Dante's *biforme fera* in *Purg.* XXXII. 43–44 ("Blessed are you, griffin, who do not lacerate this tree with your beak . . ."). The verb *discindere* ("to lacerate") may possibly be an echo of Isidore's *discerpere*. More to our purpose, however, this *hapax* calls to mind Dante's use of *scindere* in *Mon.* III. x. 5, when he states that it is forbidden for the Emperor to *scindere Imperium* ("rend the Empire").[31]

Since the griffin appears so prominently in a procession filled with biblical allusions, we must note that in the Bible the griffin is one of the birds to be avoided as unclean, according to Deuteronomy 14. 12 (cf. Leviticus 11. 13). Albertus Magnus, in his *Libri XXIII de animalibus*, mentions their enmity to horses and men (as does Aquinas in *S. Th.* 1.2.102.6.1).[32] Professor Armour insists that "the griffin of tradition was a large, swift, and terrifying predator." Thus "if the griffin symbolizes Christ, the image is not only crudely zoomorphic but also a violent and unprecedented distortion of the entire classical, biblical, and medieval tradition concerning griffins."[33] As a symbol of Christ, Dante's *biforme fera* is "monstrous, crude, theologically misleading," since Christ did not possess two forms but two natures in the same person, and the Incarnation, "one of the most transcendent of Christian mysteries . . . pertains . . . to the realm not of the earthly but of the heavenly Paradise."[34] Moreover, the griffin's action in peacefully drawing the chariot is out of character: "In thus doubly upsetting his reader's expectations, Dante is indicating that his griffin is not Christ the Lamb but a powerful potential enemy of Christ which here, however, enters fully and miraculously in accord with God's will, placidly drawing the triumphal chariot . . . of Christ's representative, Beatrice."[35]

What, then, does the griffin represent? What in history constituted a terrible threat to Christianity as "a powerful potential enemy of Christ," and yet fulfilled a mission willed by God? The answer is Rome and its Emperor (and we note that the persecutions of the early Christians are indeed ascribed to the eagle, symbol of the Empire, in *Purg.* XXXII. 109–17).[36] It would surely have been strange if, in that very same Earthly Paradise, which for Dante reflected the happiness attainable through Justice and the teachings of philosophy, the poet had placed no signifier of the imperial office and its divinely appointed mission to guide the human race, *humana civilitas*, to the *beatitudo huius vite* (*Mon.* III. xv. 10).

Far from denying the christological echoes in the epithets *biforme, doppia* or the phrase "the animal that is one person with two natures" (*Purg.* XXXI. 80–81), the former are in fact a valuable pointer to the concept of the Emperor as "a *gemina persona*, human by nature and divine by grace."[37] This concept is graphically illustrated in Dante's Paradise, where the only soul to have two halos of light is that of the Emperor Justinian (*Par.* VII. 6). This double halo is truly a striking poetic image, reinforced by the *hapax* "s'addua" and created precisely in order to illustrate "Justinian's christological dimension."[38] We can now see that the *doppia fiera* ("the twofold animal") of *Purgatorio* XXXI. 122 and the *doppio lume* ("twofold light") of *Paradiso* VII. 6 are but two aspects of the same truth, personified in the edenic procession by the Griffin; "the person of the ideal Roman Prince is—or should be—the image of Christ on earth, human but also divine."[39] The chariot represents humanity as Christendom, which at various allegorical levels will be interchangeable with Christ's Church on earth.[40]

The Pilgrim's Confession

It is to this chariot that the elders representing the books of the Old Testament turn "as to their peace," in *Purgatorio* XXX. 9. One of them cries out three times "*Veni, sponsa, de Libano*" (ll. 10–21) followed by a chorus chanting "*Benedictus qui venis!*" and "*Manibus, oh, date lilïa plenis!*" ("Oh, give handfuls of lilies!"). Erich Auerbach refers to "the spontaneous reaction of every mediaeval Christian to the words *sponsus* ['bridegroom'] and *sponsa* ['bride']: they meant for him Christ and the Church," and Professor Ferrante makes the pregnant suggestion that "Beatrice is heralded by three phrases which connect her first with the church as Christ's spouse, then with Christ himself, and finally with the emperor."[41] Dante's equation of the bride with theology in *Convivio* II. xiv. 19–20 may also help to prepare us for Beatrice's role as a *figura* pointing to Divine Wisdom. The specific reference to the Last Judgment (*novissimo bando*) comes in lines 13–15. This, combined with the words used to acclaim Christ's triumphal entry into Jerusalem on Palm Sunday—"Blessed is he who comes in the name of the Lord" (Matt. 21. 9; Mark 11. 10)—together with the allusion to the rising sun in lines 22–27, would certainly have led a medieval Christian to expect the Second Coming of Christ in His role as world judge. Instead:

> sovra candido vel cinta d'uliva
> donna m'apparve, sotto verde manto
> vestita di color di fiamma viva.[42]

The climax "DONNA m'apparve"—prepared for by a crescendo of ten verses—shatters the reader's expectations. How can the masculine *benedictus* refer to a woman, even one clothed in the colors of the three theological virtues?

As I suggested in a previous study, the care with which Dante has changed the biblical quotation to "Blessed are *you* who come" (*venis*), offset by the masculine *benedictus*, in fact suggests that the poet fully intended to surprise, to shock his readers into the realization that he was bent on establishing an analogy, *analogia entis*, between Beatrice and Christ. There is, of course, no suggestion that Beatrice *is* Christ, that she can replace Him, or that she is in any sense divine: the absolute distinction between creature and Creator remains intact. Both, however, may be seen to perform similar actions *on different planes*, which, like parallel lines, remain distinct yet interconnected. Coming from the heavenly Jerusalem, Beatrice is greeted by the words with which Christ was hailed upon his entry into Jerusalem on earth. And, even as Christ will come to judge all men at the end of time, so Beatrice comes to judge Dante once the procession, like time, has come to a halt. Her role as judge and *typus Christi* is once again hinted at in the quintessentially masculine image of the "admiral" in line 58.[43] The climax of her *Parousia* is also highlighted, and her role as a type of Christ (*typus Christi*) indicated by a backward glance to the *Vita Nuova*, where (XXXIX. 3) the fact that Beatrice was accompanied by the number nine in her life on earth revealed her to be a miracle "whose root . . . is the miraculous Trinity alone." In Eden, she first appears to judge her lover and ultimately to lead him to Paradise in the thirtieth canto of *Purgatorio*, after a prelude of 30 verses (the trinitarian unit, multiplied by the perfect number 10).

Beatrice's reproaches in Cantos XXX and XXXI provide one of the thorniest problems in Dante scholarship. What exactly do her accusations signify? To what transgressions do they refer?[44] The textual evidence is scant. After receiving the brunt of his lady's attack, the Pilgrim confesses through his tears:

> . . . "Le presenti cose
> col falso lor piacer volser miei passi,
> tosto che 'l vostro viso si nascose."[45]

Nothing could be more generic than this admission that, in the ten years from 1290 to 1300, Dante had been led astray by the false allurements of the things of this world, *le presenti cose*. Nevertheless, we note that the decade pinpointed by his lady saw Dante become involved in both the study of philosophy and political life. As far as philosophial error is concerned, for the present I shall merely quote Michele Barbi's summation, that in Beatrice's speech for the prosecution: "Never is mention made of anything but an excessive love for secondary goods . . . that is to say, for the goods and things of this world; there is absolutely no reference to philosophical doctrine . . ."[46]

Let us instead return to Dante's experience of Florentine politics. It is surely possible that Dante's moral transgressions included at least certain aspects of his political activities as a companion of those White Guelphs whom he condemned as that "evil, stupid company" in *Paradiso* XVII. 61–

69, where he also boasted of having risen above all political factions. It was in fact none other than Guido Cavalcanti who complained that Dante no longer shunned the vulgar crowd, whereas in the heyday of their friendship:

> Solevanti spiacer persone molte;
> tuttor fuggivi l'annoiosa gente . . .
> Or non ardisco, per la vil tua vita,
> far mostramento che tu' dir mi piaccia,
> né 'n guisa vegno a te, che tu mi veggi.[47]

Cavalcanti accuses Dante of mixing with *l'annoiosa gente*, and we must take account of the fact that "noioso" and its cognates had a far stronger pejorative meaning in old Italian, indicative of the behavior of the *villani* (at the opposite end of the moral scale from those endowed with a noble heart or *cor gentil*). As Corrado Calenda glosses: "Cavalcanti's violent rebuke is certainly directed against Dante's political activities on behalf of the popular elements in the Commune . . ."[48] Taken together with lines 88–90 of the canzone *Tre donne intorno al cor mi son venute* (*Rime*, CIV) and their enigmatic reference to possible political wrongdoing on Dante's part, it is not improbable that the errors confessed in *Purgatorio* XXXI included certain compromises and adjustments imposed by the realities of Florentine political life; in other words, a line of conduct far removed from the idealism that had inspired the *Vita Nuova* and Dante's youthful love for Beatrice.

We also notice that, immediately after the Pilgrim's admission that he had been led astray by *le presenti cose* (*Purg.* XXXI. 34–35), Beatrice exhorts him to be more steadfast *altra volta, udendo le serene* (ll. 44–45: "another time, when you hear the sirens"). Commentators are at one in pointing out that this reference to *le serene* is linked to the Pilgrim's second dream on the mountain, when he had been tempted by the false allurements of a "sweet siren" (*Purg.* XIX. 19–21). As we have already noted in chapter 9, the "femmina balba" represents the four sins purged on the last three terraces of Mount Purgatory (avarice, prodigality, gluttony, and lust): they are truly the things of this world, *le presenti cose*. Dante's apparent proclivity to lust has already been mentioned. And, as we have seen in the case of Pope Adrian in *Purgatorio* XIX, avarice (and also prodigality, its antithesis) may well be one of the concomitants of ambition. It may be pertinent, therefore, to recall that by the time of his exile Dante was heavily in debt, and (as we learn from *Purg.* XIII. 136–38) his soul was greatly oppressed by the sin of pride, the beginning of all sin and the mother of ambition in the political as in every other sphere of human activity.[49]

It is obvious that the poet went to a great deal of trouble to use words and expressions that have only a generic import, pointing to a broad area of sin. More importantly, we should bear in mind that the trial and confession of Dante the individual are over, described as they are in Cantos XXXI and XXXII of *Purgatorio*, in what is the most intensely autobiographical section of the whole *Comedy*. Before arriving at the pageant described in Canto XXXII, the Pilgrim looks at Beatrice, who is "turned toward the animal / that is but one person with two natures" (XXXI. 80–81). Then, accompanied by the penitential *Miserere* (Psalm 50 [51]) — "Wash me clean, cleaner yet, from my guilt, and purge me from my sin . . . blot out the record of my guilt . . . renew the spirit of righteousness within me . . . I will teach the wicked thy ways . . . and my mouth shall sing forth thy praise" — he is first immersed by Matelda in the waters of oblivion (Lethe), and then placed under the protection of Beatrice's handmaidens representing the four cardinal virtues. They lead the purified sinner "to the griffin's breast . . . where Beatrice stood, turned toward us" (ll. 113–34), and tell him to look into her emerald eyes "from which Love once aimed his shafts at you" (l. 117). Within those eyes:

> Come in lo specchio il sol, non altrimenti
> la doppia fiera dentro vi raggiava,
> or con altri, or con altri reggimenti.[50]

This *terzina* is misleading, if the simile of the sun's reflection in a mirror is taken to signify that the sun (God) was reflected in Beatrice, *speculum Dei*. This is, of course, the most likely meaning, but only if we divorce the image from its context and, moreover, give a unique signification to the word *reggimenti* forcing it to refer to the two natures of the incarnate God. The primary meaning of the term *reggimenti* is found in *Purg.* XVI. 128, where it refers to the two supreme authorities on earth; however, it is also used by Dante to signify the governance of human nature whereby passions are controlled by reason to produce noble behavior (*Le dolci rime*, l. 24). Here, in Eden, as Professor Armour writes: "Dante can see, unchanged, a 'double beast,' the griffin which has parts as of an eagle and parts as of a lion, and at the same time he can see alternately the two other creatures whose similitudes are joined in it."[51]

Of the six objections raised by Armour to the idea that the Pilgrim is supposed to be experiencing a vision of the mystery of the Incarnation, I would stress the fact that at this point he has not yet reached the theological virtues. Moreover, when they do come forward, these supernatural virtues beg Beatrice to turn her gaze toward her faithful lover:

> . . . "al tuo fedele
> che, *per vederti*, ha mossi passi tanti!
> *Per grazia fa noi grazia che disvele*
> *a lui la bocca tua*, sí che discerna
> la seconda bellezza che tu cele."[52]

The words emphasized show that it is above all in order to see his beloved Beatrice that Dante has made this journey, and that it is inconceivable that the three theological virtues—faith, hope, and charity—could be pleading with her to reveal her full beauty to the Pilgrim, if the mystery of Christ's dual nature were already revealed to him through the Griffin. Instead, as Mazzoni has rightly insisted, with the words *la seconda bellezza che tu cele* ("the second beauty you conceal") the poet is here pointing to Beatrice's ability to reflect the beauty of her Creator (cf. *Par.* XVIII. 16–18), as expressed in line 139, *O isplendor di viva luce etterna* ("O splendor of eternal, living light").[53]

It should be clear by now that the Griffin is in fact subordinate to Beatrice in her role as *typus Christi*. This composite creature is found *only* in the Earthly Paradise, where the four cardinal virtues lead the Pilgrim "to the Griffin's breast" (*Purg.* XXXI. 113), so that in Beatrice's eyes he may discover "the previously hidden heavenly mystery of its [the Griffin's] two constituent aspects . . . united as one and at the same time, paradoxically, both coextensive and amenable to separate consideration." We therefore come to see in Dante's Griffin "the Rome in which the potential for violence and hostility towards Christianity has been entirely superseded, for here Rome is revealed as harnessed within God's design, as Rome . . . the bringer of Beatrice."[54]

The Pageant

Canto XXXII opens with a declaration that Dante's eyes, feasting on Beatrice in their attempt to quench their ten-year old thirst, had extinguished his other senses. His eyesight, too, is then overcome by the "splendor of light eternal"; when it returns, he sees the "glorious host" turn to the right and move toward the east. As Charles Singleton observes: "The scene changes radically now, and the action centers around a tree in Eden."[55]

Dante, Statius, and Matelda follow the right-hand wheel of the chariot through the forest, otherwise empty as a result of Eve's sin (*Purg.* XXXII. 32). Beatrice descends from the Chariot, while everyone murmurs the name "Adam" and then surrounds "a plant whose every branch was stripped of all foliage and flowers" (ll. 37–39) but is of immense height. They all praise the Griffin (ll. 43–8):

> "Beato se', grifon, che non discindi
> col becco d'esto legno dolce al gusto,
> poscia che mal si torce il ventre quindi."
> Cosí dintorno a l'albero robusto
> gridaron li altri; e l'animal binato:
> "Sí si conserva il seme d'ogne guisto."[56]

The reference to Adam makes it clear that this is the tree of the knowledge of good and evil planted by God in Eden and signifying human obedience to God's law (Gen. 2. 16–17: "From every tree of the garden you may eat; but from the tree of the knowledge of good and evil you must not eat; for if ever you eat of it, you shall die"). An essential clue is provided only in the next canto (XXXIII. 71–72), when Beatrice tells the Pilgrim that the forbidden tree is to be interpreted tropologically as signifying God's Justice. This tree (already mentioned in *Purg.* XXIV. 116) symbolizes the divine origin of all justice and of the true laws administered by the Emperor; the unrighteous and the opponents of the divinely-willed Empire—like Adam and Eve—feed on false nourishment, which eventually poisons their whole being.

The other essential clue to the tree's allegorical meaning is contained in the Griffin's only pronouncement *Sí si conserva il seme d'ogne giusto* (l. 48: "In this way is the seed of all justice preserved"); *giusto* is neuter, meaning "just things" rather than abstract Justice. As others have noted, the tree represents "*ius*, law, and law in this conception is identical with God's will and providential plan."[57] We recall that "the Empire's foundation is human law/justice [*ius humanum*]" (*Mon.* III. x. 7) and that, since Adam's sin, only under the Emperor's universal rule can Justice be allpowerful on earth: "soli Monarche insistens iustitia in mundo potissima est" (*Mon.* I. xi. 8). The way—the only way—to defend and dispense Justice in the world

is illustrated in the Griffin's action, whereby the tree is restored to health
(ll. 49–60):

> E vòlto al temo ch'elli avea tirato,
> trasselo al piè de la vedova frasca,
> e quel di lei a lei lasciò legato . . .
> . . . s'innovò la pianta,
> che prima avea le ramora sí sole.[58]

Commentators have long noted the echo between line 48 and
Matthew 3. 15, in which Christ underlined his humility in receiving baptism from a mere man: "Thus it behoves us to fulfill all justice." That
biblical phrase was given a political meaning in Epistle VII, when Dante
claimed that if the decree issued by Augustus at the time of Christ's birth
had not proceeded from the court of the most just Emperor (*iustissimi
principatus*), the only Son of God would have refused to be born of the Virgin Mary: "He who was called 'to fulfill all justice'" (*Ep.* VII. iii. 14: *quem
"omnem iustitiam implere" decebat*). Hence, as Armour contends, the Griffin's declaration is "polemical, an admonition to the present opponents of
the Empire . . . and a lesson to its supporters on the true nature and goal
of earthly justice."[59]

The Griffin's act points to the Emperor's fundamental role, which is
to bind together in perfect harmony divine, natural and human law by providing the essential link between *ius divinum* and *ius humanum*. The Em-
peror/Griffin thus brings about the renovation of the Tree of Justice, found
in that Earthly Paradise to which the Emperor must lead humanity according to both the *Monarchia* and the basic allegory of the *Comedy*, which
requires that Virgil, the herald of the Empire, bring Dante and leave him
in Eden to observe the spectacle of God's providential plan for the world.

If we take the three *terzine* from lines 43–48, I believe the meaning of
the text's allegorical message is clear. First, we find the Griffin praised for
not harming the Tree of Justice. The literal meaning is that the Griffin does
not forcefully remove any part of it—"who do not lacerate [*discindi*] this
tree with your beak" (*Purg.* XXXII. 43–44). As already hinted, the *hapax*
"discindi" is to be placed beside *Monarchia* III. x. 9, in which we are told
that the Emperor is not allowed to do anything contrary to justice, nor is
he allowed to remove any part of the Empire or give it away. The reference
to the Donation of Constantine is the immediate cause for the assertion
that the Emperor is not allowed to divide the Empire (*scindere Imperium*

non licet, with the alternative form *discindere* in the striking parallel of *Mon.* III. x. 12).[60] Then, in lines 46–48, we are told by the Griffin that this is the supreme way of pre/serving Justice. In lines 49–51, his action illustrates this exemplary way; *e quel di lei a lei lasciò legato* ("and bound to it what had come from it") must refer to the legend that the wood of the cross on which Christ died to redeem humanity came from the tree of the knowledge of good and evil. Thus, in the first *terzina* we are told that God created this tree for His use alone (*Purg.* XXXIII. 60) and the Griffin is praised for not detaching anything from it; in the second, the Griffin warns that this is the only way to pre/serve Justice; in the third, we see that *l'animal binato* ("the dual-nature animal," representing Rome and the ideal Emperor, restores something to the tree. As a result, the tree blossoms anew.

In an important study, Edward Moore concluded that line 51 implies "that the Cross was made from the wood of the Forbidden Tree in the Garden of Eden."[61] Others, however, reject the idea that the chariot's pole-shaft can represent the Cross "because Dante later describes it as the piece of the chariot which becomes especially corrupt when it puts forth a full three of the monster's seven heads (*Purg.* XXXII. 144)."[62] It would certainly seem far-fetched to claim that the Cross was in any way corrupted. What has not been appreciated, however, is that the Cross is above all the symbol of Christ's absolute humility and His obedience to God's Justice, as is made clear in *Par.* VII. 97–100 (my emphasis):

> "Non potea l'uomo ne' termini suoi
> mai sodisfar, per non poter ir giuso
> *con umiltate obedïendo* poi,
>   quanto disobediendo intese ir suso;"[63]

Or, as St. Paul wrote (Phil. 2. 8): Christ "humbled Himself, making Himself obedient unto death, even death on the cross" (*Humiliavit semetipsum factus obediens usque ad mortem, mortem autem crucis*).

And yet, Dante claimed in *Monarchia* II. i. 1 that even this supreme act of obedience and reparation would have been void, if the Empire had not been based on right (*Et si Romanum Imperium de iure non fuit, peccatum Ade in Cristo non fuit punitum*) or if "Christ had not suffered under the appropriate judge, that penalty would not have been a [just] punishment" (II. xi. 5: *Si ergo sub ordinario iudice Christus passus non fuisset, illa pena punitio non fuisset*). Christ's act of redemption through obedience unto death had to be sanctioned by the Emperor's authority, which was the only one that could justify His death on the cross, as we are told in the canto of the Empire (*Par.* VI. 82–90):

> "Ma ciò che 'l segno che parlar mi face
> fatto avea prima e poi era fatturo . . .
>   diventa in apparenza poco e scuro,
> se in mano al terzo Cesare si mira . . .
>   ché la viva giustizia che mi spira,
> li concedette, in mano a quel ch'i' dico,
> gloria di far vendetta a la sua ira." [64]

In short, it was through the Emperor's supreme temporal authority that fallen humanity (the chariot) was bound once more to God's Tree of Justice and obedience to God's law. And it is as the supreme symbol of obedience—"not my will, but Thine, be done" (Luke 22. 42)—that the shaft now sprouts three heads, symbolizing humanity's disobedience to God's law, a rebellion that corrupts or distorts Christ's act of supreme obedience by rejecting the right order signified by the two suns of *Purg.* XVI. 106–8.

Like the Pilgrim, we have watched as the Griffin draws the chariot— a symbol of humanity and, at another level, of the Church—to the Tree of Justice. In its role as a remedy for the weakness of sin (*Mon.* III. iv. 14), the Griffin-Emperor binds the chariot and the tree fast together (even as Titus' imperial authority had done in decreeing Christ's death: *Par.* VI.90), thus bringing about a glorious rebirth of justice and happiness on earth—a state that will be shattered in six catastrophic stages, culminating in a picture of total corruption. We now enter into the heart of Dante's Apocalypse, "an enactment of ruin, almost a second Fall, a swiftly moving allegory of the woes and sins of the historical Church, culminating in the alternate kissing and conflict of the harlot-papacy and the king of France." [65]

The last fifty-two verses (*Purg.* XXXII. 109–60) offer a nightmarish vision of universal catastrophe. The Griffin and the positive symbols of the sacred procession ascend to heaven (ll. 89–90), while Beatrice, surrounded by the seven virtues, remains to guard the Chariot now reunited with the tree (ll. 93–96). The Griffin, as God's ideal of earthly Rome which had been realized possibly twice in history (the universal peace achieved at Christ's birth, and the instrument of universal justice fashioned by Justinian), has returned to its heavenly home and is replaced by a highly-charged symbol of Roman imperial power on earth, an eagle, which will figure in two of the seven dramatic scenes that now unfold.

Beatrice herself emphasizes the universal import of what the Pilgrim is about to witness by telling him to keep his gaze fixed on the chariot (ll. 103–5):

> "Però, in pro del mondo che mal vive,
> al carro tieni or li occhi, e quel che vedi,
> ritornato di là, fa che tu scrive."[66]

The first episode (ll. 109–17) is the faster-than-lightning descent of the eagle (l. 112: "God's bird"), damaging the tree's bark, its flowers and new foliage, and striking the chariot so violently that it reels under the blow like a ship in the grip of a typhoon. The early commentators unanimously interpreted this as signifying the persecutions of the early Church by the Roman Empire, from Nero to Diocletian.[67] The second shows a famished fox making its way into the body of the chariot and then put to flight by Beatrice as the representative of Divine Wisdom and orthodoxy—the former, an image based on Ezek. 13. 4 ("Thy [false] prophets are like the foxes in the desert") and The Song of Solomon 2. 15 (where the small foxes "destroy the vines"), indicating the threats to sound doctrine (*ogne pasto buon*) posed by heretics and their false teachings.[68]

The next tableau (ll. 124–29) occupies a central position in the sequence, preceded as it is by the two frames of the eagle and the fox, and followed by another two, detailing the attack made by a dragon (ll. 130–35) and the terrible transformation of the chariot (ll. 136–60). This central tableau shows the descent of the eagle onto the chariot's center as it covers that central part with its own feathers, while a voice is heard from heaven exclaiming "O my ship, what an evil cargo you have taken on board" (l. 129). This is generally interpreted as a dramatic visual representation of the terrible effects of the Donation of Constantine, with Christ's (less likely, St. Peter's) exclamation a variation on the legendary cry "Today, poison has been injected into the Church of God."[69] The omission of any reference to poison in Dante's version means that the poet emphasizes the wrongful acceptance of Constantine's well-intentioned gift on the part of the Pope described in a pregnant phrase as "the first rich father," in *Inf.* XIX. 117.[70]

A dragon then attacks the chariot and, removing part of it with its tail, makes off with it (ll. 130–35). The imagery is derived from Rev. 12.4, in which the dragon's tail "drew the third part of the stars of heaven, and did cast them down to the earth." For Lana, Benvenuto, and Buti the dragon symbolizes Mahomet, who proclaimed himself the greatest of the prophets

c. 610 and whom Dante placed among the sowers of discord and schism (*Inf.* XXVIII. 22–63). For Pietro di Dante (and perhaps L'Ottimo),[71] it stands for Antichrist. For some modern scholars, the description of the dragon as a serpent in *Purg.* XXXIII. 34 leads them to suppose that it is but another manifestation of the devil.[72] Since it is impossible to prove that any interpretation is exclusively correct, the episode of the serpent's theft merely goes to show both the wealth and the weakness of this type of allegory.

On the other hand, the dragon serves as the conceptual link with the apocalyptic transformation of "what remained" of the chariot (l. 136), which is overgrown by the eagle's feathers like fertile ground by weeds and then puts forth seven heads with ten horns (ll. 136–46). In order to bring home the horror of the scene and the totality of the corruption of the "holy structure" (l. 142), the poet adds "such a monster was never seen before" (l. 147) — but, of course, although such a hideous monster has not yet been seen on earth, it is already found in Rev. 12.3: "And there was seen another sign in heaven: and behold a great red dragon having seven heads and ten horns . . ."[73] By now, most commentators have made the Chariot synonymous with the Church as an institution on earth. It is in fact more consistent to see the Chariot as still representing humanity, which, after Christ's founding of His Church, is synonymous with the Church militant. Thus at the end of the Book I of the *Monarchia* (I.xvi.4), Dante inveighs against the human race, constantly beset by storm and shipwreck and now transformed into a multi-headed monster (*bellua multorum capitum factum*).

Then humanity's spiritual guide, seated on the monstrously transformed chariot and placed "like a fortress on a great mountain," appears as a lascivious whore "whose eyes were quick to rove" (ll. 149–50). Standing next to her is a giant. They embrace a number of times, but as the whore turns her "wanton, wandering eye" toward the Pilgrim, the giant flogs her from head to foot; he then completes the Griffin's destructive work by untying the chariot from the tree and dragging it off into the wood, where both the whore and the monstrous chariot-beast are hidden from the Pilgrim's sight.

The horror felt in the Middle Ages for anything monstrous and outside the norms of nature (God's daughter: *Inf.* XI. 105), is hinted at in the epithet *nova belva* ("new" beast), as applied to the deformed chariot in the last line of the canto and echoing the unnatural roots — *le nove radici* — of the suicide's tree in *Inf.* XIII. 73. It is something never seen before, something so "new" but so terrible that it goes beyond past human experience.

The "fornication" (to use the biblical term) of the whore with the giant reflects the "adultery" of the Holy See, its flirtation and conspiracy with the
kings of France under Popes such as Urban IV (1261–1264), the Frenchman who did all in his power to destroy Manfred and install Charles of
Anjou in Italy; his successor, Clement IV (1265–1268), another Frenchman, who used his influence to finance Charles's expedition against Frederick's heir; or Nicholas III (1277–1280), damned by Dante for his simony
(*Inf*. XIX, 46ff.) and guilty of securing from the Emperor Rudolf of Habsburg the formal cession of Ferrara, Bologna, and towns in the Romagna
to the papal state. But it is above all the whole drift of pro-French and anti-
imperial papal policy throughout the thirteenth century that is incrimi-
nated, a policy which reached both its zenith and its nadir in the reigns of
Boniface VIII (1294–1303) and Clement V (1305–1314).

The identification of the harlot with the corrupt papacy or Roman
curia suggested itself immediately to Dante's first commentators, based as
it is on the image in Revelations 17. 1–2 of the "great whore . . . with whom
the kings of the earth have committed fornication." The giant is primarily
Philip IV of France, who inflicted the "shame of Anagni" on Boniface and
who dominated Clement utterly. It is in fact noteworthy that Dante never
refers to Philip by name, although the French king played such an important role in the contemporary drama as the nameless villain depicted in
each of the three parts of Dante's poem (*Inf*. XIX. 87; *Purg*. VII. 109–
10, XX. 85–93, XXXII. 152–60; *Par*. XIX. 118–20). In the pit of Hell (*Inf*.
XXXI. 31ff.) the giants, who prefigure Satan and whose storming of Mount
Olympus, like Nimrod's disobedience at Babel, "was a conspiracy to usurp
heaven, to snatch the rule of heaven from God,"[74] may be regarded as symbolizing *inter alia* the rulers who rebelled against the Empire, opposing
the will of Heaven.[75] At the end of the *Purgatorio*, the king of France
who refused to acknowledge the Emperor's overlordship is portrayed as a
giant dragging the *nova belva* into the *selva* of Eden (l. 158: the "divine forest" is distorted in this apocalypic nightmare into a mirror-image of the
"savage wood" or *selva selvaggia* of *Inferno* I, with the latter's three beasts
conflated in this unique monster). The reference to the removal and exile
of the papacy to Avignon during Philip IV's reign is the most immediate
allusion on the contemporary plane, showing Dante's poetic exploitation
of apocalyptic imagery in his savage denunciation of both the Church's
corrupt leaders and the royal house of France as the prime example of rebellion against the divinely-instituted Empire.[76]

The polysemy of Dante's allegory, however, justifies other interpretations. Among these, the fact that "the Antichrist . . . appears prominently as a giant in almost all medieval commentary on the famous number 666 in Apocalypse 13. 18" and "the Antichrist is very frequently portrayed as sitting above or upon the corrupted Church" means that Dante's giant may also point to the Antichrist, with Philip as *typus Antichristi* and the whore as an Anti-Beatrice.[77] The links with the use of the *Apocalypse* made by the Spiritual Franciscans in their polemic against what they perceived to be the corruption of certain Popes are clear (although it is important to remember that their general anti-imperialism was anathema to Dante). Nevertheless, the role of the apocalyptic imagery in their leading exponents who had contacts with Florence is striking and similar; so much so that "Dante's Whore also suggests the mystical Antichrist of Spiritual Franciscans like Olivi and his follower Ubertino, just as his giant suggests their open Antichrist."[78]

Following this section is the longest canto in the whole poem. It carries the central lesson for Dante's audience, the need to restore the supreme institutions of both Church and State to the roles assigned to them by God, and the "following canto . . . assures us of that restoration."[79]

The Epilogue

The last act of the drama begins with the words "*Deus, venerunt gentes*" of Psalm 78 [79: "O God, the heathen have broken into thine inheritance; they have profaned . . . thy sanctuary"], lamenting the defilement of the Temple and the destruction of the Holy City, Jerusalem, and calling upon God to avenge these crimes and to punish the transgressors (ll. 1–10): "help us, O God, our saviour, and deliver us for the glory of Thy name . . . let not the heathen cry out: 'Where is their God?'" This terrible lament is chanted by the theological and the cardinal virtues alternately, while Beatrice listens with a mien not unlike that of Mary as she stood at the foot of the Cross.

Then, changing color and flashing red with righteous anger, Beatrice quotes Christ's words to his disciples, which had left some wondering about the meaning of his strange prophecy (John 16. 16–18), and especially the word *modicum* ("a little while"). Christ had comforted them in their confusion (John 16. 20: "you shall be sorrowful, but your sorrow shall be turned to joy") and promised that the truth would be made manifest (John 16. 25: "the time is approaching, when I shall no longer speak to you in parables, but I shall tell you openly about the Father"). Likewise, Beatrice in Eden forecasts the coming of the eagle's heir and of a messenger sent by God to destroy the harlot and the giant. But soon—in Heaven (*Purg.* XXXIII. 100–102)—she will reveal the open truth about God and providence to the Pilgrim.

The literal level in the poem's economy is complemented by the allegorical sense whereby Beatrice speaks as the representative of Divine Wisdom and doctrine, announcing to the world that the Church in 1300 will soon be so corrupt that its divine inspiration will be blocked out and the papacy removed to Avignon. Nevertheless, surrounded by her seven handmaidens, she assures humanity that divine inspiration will soon return to and be made visible once again in Christ's Church on earth, the true *Ecclesia spiritualis*. In her long speech to Dante (ll. 51–78), culminating in the assertion placed at the center of the canto (ll. 71–72) that the tropological meaning of the tree signifies God's Justice, Beatrice tells the Pilgrim that the chariot "broken" by the serpent "was and is not," while the one responsible (literally, the serpent, dragon, or devil) must know that God's just punishment cannot be avoided.[80] In this echo of Rev. 17. 8, we may note that "the phrase 'bestia, quam vidisti, fuit et non est' ['the beast which you saw was and is not'] was applied by Joachim of Floris to the future liberation of the Church."[81] In lines 37–39, Beatrice asserts that the eagle, which had initiated the Church's decadence by leaving its features on the chariot, "will not always be without an heir"—and we know from *Convivio* IV.iii.6 that for Dante in 1300 the Empire was vacant:

> "ch'io veggio certamente, e però il narro,
> a darne tempo già stelle propinque,
> secure d'ogn' intoppo e d'ogne sbarro,
>   nel quale un cinquecento diece e cinque,
> messo di Dio, anciderà la fuia
> con quel gigante che con lei delinque."[82]

The two parts of the prophecy—"The eagle shall not be for all time without an heir" (ll. 37–38) and "a Five Hundred and Ten and Five . . . shall slay the thievish whore . . ."—are indissolubly and syntactically linked by the conjunction *che*, which would surely receive the diacritical marker *ché* in modern editions to indicate the meaning "for I can clearly see," a point further emphasized by the second part of line 40: "for I see plainly *and therefore I speak out*"). It may therefore seem strange, not to say perverse, to discover that scholars have not unanimously associated the "Five Hundred and Ten and Five," sent by Heaven, with the eagle's heir, in other words, an Emperor. On the other hand, the deciphering of riddles and prophecies in Dante's poem is never a straightforward matter; in this case, the relevant entry in the *Enciclopedia Dantesca* runs to no fewer than five pages.[83] From it we learn that the earliest commentators "regarded the DXV as an anagram of DUX, pointing generically . . . to a leader, emperor or prince, who would be sent by God to succor humanity led astray." Indeed, Dante's friend (most probably, the Florentine notary, Ser Andrea Lancia) states categorically: "What the Author has in mind is a great revolution of the heavens signifying the coming of a most just and most holy prince, who shall reform the state of the Church and of all faithful Christians."[84]

By taking into account Virgil's prophecy of the *veltro* ("greyhound"), who will save Italy and destroy the power of the *lupa* by sending her back to Hell (*Inf*. I. 100–11), Beatrice's announcement of the *Cinquecento diece e cinque* (*Purg*. XXXIII. 37–45), who will kill the giant and the whore, and St. Peter's forecast that God who willed that the universal Empire be given to Rome will intervene to save the world gone astray (*Par*. XXVII. 60–63), Professor Davis concludes:

> It seems clear . . . that Virgil . . . and Beatrice . . . [in] looking forward to the coming of a 515 who would be the heir of the Eagle, were looking forward to the coming of a secular leader powerful enough to imitate the achievement (which, according to Dante, had been unique) of the great Augustus: bringing peace to the whole world and especially to Italy. Who but an emperor could, in Dante's mind, assume such a role?[85]

Davis points out that the "messo di Dio" (*Purg*. XXXIII. 44) will be an extraordinary Emperor, whose task and accomplishments will transcend even those of Augustus by driving the wolf of cupidity back to her home in Hell. In the words just quoted from L'Ottimo, such an Emperor will be a "most just and most holy prince, who shall reform the state of the Church and of all faithful Christians." Thus harking back to Pietro di Dante's belief that his father may well have had in mind the *rex christianorum* prophesied by Methodius, Davis suggests that "the last ruler [Emperor] prophesied by the Tiburtine Sybil is an even more suitable model, since he will not merely defeat the Saracens and establish peace and prosperity but also convert the Moslems and the Jews. How else can the conquest of cupidity be complete?"[86] Moreover, we note that, owing to the influence of Joachite ideas, such prophecies had often been given a religious dimension, whereby the Last World Emperor took on the role not only of conqueror of the Antichrist but also that of reformer of the *Ecclesia carnalis*.[87] This tempo-

ral saviour would fit in with everything known about Dante's political and
religious thought, which leads Beatrice from the heights of Paradise to repeat the fundamental political message of the whole *Comedy*:

> "pensa che 'n terra non è chi governi;
> onde si svïa l'umana famiglia." [88]

To return to the DXV riddle, Gian Roberto Sarolli has given perhaps
the most detailed analysis of this crux. Taking his cue from the monogram
frequently placed before the *Prefatio* of the Mass, *Vere dignum et iustum est*,
and formed by the initials of the first two words (**VD**), joined together by
a cross (**X**), Professor Sarolli claims that Dante translated the christological
sign **VXD** into numbers and applied it to the ideal Emperor to come, thus
following the numerological technique employed by interpreters of the
Apocalypse—as well as by Dante himself in the *Vita Nuova*.[89] Following
the example of the Book of Revelation, where the number of the Beast "is
six hundred threescore and six" (Rev. 13. 18), the poet decided to place the
highest number first, thus reversing the order and giving D (*cinquecento*) X
(*diece*) V (*cinque*), while maintaining the link with the christological sign
through the concept of the Emperor regarded as *typus Christi*.[90]

The idea that the poet gave his letters in descending order would explain why he decided to place in the rhyming position the word "cinque,"
which, as Edward Moore pointed out in 1900, is used only once in the
whole *Comedy*. In fact, it is worthwhile to consider Moore's scepticism regarding the transposition of DXV into DVX ("a leader"):

> . . . if "Dux" were intended either exclusively or even primarily, why should not
> Dante have said,
>   "Un cinquecento cinque e diece," since "diece" would be a much easier
> rhyme? Thus, in the *Divina Commedia, -ece* occurs in ten *terzine*, and *-inque* in one
> only, viz. in the present passage.[91]

Moore comes to the conclusion that Henry VII is "the primary interpretation," and the "DVX" transliteration is "at most a subordinate one." [92]
Other scholars have categorically rejected the latter as an unwarranted
modification of what Dante actually wrote.[93]

Most scholars ignore or dismiss the fact that "DVX" was—as the late
Professor Renucci reminded us in 1965—"a term commonly used in Joachite prophecies, where the Last Emperor, whose task it will be to chastise
the corrupt Church, is specifically designated by the formula *novus DVX*." [94]
Renucci referred his readers to the seminal work by Norman Cohn, *The*

Pursuit of the Millennium, first published in 1957 (and on which my own conclusions are based). In a section entitled "Joachite Prophecy and Frederick II," Cohn stresses the all-pervading influence of a new prophetic system, "which was to be the most influential one known to Europe until the appearance of Marxism," specifically the one initiated by Joachim of Floris (1145–1202).[95] Quite apart from the vexed question whether or how far Dante was influenced by "the Calabrian abbot Joachim, who had the gift of prophecy" (*Par.* XII. 140–41), the idea of palingenesis, the need for reform (bolstered by elements taken from the Book of Revelation, and especially as these were developed by the Spiritual Franciscans), together with the belief that reformation would be accomplished by a temporal leader, obviously influenced the Florentine poet in exile.[96]

It is therefore pertinent to record the Joachite belief in the advent of "one supreme teacher, *novus dux*, who would lead all mankind away from the love of earthly things . . . ," a belief which, mingled with eschatological legends inspired by the figure of Frederick II, led to the expectation of "a saviour whose role now included the chastisement of the Church; a figure in whom the Emperor of the Last Days merged into the *novus dux* of Joachite prophecy."[97] If, as we have good reason to believe, this idea of a *novus dux* was accessible to Dante, we then have a strong possibility that the poet did in fact expect his ideal readers to read "cinquecento diece e cinque" not only as DXV but also as DVX.

Why, however, as Moore asked in 1900, did he not change his words to "cinquecento cinque e diece"? The answer, I would suggest, lies in the numerological significance of "cinquecento diece e cinque" and its fundamental connection with St. John's 666. In arabic numerals, 515 displays a central **5** flanked by two **1**s (while 515 subtracted from 666, the beast's number, gives the symmetrical transposition **515 > 151**).[98] The Pythagorean belief in the superiority of odd numbers over the even (*Conv.* II.xiii. 18) had been affirmed by Aristotle, Boethius, and others; and Dante found it expressed succinctly in Virgil's eighth Eclogue, in which the pagan sage had asserted that God Himself delights in the uneven numbers (l. 75: "numero Deus impare gaude"; cf. *DVE* I.xvi. 5). It is therefore possible to claim that, in the *Comedy*, the number 5 represents the perfection of the ideal rational human being (cf. *Conv.* IV. vii. 14–15). It is the number assigned to Solomon, the wisest of kings (*Par.* X. 109: "The fifth light, the most beautiful among us"), and to Rhipeus, the most just, fifth among the souls (*Par.* XX. 69) that appear to the Pilgrim in the Heaven of Justice, where the Eagle, "the blessed sign" of the Empire, admonishes all earthly rulers to love Justice above all else (with words taken from the opening of Solomon's Book of Wisdom).[99] DXV or 515 must therefore signify the ideal Emperor, who will combine human perfection with what Kantorowicz defines as "Christ-centered Kingship" and who—with the help of Christ or the 151, God and Man[100]—shall in his role as God's messenger destroy both the whore and the giant, restore justice on earth, and thus be the new DVX.

The Emperor to come will chastise the degenerate papacy and all opponents of the Empire, purging the former of its temporal possessions, the Eagle's feathers that were the source of its corruption. One of the cardinal beliefs of the Spiritual Franciscans was that a new Emperor would take away from the *Ecclesia carnalis* the poisonous gifts made to Christ's Church by the Emperor Constantine and others, and it is interesting to note that Benvenuto took up this idea in his commentary.[101] Whether or not this Emperor would be the Last Emperor is still open to conjecture. On the one hand, it is certainly true that Christ's Second Coming with the consequent end of time was regarded as imminent throughout the Middle Ages, with Dante echoing this belief in his *Convivio*.[102] On the other hand, in *Par*. XVII. 119–20, Dante speaks of "those who shall call this time ancient." Combined with Beatrice's assertion in *Par*. XXV. 52–53 that no Christian possessed to a fuller degree than Dante the theological virtue of hope, it is, I believe, impossible to decide whether the poet's prophecy of a reforming Emperor implied of necessity the idea that he would be the Last Ruler or whether Dante (as so often) adapted the various millennarian myths to suit his own purpose, which was to act as the prophet of a new Augustus—(*Mon*. I. xi. 12)—who, immune from greed, would usher in a golden age of peace and unity, as both St. Peter and Beatrice proclaim from the heights of Paradise:

> "Ma l'alta provvedenza, che con Scipio
> difese a Roma la gloria del mondo,
> soccorrà tosto, sí com'io concipio . . .
> . . . la fortuna che tanto s'aspetta
> le poppe volgerà u' son le prore,
> sí che la classe correrà diretta;
> e vero frutto verrà dopo 'l fiore."[103]

Beatrice realizes that her prophecy is obscure (*Purg*. XXXIII.46), but she assures the Pilgrim that events will soon clarify "this hard enigma" (l. 50); in the mean time, he must simply note her words and point out in what state he has seen the tree "which has now twice been despoiled here" (l. 57)—most probably, a reference to Adam's sin (*Purg.* XXXII. 37–39) and the giant's forceful removal of the chariot from the tree (to which it had been united by the Griffin, *Purg.* XXXII. 49–60, thus restoring the *pianta dispogliata* or "despoiled tree"). Here, Beatrice identifies this tree as the Tree of Knowledge desecrated by Adam, and—interpreted tropologically—it signifies God's Justice through the prohibition not to eat of its fruit (*Purg.* XXXIII. 58–72; cf. Genesis 1. 17).

The Pilgrim promises to tell the world what he has seen, but asks why he cannot understand Beatrice's prophecy, however much he struggles to make sense of her words. She tells him that this is to show him the worthlessness of the "school" he has followed, so that he may see for himself how helpless its teachings are to explain her message and how different the ways of the followers of that school are from the ways of God (ll. 85–90):

> "Perché conoschi", disse, "quella scuola
> c'hai seguitata, e veggi sua dottrina
> come può seguitar la mia parola;
>   e veggi vostra via da la divina
> distar cotanto, quanto si discorda
> da terra il ciel che piú alto festina." [104]

Which "school" had Dante followed? For once, commentators are virtually unanimous in claiming that it is the school of philosophy, whose teachings (*dottrina*) are rooted in the wisdom of this world, which is foolishness opposed to God's wisdom and its *sacra dottrina* (1 Corinthians 3.19).

Instead, I would agree with Parodi that the word *scuola* alludes to the fact that in 1300 as a member of a fiercely independent Guelf Commune, Dante followed a school of thought that was incapable of understanding that the Empire, no less than the Church, was of divine origin.[105] I must also add that I cannot understand why the teachings of philosophy should be an obstacle to an understanding of Beatrice's words in lines 31–72 and their relevance to what the Pilgrim has just witnessed. I discard the idea that the author of the *Comedy* had turned away from philosophy; such a rejection is utterly incompatible with his description of himself in 1315 as a disciple of philosophy (*Ep.* XII. iii. 6) and his placing of Siger of Brabant in Heaven (*Par.* X, 136–38)—to which must be added the evidence of the very last pages of the *Monarchia*, in which the Emperor's task is specifically to guide humanity to Eden (i.e., blessedness in this life) according to the teachings of philosophy. In fact, training in the investigation of philosophical truths, such as Dante had received in "the schools of the religious" (*Conv.* II. xii. 7), would surely have helped him to understand the spectacle revealed in his Eden of the progressive corruption of the Church after the Donation of Constantine as well as the tragedy of the removal of the papacy to Avignon under the wing of the French monarchy.

Above all, the study of philosophy would have encouraged the Pilgrim to acknowledge the providential role played by the Eagle/Empire in history. Beatrice's words merely highlight the overall lesson, illustrating the tragic fortunes of the historical Church and driving home the need for a reformed Church, immune to greed and the pitfalls of temporal power and wealth, ready and able to offer spiritual guidance and co-operation with the Emperor. The tree, which God sanctified "solely for His use" (*Purg.* XXXIII. 60), may not signify the Empire; it is nevertheless true that the Eagle should nest in the tree of God's Justice and thereby demonstrate the divinely-instituted link between the latter and the Emperor (cf. *Par.* VI. 88).[106]

Let me stress once more that the triptych in Eden consists of an autobiographical central episode (Cantos XXX–XXXI), flanked by two panels, each illustrating a pageant of universal significance: God's providential workings from Creation to Apocalypse in Canto XXIX, paralleled by—and implicitly contrasted with—the universal tragedy of sin and the corruption of Christ's Church as portrayed in Canto XXXII. The same nexus between individual experience and God's universal truths is present in Beatrice's words: "Perché conoschi . . . quella scuola / *c'hai seguitata* . . . / e veggi *vostra via* da la divina / distar cotanto . . ." (ll. 85–89; my emphasis).[107]—It is not Dante's love of philosophy (hardly a universal predilection!) that is implied by the plural "vostra via," the ways of erring human beings on earth; instead, it should remind us of the only specific confession ever made by Dante. This is found at the beginning of the second book of the *Monarchia*, which opens with a highly significant quotation from the second Psalm:

What means this turmoil among the nations? Why do the peoples cherish vain dreams? See how the kings of the earth stand in array, how its rulers make common cause against the Lord, and against the King he has anointed, crying: "Let us break away from their bondage, rid ourselves of the toils!" (*Mon.* II. i. 1)

In Dante's text (and in the Vulgate cited by him) the phrase "against the King he has anointed" bears the highly charged words *adversus Christum eius*.[108] After quoting this sacred text, Dante makes his confession:

I must admit that there was a time when I too was struck with wonder at the fact that the Roman people had managed to acquire dominion over the whole world without encountering any valid resistance—because, looking at things in a purely superficial way, I believed that they had achieved such universal dominion merely through force of arms and not by right [*illum nullo iure sed armorum tantummodo violentia obtinuisse arbitrabar*]. However, after turning my mind's eyes to scrutinize the question and realizing from incontrovertible signs that divine providence was in fact the cause, my wonder gave way to a certain scornful contempt at the thought that the nations had been able to rise up against the supremacy of the Roman people, while I also saw others imagining vain things (as formerly I too had done) and—what is more—I was struck with sorrow at the fact that kings and rulers were united in one thing alone, in opposing their Lord, their Anointed One, the Roman Emperor. (*Mon.* II. i. 2–3)

Although it is well known, I doubt that this confession (I repeat: the only specific one found in Dante's writings) has been accorded its due importance.[109]

The author of the *Inferno* took great pains to show the Pilgrim as he himself truly was in 1300, enmeshed in Guelf party politics. The most obvious example is to be found in the Pilgrim's aggressive reaction to Farinata degli Uberti's proud boast that he had twice exiled Dante's Guelf ancestors. The Pilgrim's riposte (*Inf.* X. 49–51) causes the Ghibelline leader greater suffering than his infernal bed (ll. 77–78). At that stage in his life, Dante believed—as did St. Augustine (*De Civitate Dei* XIV. 28) and the Guelf extremists—that the power of Rome and her Empire was not obtained "by virtue of reason or a decree of a council representing the whole of humankind but by force, which seems opposed to reason." (*Conv.* IV. iv. 8). It was this "school," with its rejection of the Empire's providential mission in God's plan for the world, that had led to the tragedy of 1312–13, when Henry VII arrived to set Italy straight before she was ready (*Par.* XXX. 137–38), while the peoples of the peninsula cherished vain thoughts and "kings and rulers were united in one thing alone, in opposing their Lord, their Anointed One, the Roman Emperor" (*Mon.* II. i. 3). In this, their way —*vostra via*, as Beatrice calls it in *Purg.* XXXIII. 88—inspired by the beliefs that Dante had shared in 1300 (*ut ipse solebam*), was truly as distant from God's providential design as this earth is from the highest heaven (l. 90).

After his conversion and before he began to write the *Comedy*, Dante came to realize how terribly mistaken he had been: he now saw that the Empire was not only founded on Justice, but that only under the Emperor could Justice reign supreme on earth (*Mon.* I. xi. 2, 8, 13, 19). This is in fact the central lesson of the tableau described in Canto XXXII, in which the Griffin—representing the ideal Empire—provides the essential link between divine, natural, and earthly Justice by binding the chariot to God's Tree, thus restoring it to health (*Purg*. XXXII.43–60). As we have observed, this symbolic renewal of justice and harmony on earth is then shattered in the six catastrophic stages that culminate in the picture of universal corruption dominated by the evil force of the Giant exemplifying both the anti-imperial house of France and the Antichrist.

The Pilgrim records this lesson "for the sake of the world that lives badly" (*Purg*. XXXII. 103), although it could not be comprehended by him as he truly was in 1300. He followed the school of thought then which, by maintaining that the Roman Empire had been acquired unjustly (*nullo iure*), denied the very premise on which the Empire was founded by God: namely, that the foundation of the Empire is human justice (*Imperii fundamentum ius humanum est: Mon*. III. x.8). Moreover, the Roman Empire's mission of justice was willed by God, and justice on earth is but a reflection of the divine will (*ius in rebus nichil est aliud quam similitudo divine voluntatis: Mon*. II. ii. 5). However, all memory of the Pilgrim's errors has been washed away by the waters of Lethe; now, after being led by the Cardinal and Theological Virtues, he drinks of the River Eunoë thereby reviving the memory of his good works. Like a tree renewed in its foliage (and like God's Tree of Justice renewed by the Griffin's action), the fully justified Pilgrim is ready to begin his ascent to God (ll. 142–45):

> Io ritornai da la santissima onda
> rifatto sí come piante novelle
> rinovellate di novella fronda,
>   puro e disposto a salire a le stelle.[110]

Conclusion

THE READER MAY NOW GAZE BACK AT THE whole range of Dante's second *cantica*, the section of the poem that offers "the most truthful portrayal of the human condition."[1] This is so not merely because the *Purgatorio* is the only part of the poem subject to time and change, but also because it portrays "public figures, statesmen, poets" who "embody political virtues" set squarely within a social and political context.[2] The *Inferno* has comparatively little to say about the relationship between Church and Empire (although traitors to the founders of both institutions are punished in the jaws of Satan). The *Paradiso* will focus more and more on the need to reform the corrupt Church (although never abandoning the political diagnosis and remedy most clearly stated in *Pur.* XVI).

Instead, the central part of Dante's poem, composed most probably at some time between 1310 and 1314 — and therefore set against the backdrop of Henry VII's tragic enterprise — is replete with the poet's vital political message. This is particularly evident in the encounter with Cato (symbolizing the cardinal virtues of Republican Rome, on which God founded his Empire), the meeting with Sordello (Italy's subjection to anarchy and self-destruction; the Negligent Rulers) and with Hugh Capet (the Pope's crucifixion at Anagni); finally, in the pageant of Church, Empire, and France witnessed in the Earthly Paradise. This closing scene culminates in the portrayal of the papacy's Babylonian exile at Avignon and the prophecy of a temporal saviour who shall destroy universal corruption and restore justice on earth. The author of the *Comedy* is not inspired to reveal religious mysteries or dogma. Instead, he is charged with a divinely inspired mission to announce the imminent arrival of a messenger from God on the political plane (which must perforce include the religious plane as well) who shall set the Christian fleet on its proper course toward the harbor of temporal safety.

To return once more to the poem's trinitarian symmetry, we find that at three major landmarks in his second *cantica* Dante took care to highlight the essential need for a right ordering of this world, something he was convinced could be attained only when the supreme spiritual and political authorities labored together in harmony according to God's plan: in Ante-purgatory (*Purg.* VI. 91–96); once in Purgatory proper (*Purg.* XVI. 97–114); and a third time in the Earthly Paradise (*Purg.* XXXII. 48–60). That lesson will be triumphantly illustrated in Paradise. We find exalted (*Par.* VI. 22–24) the ideal collaboration between Justinian, Emperor and law-giver, and Pope Agapetus, who converted the Emperor from his mono-physite heresy, thus enabling the Just-One to carry out his God-given task of refitting humanity's bridle (*Purg.* VI. 88–89). In preparation for this, the Pilgrim watches in Eden the spectacle of human history, from creation to apocalypse, and the momentous consequences of obedience and disobedi-ence to God's will as it shines through, or is eclipsed, with His two suns, created by Him to light up the way to happiness in this life and the next.

Dante, as always, raises up the particular and invests it with univer-sal significance *in pro del mondo che mal vive*, in a desperate attempt to save errant humanity from its precipitous path toward chaos in this life and eternal damnation in the world to come. After the Pilgrim's purification in Purgatory, his role as a poet-prophet or *vates* receives its solemn investi-ture in Eden, where humanity had once enjoyed a state of original Justice and happiness and where it now faces an apocalyptic cataclysm. No one before Dante had seen in the myth of Eden a symbol of the "political" goal for humanity on earth. No one had placed the Earthly Paradise next to—and above—Purgatory. In his *Purgatorio* Dante achieved a unique fusion of political and religious elements that is emblematic of Dante's world vision as expressed in his poetic masterpiece.

Notes

Chapter 1. Dante's Political Experience (1265–1302)

1. Cf. W. Ullmann, *Medieval Political Thought* (Harmondsworth, 1975), 16: "We view human activities from certain angles and put them into more or less neatly confined departments . . . we speak of religious, moral, political, economic norms. . . . But this atomization of the norms determining human actions is of rather recent date. For the larger part of the Middle Ages there was no such splitting up of human actions into different compartments . . . religion was not separated from politics, politics not separated from morals."

2. For accounts of the overall situation, see C. T. Davis, *Dante's Italy and Other Essays* (Philadelphia, 1984), 1–22; J. Larner, *Italy in the Age of Dante and Petrarch: 1216–1380* (London, 1980), esp. 38–54; J. H. Mundy, *Europe in the High Middle Ages: 1150–1309* (London, 1973); N. G. Pounds, *An Economic History of Medieval Europe* (London, 1974), 313–433. D. Waley, *Late Medieval Europe: From St. Louis to Luther* (London, 1975), 34, warns: "To interpret the history of twelfth- and thirteenth-century Europe as 'the struggle of pope and emperor' is to impart a fictitious unity to a complicated theme and, above all, to neglect the feeble temporal resources of these two contestants." He points out that "After Frederick's death (1250) the Italian political scene lacked a pattern; the cities were like filings meaninglessly dispersed after the removal of a magnetic source." It is perhaps interesting to recall that in the sixteenth century Guicciardini (*Considerazioni intorno ai Discorsi del Machiavelli* I. 12) claimed that it was normal for Italy not to be united under one central government, which would have inhibited the wealth and variety of the regions.

3. J. N. Najemy, "Dante and Florence," in *The Cambridge Companion to Dante*, ed. R. Jacoff (Cambridge, 1993), 87–88. Najemy points out, moreover, that "when Dante attempts in the *Commedia* and elsewhere, to give some idea of the principles and assumptions that he considers fundamental to a properly organized society, he does so in the language of the *popolo*" (93).

4. *Inf.* III. 58–60. Cf. M. Picchio Simonelli, *Lectura Dantis Americana: Inferno III* (Philadelphia, 1993). It should be remembered that all the earliest commentators (Jacopo, the poet's son; his brother Pietro, in the first version of his commentary; Graziolo de' Bambaglioli; Guido da Pisa; Jacopo della Lana) were categorical in their identification of Celestine. We must also bear in mind the fact that *Inferno* III was most probably written c. 1308, years before Celestine was canonized (May 1313, after years of French anti-Bonifacian pressure), while a contemporary must have been intended by the poet—witness the pilgrim-narrator's im-

mediate recognition (59: *vidi e conobbi*, "I saw and I recognized") and the author's assumption that the *gran rifiuto* or "great refusal" (60) would easily be deciphered by his audience in the first years of the fourteenth century.

5. See the poem *Che farai, Pier da Morrone?* in Jacopone da Todi, *Laude*, ed. F. Mancini (Bari, 1974), 218–20. From Dante's anti-French, anti-Angevin standpoint, Celestine's policies had been a total disaster: with only seven cardinals in the Sacred College, he created twelve new members, of whom no less than five were French. Moreover, Celestine poured huge sums into the Angevin coffers to finance Charles II's war in Sicily.

6. On this topic see the fine essay "Poverty and Eschatology in the *Commedia*," in C. T. Davis, *Dante's Italy*, 42–70.

7. Dante was inevitably conditioned by some of the legalistic aspects of western Christianity. However, he strongly condemned the desire for monetary gain that all too often inspired the study of Canon Law (*Conv.* III. xi. 10) and, in particular, denounced the way contemporary churchmen neglected the Gospels and the Church Fathers in order to exploit the decretals (to which Boniface VIII added the *Liber sextus* in 1298): cf. *Par.* IX. 133–38, XI. 82–85; *Ep.* VIII. vii. 6; *Mon.* III. iii. 9–16.

8. G. Barraclough, *The Medieval Papacy* (London, 1968), 142.

9. For Brunetto's attitude toward the Empire, see lines 6–11 of his dedication of his *Tesoretto* to Alfonso the Wise (elected Emperor in 1260), and A. Pézard's judgment, *Dante sous la pluie de feu* (Paris, 1950), 42: "Dante's master was therefore irreproachable in his political views." R. Kay, however, argues (*Dante's Swift and Strong: Essays on "Inferno" XV* [Lawrence, Kansas, 1978], 11, 21) that the author of the *Comedy* placed Brunetto among those who sinned against Nature, because he was one of those "politicians" who refused "to recognize the natural authority of the empire"; moreover, in 1281, "he had perverted his profession of rhetoric by turning it against the natural lord of the world, the Roman emperor."

10. *Il Tesoro di Brunetto Latini volgarizzato da Bono Giamboni* (Bologna, 1880), III, 479–80. See also Brunetto Latini, *Li livres dou Tresor*, ed. F. J. Carmody (Berkeley-Los Angeles, 1948), II. 120 ("De Glore," 303): "glory gives a second life to the good man, that is to say after his death the renown of his good works makes him appear to be still alive."

11. C. T. Davis, *Dante's Italy*, 191.

12. *Il "Commentarium" di Pietro Alighieri nelle redazioni ashburnhamiana e ottoboniana*, ed. R. Della Vedova and M. T. Silvotti (Florence, 1978), 256.

13. E. H. Kantorowicz, *The King's Two Bodies: A Study in Medieval Political Theology* (Princeton, N.J., 1957), 245.

14. C. T. Davis, "An Early Florentine Political Theorist: Fra Remigio de' Girolami," *Proceedings of the American Philosophical Society* 104, 6 (1960), 662–75.

15. J. P. Canning, "Introduction: Politics, Institutions and Ideas," in *The Cambridge History of Medieval Political Thought, c. 350–c. 1450*, ed. J. H. Burns (Cambridge, 1991), 360.

16. On Remigio and Dante, see note 19. Also C. T. Davis, *Dante's Italy*, 157–65, 198–223, 260–62, 279–81; L. Minio-Paluello, "Remigio Girolami's *De bono communi*," *Italian Studies* 11 (1956), 56–71.

17. C. T. Davis, "An Early Florentine Political Theorist: Fra Remigio de' Girolami."

18. The reader of the *Comedy* will recall that the family straddles the three realms of the afterlife in Dante's poem: Corso, destined for Hell in 1308 (*Purg.* XXIV. 82–87); Forese in Purgatory (*Purg.* XXIII–XXIV), where his exchange with the pilgrim constitutes one of the outstanding autobiographical episodes in the whole *Comedy*; and the gentle figure of Piccarda, saved according to *Paradiso* III.

19. D. Compagni (*Cronica* I. 27) offers yet another example of the Cerchi's political naivety: "Their enemies began to slander them among the Guelfs, saying that they were colluding with the Aretines, Pisans, and the Ghibellines. And this was not true . . . but they did not deny this to their critics, thinking that they would be the more feared and thus overcome them, saying: 'They will fear us all the more, since they will be afraid that we may join them [the Ghibellines], while these will love us the more, having hope in us.'" J. M. Najemy, "Dante and Florence," 81, claims that "Why some families ended up among the so-called Blacks . . . and others among the White Guelfs . . . is one of the great mysteries of Florentine history. No clear demarcation of ideology, economic interest, or class has ever been demonstrated as the cause of the split. . . . It is usually claimed that Dante belonged to the party of faction of the Whites, which is accurate to the extent that he held a number of important posts during the year and a half of White dominance early 1300 . . . until the fall of 1301."

20. *CDD*, no. 73. G. Holmes, "Dante and the Popes," 25: "One of the pope's later complaints about Florence was that the *Tallia* had not yet been organized. The other evidence suggests that this was a misrepresentation: the Florentines had been actively promoting it, and it was held up by the usual reluctance of the smaller communes to contribute. Boniface was either blind or misinformed about the real aims of the Florentine government."

21. "Tutti li mali e l'inconvenienti miei dalli infausti comizi del mio priorato ebbono cagione e principio" (*Le vite di Dante, Petrarca e Boccaccio*, ed. A. Solerti [Milan, 1904], 100).

22. G. Holmes, "Dante and the Popes," 26. B. Barbadoro, "La condanna di Dante e le fazioni politiche del suo tempo," *Studi Danteschi* 2 (1920), 35ff., puts forward the convincing hypothesis that Dante also spoke out against Charles of Valois' requests in the Council of One Hundred on 15 March 1301. On 27 January 1302, Dante and others were accused of fraud and barratry against the Florentine Commune, that they had used their political office and ill-gotten gains in order to oppose the Pope and Charles of Valois, and against the peace of Florence and the Guelf party (*CDD*, no. 90; *Il processo di Dante*, ed. D. Ricci [Florence, 1967], 205).

23. D. Compagni, *Cronica*, II. 25, lists among the White leaders condemned in 1302 "Dante Alighieri who was ambassador at Rome." G. Petrocchi, *La selva del protonotaro* (Naples, 1988), 37, suggests Compagni was in fact referring to the fact that Dante had been a member of the Florentine embassy to the Pope in November 1300, and claims that Dante visited Rome on two occasions (42). P. Armour, *The Door of Purgatory: A Study of Multiple Symbolism in Dante's "Purgatorio"* (Oxford, 1983), 173ff., takes up the idea that Dante had been sent with Lapo Saltarelli and others to Rome in March–April 1300.

24. For the text of the sentences (from 1302 to 1315), see: *CDD*, nos. 90–91 and 115, or *Il processo di Dante*, 204–22.

Chapter 2. Dante's Political Experience: Exile and Conversion (1302–1305)

1. Cf. *Par.* XVII. 70–75. For the chronology, see G. Petrocchi, *Vita di Dante* (Bari, 1983), 94–95, his *Itinerari danteschi* (Bari, 1969), 119–28, his biography in *ED* VI, 32–33, and *La selva del protonotaro* (Naples, 1988), 59–62.

2. Cf. D. Matthew, *Atlas of Medieval Europe* (Oxford, 1983), 119. For a bibliography on Frederick II, see J. Larner, *Italy in the Age of Dante and Petrarch*, 36, to which may be added D. Abulafia, *Frederick II: A Medieval Emperor* (London, 1988). For Dante and Frederick, see A. Vallone, "La componente federiciana della cultura Dantesca," in *Dante e Roma* (Florence, 1965), 347–69; P. Renucci, "Dante e gli Svevi," in *Dante e l'Italia meridionale* (Florence, 1966), 131–47; G. Tarugi, "Federico II e il suo umanesimo," in *Dante e la cultura sveva* (Florence, 1970), 207–30. For an evaluation of the pontificate of Innocent III (1198–1216), see C. Morris, *The Papal Monarchy: The Western Church from 1050 to 1250* (Oxford, 1989), especially 430: "Innocent III involved himself in political actions to a greater extent than previous popes"; as well as Morris's judgment: "The thirteenth century was the high point of the papal monarchy" (569).

3. Of the formula *indignus haeres beati Petri*, Ullmann writes (*Medieval Political Thought*, 25): "It is a formula which, because it was so succinct, has not yet been properly appreciated." For the title "Vicar of Christ," see the exhaustive study by M. Maccarrone, *"Vicarius Christi": storia del titolo papale* (Rome, 1952). As C. T. Davis (*Dante's Italy*, 63–65) points out, Dante shared some of the views of the Spiritual Franciscans. Like Petrus Johannis Olivi, the poet accepted Boniface's legitimacy, whereas Ubertino da Casale (*Par.* XII. 124–26) condemned Boniface as a usurper and personification of the Antichrist.

4. For the texts of Boniface's *Allegatio* and Albert's *Promissio*, see *MGH* 4:1, 139–55.

5. For the texts, see B. Tierney, *The Crisis of Church and State: 1050–1300* (Englewood Cliffs, N.J., 1980), 185–86; and *Les Registres de Boniface VIII*, 3: col. 328–32; P. Dupuy, *Histoire du différence d'entre le pape Boniface VIII et Philippe le Bel Roy de France* (Paris, 1655), 48. For a detailed account of the struggle, see G. Digard, *Philippe le Bel et le Saint-Siège de 1285 à 1304*, 2 vols. (Paris, 1936); J. Rivière, *Le Problème de l'Église et de l'État au temps de Philippe le Bel* (Louvain-Paris, 1926); and J. Favier, *Philippe le Bel* (Paris, 1988).

6. C. Mitchell, "The Lateran Fresco of Boniface VIII," *Journal of the Warburg and Courtauld Institutes* 14 (1951), 3.

7. All quotations from *Unam sanctam* are taken from B. Tierney, *The Crisis of Church and State*, 189.

8. Tierney, 182.

9. Traditionally, from the collapse of the Roman Empire in the West, relations between the spiritual and temporal authorities had been governed—in theory—by the "Gelasian" principle. This was based on a theoretical separation of

the two powers, outlined in a letter sent by Pope Gelasius I in 492 to the eastern Emperor Anastasius: "The world is chiefly governed by these two: the sacred authority of bishops and the royal power . . . although you rule over the human race in dignity, you nevertheless devoutly bow the neck to those who are placed in charge of religious matters and seek from them the means of your salvation." Gelasius stressed the complementary nature of the two powers (see *Cambridge History of Political Thought: c. 350–c. 1450*, 288–89).

10. *Inf.* XXVIII. 96–102. As is well known, Curio had been swayed by Caesar's gold. Nevertheless, the responsibility for waging civil war in 1304 must have weighed heavily on Dante's conscience (and it may have hastened his break with the other White exiles). Despite the assertions of commentators, however, there is in fact no real contradiction between Curio's words as reported in *Inferno* XXVIII and those same words used by Dante in the exhortation to Emperor Henry VII in *Ep.* VII. 4. 16. Scholars have simply failed to grasp the fact that the words attributed to Curio by Lucan, "Make haste; delay is ever fatal to those who are prepared" (*Pharsalia* I. 281), were frequently quoted by medieval encyclopedists as a spur to *magnanimitas* (in the sense of the courage needed to undertake great exploits in the face of dangerous odds): e.g., Brunetto Latini, *Li Livres dou Tresor* II. 82 ("De Magnanimité": 261), "Lucan says, remove all delay, for it always harms those who are ready to act."

11. *Par.* XVII. 62–69: "the evil, stupid company . . . will turn against you in their wicked madness and ingratitude . . . but their fate will bear witness to their bestiality . . . so that it will be to your credit to have formed a party for yourself alone." E. Peters points out that Cacciaguida's prophecy that Dante will make a party for himself "is *not* honorific. It is certainly not, as some commentators have read it, a kind of paean to Dante's romantic political individualism" but "the honor that exists in the face of the shame of factionalism, not an honor that justifies it" ("*Pars, Parte*: Dante and an Urban Contribution to Political Thought," in *The Medieval City*, ed. H. A. Miskimin et al. [New Haven, Conn., 1977], 116).

12. A. Passerin d'Entrèves, *Dante as a Political Thinker* (Oxford, 1952), 34.

13. J. A. Scott, "Politics and *Inferno X*," *Italian Studies* 19 (1964), 1–13, and *Dante magnanimo*, 47–73. Regarding Dante's denunciation of Florence and his fellow-citizens in the *Comedy*, it is important to realize that "much of what at first glance seems to be Dante's polemic against Florence is actually directed against its upper class of large, rich, and politically influential families, the class that led the city into two tragic periods of civil conflict" (J. Najemy, "Dante's Florence," 87).

14. A. Passerin d'Entrèves, *Dante as a Political Thinker*, 32–33.

15. A. Passerin d'Entrèves, 76–97.

16. *DVE* I. xii. 4 (cf. Ulysses' stirring call to his men in *Inf.* XXVI. 118–20: "Consider your origins: you were not made to live like brutes, but to follow virtue and knowledge"). The *terminus ante quem* for this section is provided by the reference in *DVE* I. xii. 5 to the Marquis Giovanni of Monferrato as still alive (he died in February 1305).

17. P. V. Mengaldo, *DVE* (Naples, 1979), 2: 100–101, n. 2.

18. J. L. Huilliard-Bréholles, *Historia diplomatica Friderici II* (Paris, 1854), 4: 1, 384: "totum in lectionis exercitatione gratuite libenter expendimus, *ut anime*

clarius vigeat instrumentum in acquisitione scientie, sine qua mortalium vita non regitur liberaliter" (emphasis mine).

19. B. Nardi, *Dante e la cultura medievale* (Bari, 1942), 176–209; *Nel mondo di Dante* (Rome, 1944), 41–90; *Dal "Convivio" alla "Commedia": sei saggi danteschi* (Rome, 1960), 37–83; *Saggi di filosofia dantesca* (Florence, 1967), 341–80. In a stimulating study (*Dante a un nuovo crocevia*, Florence, 1981), Maria Corti claims that in the *De Vulgari Eloquentia* Dante was greatly influenced by the theories on language and speculative grammar propounded by Boethius of Dacia, who was, with Siger of Brabant, the leading representative of radical Aristotelianism in western Europe.

20. For the text of the *De pomo*, see B. Nardi, *"Lecturae" e altri studi Danteschi* (Florence, 1990), 113–25.

21. While an *argumentum ex silentio* is inevitably fragile, I would suggest that the absence of any direct criticism of the papacy (but not of the populace governed by contemporary popes) is due to both the subject matter of the *De Vulgari Eloquentia* and the moment of its composition: the work's primary purpose is the quest for an illustrious Italian vernacular. Dante wrote it (c. 1304) at a time when the pontificate of Benedict XI (22 October 1303–July 1304) held out great hope for the return to Florence of the White and Ghibelline exiles (cf. Villani's judgment on this "wise man who led a holy life": *Cronica*, IX. 86).

22. For the most convincing explanation of this phrase, see A. P. d'Entrèves, *Dante as a Political Thinker*, 96: "The gracious light of reason can and must unite the Italians in revealing to them what is the greatest and strongest bond of a nation: the unity of language."

23. *De Vulgari Eloquentia*, ed. A. Marigo (Florence, 1968), 155–56, n. 29. For the teleological process whereby God willed that Rome should be founded and then become the seat of world empire as well as "the holy place where the successor of great Peter has his seat" (*Inf.* II. 20–24), see: C. T. Davis, *Dante and the Idea of Rome*, passim.

24. *Purg.* VI. 112–14: "Come and see your Rome in tears, widowed and alone, crying out: 'My Caesar, why are you not here with me?'"

25. F. Ercole, for example, claimed (*Il pensiero politico di Dante* [Milan, 1927]) that at the time of writing the *De Vulgari Eloquentia* Dante pinned his hopes on national unity embodied in the *regnum italicum*. Ercole's thesis won favor with M. Barbi, *Problemi fondamentali per un nuovo commento della Divina Commedia* (Florence, 1956), 69–89, but was subjected to detailed criticism by B. Sumner, "Dante and the *Regnum Italicum*," *Medium Aevum*, I (1932), 2–23, and refuted by B. Nardi in *Saggi di filosofia dantesca* (Milan-Genoa-Rome-Naples, 1930), 239–345. Nevertheless, the idea lingers of an intermediate stage when the poet was concerned primarily with an Italian kingdom (see, e.g., the inaccuracies in A. Marigo's introduction to his edition of the *DVE*, lxxxii–iv).

26. G. Petrocchi (*Vita di Dante*, 98) suggests that at the time of this ignominious defeat Dante was probably in Arezzo, where Petrarch, the son of a friend and fellow exile, was born on 20 July 1304.

27. *Inf.* XV. 70–72: "Your fortune reserves for you the honor of being hungered after by both parties; but the grass will be far from the hungry beak."

Chapter 3. Exul Inmeritus *(1305–1321)*

1. Both quotations in G. Holmes, *Florence, Rome and the Origins of the Renaissance* (Oxford, 1988), 184–85.

2. C. T. Davis, *Dante and the Idea of Rome*, 267. In fact, Clement repeatedly announced his intention of going to Italy. G. Mollat, in *The Popes at Avignon: 1305–1378* (New York, 1965), xx, summarizes well his reasons for not doing so: "the need to put an end to the suit brought against Boniface VIII and to wind up the trial of the Templars [1312] . . . the imminence of the crusade . . . the attempts at conciliation between France and England, and above all . . . the unsettled state of Italy," to which must be added the ill-health that plagued him during the whole of his pontificate, and became acute just after the end of the Council of Vienne (6 May 1312; on 9 June, Clement dictated his will). It should also be noted that medieval Popes were often away from Rome; in fact, according to V. H. R. Green, *Medieval Civilization in Western Europe* (London, 1971), 126, the pontiffs spent a total of "one hundred and twenty-two years away and eighty-two in the city between 1100 and 1304."

3. *Inf.* XIX. 82–87: "there will come from the west a lawless shepherd of filthier deeds, such that he will fittingly cover both him [Boniface VIII] and me. He will be a new Jason, like the one of whom we read in Maccabees; and just as the latter was compliant to his king, so will he be towards the one who rules France."

4. G. Holmes, *Florence, Rome*, 182. E. Renan judged this change in the balance of power in the Sacred College to be "one of the most abrupt revolutions recorded in ecclesiastical history" (quoted by G. Mollat, *The Popes at Avignon*, 6).

5. Cf. G. Petrocchi, *Vita di Dante*, 98–99; P. Renucci, *Dante, disciple et juge du monde gréco-latin* (Paris, 1954), 87. Dante displays a remarkable acquaintance with the nuances of Bolognese speech in *DVE* I. ix. 4. A first visit to Bologna before his exile (c. 1286–87) is probable: cf. *Rime*, LI. It is highly unlikely that the exiled poet could have revisited Bologna after 1306, when the city became fiercely Guelf; it later opposed Henry VII and became a place where Dante feared for his safety (*Eclogue* IV). M. Corti, while emphasizing the ideological and chronological "break" between the first three books and Book IV of the *Convivio*, makes the well-argued claim that at some time, "during the composition of the *De Vulgari Eloquentia* and Book IV of the *Convivio*, Dante must have gone to Bologna" (*La felicità mentale: nuove prospettive per Cavalcanti e Dante* [Turin, 1983], 132).

6. For a detailed survey of the exegesis of *Inf.* I. 63, see R. Hollander, *Il Virgilio dantesco: tragedia nella "Commedia"* (Florence, 1983), 23–79. For Dante's own use of an allegorical interpretation of Virgil's epic, see *Conv.* IV. xxiv. 9, where this medieval incrustation has its origin in Fabius Fulgentius Planciades (c. 480–550), *Expositio virgilianae continentiae*.

7. Cf. *Aeneid* I. 278–79: "His ego nec metas rerum nec tempora pono: / imperium sine fine dedi." Dante rejects the Augustinian view of the Empire as founded on force, which he himself had accepted in earlier years (cf. *Mon.* II. i. 2–3, and chapter 10), as well as Augustine's claim that Virgil was guilty of mere adulation, placed in the mouth of a lying god (see *PL* 38. 622–23).

8. The first scholar to pinpoint this valuable evidence was Ulrich Leo, to whom we are all much indebted. See his "The Unfinished *Convivio* and Dante's Rereading of the *Aeneid*," first published in 1951 and reprinted in U. Leo, *Sehen und Wirklichkeit bei Dante (mit einem Nachtrag über das Problem der Literaturgeschichte)* (Frankfurt-am-Main, 1957), 71–104.

9. U. Leo, "The Unfinished *Convivio*," 98–99. For Cacciaguida as a father-figure in Dante's poem, see M. De Rosa, *Dante e il padre ideale* (Naples, 1990).

10. Cited in R. Hollander, *Allegory in Dante's "Commedia"* (Princeton, 1969), 257. See also his closely argued "Dante *Theologus-Poeta*," in his *Studies in Dante* (Ravenna, 1980), especially 71: "perhaps the most important thing, for his own poetic development, which Dante learned from the *Aeneid* was . . . how to compose a narrative poem which describes actions as though they were historical, to compose a fiction that is intended to be taken as historically true." For Virgil's poem as the "Bible of the Empire," see "Dante profeta," in B. Nardi, *Dante e la cultura medievale*, 301, and M. Frankel, "Dante's Conception of the Ideology of the *Aeneid*," in *Proceedings of the Xth Congress of the International Comparative Literature Association* (New York-London, 1985), 406: "for Dante the *Aeneid* contains a religious message, an anticipation of Christian revelation. . . . Just as the Old Testament was adopted by Christian theologians and re-interpreted to make it conform to Christian Revelation, so does Dante retrieve and reinterpret the pagan poem to disclose a Christian subtext."

11. R. Hollander, *Studies in Dante*, 50–51.

12. For all aspects of this central episode in Dante's exile, see the standard work by W. M. Bowsky, *Henry VII in Italy: The Conflict of Empire and City-State (1310–1313)* (Lincoln, Neb. 1960).

13. D. Compagni, *Cronica* III. 35 (cf. Villani, *Cronica* IX. 120). For the "clear statement of policy" contained in the reply of 1281, see: A. Passerin d'Entrèves, *Dante as a Political Thinker*, 22, who quotes the declaration: "The Commune of Florence has never given allegiance to any emperor: it has always been free" (*Nunquam Comune Florentie fidelitatem fecit alicui imperatori . . . quia semper vixit et fuit liberum*).

14. W. M. Bowsky, *Henry VII in Italy*, 46–47.

15. *Ep.* V. x. 30: "Hic est quem Petrus, Dei vicarius, honorificare nos monet; quem Clemens, nunc Petri successor, luce Apostolice benedictionis illuminat; ut ubi radius spiritualis non sufficit, ibi splendor minoris luminaris illustret."

16. *Ep.* V. vi. 17: "a quo velut a puncto biffurcatur Petri Cesarisque potestas." The point is reinforced in ix. 27: "He [Christ] divided all things between Himself and Caesar, as though marking out two kingdoms, by saying 'give unto each the things that are his'" (cf. Matthew 22. 21 and *Purg.* VI. 91–93).

17. E. H. Kantorowicz, *The King's Two Bodies: A Study in Medieval Political Theology*, 65.

18. See: G. R. Sarolli, *Prolegomena alla "Divina Commedia"* (Florence, 1971), especially 64–74; N. Mineo, *Profetismo e apocalittica in Dante: strutture e temi profetico-apocalittici in Dante (dalla "Vita Nuova" alla "Commedia")* (Catania, 1968), 143–60; also, the classic study "Dante profeta" in B. Nardi, *Dante e la cultura medievale*, 265–326. As Mineo points out, medieval theologians accorded a purely moral

role to Christian prophets; hence, as the prophet of "a political and moral reformation," Dante is closer "to the classical poet-prophet model" (348–49).

19. *Ep.* VI. i. 3: "solio augustali vacante, totus orbis exorbitat . . . et quod Ytalia misera, sola . . . quanta ventorum fluentorumve concussione feratur verba non caperent" (cf. *Mon.* I. xvi. 4).

20. *Ep.* VI. ii. 8. L. Minio-Paluello, "Tre note alla *Monarchia*," in *Medioevo e Rinascimento: studi in onore di Bruno Nardi*, 2: 520, points out that Dante uses the term *civilitas* almost always with the meaning of a state or political organization.

21. *Ep.* VI. vi. 25: "sua sponte penas nostras participans, tanquam ad ipsum, post Christum, digitum prophetie propheta direxerit Ysaias, cum, spiritu Dei revelante, predixit: 'Vere languores nostros ipse tulit et dolores nostros ipse portavit.' "

22. *Ep.* VII. ii. 10: "Tunc exultavit in te spiritus meus, cum tacitus dixi mecum: 'Ecce Agnus Dei, ecce qui tollit peccata mundi.' " D. Compagni, *Cronica*, III. 24, describes Henry's actions in apparently similar terms: "and he came down [into Italy], moving from city to city, making peace as though he had been an angel of God." The latter phrase is, however, quite isolated, whereas Dante's scriptural quotation (given in Latin: cf. *Purg.* XVI. 19 and *Par.* XVII. 33) is part of a Christological mosaic of incomparable significance Cf. G. Padoan, *Il lungo cammino del "poema sacro"* (Florence, 1993), 134: "Not even the most partisan Ghibelline nor the most tenacious defender of imperial rights had ever asserted as much."

23. B. Nardi, "Dante profeta," in *Dante e la cultura medievale*, 295.

24. W. M. Bowsky, *Henry VII in Italy*, 108.

25. G. Villani, *Cronica* X, 15. Cf. G. Holmes, *Florence, Rome*, 191: "Henry would probably have done better to follow the poet's advice."

26. W. M. Bowsky, *Henry VII in Italy*, 126–27.

27. W. M. Bowsky, 165.

28. *MGH*, No. 801, p. 802: "just as all the orders of the celestial host carry out their duties under the one God, so the universality of mankind, while divided into distinct kingdoms and provinces, must be subject to one ruler and emperor" (cf. the conclusion of Boniface VIII's notorious bull *Unam sanctam*: "we declare, state, define, and pronounce that it is altogether necessary to salvation for every human creature to be subject to the Roman Pontiff").

29. A. Solerti, ed., *Le vite di Dante, Petrarca e Boccaccio*, 103–104.

30. W. M. Bowsky, *Henry VII in Italy*, 180.

31. *Par.* XXX. 136–44: "of noblest Henry, who will come to straighten Italy before she is ready. . . . And the one who will then be governor in the forum of things divine will not tread the same path with him openly and secretly."

32. Most recently, the dating of the *Purgatorio* has been drastically revised by G. Padoan, who claims that "the composition of the *Purgatorio* took up most of 1315 and the first part of 1316" (*Il lungo cammino del "poema sacro,"* 93. See also the whole chapter, 93–120, as well as the "Conclusione" 121–23). While indicating the period 1308–12 as the most likely for the first draft of the *Purgatorio*, G. Petrocchi (*Vita di Dante*, 156) distinguishes a clear break between the first twenty-four cantos and the last nine, when Henry VII's departure from Tuscany for Rome is supposed to have brought about a "detachment from the world" and graver spiritual concerns in Dante's outlook. In *Il Purgatorio di Dante* (Milan, 1978), 57–58, Petrocchi

sounds a warning that it is especially dangerous to attempt to set up links between Dante's "biographical experiences" and the second part of the *Comedy*, "where the serene, refined atmosphere . . . would be hard to reconcile with the turbulent events of Henry VII's expedition." Too much has been written about the serenity that supposedly characterizes the whole of the second third of the poem: while true for certain sections, a reading of *Purgatorio* VI, XVI, XX or XXIX–XXXIII should quickly serve to redress the critical balance and make us aware of the broad scope and richness of the *cantica*'s poetic tonality.

33. *MGH*, No. 1252, 1362–69.

34. Ibid. No. 1253, 1369–73.

35. W. M. Bowsky, *Henry VII in Italy*, 191. In chapter 5 ("Henry VII and Robert of Naples") of his *The Prince and the Law, 1200–1600: Sovereignty and Rights in the Western Legal Tradition* (Berkeley-Los Angeles-Oxford, 1993), K. Pennington veers away from the traditional emphasis on the challenge to the Emperor's jurisdiction in order to stress the fact that the clash was "an event of the first rank in legal history" (171), in that it led the Pope to issue two decrees (*Pastoralis cura* and *Saepe*) destined to become "milestones for the development of a doctrine of due process in the *ius commune*" (172). The dispute between Henry and Robert is in fact memorable as "a rare example of a great dispute in the public forum having a substantial and immediate impact on a legal system" (190).

36. *MGH*, Nos. 1165–66, 1207–13.

37. Dante used the opening verse of Lamentations in *Vita Nuova*, XXVIII, 1, to announce the desolation of Florence when Beatrice died and to foreshadow the analogy Florence-Jerusalem/Beatrice-Christ. R. Jacoff, "Dante, Geremia e la problematica profetica," in *Dante e la Bibbia*, ed. G. Barblan (Florence, 1988), 119, has recently reminded us that Jeremiah is central to Dante's role as a prophet.

38. R. Morghen, *Dante profeta: tra la storia e l'eterno* (Milan, 1983), 115.

39. U. Cosmo, *Vita di Dante* (Bari, 1949), 240; F. Mazzoni, "Teoresi e prassi in Dante politico," lxv; P. G. Ricci, "L'ultima fase del pensiero politico di Dante e Cangrande vicario imperiale," in *Dante e la cultura veneta* (Florence, 1966). See also "Monarchia," *ED* III, 1002: "1317 or just after"; G. Petrocchi, *Vita di Dante*, 192: "the hypothesis favoring 1318 now prevails"; R. Hollander and A. L. Rossi, "Dante's Republican Treasury," *Dante Studies* 104 (1986), 59: "after Henry's death— in 1317 or later."

40. P. Shaw, "Sul testo della *Monarchia*," *Studi Danteschi* 53 (1981), 215–16, where B. Nardi's objections (Dante Alighieri, *Opere minori*, 1979, 2, 348–49, n. 6) are refuted.

41. The passage is worth quoting more fully in the original text (*Monarchia* III. xv. 7–13): "Duos igitur fines providentia illa inenarrabilis homini proposuit intendendos: beatitudinem scilicet huius vite . . . per terrestrem paradisum figuratur; et beatitudinem vite ecterne . . . que per paradisum celestem intelligi datur . . . ad primam per phylosophica documenta venimus, dummodo illa sequamur secundum virtutes morales et intellectuales operando; ad secundam vero per documenta spiritualia . . . dummodo illa sequamur secundum virtutes theologicas operando . . . humana cupiditas postergaret nisi homines, tanquam equi, sua bestialitate vagantes 'in camo et freno' compescerentur in via. Propter quod opus fuit homini duplici

directivo secundum duplicem finem: scilicet summo Pontifice, qui secundum reve-
lata humanum genus perduceret ad vitam ecternam, et Imperatore, qui secundum
phylosophica documenta genus humanum ad temporalem felicitatem dirigeret . . .
[romanum Principem] solus eligit Deus, solus ipse confirmat."

42. F. Mazzoni, "Teoresi e prassi," xci–xcii. See lxxxviii, for the assertion that
the final chapter of the *Monarchia* offers us a "declaration of [the poem's] fundamental allegory in terms that are as clear and significant as they have often been
forgotten and ignored by critics."

43. *Ep.* XIII [X]. xvi. 40: "non ad speculandum, sed ad opus inventum est
totum et pars." Doubts about the authenticity of this epistle abound. See, for example, P. Dronke, *Dante and Medieval Latin Traditions* (Cambridge, 1986), 103–11;
R. G. Hall and M. U. Sowell, "*Cursus* in the Can Grande Epistle: A Forger Shows
His Hand?" *Lectura Dantis* 5 (1989), 89–104; H. A. Kelly, *Tragedy and Comedy
from Dante to Pseudo-Dante* (Berkeley-Los Angeles-London, 1989); Z. G. Barański,
"*Comedía*: Notes on Dante, the Epistle to Cangrande, and Medieval Comedy,"
Lectura Dantis 8 (1991), 26–55. The epistle's authenticity has been strongly defended by many leading scholars, including E. Moore, "The Genuineness of the
Dedicatory Epistle to Can Grande," *Studies in Dante: Third Series* (Oxford, 1903),
284–362; F. Mazzoni, "L'Epistola a Cangrande," *Atti della Accademia Nazionale dei
Lincei. Rendiconti. Classe di scienze morali, storiche e filologiche*, Series VIII (10: 1955),
157–98; G. Padoan, "La 'mirabile visione' di Dante e l'Epistola a Cangrande," in *Il
pio Enea, l'empio Ulisse* (Ravenna, 1977), 30–63; L. Pertile, "*Canto-cantica Comedía*
e l'Epistola a Cangrande," *Lectura Dantis* 9 (1991), 105–23; R. Hollander, *Dante's
Epistle to Cangrande* (Ann Arbor, 1993). Whatever the outcome of the debate, I
agree with Étienne Gilson who stated that the Epistle offers "certain ideas which,
even if Dante himself did not pen them in this work, it is fortunate that someone else did so in his name. They are a faithful reflection of his attitude concerning
those problems" (E. Gilson, "Poésie et théologie dans la *Divine Comédie*" in *Atti
del congresso internazionale di studi danteschi* [Florence, 1965], 1, 220, n. 7). One is
tempted to add: *se non è autentica [l'Epistola], è ben trovata.*

44. *Purg.* XVI. 106–12: "Formerly, Rome, which made the good world, had
two suns, which made clearly visible both paths, that of the world and that of God.
One has extinguished the other; and the sword has been joined to the crook, and
of necessity they go ill together; because, when joined, neither fears the other."
For the vital function of this unscientific image of two suns, see J. A. Scott, "Una
contraddizione scientifica nell'opera dantesca: i due soli di *Purgatorio* XVI. 107," in
Dante e la scienza, ed. P. Boyde and V. Russo (Ravenna, 1995), 149–55.

45. *Purg.* XVI. 127–29: "Say henceforth that the Church of Rome, by confounding two powers in herself, falls into the mire and befouls both herself and her
burden."

46. E. Gilson, *Dante the Philosopher*, trans. D. Moore (London, 1948), 211;
B. Nardi, *Dal "Convivio" alla "Commedia"*, 311.

47. F. Mazzoni, "Teoresi e prassi," xcii–iv. The passages quoted by Mazzoni
are *S. Th.* 1.2.5.5, resp. and 1.2.62.1, resp. (the latter, where "earthly happiness seems
to acquire a certain independence and autonomy"). Cf., however, *Summa Theologica*
2-2, 60, 6, ad 3, where Aquinas categorically asserts that the secular authority must

be subject to the spiritual power, just as the body must be governed by the soul. For the whole question, see *Aquinas: Selected Political Writings*, edited and with an introduction by A. P. d'Entrèves (Oxford, 1959). See also M. Trovato, "Dante and the Tradition of the 'Two Beatitudes'," in *Lectura Dantis Newberryana*, ed. P. Cerchi and A. Mastrobuono (Evanston, 1988), 1: 19–36, especially 31: "The *duo ultima* does not imply any dualism: rather, they are the outcome of one principle or operation. . . . When considering the continuum of intellectual activity—from time to eternity—Dante strongly agrees with Albert and Thomas: 'That happiness, which is subject to mortality, in a sense is ordered to the immortal happiness.'"

48. See M. Maccarrone, "Il terzo libro della *Monarchia*," *Studi Danteschi* 33 (1955), 5–142, and "Papato e Impero nella *Monarchia*," in *Nuove letture dantesche* (Florence, 1976), 259–322; B. Nardi, *Saggi di filosofia dantesca*, 285, and *Dal "Convivio" alla "Commedia*," 116–17, 301; L. Minio-Paluello, "Tre note alla *Monarchia*," 522–24; E. Williamson, "De Beatitudine Huius Vite," *Annual Report of the Dante Society* 76 (1958), 1–22; G. Vinay, *Interpretazione della "Monarchia" di Dante* (Florence, 1962), 19–24; O. Capitani, "*Monarchia*: il pensiero politico," in *Dante nella critica d'oggi*, ed. U. Bosco (Florence, 1965), 733–36; A. M. Chiavacci-Leonardi, "La *Monarchia* di Dante alla luce della *Commedia*," *Studi Medievali*, Terza Serie 18 (1977), 147–83.

49. M. Maccarrone, "Il terzo libro," 16. See also G. Di Scipio's essay, "Dante and Politics" in *The "Divine Comedy" and the Encyclopedia of Arts and Sciences*, ed. G. Di Scipio and A. Scaglione (Amsterdam-Philadelphia, 1988), 267–84, especially 276: "The understanding of the concept 'reverentia' (cf. *Conv.* IV. viii. 11–14) is, therefore, the key to the whole theoretical discourse on the Empire and the Church . . . Moreover, if this word 'reverentia' is understood in the terms of the *Convivio*, it eliminates any notion that Dante, having gone too far in the *Monarchia* in attacking the Pope, has retracted his position and added the last paragraph." B. Martinelli, "Sul 'Quodammodo' di *Monarchia*, III xv. 17," in *Miscellanea di studi in onore di Vittore Branca* (Florence, 1983), 2: 193–214, gives an exhaustive analysis of the whole question.

50. The whole concept of the Empire in the fourteenth century has been dismissed as an anachronism devoid of any real significance in the *Realpolitik* of the times. W. M. Bowsky, however, is not alone in pointing out that, long after Henry's death, many "still believed that only the Emperor had the right of sovereignty or God-given rule in Lombardy and Tuscany. . . . For many years communes condemned by Henry VII expressed the desire to procure the cancellation of their sentences. . . . Florence alone paid one hundred thousand florins [to the Emperor Charles IV], and Padua too bought a cancellation of the sentence pronounced against it by the Emperor it had banned" (*Henry VII in Italy*, 183).

51. *Ep.* XII. iii–iv. 5–9 (cf. *Par.* XXV. 1–9). The hardening of the poet's stance regarding the charges brought against him is obvious if we compare this assertion of his total innocence with the virtual admission of some fault in *Rime* CIV. 88–90.

52. *CDD*, Nos. 114–15: they were condemned to death by decapitation, and anyone was entitled to attack them and other "Ghibellines and rebels" with impunity "both in their possessions and their persons."

53. *Par.* XVIII. 127–36: "In the old days, wars were waged with the sword,

but now they are fought by taking away—now here, now there—the bread the tender Father withholds from no one. But you, who write only in order to cancel what you have written, remember that Peter and Paul, who died for the vineyard laid waste by you, are still alive. You can certainly say: 'My desire is so fixed on him who chose to live alone and was brought to martyrdom through a dance, that I know not the Fisherman nor Old Paul.'"

54. *MGH*, V, No. 401.

55. G. Mollat, *The Popes at Avignon*, 81 (with the extract quoted from the *Annales Mediolanenses*).

56. G. Petrocchi, *Vita di Dante*, 190.

57. G. Boccaccio, *Trattatello in laude di Dante*, ed. P. G. Ricci, in *Tutte le opere*, ed. V. Branca (Milan, 1974), 3: 464.

Introduction to Part Two

1. Cf. A. Morgan, *Dante and the Medieval Other World* (Cambridge, 1990), 160.

2. "And because of that sin the place [Eden] was forbidden to everyone for all time" (see *Poeti del Duecento*, ed. G. Contini (Milan-Naples, 1960), 2: 192. Cf. Brunetto's *Tresor* I. 122 (114): "And know that, after the first man's sin, this place was closed to all men"; see also Aquinas, *S. Th.* 1.102.1.3. In this second part (which concentrates on the *Purgatorio* text), I shall normally quote the Italian text and given an English translation in the notes.

3. According to popular belief (mentioned by Aquinas and one of Dante's early commentators, Francesco da Buti), Elijah and Enoch were in fact to be found in the Earthly Paradise. Ariosto is the last Italian writer to refer to this legend, when (*Orlando Furioso* XXXIV. 48ff.) Astolfo is welcomed to the Earthly Paradise by Elijah, Enoch, and St. John. This legend, that Elijah had been carried up not to Heaven but to the Earthly Paradise, would help to illuminate the reference to Elijah's fiery chariot in *Inf.* XXVI. 35, by setting up Elijah's providential elevation as the direct antitype of Ulysses' disastrous attempt to reach the Earthly Paradise, which ended in a downward trajectory to Hell.

Chapter 4. Cato: A Pagan Suicide in Purgatory

1. The ambiguity is intentional. Line 39 ("ch'i' 'l vedea come 'l sol fosse davante") can mean either "I saw him as though he had been facing the sun" (lit up by the sun's rays) or "I saw him as though I had been facing the sun" (Cato compared to the sun). The latter interpretation would agree with the extraordinary exclamation in *Conv.* IV. xxviii. 15: "And what man on earth was worthier of signifying God than Cato? None, certainly," as well as with the biblical passages frequently quoted by commentators (e.g., Rev. 10. 1: "His face was like the sun" [*facies eius erat ut*

sol]; Matthew 13.43, "Then the righteous will shine like the sun in their Father's kingdom").

2. *S. Th.* 2.2.59.3.2: "the person who commits suicide harms . . . the commonwealth and God"; 2.2.6.4.5.3; III.47.6.3.

3. C. T. Davis, *Dante's Italy*, 263; *Dante and the Idea of Rome*, 84.

4. T. Silverstein, "On the Genesis of *De Monarchia*, II, v," *Speculum* 13 (1938), 326–49, now reprinted in *Dante in America: The First Two Centuries*, ed. A. Bartlett Giamatti, Medieval and Renaissance Texts and Studies 23 (Binghampton, N.Y., 1983), 186–218 (passage quoted, 209).

5. *Mon.* II. v. 17. Dante's own character would seem—especially in his later years—to have been modelled on such stoic ideals, which made him feel "truly impervious to fortune's blows" (*Par.* XVII. 24: *ben tetragono ai colpi di ventura*): witness his uncompromising refusal to accept the offer of amnesty during his exile (1315: *Ep.* XII. iii–iv. 5–9).

6. See especially F. Forti, *Magnanimitade: Studi su un tema dantesco* (Bologna, 1977) and J. A. Scott, *Dante magnanimo* (Florence, 1977), esp. 239–345.

7. B. Latini, *Li Livres dou Tresor* II. 82 (261).

8. Ibid., 194.

9. *ED* III, 243.

10. *Mon.* II. v. 15: "illud inenarrabile sacrifitium severissimi [vere] libertatis tutoris Marci Catonis . . . ut mundo libertatis amores accenderet, quanti libertas esset ostendit dum e vita liber decedere maluit quam sine libertate manere in illa."

11. Seneca, *Epistulae Morales*, XC. 72: "Catonis illud ultimum ac fortissimum vulnus, per quod libertas emisit animam"; *De Providentia* II. 10: "ferrum istud . . . libertatem, quam patriae non potuit, Catoni dabit"; *De Constantia Sapientis* II. 3: "neque enim Cato post libertatem vixit, nec libertas post Catonem."

12. *Purg.* I. 69–75: "May it now please you to welcome his coming: he is seeking true freedom, which is so precious, as the person knows who abandons life for it. You know: for death in Utica was not bitter because of it, when you left the body that will be so bright on the great day [of Judgment]."

13. The probable dating of the *Monarchia* as c. 1315–17 suggests that the praise of Cato found in that treatise is to be read as further proof of Dante's admiration for the Roman hero, bolstering the evidence of *Purgatorio* I and II and eliminating (at least for this writer) the possibility that Virgil's words in his encounter with Cato on the shores of Purgatory should be downgraded as a mere *captatio benevolentiae*.

14. *Mon.* I. xii. 8: "Sed existens sub Monarcha [genus humanum] est *potissime liberum*" (emphasis mine). To appreciate the essential link between freedom and peace see e.g. the end of the treatise: "And since none or very few would reach this haven, if the waves of seductive greed were not assuaged and the human race left free to rest in the tranquillity of peace, this is the task to which he who has charge of the world and is called *Roman Emperor should chiefly devote his energies*, namely, that on this threshing floor of mortality *life should be lived in freedom and in peace*" (*Mon.* III. xv. 11; emphasis mine).

15. E. Proto, "Nuove ricerche sul Catone dantesco," *Giornale Storico della Letteratura Italiana* 59 (1912), 230: "La libertà politica, per la quale si uccise Catone, si trasforma nella libertà morale, spirituale del cristiano."

16. *Ep.* VI. v. 22–23: "dominantem cupidinem . . . captivantem vos in lege peccati, ac *sacratissimis legibus que iustitie naturalis imitantur ymaginem, parere vetantem; observantia quarum, si leta, si libera, non tantum non servitus esse probatur, qui ymo perspicaciter intuenti liquet ut est ipsa summa libertas.* . . . Itaque solis existentibus liberis qui voluntarie legi obediunt, quos vos esse censebitis qui . . . contra leges universas in legum principem conspiratis?" (emphasis mine). As E. Peters states in "The Frowning Pages: Scythians, Garamantes, Florentines, and the Two Laws" (*The Divine Comedy and the Encyclopedia of Arts and Sciences*, ed. G. Di Scipio and A. Scaglione [Amsterdam-Philadelphia, 1988], 289; "In Dante's eyes Roman law was that human institution which best aligned itself with the law of nature and created the ideal conditions by which the divine law of revelation might be followed."

17. E. Auerbach, *Scenes from the Drama of European Literature* (New York, 1959), 66.

18. *Purg.* I. 103–5: "No other plant can live there, despite its leaves or strength, since it cannot yield to the blows."

19. *Mon.* II. v. 1: "Quicunque preterea bonum rei publice intendit, finem iuris intendit."

20. See L. Minio-Paluello, "Remigio de' Girolami's *De bono communi*," *Italian Studies* 11 (1956), 56–71. Already in 1957 C. T. Davis pointed out that Remigio's "instruction and example were significant not only for the formation of Dante's theological and philosophical theories, but for the *alteration of his historical view of Rome*" (*Dante and the Idea of Rome*, 83; emphasis mine).

21. E. H. Kantorowicz, *The King's Two Bodies*, 242–43.

22. E. H. Kantorowicz, 245. Cf. A. Graf, *Roma nella memoria e nelle immaginazioni del Medio Evo* (Turin, 1923), 574ff.; G. Mazzotta, *Dante, Poet of the Desert: History and Allegory in the "Divine Comedy"* (Princeton, N.J., 1979), 58.

23. Seneca, *Epistulae morales*, LXXXII.12: "mors enim illa, quae in Catone gloriosa est, in Bruto statim turpis est et erubescenda . . ."

24. *Phar.* II. 302–3: "tuumque / Nomen, Libertas, et inanem prosequar umbram"); IX. 566–67: "Quid quaeris, Labiene, iubes? an liber in armis / Occubuisse velim potius quam regna videre?" Cf. the passage from Cicero quoted by Dante in *Mon.* II. v. 17: "moriendum ei potius quam tyrampni vultus aspiciendus fuit" (for which see above). I quote the text and translations as given in Lucan, *The Civil War* (*Pharsalia*) (London-Cambridge, Mass.), 1962.

25. Cf. Isidore of Seville, *Etymologiae* VIII. vii. 10: "Lucan is not listed among the poets, for it seems that what he wrote was not a poem but history."

26. See J. A. Scott, *Dante magnanimo*, 244ff.

27. C. T. Davis, *Dante and the Idea of Rome*, 90.

28. Thus T. B. Macaulay, in an annotation dated 30 August 1835, in which he also reproaches Lucan for his "furious partiality" in setting up Cato in this way, "while Caesar . . . is a bloodthirsty ogre" (quoted by J. Duff in Lucan, *The Civil War*, xv). Cf. P. F. Widdows, who describes Cato as "Lucan's ideal, the Stoic saint," in *Lucan's Civil War*, translated into English verse by P. F. Widdows (Bloomington and Indianapolis), 1988.

29. "Catonem certius exemplar sapientis viri nobis deos immortales dedisse quam Ulixen et Herculem prioribus saeculis . . . cum ambitu congressus . . . et cum potentiae immensa cupiditate, quam totus orbis in tres divisus satiare non pot-

erat" (*De Constantia Sapientis* II. 2). For the role played by the opposition between Ulysses and Cato in the economy of Dante's poem, see J. A. Scott, *Dante magnanimo*, 147ff.

30. *Phar.* IX. 601–4: "Ecce parens verus patriae, dignissimusn aris, / Roma, tuis . . . / Et quem, si steteris umquam cervice soluta / Nunc, olim, factura deum es . . ."

31. R. Hollander makes a far more convincing case (*Allegory in Dante's "Commedia*," 124–26) for the "figural presence" of Moses "that emanates from Cato." We would do well to heed Hollander's warning: "Whatever rationale we may find for his salvation by Dante, we must remember that Dante expected us to be amazed . . ." I would add that, even as Moses was not allowed to enter the Promised Land, so Cato was not able to witness the fulfillment of Rome's imperial destiny. For Dante's praise of Cato as signifying the divinity, scholars have pointed to a possible "source" in Seneca, *Controversiae* I, preface 9: "and what high priest could the divinity have found more holy than Marcus Cato?" (*"et quem tandem antistitem sanctiorem sibi invenire divinitas potuit quam M. Catonem . . . ?"*).

32. R. Hollander, *Allegory in Dante's "Commedia*," 126.

33. *Phar.* II. 304–12: "Sic eat: inmites Romana piacula divi / Plena ferant . . . / O utinam caelique deis Erebique liceret / Hoc caput in cunctas damnatum exponere poenas! . . . Hic redimat sanguis populos, hac caede luatur, / Quidquid Romani meruerunt pendere mores"* (emphasis mine).

34. See Lucain, *La Guerre civile*, texte établi et traduit par A. Bourgery, (Paris, 1926, 1: 45). Cf. E. Malcovati, *M. Anneo Lucano* (Milan, 1940), 117ff. For a Christian, the parallel with Christ might well appear reinforced by the portrait, some seventy lines further on (ll. 380–83), which sums up "the character . . . the inflexible rule of austere Cato—to observe moderation and hold fast to the limit, to follow nature, to give his life for his country, *to believe that he was born to serve the whole world and not himself*" ("Hi mores, haec duri immota Catonis / Secta fuit, servare modum finemque tenere / Naturam sequi patriaeque inpendere vitam / *Nec sibi sed toti genitum se credere mundo*"). Dante refers directly to the words italicized in his praise of Cato as a political animal: "as Aristotle says, man is a political animal, so that he must bring benefit not only to himself but also to others. Hence, we read about Cato that he considered that he had been born not for his own good, but for that of his country and of the whole world" (*Conv.*, IV. xxvii. 3: "Onde si legge di Catone che non a sé, ma a la patria e a tutto lo mondo nato esser credea"). We may also note that Seneca (*De Providentia* III. 4) claimed that Fortune had tested the endurance of the bravest of men, with fire in the case of Mucius Scaevola, poverty (Fabricius), exile (Rutilius), torture (Regulus), poison (Socrates), and death (*mortem in Catonem*): thus a parallel with Christ's trial and victory over death might impose itself on the mind of a Christian reader.

35. *S.Th.* 2.2.2.7.3: "multis gentilium facta fuit relevatio de Christo . . . Si qui tamen salvati fuerunt quibus revelatio non fuit facta, non fuerunt salvati absque fide Mediatoris; quia etsi non habuerunt fidem explicitam, *habuerunt tamen fidem implicitam in divina providentia*, credentes Deum esse liberatorem hominum secundum modos sibi placitos" (emphasis mine).

36. A. Pézard, "Le Chant premier du *Purgatoire*," in *Letture del "Purgatorio*," ed. V. Vettori (Milan, 1965). 14.

37. *Mon.* III. xv. 8: "Nam ad primam [beatitudinem huius vite] per phylosophica documenta venimus, dummodo illa sequamur secundum virtutes morales et intellectuales operando; ad secundam [beatitudinem vite ecterne] vero per documenta spiritualia que humanam rationem transcendunt, dummodo illa sequamur secundum virtutes theologicas operando, fidem spem scilicet et karitatem."

38. E. Proto, "Nuove ricerche sul Catone dantesco," 224–25. Cf. M. Sansone, "Il canto I del *Purgatorio*," in *Nuova Lectura Dantis* (Rome, 1955), 8–9.

39. R. Hazelton, "The Christianization of 'Cato': The *Disticha Catonis* in the Light of Late Mediaeval Commentaries," *Mediaeval Studies* 19 (1957), 157. I am indebted to this seminal essay for my observations regarding the significance of the *Disticha*. For Cato's place in the medieval canon, see P. F. Grendler, *Schooling in Renaissance Italy: Literacy and Learning, 1300–1600* (Baltimore, 1989), 114.

40. R. Hazelton, "The Christianization of 'Cato'," 173.

41. R. Hazelton, 157–63.

42. R. Hazelton, 167, n. 41. On p. 165, we read in an extract from one of those commentaries: "Cato's subject in this work is the four principal virtues, namely, justice, prudence, fortitude, temperance."

43. K. Foster, *The Two Dantes and Other Studies* (London, 1977), 180–81.

44. J. Le Goff, *La Naissance du Purgatoire* (Paris, 1981), 449.

45. J. A. Scott, *Dante magnanimo*, 317–18. As D. Thompson has noted, this peculiarity is a feature of Latin literature: "An exhaustive study of Roman *exempla virtutis* showed that of the twenty-seven major *exempla* not a single one post-dated Julius Caesar, and most were a good deal earlier" ("Dante's Virtuous Romans," *Dante Studies* 96 [1978], 151). A possible link between republican Cato and the ideal Emperor may be found in the fact that Luca de Penna, a Neapolitan jurist, quoted (c. 1350) Lucan's description of the Republican hero as *urbi pater urbique maritus* (*Phar.* II. 388, grammatically *urbi* can mean not only "for" but also "to": "father and husband to the state") to signify the marriage between the prince and the state (E. H. Kantorowicz, *The King's Two Bodies*, 214).

46. Cf. J. H. Whitfield, "Dante and the Roman World," *Italian Studies* 33 (1978), 9: "With Fabricius, Cincinnatus, Camillus candidates for Limbo, it would have been inconvenient if Caligula, Nero, Commodus were in Hell. They are none of them in the *Inferno*, though Nero for the Middle Ages was the greatest scoundrel after Judas. Not even Julian the Apostate qualifies for Hell"; also, P. Renucci, *Dante disciple et juge du monde gréco-latin*, 313–14.

47. R. Hollander and Albert L. Rossi, "Dante's Republican Treasury," 60.

48. *Phar.* II. 439–46: "Caesar in arma furens . . . Concessa pudet ire via civemque videri."

49. This is the version given by Orosius (*Historiae Adversum Paganos* VI. xv. 28), in which the "advocate of the Christian age" (*Par.* X. 119) claims that the young Ptolemy ordered Pompey's murder in order to ingratiate himself with Caesar ("iussu Ptolomaei adulescentis in gratiam Caesaris occisus est": quoted by C. Kraus, "Tolomeo," *ED* V, 621). For the importance of Orosius' influence on Dante, see especially: C. T. Davis, *Dante and the Idea of Rome*, 55ff.; and A. Martina, "Orosio," *ED* IV, 204–8.

50. As readers will recall, the third zone of the ninth circle of Dante's Hell (reserved specifically for traitors to their guests) is named "Tolomea." According to

many commentators, "Tolomea" (*Inf.* XXXIII. 124) is derived from Ptolemy, the son of the High Priest (1 Maccabees 16. 11ff.), who slaughtered his guest, a public official charged with keeping the country in order. However, as E. Bigi observes (*ED* V, 618), Dante may well have had in mind the two characters Ptolemy, governor of Jericho, and Ptolemy, king of Egypt—a hypothesis reinforced by Dante's reference (*Mon.* II. viii. 9) to Lucan's invective against Ptolemy of Egypt in *Phar.* VIII. 692ff. The dual inspiration (biblical and classical) is accepted by both the present writer and J. Ferrante, who observes that "this name has meaning for the histories of both chosen nations, Rome and Israel. Perhaps implicit in the ambiguity of the name is the confusion between church and state, the interference of the church in secular affairs" (*The Political Vision of the Divine Comedy* [Princeton, N.J., 1984], 190). We may further note Ptolemy's words to Caesar (*Phar.* IX. 1028ff.), especially the description of Pompey as *Hospes avitus*, in which the semantic ambiguities range from "our friend" to "our guest of old" (with the latter meaning probably uppermost in the mind of an Italian reader). Dante's abhorrence of treachery led him to go against the authoritative judgment of Aquinas in placing fraud below violence as the worst category of sin; in the *Comedy*, "the devil's city is its [Heaven's] antithesis, based as it is on sin and, finally, on treachery" (J. A. Scott, "Treachery in Dante," in *Studies in the Italian Renaissance: Essays in Memory of Arnolfo B. Ferruolo*, ed. G. P. Biasin et al. [Naples, 1985], 35).

51. See under "Triumphus" in Uguccione's *Magnae Derviationes*. It is well-nigh impossible to accept the comment in the Bosco-Reggio edition of the *Commedia*, 2: 446: "It is, however, difficult to suppose that Dante accepted as true the accusation of sodomy made against Caesar; otherwise, he would not have placed him among the great souls [in Limbo] but next to Brunetto Latini. . . . *This is merely a periphrasis used to designate the sin clearly but not crudely*" (emphasis mine). Caesar's vice has nothing to do with the celerity of his conquests in establishing the Empire, celebrated in the sixth canto of *Paradiso* (where the rapidity of his "flight . . . swift as lightning" echoes Lucan's comment in *Phar.* X. 507–8 that "Caesar had ever made successful use of haste in warfare").

52. R. Hollander and Albert L. Rossi, "Dante's Republican Treasury," 66. B. Stambler, *Dante's Other World: The "Purgatorio" as Guide to the "Divine Comedy"* (New York, 1957), 94 makes the interesting conjecture: "Cato's rebellion was against a Caesar engaged in tearing down an established state of things . . . Cato's act of freedom . . . took place at the last possible moment. After the establishment of the Empire such an act would have been disobedience of the divine order and not the *summum bonum* within a pagan order."

53. Seneca, *Epistulae Morales*, CIV. 30–32: emphasis mine (*"solus Cato fecit aliquas et rei publicae partes . . . duos in medio relictos, rem publicam et Catonem"*).

54. P. Armour, *Dante's Griffin and the History of the World: A Study of the Earthly Paradise ("Purgatorio" cantos xxix–xxxiii)* (Oxford, 1989), 286 and 37.

55. P. Armour, *Dante's Griffin*.

56. Cf. P. Armour, *Dante's Griffin*, 174–75: "The principal meaning of Dante's extraordinary image of the griffin's 'two natures' united but also, as 'reggimenti', open to separate consideration is, however, political and constitutional . . . Dante's amazing vision may also be interpreted diachronically . . . at the same time he

learns about the secret process of its creation through history, when God worked through the Roman people . . . up to the point when both aspects of both regimes, the imperial and the popular, were united in the single institution and the single Prince." Armour also reminds the reader of his essential thesis (supported by the study of "Christ-Centered Kingship" in Kantorowicz, *The King's Two Bodies*, 42ff.), that the griffin or ideal Emperor is "the very image on earth of him [Christ] who, both God and man, is the ultimate heavenly source of all earthly power" (175).

57. G. Mazzotta, *Dante, Poet of the Desert*, 59.

58. Mazzotta, *Dante, Poet of the Desert*, 64.

59. Augustine, *City of God*, I. 33.

60. Augustine, *City of God*, IV.4 (*magna latrocinia*); cf. Dante, *Mon.* II. v. 5; *Ep.* V. iii. 7.

61. A similar contradiction exists within the *Comedy* itself: in *Pg.* II. 98–99 and *Purg.* XX 86–90 Boniface VIII is presented as the true Vicar of Christ, while in *Par.* XXVII. 22–27 no less an authority than St. Peter himself declares that his seat is vacant in the eyes of Christ (a message hammered home by the repetition of the words "my place" in lines 22–23: "il luogo mio, / il luogo mio, il luogo mio").

62. I quote from the translation by "I. T.," revised by H. F. Stewart for the Loeb Classical Library: Boethius, *The Theological Tractates and The Consolation of Philosophy* (London-Cambridge, Mass., 1953), 347. The essential words in the Latin text are: "de hoc quem tu *iustissimum et aequi servantissimum* putas omnia scienti *prouidentiae diuersum uidetur*; et uictricem quidem causam dis, uictam uero Catonia placuisse familiaris noster Lucanus admonuit" (emphasis mine).

63. For an elaboration of this point, see my article "Dante, Boezio e l'enigma di Rifeo," *Studi Danteschi* 61 (1989), 187–92.

64. *Par.* VI. 1–6 (emphasis mine): "After Constantine turned back the eagle, *against the course of heaven, which it had followed behind the ancient one who took Lavinia,* a hundred and a hundred years and more the bird of God remained on Europe's limit, *near the mountains from which it first had come.*"

Chapter 5. Manfred and Bonconte

1. See J. Larner, *Italy in the Age of Dante*, 42. Cf. G. Leff, *Heresy in the Later Middle Ages* (Manchester-New York, 1967), 1: 23: "The cost of these plans . . . forced the popes to turn to every available resource, financial, political and ecclesiastical, to realize them: the exploiting of dispensations and provisions to benefices . . . the raising of loans from Tuscan bankers at usurious rates (a practice banned by the church); and above all the levying of wars."

2. See J. Larner, *Italy in the Age of Dante*, 43–44.

3. B. Latini, *Li livres dou Tresor*, I. 97 (79).

4. Adam de la Halle: "Manfred was a handsome, virtuous and wise knight, endowed with every good quality and courtesy"; Aimeric de Péguilhan claimed that Manfred was most worthy of love and glory among the sons of men. Quoted by E. Caccia, "Canto III," in *Lectura Dantis Scaligera* (Florence, 1967), 100, n. 1. W. Binni, "Il canto III del *Purgatorio*," in *Letture dantesche*, ed. G. Getto, 2: 737) has

drawn our attention to the description "he was handsome and strong and of great prowess" (bels fut e forz e de grant vasselage, referring, however, to Roland's Saracen enemy, and not the Christian hero, as Binni states) in the Chanson de Roland (l. 2278). A parallel with the portrait of King David given in 1 Samuel [Kings] 16. 12 ("Now he was ruddy, of a beautiful countenance, and goodly to look at"), mentioned by a number of commentators, is taken to its limits by G. R. Sarolli, Prolegomena alla "Divina Commedia" (Florence, 1971), 319–20, n. 1, in his claim that Manfred is a typus Christi through the equation David-Christ-Manfred.

5. See chapter 2.

6. See, e.g., G. Bàrberi Squarotti, "Manfredi (Purg. III)," in L'uomo di Dante e Dante uomo: Lectura Dantis Pompeiana, ed. P. Sabbatino (Naples, 1985), 185, who claims that there was certainly no "precise political intent" in the poet's decision to place Manfred among the "elect . . . the problem concerns the faith, not politics."

7. See R. Morghen, "Il trapasso dal Medio Evo alla nuova età nella testimonianza dei contemporanei," in his Medioevo cristiano (Bari, 1951), 328–31, where he shows that the idea that excommunication was merely a "poena medicinalis" which could be nullified by Grace can be put forward only on the basis of canon law after Boniface VIII and for minor excommunication, but not in Manfred's or Dante's times, "when the major form of excommunication, such as that launched against Manfred on 10 April 1259, was essentially still identified with the anathema of the early Middle Ages, in other words with the solemn curse pronounced in the name of God and the Apostles, which excluded the excommunicate from all participation in the life of the Church . . . cum Juda traditore in ignem et cum diabolo" (329–30).

8. Purg. III. 121–23: "My sins were horrible, but the arms of Infinite Goodness are so wide that it clasps whatever turns to it."

9. Par. XX. 67–69: "Who down in the errant world would believe that Rhipeus from Troy is the fifth of the holy lights?"

10. Cf. Matthew Paris's judgment of Manfred's father as "Frederick, greatest of the princes of this world and wonder of the world [stupor mundi]" (quoted by J. Larner, Italy in the Age of Dante, 21). The element of surprise is vital, since it emphasizes the greatness of God's mercy in accepting the sinner's repentance in articulo mortis. We must, therefore, believe in the enormity of Manfred's sins (as he himself states in line 121) and thus the justification of the sanctions imposed by "Santa Chiesa" (l. 137): all this, in order to throw into relief the unjustifiable persecution of the sinner after death and the efficacy of his turning to God in his last moments. Dante may have been inspired by a popular legend that king Manfred's last words had been addressed to his Creator, "May God have mercy on me, sinner that I am"; see F. Novati, "Come Manfredi s'è salvato," Indagini e postille dantesche (Bologna, 1899), 117.

11. J. Freccero, in an essay entitled "Manfred's Wounds" (see his Dante: The Poetics of Conversion, ed. R. Jacoff [Cambridge, Mass., 1986], 206), suggests that Manfred in fact refers to his own face in line 126: "In God's book, Manfred's brow is clear. This is implied by a verse [l. 126: "avesse in Dio ben letta questa faccia" that has always presented a certain difficulty for commentators. Speaking of the bishop who had his body disinterred and thrown into the river, Manfred says that had the pastor realized that Manfred was saved, he would have spared his body. . . .

God's book has no marks that are subject to misinterpretation; Manfred's wounds, however, might have been taken as signs of his damnation when read from a purely human perspective, without benefit of their radiant smile." R. Lansing ("*Purgatorio* III," *Lectura Dantis* 9 [1991], 66) makes the interesting point: "Whether real or invented, the chronicling of Manfredi's burial and later disinternment by order of the Pope is consciously meant to contrast with Vergil's death in Brundisium and the subsequent transport of his body to its final resting place in Naples, by order of Augustus." The great pagan Emperor, we may add, displayed a sense of *pietas* rejected by a politically motivated Pope.

12. B. Nardi, "*Lecturae*" *e altri studi danteschi*, 99.

13. Nardi, "*Lecturae*", 124: "Nulla scientiarum est similis scientie philosophie, que clarificat animam et facit eam delectari in hoc seculo in perfectione et rectitudine, quod est principium bene esse sui; et per illam datur ei comprehendere et intelligere bonum alterius seculi, et qui invenit eam, vitam invenit in utroque seculo."

14. Nardi, "*Lecturae*", 101: "Quamvis de nostre perfectionis premio possidendo non nostris inniteremur iustitie meritis, *sed soli misericordie creatoris*" (emphasis mine).

15. Nardi, "*Lecturae*", 98. As R. Lansing points out ("*Purgatorio* III," 62): "If Manfred once represented for Dante a pinnacle of contemporary secular humanity . . . he becomes in the *Purgatorio* the prime example of Christian redemption and pardon, achieved through a brief act of humility."

16. J. Freccero, "Manfred's Wounds," 200. Cf. G. Bàrberi Squarotti, "Manfredi ('Purgatorio', III)", in *L'uomo di Dante e Dante uomo: Lectura Dantis Pompeiana*, ed. Pasquale Sabbatino (Naples: 1985), 177. Moreover, as R. Lansing points out ("*Purgatorio* III," 64): "if there is any one element that reinforces the Christological associations, it is that Manfredi's death, like that of Christ, was brought about by a betrayal."

17. *Purg*. III. 109–10: " 'Look now,' and he showed me a wound high up on his breast."

18. *Purg*. V. 91–93: "And I asked him: 'What violence or what chance took you so far from Campaldino that your burial place was never known?' "

19. Cf. chapter 3 "Meteorology" in P. Boyde, *Dante Philomythes and Philosopher: Man in the Cosmos* (Cambridge, 1981), 74–95.

20. G. Toja, "Buonconte da Montefeltro e l'epos dell'eroe morente," in *Studi in onore di Alberto Chiari* (Brescia, 1973), 2: 1272–74.

21. "Cum Michael Archangelus cum diabolo disputans altercaretur de Moysi corpore, non est ausus iudicium inferre blasphemiae: sed dicit: Imperet tibi Dominus." Cf. G. Petrocchi, "Bonconte da Montefeltro," *ED* III, 1018. Strangely enough, D. Pietropaolo quotes W. W. Vernon but not Petrocchi to substantiate his claim that "several Dante scholars refer to this passage in Jude . . . [yet] none explains the actual significance that it has in the *Commedia*" ("The Figural Context of Buonconte's Salvation," *Dante Studies* 102 [1984], 124). According to Pietropaolo, "Buonconte's salvation is typologically linked to the death and assumption of Moses, to the inheritance of Moses' role by Joshua, and to his final succession by Jesus. It is also a reminder of the first as well of the final defeat of the devil" (132).

22. J. Larner, *Italy in the Age of Dante*, 23–24, mentions *inter alia* the rumor

that the Emperor "held Moses, Christ, and Mohammed to be three impostors," and concludes: "Any certain resolution of Frederick's real religious sentiments is impossible . . . when he was in the East Ibn-al-Jazi remarked that: 'one saw from the way he spoke that he was a materialist who made a simple game of Christianity'. . . . Against it one sets the Frederick who . . . [as a] member of a Cistercian prayer community, loaded the order with gifts, and who promoted devotion to his relative, St. Elizabeth of Hungary." G. Padoan, *Il lungo cammino del "poema sacro*," 45, claims that it was Dante's hopes of reconciliation with the Black Guelfs that led the poet to emphasize his family's anti-Ghibellinism in *Inferno* X, where the presence of Frederick II among the heretics constitutes the greatest concession ever made by the exile in his attempt to reach a compromise with his former political adversaries.

23. For the text of *Unam sanctam* in translation, see B. Tierney, *The Crisis of Church and State*, 188–89: "We are taught by the words of the Gospel that in this church and in her power there are two swords. . . . Both then are in the power of the church, the material sword and the spiritual . . . if the earthly power errs, it shall be judged by the spiritual . . . if the supreme spiritual power errs it can be judged only by God."

24. R. Manselli, "Dante e l'*Ecclesia Spiritualis*," in *Dante e Roma* (Florence, 1965), points to the fact that Dante uses the language of the Spiritual Franciscans in their repeated attacks "contro la Curia, 'ob novorum phariseorum superbiam'" (120) For the appellation "novi pharisei," see note 24 (130–31): "a similar expression . . . is not to be found either in the New Testament or in contemporary exegesis, but only in fact in the world of Joachite prophecy, and more precisely, of the Spiritual Franciscans."

25. *Inf.* XXVIII. 83–84: "and I with repentance and confession became a monk; and—miserable wretch that I am!—it would have availed me."

26. It would have been easy for the poet of Hell to fall into the trap of making all his damned sinners repeat the catechistical formula used by Ciacco (*Inf.* VI. 53–54: "for the baneful sin of gluttony, as you see, I languish in the rain"); but such a procedure would have been foreign to Dante's narrative genius, which delights in characterization.

27. *Inf.* XIX. 104–5: "your avarice corrupts the world, crushing the good and raising up the wicked."

28. *Purg.* III. 34–45: "'Anyone is mad who hopes that our reason may compass the infinite course taken by one substance in three persons. Mortals, be satisfied with the *quia*; for, if you had been able to see everything, Mary would not have had to give birth; and you have seen men desire in vain who would otherwise have fulfilled their desire, which has been given to them to grieve over for all eternity: I mean Aristotle and Plato and many others'; and at this point he bent his brow and spoke no more, but remained troubled."

29. *Purg.* III. 133–35: "By their curse the Eternal Love is not lost to such an extent that it cannot return while hope still flowers."

30. Manichaean heretics such as the Cathars denied the possibility that prayer could influence God in any way (cf. *Purg.* VI. 28–42). For the question of indulgences, see M. Aurigemma, "Manfredi e il problema delle indulgenze," in *Dante nella cultura d'oggi*, ed. U. Bosco (Florence, 1965), 540–50.

31. G. Padoan, *Il lungo cammino*, 94, insists on the striking parallels with the *Inferno* in the first five cantos of *Purgatorio*.

Chapter 6. The Sordello Episode

1. T. Barolini, *Dante's Poets* (Princeton, N.J., 1984), 170–71.

2. T. Barolini, *Dante's Poets*, 183–84.

3. Benvenuto, 3, 178. For the physical description of the *magnanimus* and his self-control, see also Brunetto Latini, *Tresor*, II. 23, 194.

4. *Purg.* VI. 64–66: "He said nothing to us, but let us go on our way, merely watching like a lion at rest."

5. As Z. G. Baranski points out ("Canto VI," in *Dante's "Divine Comedy." Introductory Readings, II: "Purgatorio,"* ed. Tibor Wlassics [Charlottesville, Virginia, 1993], 83): "We are confronted with political poetry at its most quintessential—a powerful blend of its two most potent sub-genres, the invective (*vituperatio*) and the lament (*lamentatio*). . . . Yet, these are only the two most easily recognizable political discourses that can be heard in the second half of *Purgatorio* VI . . . lines 76–151 . . . present a veritable encyclopaedia of political writing."

6. *Purg.* VI. 76–78: "Italy, you slave, home of suffering, ship without a helmsman in a mighty storm, no mistress of provinces, but a brothel!"

7. *Ep.* VI. I. 3: "solio augustali vacante, totus orbis exorbitat . . . et quod Ytalia misera . . . omnique publico moderamine destituta, quanta ventorum fluentorumve concussione feratur verba non caperent . . ." For the vexed question of the chronology of Dante's life and works, see G. Petrocchi, *Vita di Dante*, as well as his "Biografia di Dante" in *ED* VI, 3–53. According to Petrocchi, the *Purgatorio* was composed mainly in Tuscany during the years 1308–1312, revised, and then published at Verona in the autumn of 1315. Maurizio Perugi is, however, correct in pointing out that Petrocchi does not give sufficient weight to the fundamental role played in the *Comedy* by Henry VII's Italian enterprise (1310–1313); Perugi goes so far as to claim that the invective in Canto VI is in fact a *planctus* for the Emperor (M. Perugi, "Il Sordello di Dante e la tradizione mediolatina dell'invettiva", *Studi Danteschi*, 55 (1983), 104–5. G. Padoan's hypothesis that the years 1315–1316 saw the composition of the whole of the second *cantica* (*Il lungo cammino del "poema sacro,"* 93–123) would add even greater poignancy to the lament on Italy's ills in the sixth canto and the whole *cantica*.

8. Cf. E. Auerbach, "Sacrae Scripturae sermo humilis," *Studi su Dante*, ed. D. Della Terza (Milan, 1977), 165–73. For a recent discussion of the problem of Dante's concept of comedy, see Z. Baranski, "*Comedía*: Notes on Dante, the Epistle to Cangrande, and Medieval Comedy," *Lectura Dantis* 8 (1991), 26–55. In an important essay, Lino Pertile has shown *inter alia* that "in a indisputably sacred book [the *Song of Songs*] the sublime, the comic and the humble styles all intermingled," declaring his intention of studying the specific problem of the poem's title. See "*Cantica* nella tradizione medievale e in Dante," *Rivista di storia letteratura religiosa* 25 (1992), 389–412.

9. Lamentations I. I: "Facta est quasi vidua domina Gentium: princeps provinciarum facta est sub tributo." G. Padoan, *Il lungo cammino del "poema sacro,"* 135, observes that the abandonment of Rome is a dominant theme in the *Purgatorio*.

10. T. Barolini, *Dante's Poets*, 179–82 (the text quoted is from lines 70–74 and 106 of Guittone's poem: "the best mistress of the province and also queen . . . virtually become a handmaid").

11. *Monarchia* I. xvi. I: "Nam si a lapsu primorum parentum . . . dispositiones hominum et tempora recolamus, non inveniemus nisi sub divo Augusto monarcha, existente Monarchia perfecta, mundum undique fuisse quietum." Cf. *Convivio* IV. iv. 3–4, and IV. v. 8.

12. *Mon.* II. i. 3: "cum videam populos vana meditantes . . . cum insuper doleam reges et principes in hoc unico concordantes: ut adversentur Domino suo et Uncto suo, romano principi."

13. See F. Mazzoni, "Pietro Alighieri interprete di Dante," *Studi Danteschi* 40 (1963), 334–38, where a passage from Pietro's commentary is quoted to the effect that the world, a microcosm, should be ruled by only one "mover," just as the universe is governed by one God (cf. *Mon.* I. ix. 2–3, *Purg.* XIV. 148–51, and *Par.* I. 103–105). For the medieval view of the government of the universe, see J. A. Mazzeo's fine essay, "The Mediaeval Concept of Hierarchy," in his *Mediaeval Tradition in Dante's "Comedy"* (Ithaca, N.Y., 1960), 1–55.

14. *Mon.* I. xi. 11–12: "iustitie maxime contrariatur cupiditas, ut innuit Aristotiles . . . Remota cupiditate omnino, nichil iustitie restat adversum . . . Sed Monarcha non habet quod possit optare: sua nanque iurisdictio terminatur Occeano solum: quod non contingit principibus aliis. . . . Ex quo sequitur quod Monarcha sinceerissimum inter mortales iustitie possit esse subiectum." Cf. Nardi's note (*Monarchia*, ed. cit., 337): "*avarice* for Dante . . . is greed for riches and power"; also, the penetrating study by G. Berretta, "Il mal che tutto il mondo occúpa," *Filologia e Letteratura* 14 (1968), 163–91.

15. "quasi ad nihilum" (quoted in J. H. Mundy, *Europe in the High Middle Ages: 1150–1309*, 368).

16. D. Waley, *Later Medieval Europe: From St. Louis to Luther*, 78.

17. H. S. Offler, "Aspects of Government in the Late Medieval Empire," in *Europe in the Late Middle Ages*, ed. J. Hale et al. (London, 1965), 228–29.

18. *MGH* IV:I, 139: "Mentiuntur, quia de iure sunt et esse debent sub rege Romano et imperatore . . ."

19. *MGH* IV: I, 155. In his reply to Boniface Albert's Chancellor had spoken of the "unbounded authority" (*inlimitata auctoritas*) of the Holy See, followed by unconditional recognition of the Pope's *plenitudo potestatis* (143). T. S. R. Boase (*Boniface VIII*, 330) comments that in Albert's oath to the Pope "for the first and only time the terms *fidelis et obediens* are found in an imperial pledge . . . its clauses provided analogies for almost any papal pretension. . . . All imperial care about the subtlety of papal formulae had been completely abandoned."

20. *Mon.* III. x. 10–20: "Ex quo patet quod Imperator ipsam [iurisdictionem temporalem] permutare non potest in quantum Imperator, cum ab ea recipiat esse quod est. . . . Adhuc dicunt quod Adrianus papa Carolum magnum sibi et Ecclesie advocavit . . . et quod Carolus ab eo recepit Imperii dignitatem . . . Propter quod dicunt quod omnes qui fuerunt Romanorum Imperatores post ipsum, et ipsi

advocati Ecclesie sunt et debent ad Ecclesia advocari [N.B. the play on the words *advocati/advocari*, impossible to reproduce in translation]: ex quo etiam sequeretur illa dependentia quam concludere volunt. Et ad hoc infringendum dico quod nichil dicunt: usurpatio enim iuris non facit ius." Cf. Ullmann, *Medieval Political Thought*, 108: "The papal doctrine concerning the empire was classically expressed by Innocent III [1198–1216], who maintained that, because no one had a right to a favour, the German king could have no claim to emperorship."

21. Regarding the verb *vergognarsi* ("to be ashamed"), A. Bufano in *ED* V, 959 observes that it acquires a particular intensity of meaning in this context and quotes Buti's gloss: "come at least, in order to show that you are ashamed of having such a reputation, that you remain in Germany through avarice and allow Italy to be undone." French readers may turn to the vigorous translation of lines 116–17 offered by André Pézard: "et si pitié de nous point ne t'émeut, / viens de ton bas renom prendre vergogne" (Pézard, 1159). For the stress in lines 112–14 ("*your* Rome . . . *widowed and alone* . . . 'O *my* Caesar, why are you not here with me?' "), I would refer readers to the illuminating essay "Rome and Babylon in Dante," in which Charles Davis puts forward the original and convincing idea that the husband in *Inf.* XIX. 111 is Rome's husband, the Emperor. However, although Professor Davis rigorously adheres to the evidence of Dante's Epistle XI in pointing out that "Rome has another husband. . . . Even though one of her husbands, the pope, is in the city in 1300, the fictional date of the *Commedia*, Dante thinks that she is a widow without the other" (26), I would claim that in the *Comedy*'s poetic universe—and, more than ever, in *Purgatorio* VI—Rome's husband is solely the Emperor.

22. Cf. P. Renucci, *Dante, disciple et juge*, 352, n. 9; J. A. Scott, "Myth in Dante and Petrarch," in *Myth and Mythology*, ed. F. West (Canberra, 1987), 91. Cf. Petrarch's more traditional use of the classical deity in, e.g., *Rime sparse*, CLXVI. 13 and CCXLVI. 7 ("O living Jove").

23. *Purg.* VI. 124–26: "For Italy's cities are full of tyrants, and any bumpkin playing the partisan becomes a Marcellus."

24. G. Favati, "Sordello," in *Dante nella critica d'oggi*, ed. U. Bosco, (Florence, 1965), 561, notes that the reference to the conqueror of Syracuse is filtered through Virgil's portrait in the *Aeneid*, in which Marcellus appears above all as the man who restored order to Italy, thus explaining Dante's ironic statement: "no one has been able to be a second Marcellus: not even the youth who seemed best qualified, Octavian's son-in-law . . ." For the other identification, see T. Barolini, *Dante's Poets*, 182, and her pregnant parallel with Guittone: "Dante's point is that his contemporaries have modeled themselves not on good Romans, but on the bad ones like Marcellus."

25. *Purg.* VI. 136–38: "Now be happy, for you have good reason to be so: with your riches, your peace, and your good government! Reality shows whether or not I speak the truth."

26.   Godi, Fiorenza, poi che se' sí grande
        che per mare e per terra batti l'ali,
        e per lo 'nferno tuo nome si spande! (*Inf.* XXVI. 1–3)

27. J. Bernard, "Trade and Finance in the Middle Ages," in *The Fontana Economic History of Europe: The Middle Ages*, ed. C. M. Cipolla (London, 1972), 296,

310. Contemporary Florence's vast program of building and townplanning is well documented in G. Pampaloni, *Firenze al tempo di Dante: documenti sull'urbanistica fiorentina* (Rome, 1973).

28. For the revenues of the French Crown, see J. Larner, *Italy in the Age of Dante*, 87; also G. Holmes, "The Supremacy of Florence, 1277–1294," in *Florence, Rome*, 25–43. For a general survey, see P. J. Jones, "La storia economica: dalla caduta dell'Impero romano al secolo XIV," in *Storia d'Italia*, vol. 2 (Turin, 1974), especially 1688–1810. For the Florentine economy in particular, see F. Melis, "La vita economica di Firenze al tempo di Dante," in *Atti del Congresso Internazionale di studi danteschi* (Florence, 1966), 2: 99–128.

29. J. Larner, *Italy in the Age of Dante*, 36; cf. A. Frugoni, *Incontri nel Medio Evo* (Bologna, 1979), 138 and 171, n. 287. Cf. the inscription placed in 1255 on the façade of the Palazzo del Podestà claiming that Florence owned the earth, the sea, the whole globe—*quae mare, quae terram, quae totum possidet orbem*.

30. Quoted in C. T. Davis, *Dante's Italy*, 206.

31. For a concise survey of the period of conflict and turmoil in Florence (c. 1250–1300), see L. Baktin, *Dante e la società italiana del Trecento* (Bari, 1979), 107–23, and "Party Conflict and the *Popolo*" in J. Larner, *Italy in the Age of Dante*, especially 119–22.

32. G. Holmes, *Florence, Rome*, 35. Referring to this invective against Florence, J. Najemy ("Dante and Florence," 92) rightly observes: "This *popolo* is clearly the political movement . . . [the episode] is a precise denunciation of the fundamental institutions and language of the *popolo*: its notions of justice, its ethic of citizen participation, and its emphasis on law and constitutional reform. Here Dante has gathered the characteristic terms of the *popolo*'s discourse of politics . . . 'giustizia,' 'consiglio,' 'comune,' 'leggi,' 'civili,' 'viver bene,' 'provedimenti,' 'officio,' and 'membre.'"

33. J. Ferrante, *The Political Vision*, 61ff. The image of Florence as the good mother nurturing and protecting her young is most clearly subverted in *Par.* XVII. 46–48. In Purgatory we are offered instead the vision of Dante's beloved city seen as a sleepless woman, wracked by fever, incapable of finding peace or health, while her constant metamorphoses, resulting in "renewed members," are reminiscent of the grotesque physical mutations that afflict the thieves and other denizens of nether Hell.

34. Cf. Brunetto Latini, *Tresor*, II. 108 (292, "On Concord"): "Solomon says that every kingdom that is divided shall be destroyed in itself." Regarding the poet's lengthy "digression," F. Masciandaro makes the following penetrating comment: "Dante's invective dramatically represents the longing for the happiness 'figured' by the Earthly Paradise as the longing to transform the desert into a garden in the here and now of this life. Thus the poet's vision at once departs from and perfects the pilgrim's nostalgia for Eden" (*Dante as Dramatist: The Myth of the Earthly Paradise and Tragic Vision in the "Divine Comedy"* [Philadelphia, 1991], 153).

35. Benvenuto, III, 178: "in hoc ostendit eum magnanimum. Leo enim magnanimus non movetur nec curat eum qui non molestat eum." The lion as a symbol of magnanimity is a *topos* found in late antiquity, as well as in a contemporary of Dante's, who noted in the *Somme-le Roi* (1279), "Magnanimity is greatness and

nobility of heart, which makes man courageous like the lion" (quoted in R. A. Gauthier, *Magnanimité: l'idéal de la grandeur dans la philosophie païenne et dans la théologie chrétienne* [Paris, 1951], 293).

36. All quotations are taken from Sordello, *Le poesie*, ed. Marco Boni, (Bologna, 1954). The lines quoted are from *Planher vuelh en Blacatz en aquest leugier so* (no. VI. 41–42): "The great and powerful will hate me for the way I speak out / But let them know that I care as little for them as they do for me"). Cf. XX. 41–43, where the poet declares that he has surely gained the enmity of James I of Aragon and the Counts of Toulouse and Provence, because he has dared to tell them some unpalatable truths.

37. T. Barolini, *Dante's Poets*, 179.

38. Quoted by F. Coletti, *ED* IV, 1026. For Dante's possible rejoinder, see *Par.* IX. 32–36.

39. C. M. Bowra, "Dante and Sordello," *Comparative Literature* 5 (1953), 7.

40. Sordello, *Le poesie*, XXII. 22–24: "Ai, com pot tan esser desvergoignatz / nuls hom gentils, que an enbastarden / son lignage per aur ni per argen?"

41. *Purg.* XX. 79–81: "O avarice, what else can you do to us, now that you have my family so much in your clutches that it does not care for its own flesh?"

42. C. M. Bowra, "Dante and Sordello," 7.

43. T. Barolini, *Dante's Poets*, 161.

44. T. Barolini, *Dante's Poets*, 161 (emphasis mine). Cf. Z. Barański, "Canto VI," 89–90: "It is thus difficult to escape the startling conclusion that the world evoked in the invective is precisely the world as fashioned by Sordello and his ilk . . . Sordello seems to stand in contrast to his author."

45. T. Barolini, *Dante's Poets*, 161.

46. M. Perugi, "Il Sordello di Dante," 78.

47. M. Perugi, "Il Sordello di Dante," 79.

48. E. Gilson, *Dante the Philosopher* (London, 1948), 267. Cf. I. Brandeis, *The Ladder of Vision: A Study of Dante's "Comedy"* (New York, 1962), 84: "Dante in his *Comedy* never *serves* history; he uses it . . ."

49. *De Vulgari Eloquentia*, I. xv. 2: "Dicimus ergo quod forte non male opinantur qui Bononienses asserunt pulcriori locutione loquentes, cum ab Ymolensibus, Ferrarensibus et Mutinensibus circunstantibus aliquid proprio vulgari asciscunt, sicut facere quoslibet a finitimis suis conicimus, ut Sordellus de Mantua sua ostendit, Cremone, Brixie atque Verone confini: qui, tantus eloquentie vir existens, non solum in poetando sed quomodocunque loquendo patrium vulgare deseruit." See the penetrating discussion of this passage in Z. Barański, "*Sordellus . . . qui . . . patrium vulgare deseruit*: A Note on *De Vulgari Eloquentia*, I, 15, sections 2–6," in *The Cultural Heritage of the Italian Renaissance (Essays in Honour of T. G. Griffith)*, ed. C. E. J. Griffiths and R. Hastings (Lewiston-Queenston-Lampeter, 1993), 19–45. Regarding Barański's writings on Sordello (see also note 5), I am delighted to note the convergence of views in our studies, which have been developed independently and at such great remove.

50. P. V. Mengaldo, in Dante Alighieri, *Opere minori*, 2:120, n. 1.

51. M. Shapiro, *De Vulgari Eloquentia: Dante's Book of Exile* (Lincoln, Nebraska and London, 1990), 4: "On internal evidence, the first book of *De vulgari*

eloquentia was written between the spring of 1303 and the beginning of 1305. . . . Adducing the many elements of Bolognese culture present in *De vulgari eloquentia* as evidence of a 1304–15 sojourn in that city, Mengaldo concedes the possibility, and Corti adds emphasis to the argument, that *De vulgari eloquentia* was composed after the first part and certainly before the fourth of the vernacular work [*Convivio*]." For the chronology of the *Convivio*, see Cesare Vasoli, in Dante Alighieri, *Opere minori* (Milan-Naples, 1988), I: 2, xiv.

52. Dante Alighieri, *Opere minori* (Milan-Naples, 1988), I: 2, 78, note: "coloro che preferiscono al volgare proprio quello altrui sono colpevoli di adulterio verso la loro lingua e, quindi, 'traditori'; e la loro bocca è *meretrice* perché servile e spregevole, in quanto loda vilmente una lingua estranea alla quale non si è legati da 'lo naturale amore de la propria loquela' (X. 5)."

53. Pézard, 1156, n. 58. For Pézard's thesis on the reason for Brunetto's damnation, see A. Pézard, *Dante sous la pluie de feu*.

54. C. M. Bowra, "Dante and Sordello," 4.

55. *S. Th.* 2.2.54.1. Cf. E. Peters, "I principi negligenti di Dante e le concezioni medievali del *rex inutilis*," *Rivista storica italiana* 80 (1968), 741–58, especially 742: the concept of the *rex inutilis* (as distinct from the *tyrannus*) "was a political type that grew up in the popular imagination and in juridical thought between the eighth and the thirteenth century," a type that characterized rulers who were negligent "in regard to both their own salvation and the well-being of the kingdoms entrusted to their care."

56. For this theoretical supremacy of the vernacular, see C. Grayson, "*Nobilior est vulgaris*: Latin and Vernacular in Dante's Thought," in *Centenary Essays on Dante*, ed. C. Grayson (Oxford, 1965), 54–76.

57. *Conv.* I. xiii. 12: "Questo sarà luce nuova, sole nuovo, lo quale surgerà là dove l'usato tramonterà, e darà lume a coloro che sono in tenebre e in oscuritade, per lo usato sole che a loro non luce."

58. *S. Th.* 2.2.54.3.1.

59. M. Shapiro, *De Vulgari Eloquentia*, 6, merely observes: "*Convivio* speaks ill of those who overvalue this language [Provençal] to the detriment of Italian. And when praising Sordello, Dante withholds the information that Sordello composed in Provençal."

60. *Purg.* XXVI. 117. See C. S. Singleton's warning ("The Vistas in Retrospect," in *Atti del congresso internazionale di studi danteschi* [Florence, 1965], 1: 303): "he who does *not* look back will deny himself vistas in memory, dimensions of meaning, that could not lie closer to the heart of Dante's poetry."

61. T. Barolini, *Dante's Poets*, 176.

62. *Purg.* VIII. 19–21: "Reader, here sharpen well your eyes to the truth, for the veil is now so very fine that to pass within is surely easy."

63. F. Forti, *Magnanimitade*, 87 (with the passage from Pietro's commentary).

64. J. Ferrante, *The Political Vision*, 218. Cf. chapter 5 of F. Masciandaro, *The Myth of the Earthly Paradise*, esp. 183: "in the Valley of the Princes Dante gives expression to the problematic recovery of the true garden and its inherent tragic vision." Professor Masciandaro's different approach and stimulating insights will, I trust, be welcomed as complementary to my own for students of the *Purgatorio*.

65. W. Ullmann, *Medieval Political Thought*, 110.

66. See chapter 2.

67. B. Tierney, *The Crisis of Church and State*, 157.

68. F. Forti, *Magnanimitade*, 97.

69. *Monarchia* III. iv. 14: "cum ista regimina sint hominum directiva in quos-dam fines . . . si homo stetisset in statu innocentie in quo a Deo factus est, talibus directivis non indiguisset: sunt ergo huiusmodi regimina remedia contra infirmi-tatem peccati."

70. Forti, *Magnanimitade*, 95. The passage reads: "*velut fecunda vallis* con-cipite ac *viride* germinetis, viride dico fructiferum *vere pacis* . . . Itaque, si *culpa vetus* non obest, que plerunque supinatur *ut coluber* et vertitur in se ipsam . . . Evigilate igitur omnes et assurgite regi vestro" (*Ep.* V. v–vi. 16–19; emphasis mine).

71. *Ep.* V. x. 30: "ut ubi radius spiritualis non sufficit, ibi splendor minoris lu-minaris illustret" (for the rejection of the sun-moon analogy, see chapter 8).

72. J. A. Watt, "Spiritual and Temporal Power" in *Cambridge History of Medi-eval Political Thought: c. 350–c. 1450*, ed. J. H. Burns (Cambridge, 1991), 387.

73. *Mon.* III. x. 9: "Cum ergo scindere Imperium esset destruere ipsum, con-sistente Imperio in unitate Monarchie universalis, manifestum est quod Imperii auctoritate fungenti scindere Imperium non licet."

74. *Purg.* VII. 91–96: ". . . with the look of one who neglected what he ought to have done . . . who could have healed the wounds that have proved to be the death of Italy, so that it is late for her to be saved by another."

75. Dante's Rome-centered vision of the Empire was contradicted by the political reality: see P. G. Ricci's observation that "The *Rex Romanorum*, elected in Frankfurt and crowned at Aix-la-Chapelle and confirmed by the Pontiff, possessed full juridical authority to administer the Empire without the need to be crowned in Rome" ("Dante e l'impero di Roma," in *Dante e Roma*, [Florence, 1965], 148, n. 53).

76. G. Villani, *Cronica* VIII, 55 (emphasis mine).

77. Cf. *DVE* I. xii. 5: "*Racha, Racha!* [cf. Matt. 5.22] What does the trumpet of the new Frederick proclaim . . . if not: 'Come, you murderers; come all traitors; come you followers of avarice?' "; see also the historian's judgment in K. Penning-ton, *The Prince and the Law*, 169: "[Dante's Emperor, Henry VII] committed an even graver error by binding himself with the Aragonese king, Frederick II, who would prove a completely ineffective ally."

78. *Purg.* VII. 16–19: " 'O glory of the Italians', he said, 'through whom our language showed what it could achieve, o eternal pride of the place where I was born, what merit or what grace shows you to me?' "

79. Reference must be made to C. Grayson's attractive hypothesis that *la lin-gua nostra* ("our language") refers to language in general, with the rider that, "what greatness human language showed through Virgil using Latin, may still be paral-leled through Dante using Italian" ("Latin and Vernacular in Dante's Thought," in *Centenary Essays on Dante* [Oxford, 1965], 75–76). It is in any case important to remember that Dante saw Latin as an amalgam, made up of elements drawn from the various pre-existing "Romance" languages (Italian, French, Provençal: *DVE* I. x. 1–2): from this (antihistorical) viewpoint, Latin could truly be described as "our language," uniting the various members of the Empire.

Chapter 7. The Dream and the Entrance to Purgatory

1. *Purg.* IV. 127–32: "And he: 'Brother, what is the point of going up? Because God's angel who sits at the gate would not allow me to pass through to the torments. First the heavens must revolve around me outside it as many times as they did in life, since I put off the good sighs until the end.'"

2. J. Le Goff, *La Naissance du purgatoire* (Paris, 1981), 453–54: "Of all the geographical images offered to Dante over so many centuries by the way the other world had been imagined, he chose the only one that expresses the true logic of Purgatory, one where there is an ascent: a mountain."

3. Recently, Z. Barański has argued that, "Rather than glimpses of the future, they [the three dreams] are sophisticated signs of the pilgrim's emotional, intellectual, and spiritual condition at the moments when they occur": "Dante's Three Reflective Dreams," *Quaderni d'italianistica* 10 (1989), 220. On the three dreams, see also B. Stambler, "Three Dreams," *Books Abroad: Dante Issue* (May 1965), 81–93; C. Speroni, "Dante's Prophetic Morning Dreams," in *American Critical Essays on the "Divine Comedy,"* ed. R. J. Clements (New York, 1967), 182–92; R. Hollander, *Allegory in Dante's "Commedia"* (Princeton, N.J., 1969), 136–58; G.P. Norton, "Retrospection and Prefiguration in the Dreams of *Purgatorio*," *Italica* 47 (1970), 351–65; R. Stella, "L'Expression symbolique dans les trois rêves du *Purgatoire* de Dante," *Revue des Études Italiennes* 25 (1979), 124–44; R. Stefanini, "I tre sogni del *Purgatorio*: struttura e allegoria," in *Studies in the Italian Renaissance: Essays in Memory of Arnolfo B. Ferruolo* (Naples, 1985), 43–66; D. S. Cervigni, *Dante's Poetry of Dreams* (Florence, 1986).

4. *Purg.* IX. 16–18: ". . . our mind, more of a pilgrim from the flesh and less of a captive to thoughts, is almost divine in its visions."

5. *Purg.* IX. 19–33: "in a dream I seemed to see an eagle poised in the heavens, with feathers of gold, its wings outspread, and ready to swoop down; and I seemed to be in the place where his companions were abandoned by Ganymede, when he was snatched up to the supreme court. Within myself I thought, 'Perhaps this eagle strikes only here, and perhaps it refuses to carry up any prey from any other place.' Then it seemed to me that, after wheeling a while, it swooped down terrible as lightning and snatched me upward as far as the fire. There it seemed that both he and I burned; and the imagined fire so scorched me that my sleep was broken."

6. *Purg.* IX. 52–63: "A short while ago, at dawn which precedes the day, when your soul was sleeping innerly, a woman came upon the flowers that adorn the ground down there and said: 'I am Lucy; let me take this sleeping man, that I may speed him on his way.' Sordello and the other noble spirits stayed there; she took you, and, once the day was bright, she came on upward as I followed in her footsteps. She set you down here, but first her lovely eyes showed that open entrance to me; then she and sleep both departed."

7. Stefanini argues forcefully that Lucia is a "figure of the universal Empire . . . in Dante's allegorical idiolect," and points out that the saint's liturgy opens with the eighth verse of Psalm 44: "You have loved justice [*Diligisti iustitiam*: cf. *Par.* XVIII. 91–93] and hated iniquity," which was "also chanted during the politi-

cal and religious ceremony of the Coronation. In the Middle Ages, the first two clauses of this verse had thus become a kind of imperial motto and auspice. . . . The first to act must be the Empire; so, divine Mercy (Mary) sends Lucy, precisely because she represents the [supreme] political authority" ("I tre sogni," 59–62).

8. Bosco-Reggio, 2: 153, n. 33.

9. R. Hollander, *Allegory*, 145–47.

10. See E. Auerbach, "Figurative Texts Illustrating Certain Passages of Dante's *Commedia*," *Speculum* 21 (1946), 474–89, in which the eagle is seen above all as *figura Christi*. D. S. Cervigni, *Dante's Poetry of Dreams*, 114, refers to an important study by R. Wittkover ("Eagle and Serpent: A Study in the Migration of Symbols," *Journal of the Warburg Institute* 2 [1938–1939], 293–325) and concludes that "the golden eagle represents a supernatural power and must necessarily be identified with Christ Himself."

11. *Ep.* XIII, xvi. 40–41: "Genus vero phylosophie sub quo hic in toto et parte proceditur, est morale negotium, sive ethica; quia *non ad speculandum, sed ad opus inventum totum et pars*. Nam si in aliquo loco vel passu pertractatur ad modum speculativi negotii, hoc non est gratia speculativi negotii, sed gratia operis" (emphasis mine).

12. See the famous couplet by Augustine of Dacia (d. 1282): *Littera gesta docet, quid credas allegoria, / moralis quid agas, quo tendas anagogia* ("The letter teaches things that have been done [the (hi-)story], the moral sense what you must do, the anagogical, your final aim").

13. C. S. Singleton, *"In Exitu Israel de Aegypto,"* in *Dante: A Collection of Critical Essays*, ed. J. Freccero (Englewood Cliffs, N.J., 1965), 119 and 106.

14. *Purg.* IX. 70–72: "Reader, you can clearly see how I am raising the level of my theme: therefore, be not surprised if I refine it with even greater skill."

15. Cf. Benvenuto, 3: 287: "a black eagle in a gold field was the insignia of the Roman emperors."

16. *Purg.* IX. 22–24: "and I seemed to be in the place where his companions were abandoned by Ganymede, when he was snatched up to the supreme court."

17. Bosco-Reggio, 2: 153. In fact, Sapegno, 492, had already emphasized the fact that "this detail in the dream is also based on a real sensation: the rays of the sun already high in the sky strike the poet's eyes." It will be noted that both Bosco and Sapegno refer to the "poet" when describing the experience undergone by the wayfarer or pilgrim.

18. *Purg.* XXVII. 10–12: "Then: 'It is not possible to proceed, holy souls, unless the fire first bites: enter it and do not be deaf to the chanting beyond it."

19. *Purg.* XXVII. 49–51: ". . . I would have thrown myself into molten glass to cool myself, such was the infinite heat of that fire."

20. It is equally surprising that such a perspicacious scholar as Jacques Le Goff should state: *"Often* Dante refers to what beforehand had more or less identified itself with the purgatorial suffering: fire" (J. Le Goff, *La Naissance*, 464; emphasis mine)—surprising, because no fewer than seven of the nine examples quoted by him are all taken from the fire on the cornice of lust, the eighth is the occurrence we are discussing (IX. 31–33) and the last is an example of traditional metonymy (XXVII. 127–28). D. S. Cervigni, *Dante's Poetry of Dreams*, 103, states: "The first as-

sociation which every Dante reader probably makes, in relation to the fire, conjures up the flames in Canto XXVII, the culmination and summary of Dante's purification in Purgatory." This can only be true for those readers who, when they arrive at the last terrace, look back on Dante's first dream—which is perhaps the reason why so many of them have in fact failed to make this association of ideas.

21. *Purg.* XXVII. 127–41: "and he said: 'Son, you have seen both the temporal and the eternal fire; and you have come to a place where I can discern no further. I have led you here with intelligence and skill; now, you must take your own pleasure to be your guide . . . free, upright, and whole is your will, and it would be a sin not to follow its promptings . . .'"

22. *Mon.* III. xv. 17–18: "cum mortalis ista felicitas quodammodo ad immortalem felicitatem ordinetur. Illa igitur reverentia Cesar utatur ad Petrum qua primogenitus filius debet uti ad patrem: ut luce paterne gratie illustratus virtuosius orbem terre irradiet, cui ab Illo solo prefectus est, qui est omnium spiritualium et temporalium gubernator." For the vexed question of the correct interpretation of the phrase "quodammodo . . . ordinetur" and of the whole ending to Dante's political treatise, see E. Gilson, *Dante the Philosopher*, 198–99; E. H. Kantorowicz, *The King's Two Bodies*, 457, n. 17; H. Kelsen, *La teoria dello stato in Dante* (Bologna, 1974), 139–40; B. Martinelli, "Sul 'quodammodo' di *Monarchia*"; M. Maccarrone, "Il terzo libro"; M. Maccarrone, "Papato e Impero nella *Monarchia*"; F. Mazzoni, "Teoresi e prassi in Dante politico," xci–xcvi; L. Minio-Paluello, "Tre note alla 'Monarchia'," in *Medioevo e Rinascimento: Studi in onore di Bruno Nardi* 2: 522–24; B. Nardi, *Dal "Convivio" alla "Commedia,"* 66–69, 285–313; G. Vinay, *Interpretazione della "Monarchia" di Dante* (Florence, 1962), esp. 12ff.; E. Williamson, "*De Beatitudine Huius Vite,*" *Annual Report of the Dante Society* 76 (1958), 1–22.

23. Cf. G. Mazzotta, *Dante's Vision and the Circle of Knowledge* (Princeton, 1993), 135–36: "[For Dante] Not the philosopher or the theologian but the poet, who is installed in the world of the imagination—dreams, memories, visions, representations—plays a crucial role in determining the shape of knowledge . . . knowledge is ultimately self-knowledge."

24. See P. Armour, *The Door of Purgatory: A Study of Multiple Symbolism in Dante's "Purgatorio"* (Oxford, 1983), especially 35–118. I am gratified that Professor Armour's illuminating study supports and complements my own interpretation of Dante's second *cantica* as offering "a hidden polemic and admonition to the Church on earth" (122).

25. C. Mitchell, "The Lateran Fresco of Boniface VIII," *Journal of the Warburg and Courtauld Institutes* 14 (1951), 1.

26. Regarding Dante's visit(s) to Rome, see P. Armour *The Door*, 69–185 (who believes it is likely that "Dante's Jubilee pilgrimage heightened his religious sense and, at the same time, his indignation against Boniface VIII," 182). Armour also points out (44) that the traditional symbols of St. Peter are in fact the keys and a sword.

27. P. Armour, *The Door*, 172, 185.

28. *Purg.* IX. 127–29: "'I received them from Peter; and he told me that I should err in opening the gate rather than in keeping it shut, provided that people prostrate themselves at my feet.'"

29. See the classic study by E. De' Negri, "Tema e iconografia del *Purgatorio*," *Romanic Review* 49 (1958), 81–104.

30. Benvenuto, 3: 288.

31. *Purg*. X. 93 finds an echo in John of Salisbury's *Policraticus* (V. 8), where Trajan's exemplary action is said to have been inspired by two motivating forces— "the one is the duty imposed by Justice, the other that imposed by Pity; both are equally necessary in a ruler" (*Alterum namque justitiae, alterum pietatis est; quae adeo principi necessaria sunt*)—an echo first pointed out by H. Gmelin (see G. Getto, *Letture dantesche* [Florence, 1964], 2, 877). For the legend of Trajan's "second chance", obtained through the intercession of St Gregory the Great and his salvation, see M. Pastore Stocchi, "Traiano," in *ED* V, 685–86, and A. Graf, *Roma nella memoria*.

32. *Dante Alighieri: La Commedia secondo l'antica vulgata*, ed. G. Petrocchi (Milan, 1967), 3: 163–64, n. 74.

33. *Ep*. XI. v. 9: "Forsitan 'et quis iste, qui Oze repentinum supplicium non formidans, ad arcam, quamvis labantem, se erigit?' indignanter obiurgabitis. Quippe de ovibus in pascuis Iesu Christi minima una sum; quippe nulla pastorali auctoritate abutens, quoniam divitie mecum non sunt. Non ergo divitiarum, sed 'gratia Dei sum id quod sum', et 'zelus domus eius comedit me.'" The Pauline echoes are clear (1 Cor. 15. 9–10).

34. *Ep*. XI. ii. 3: "et dictum est: Petre, pasce sacrosanctum ovile; Romam— cui, post tot triumphorum pompas, et verbo et opere Christus orbis confirmavit imperium, quam etiam ille Petrus, et Paulus . . . in apostolicam sedem aspergine proprii sanguinis consecravit" (cf. 11: "pro sede Sponse [Christi] que Roma est").

35. *Mon*. I. xi. 14–16: "charity reinforces justice, so that the more powerful she is the more force justice will have. That rightly ordered love should be found most of all in the Emperor is shown thus . . . men are closer to the Emperor than to other princes; therefore they are most greatly loved by him or they ought to be. . . . So prior and immediate tutelage over all men belongs to the Emperor" (*karitas maxime iustitiam vigorabit et potior potius. Et quod Monarche maxime hominum recta dilectio inesse debeat, patet sic . . . homines propinquius Monarche sunt quam aliis principibus: ergo ab eo maxime diliguntur vel diligi debent . . . et sic per prius et immediate Monarche inest cura de omnibus*).

Chapter 8. The Poem's Center

1. *Purg*. XI. 61–66: "The ancient blood and the splendid deeds of my ancestors made me so arrogant that, forgetful of our common mother, I held all men in such excessive scorn that it brought about my death, as the people of Siena know and every child in Campagnatico knows."

2. *Purg*. XI. 122–23: "and he is here because in his presumption he aimed at bringing all Siena under his rule."

3. For the rise of despotism in the Italian Communes, see D. M. Bueno de Mesquita, "The Place of Despotism in Italian Politics," in *Europe in the Late Middle Ages* (London, 1970), 301–31; J. Larner, *Italy in the Age of Dante*, 128–52; D. Waley, *The Italian City-Republics* (London, 1978), 128–40.

4. Boethius, *The Theological Tractates and The Consolation of Philosophy* (Cambridge, Mass. and London, 1953), 319–21.

5. *Mon.* III. xv. 9: "Has igitur conclusiones et media . . . humana cupiditas postergaret nisi homines, tanquam equi, *sua bestialitate vagantes* 'in camo et freno' [Psalm 31. 9] compescerentur in via." As E. Peters observes: "Throughout much of the *Commedia*, bestiality is associated with civil discord, probably from the frequency of the image in Aristotelian sources and commentaries" ("*Pars, Parte*," 116).

6. "It was for the empire to supply this right ordering and governance . . . To maintain peace and justice was its primary concern, as Frederick II had emphasized in 1235" (H. S. Offler, "Aspects of Government," 226). For Dante, the essential link or bridge between society and politics is created by Justice: K. Hyde, "The Social and Political Ideal of the *Comedy*," in *Dante Readings*, ed. E. Haywood (Dublin, 1987), 47–71.

7. N. Iliescu, "The Roman Emperors in the *Divine Comedy*," in *Lectura Dantis Newberryana*, ed. P. Cherchi and A. C. Mastrobuono (Evanston, Ill., 1988), 1: 4 (my emphasis); cf., however, J. A. Mazzeo, *Mediaeval Cultural Tradition*, 8: "Gravest among these [risks] is the simplification of the moral vision of the mediaeval period in order to imply that the men of that time were insensitive to moral paradox, to the antimonies present in any life of choice."

8. Since English translations mostly translate the *trista selva* of line 64 as "dismal wood," "sad wood," etc., I think it necessary to point out that *trista* in Dante can mean "evil, wicked" (as in *Inf.* XXX. 76–77: "l'anima trista / di Guido . . .".). Bosco-Reggio (2: 244, n. 64) point to the ambiguity that is perforce lost in translation: "Il termine *trista* può voler dire 'piena di malvagità', ma anche 'sventurata'. . ."

9. See A. Vasina, "Romagna," *ED* IV, 1018.

10. *Conv.* II. x. 8 (emphasis mine).

11. *Purg.* XVI. 40–42: "And if God has so gathered me into His grace that he desires that I should see his court in a manner quite unknown to modern times."

12. *Inf.* XVI. 67–69: "tell [us] if courtesy and valor still dwell in our city as was their wont, or whether they have totally left it" (emphasis mine). Note the poet's use of the singular form and feminine agreement in the verbal clause, *del tutto se n'è gita fora*, to emphasize the fact that courtesy—*cortesia*—is the keyword.

13. N. Iliescu, "The Roman Emperors in the *Divine Comedy*," 14 (emphasis mine). It is interesting to note that Villani (*Cronica* VIII. 121) makes Marco the mouthpiece for God's anger in his supposed encounter with Ugolino, then Lord of Pisa: "The wise man [Marco] immediately answered him: 'You are more likely to be struck down by misfortune than to be lord of Italy.' And the Count, fearing Marco's words, said: 'Why?' And Marco answered: 'Because the only thing you lack is God's wrath.'" Cf. *Cronica*, XIII. 74.

14. "What reason can see here, I can impart; beyond that you must wait for Beatrice, for it is a matter concerning the Faith."

15. *Par.* XXVII. 139–41: "You—in order not to be amazed—must remember that on earth no one governs, and so the human family is led astray."

16. R. Hollander, *Allegory*, 139, with particular reference to C. S. Singleton's classic study, "The Poet's Number at the Center," *Modern Language Notes* 80 (1965), 1–10.

17. *Ep.* XI. iii. 4: "et, quod horribilius est, quod astronomi quidam et crude prophetantes necessarium asserunt quod, male usi libertate arbitrii, eligere maluistis."

18. *Purg.* XVI. 85–96: "There comes forth from the hand of Him who loves it before it exists, like a child that sports, now in tears and now with laughter, the simple little soul that knows nothing, except that—created by a joyful Maker—it turns readily toward whatever attracts it. At first it savors trivial goods; and there it is beguiled and runs after them, unless a guide or bridle rules its love. Hence it was necessary to impose the laws as a bridle; it was necessary to have a ruler able to discern at least the tower of the true city."

19. *Purg.* XVI. 98–99: "No one, because the shepherd who precedes his flock can chew the cud but does not have the cloven hoof."

20. A. M. Stickler, "Concerning the Political Theories of the Medieval Canonists," *Traditio* 7 (1949–1951), 450. Cf. E. Peters, "The Frowning Pages," 290 and 302: "law and justice were for Dante metaphysical concepts, intimately linked to ethics, and thus, when applied rightly and equitably by the legitimate earthly law-giver, the emperor, they became . . . a para-sacrament . . . no Roman lawyer had ever precisely placed imperial law within a cosmological framework as spacious and detailed as Dante's."

21. See M. Maccarrone, "La teoria ierocratica e il canto XVI del *Purgatorio*," *Rivista di storia della Chiesa in Italia* 4 (1950), 389, n. 114.

22. *S. Th.* 1.2.102.6.1.

23. *Petri Allegherii super Dantis ipsius genitoris Comediam Commentarium* (Florence, 1845), 414; Benvenuto, 3: 441. André Pézard has pointed to a text by St Gregory the Great (*Moralia* I. xxix), in which we read that [the camel, as an example to the Pope] "has not a cloven hoof . . . nevertheless, it chews the cud, because by the right dispensation of temporal things it hopes to attain unto heavenly things" (Pézard, 1232, note 99).

24. W. Ullmann, *Medieval Political Thought*, 105.

25. J. A. Watt, Introduction to his translation of John of Paris, *On Royal and Papal Power* (Toronto, 1971), 25–26.

26. *Purg.* XVI. 106–8: "Rome, which made the world good, used to have two suns, which lit up the two paths, the world's path and the pathway to God."

27. *Ep.* VI. ii. 8: "ut alia sit Florentina civilitas, alia sit Romana? Cur apostolice monarchie similiter invidere non libet, ut si Delia geminatur in celo, geminetur et Delius?" The idea of a monstrosity *contra naturam* was aided by the powerful reductionism of medieval thought (cf. *Unam sanctam*: "there is one body and one head of this one and only church, not two heads as though it were a monster"). Nevertheless, although Étienne Gilson states "no one had ever thought to say that God had created two suns" (*Dante et la philosophie*, 220), already in the eleventh century Cardinal Humbert had denounced those sycophants who, at times of imperial successes, set up "two suns" (B. Tierney, *The Crisis of Church and State*, 41).

28. *Mon.* III. iv. 3: "Deinde arguunt quod, quemadmodum luna, que est luminare minus, non habet lucem nisi prout recipit a sole, sic nec regnum temporale auctoritatem habet nisi prout recipit a spirituali regimine." See the pertinent observations made by G. Di Scipio ("Dante and Politics," 268), when he relates the

disconcerting image of two suns to *Conv.* IV. xvii. 9: "This notion of the two 'fe-licitadi,' contemplative and active life, which interestingly enough Dante applies in determining the position of the Hebrew women in *Paradiso* XXXII, is at the root of the whole theory on the political system, and in the words of Marco Lombardo 'due soli,' the Empire and the Church. . ."

29. "Christi vicarius habet plenitudinem potestatis . . . potestas pape Christi vicarii habet instituere, destituere, corrigere . . . ligare et suspendere potestatem imperialem et regalem. See J. Rivière, *Le Problème de l'Église et de l'État au temps de Philippe le Bel* (Louvain-Paris, 1926), 328–29, n. 2). For the significance and elabo-ration of the title *vicarius Christi*, see M. Maccarrone, *"Vicarius Christi": storia del titolo papale* (Rome, 1952). For Dante's restrictions on the power of the Pope as *vi-carius Christi*, see *Mon.* III. iii. 7 and vii. 4–6.

30. B. Tierney, *The Crisis of Church and State*, 156.

31. E. H. Kantorowicz, "Dante's 'Two Suns'," in *Selected Studies* (New York, 1965), 338: "*Sol mundi* is Frederick in the eyes of a South Italian poet [Orfinus of Lodi], whereas Manfred, Frederick's son, styles his father *Sol mundi, auctor pacis*, and even *Sol Justitiae*."

32. Buti, 2: 381: "*Due Soli aver*; cioè due luci del mondo, come sono due luci in cielo; cioè lo papa e lo imperadore; ma notevilmente disse *Soli*, per non fare l'uno minore che l'altro . . ."

33. *Par.* VI. 13–24: "And before I was engaged on that task, I believed that there was only one nature in Christ and no more, and I was satisfied with that be-lief; but blessed Agapetus, who was the supreme pastor, directed me to the true faith by his words. I believed him. . . . As soon as I moved my steps along the Church's path, it pleased God, of His grace, to inspire me with the high task, and I gave myself entirely to it." See F. Mazzoni's fundamental essay: "Il canto VI del *Paradiso*," in *Paradiso: Letture degli anni 1979–'81* (Rome, 1989), 167–222.

34. "The one has extinguished the other; and the sword has joined the shep-herd's crook, and, joined together by unnatural force, they must perform badly; be-cause, so joined together, the one does not fear the other: if you do not believe me, look at the fruit, for every plant is known by what it seeds." M. De Rosa, "Prima che Federigo avesse briga," *Esperienze letterarie* 13 (1988), 79–88, argues for a recipro-cally destructive action (quoting Benvenuto, Landino, and Nardi), while interpret-ing line 117 "as a reference to Frederick II's attack against the Communes of north-ern Italy, rather than to the struggle between the Emperor and the Popes" (80).

35. *Purg.* XVI. 127–29: "Proclaim henceforth that the Church of Rome, be-cause she confounds two powers in herself, falls into the mire and befouls both herself and her burden."

36. J. Ferrante, *The Political Vision*, 231. I may add that the greatest example of righteous anger was given by Christ's expulsion of the moneychangers from the Temple (Mark 11. 17: "Is it not written, 'My House shall be called of all nations the House of Prayer'? but you have turned it into a den of thieves"). On virtuous anger in the *Comedy*, see P. Boyde, *Perception and passion in Dante's "Comedy"* (Cam-bridge, 1993), especially 268–9 and 274. We may also note that here in *Purg.* XVI. 127 we find the only occurrence in the *Comedy* of the appellation "the Church of Rome" (cf. the eight occurrences of "Holy Church")—as if to hammer home the

paradox that it is the Church of Rome (consecrated by the blood of Saints Peter and Paul: *Ep.* XI. ii. 3; cf. *Par.* IX. 139–41, XXVII. 40–60), now in shameful exile at Avignon and in radical opposition to "that Rome of which Christ is a Roman" (*Purg.* XXX. 102) that leads Christ's flock astray.

37. E. Peters, "Human Diversity and Civil Society in *Paradiso* VIII," *Dante Studies* 109 (1991), 64.

Chapter 9. The She-Wolf and the Shepherds

1. J. Le Goff, *Medieval Civilization: 400–1500* (Oxford, 1988), 250. Cf.M. Barasch, *Giotto and the Language of Gesture* (Cambridge, 1987), 164–65: "Under the pressure of economic developments the system of sins changed. Avarice came to be considered as the major sin . . . Dives was regarded as a prime sinner."

2. *Inf.* I. 94–99: ". . . this beast . . . does not allow anyone to pass her way, but so besets them that she slays them; and her nature is so vicious and evil that her voracious appetite is never satisfied, and after feeding she is hungrier than before."

3. Just as Lucifer, with his three monstrous heads, is the infernal antithesis or caricature of the Holy Trinity, so the she-wolf of Hell (*Inf.* I. 110) is the distorted, antithetical image of the traditional symbol of Rome, the wolf that suckled Romulus and Remus and which in medieval times had been taken over by Florence's archenemy, Siena, as a visual reminder of her Roman origins (*Saena Iulia*). As a symbol of Rome, the *lupa* ought to be associated with the Empire's role as the universal dispenser of Justice; it is therefore ironic that, when Dante visited Rome, this emblem was located in the papal palace—precisely in the Hall of Justice, "in the place where Christ is bartered all and every day" (*Par.* XVII. 51). For this detail, see F. Lanza, "Roma e l'emblema della lupa," in *Dante e Roma* (Florence, 1965), 258–59. G. P. Caprettini gives a fascinating philological and semiotic analysis of the "sign of the wolf" in medieval Italy, in his *San Francesco, il lupo, i segni* (Turin, 1974).

4. "Avarice and greed are sisters: pride is indeed their mother. Never did pride exist without greed, nor greed without avarice" (St. Bernard, *PL* 184. 126); "Avaritia est gloriae, divitiarum seu quarumlibet rerum insatiabilis et inhonesta cupiditas" (Hugh of St. Victor, *PL* 176. 1001).

5. *S. Th.* I.63.2. 2. Cf. Augustine, *De Libero Arbitrio*, 3 (*PL* 32. 1294): "Avaritia . . . non in solo argento vel in nummis . . . sed in omnibus rebus quae immoderate cupiuntur, intelligenda est." G. Berretta, "Il mal che tutto il mondo occúpa," contrasts Aquinas's moderation with Dante's radical (yet more traditional) attitude toward avarice.

6. "You have seen . . . the ancient witch that alone is now wept for above us; you have seen how to free oneself from her."

7. On personification allegory in Dante's poem, see R. Hollander, *Allegory in Dante's "Commedia,"* 239–56. Its ramifications make it possible for D. S. Cervigni to claim that "the oneiric appearance [of the *femmina balba*] embodies each one of the seven capital sins which the purging souls are expiating, from pride to lust" (*Dante's Poetry of Dreams*, 135). G. Mazzotta has a fascinating chapter on "The Dream of the Siren (*Purgatorio* XIX–XXI)" in his book *Dante's Vision*, in which

he claims: "The encounter with the Siren is a version of death's pull on and temptation for the pilgrim. Traditional mythographic accounts link the Siren with the sweetness of the story and only obliquely with death, but Dante foregrounds these dimensions of the myth."

8. G. Billanovich, *Prime ricerche dantesche* (Rome, 1947), 10.

9. Cf. Vincent of Beauvais, *Speculum Morale* III. vii. 2, who asserts that avarice deflects human beings from their proper stance, "erect toward the stars" and bends them down like beasts so that their only thought and desire is for earthly things (*ipsum ad inferiora deflectit et quem Deus creavit erectum ad sydera, ipsum ad modum bestiae incurvat ad infima, ut nihil velit cogitare, diligere, loqui, vel sapere nisi terrena*).

10. U. Bosco, *Dante vicino* (Caltanissetta-Rome, 1966), 378–90. The misunderstanding was easily made, if a reference was found to *dominus Adrianus* or to "il cardinale d'Inghilterra," since Adrian IV was English (Nicholas Breakspear) and Ottobono de' Fieschi had undertaken two missions to Henry III of England, where he had been made an archdeacon of Canterbury Cathedral.

11. R. Manselli, "Adriano V," *ED* I, 64.

12. Pézard, 783.

13. G. Paparelli, "Il canto XIX del *Purgatorio*," in *Nuove letture dantesche* (Florence, 1970), 4: 299–300.

14. G. Padoan, "Nelle cornici degli accidiosi e degli avari," in *Lectura Dantis Modenese* (Modena, 1986), 89–94.

15. See J. A. Watt, *Spiritual and Temporal Powers*, 383: "The deposition of Emperor Frederick II at the council of Lyons in 1245 was at once the papacy's most spectacular political action and the implementation of the hierocratic logic in its plentitude." Innocent IV laid claim to universal jurisdiction and power in *Quod super*, and stated that the Emperor held his authority from the Pope in *Licet* (both c. 1250: see B. Tierney, *The Crisis of Church and State*, 153–56). Frederick II rebutted these claims in, e.g., *MGH, Const.* 2, no. 262: "nowhere can it be found commanded in either divine or human law that [a pope] can transfer empires at will or punish kings temporally by depriving them of their kingdoms, or judge temporal rulers at all" (*aut terre principibus iudicare*). For Dante's attitude toward the decretalists, see E. Peters, "The Frowning Pages," 285–314 (esp. 286, "Dante here [*Par.* IX. 133–35] uses the manuscripts of the decretals as synecdoche for the larger disorder of his world: the successful envy of Satan, the papal neglect of the Holy Land, and the corruption of Florence").

16. *Purg.* XIX. 103–5: "For just over a month I learned how the great mantle weighs on the one who keeps it out of the mire, so that all other burdens seem a feather."

17. *Purg.* XVI. 127–29: "Proclaim henceforth that the Church of Rome, because she confounds two powers in herself, falls into the mire and befouls both herself and her burden."

18. *Inf.* XIX. 106–8: "The Evangelist had in mind pastors like you when she that sits upon the waters was seen by him whoring with the kings."

19. *Purg.* XIX. 106–11: "My conversion, alas! was tardy; but, as soon as I was

made the Roman shepherd, I discovered how false life is. I saw that there the heart could not find rest, nor was it possible to ascend higher in that life; therefore love for this life was kindled in me."

20. *Inf.* XIX. 70–72: "and I was truly a son of the she-bear, so greedy to advance the cubs that I pursed wealth up there and here I pursed myself."

21. Dante was, of course, unable to read Greek. For Bruno Nardi's note, see *Mon.*, 337.

22. *Par.* XVIII. 115–26: "O sweet star, how precious and how many were the gems that showed me that our justice is the effect of the heaven you make beautiful! Therefore I pray the Mind in which your motion and your force find their origin that It may look down upon the place whence comes forth *the smoke that dims your rays* . . . O hosts of Heaven whom I contemplate, pray for those who are on earth and who are all led astray by the evil example!"

23. *Purg.* XIX. 118–26 (my emphasis): "Just as our eyes, fixed on earthly things, did not look up on high, so *justice* here impels them toward the earth. Just as avarice quenched all our love of good, so that our works were lost, so *justice* here holds us captive, fettered in both hands and feet; and we shall lie here motionless and outstretched for as long as it shall please the *just* Lord."

24. For the date of composition of *Tre donne*, see K. Foster and P. Boyde, *Dante's Lyric Poetry* (Oxford, 1967), 2: 282: "the poem was probably not written much before the end of 1304." See also the significant observation on the previous page (281): "The experience of exile was of course decisive for the poet of the *Comedy*, in particular for the special stress which the idea of justice takes throughout the poem and the way the whole theme of justice is elaborated."

25. For a fuller treatment of this theme, see J. A. Scott, "La presenza antitetica di Simone Pietro in *Inferno* XIX," *Dante magnanimo*, 75–115.

26. Mark 5. 6: "Beati qui esuriunt et sitiunt iustitiam, quoniam ipsi saturabuntur." Although as we have seen, Dante in the *Monarchia* quotes Aristotle for the opposition justice-avarice, theologians like Aquinas also expressed this concept (*S. Th.* 2.2.118.4).

27. On the theme of night in the *Purgatorio*, see D. S. Cervigni, "The Purgatorial Night," in *Dante's Poetry of Dreams*, 93–95. Aquinas quotes Augustine's judgment that avarice is the poison of charity, after his own statement that the love of money darkens the soul by excluding the light of charity (*S. Th.* 2.2.118.4.3 and 5.2). P. Rajna, "Ugo Ciapetta nella Divina Commedia," *Studi Danteschi* 37 (1960), 5–20 (originally published in French, in 1924), claimed that Hugh had been guilty not of avarice but of prodigality. Despite the reader's memories of the fourth circle of Hell (*Inferno* VII), the only sin mentioned on the fifth terrace is avarice, until *Purg.* XXII. 34–54. What the reader is led to believe is surely obvious from Virgil's question (*Purg.* XXII. 22–23: "how could avarice find a place in your breast [*seno*], among such wisdom [*senno*] . . . ?"); the *coup de théâtre* so carefully prepared by the poet over three cantos would be lost, if any *exemplum* of prodigality had already been offered in Canto XX.

28. Augustine, *De Civitate Dei* V.xviii. 2. Cf. P. Renucci, *Dante disciple et juge du monde gréco-latin*, 390, n. 640, who points out that Fabricius' steadfastness was a

fairly common theme in the Middle Ages and inspired the third story in the *Conti di antichi cavalieri*.

29. Cf. E. Bonora's dismissive judgment of St. Nicholas's action in "Il canto XX del Purgatorio," in *Letture dantesche*, ed. G. Getto (Florence, 1964), 2: 1079.

30. *Par.* XI. 64–66: "This woman, deprived of her first husband, remained neglected for eleven hundred years and more, despised and obscure."

31. *Purg.* XX. 10–15: "May you be accursed, ancient wolf, who have more prey for your deep, endless hunger than all the other beasts! O heaven, in whose revolutions conditions here below are thought to be changed, when will he come to drive away this wolf?"

32. For the "Veltro" controversy, see the article by C. T. Davis, in *ED* V, 908–12, in which great emphasis is placed on Pietro di Dante's identification of the Veltro both with the DXV (*Purg.* XXXIII. 43) and with Methodius' Last Emperor. For the prophecies of the *Pseudo-Methodius*, see N. Cohn, *The Pursuit of the Millennium* (London, 1970), 31–33, where we are reminded that "uncanonical and unorthodox though they were, the Sibyllines had enormous influence—indeed save for the Bible and the works of the Fathers they were probably the most influential writings known to medieval Europe."

33. The verb *aduggiare* (l. 44) is uncommon (cf. *Inf.* XV. 2). E. G. Parodi, "Il canto XV dell'Inferno," in *Letture dantesche*, ed. G. Getto (Florence, 1964), 1: 269, felt it necessary to gloss for his Italian readers: "A plant *aduggia*, when its shadow causes all the smaller plants beneath it to wither and die."

34. An exception must of course be made for Dante's portrayal and praise of Charles Martel, the eldest son of Charles II of Anjou in *Par.* VIII. 49–148.

35. Hugh's (Dantesque) judgment that his line "was not worth much" (l. 63: *poco valea*) is contradicted by the achievements of Philip II (Augustus) and Louis IX. Of the former, Jacques Le Goff writes (*Le Moyen Age* [Paris, 1962], 167): "The welcome he received after his victory at Bouvines . . . was an expression of a truly French national feeling. . . . At his death, the royal domain had quadrupled."

36. S. Runciman, *The Sicilian Vespers: A History of the Mediterranean World in the Later Thirteenth Century* (Cambridge, 1992), 274. See also J. Favier, *Philippe le Bel*, 312: "by allowing his friends to behave in Florence as the Latin crusaders had done many years before in Constantinople, he [Charles] darkened the reputation of the Capetians in Italy for a long time to come." Cf. D. Compagni's lament (*Cronica* II. 18): "O good king Louis, who so feared God, where is the good faith of the royal house of France? . . . O evil counsellors, who have turned the blood of such a lofty crown into an assassin!"

37. *Purg.* XX. 73–75: "Without arms he comes but only with the lance with which Judas jousted, and he thrusts it so that he makes Florence's belly burst."

38. Sapegno, 624–25: "*he makes her belly burst*: the plebeian metaphor fits in with the sarcastic portrayal of that warrior without weapons and without honor . . ."

39. *Purg.* XX. 82–84: "O avarice, what else can you do to us, now that you have my family so much in your clutches that it does not care for its own flesh?"

40. For the events leading to the outrage at Anagni, see above, chapter 2. For a detailed account of the whole drama, see A. de Lévis-Mirepoix, *L'Attentat d'Anagni*

(Paris, 1969). Historians have been puzzled "by the lack of interest throughout Europe in the attack on Boniface VIII"; there were no official reports from Rome to the courts of Europe about Anagni, and "the chroniclers display no great concern about the attack." In France itself, "chroniclers who were filled with indignation over internal royal policies accepted the official version of Anagni without question: Boniface VIII got what he deserved," J. R. Strayer, *The Reign of Philip the Fair* (Princeton, 1980), 281 and 390.

41. *Purg.* XX. 91–93: "I see the new Pilate so cruel that this does not satisfy him, but, without decree, he carries his greedy sails into the Temple" [*portar* is the form accepted by Petrocchi; other editions give *porta*, the *lectio facilior*]. Philip the Fair had in fact been denounced as a second Pilate by Boniface's successor, Benedict XI, who claimed that Pilate's soldiers had despoiled and captured Christ in the person of His vicar. See P. Fedele, "Per la storia dell'attentato di Anagni," *Bullettino dell'Istituto Storico Italiano* 41 (1921), 210–11.

42. J. Favier, *Philippe le Bel*, 439. Extracts from Clement's indignant reaction are given in J. R. Strayer, *The Reign of Philip the Fair*, 286, n. 148. Regarding the whole operation, Strayer comments: "No modern dictatorship could have done a better job" (286).

43. E. Bonora, "Il canto XX del Purgatorio," 1087–88. For the (generally discarded) hypothesis of Dante's connection with the Templars, see: R. Guénon, *L'Ésotérisme de Dante* (Paris, 1925); L. Valli *Il linguaggio segreto di Dante e dei fedeli d'amore* (Rome, 1928); and R. John, *Dante* (Vienna, 1946). Cf., however, W. Anderson, *Dante the Maker* (London, 1980), 413: "There is also the fact . . . that the turning points of the two greatest vernacular poems of medieval literature, the *Commedia* and *Parzival*, are both scenes of confession set at Easter with strong Templar connotations."

44. Sapegno, 627. Cf. Pézard, 1260–61.

45. See, e.g., L. Spitzer, "Linguistics and Literary History," in *Issues in Contemporary Literary Criticism*, ed. G. T. Polletta (Boston, 1973), 499: "the indication that detail and whole have found a common denominator—which gives the etymology of the writing."

46. *Purg.* XXI. 58–60: "It quakes here when a soul feels itself purified so that it can rise or move to ascend; and then that cry is heard."

47. It will be recalled that Christ's forceful eviction of the merchants from the temple was for medieval Christians the supreme example of righteous anger, a prefiguration of the destruction of Jerusalem in A.D. 70 and a warning to all those who would turn God's house of prayer into a den of thieves, *vivi ladroni* (Matthew 21. 13; Mark 11.17).

48. *Il nuovo Zingarelli* (Bologna, 1983), 2119, gives: "*Vela* . . . [6] al pl. lett. Le ali spiegate degli uccelli", simply marking it as an archaic meaning.

49. Pézard, 1266, note 58–60: "The liberation of each soul allowed to ascend to heaven . . . reminds each one . . . by a brief tremor, Christ's ascension to heaven, when at his death the earth was shaken by a universal quake." P. Boyde, *Dante Philomythes and Philosopher: Man in the Cosmos* (Cambridge, 1981), 95, makes the complementary observation: "This is what happened to Statius; and the mountain

skipped and the earth trembled not because of 'wind in the belly,' but, as Virgil had divined with regard to the earthquake at the Crucifixion, because it had 'felt love.' "

50. J. Favier, *Philippe le Bel*, 432.

51. J. Favier, *Philippe le Bel*, 427.

52. J. R. Strayer, *The Reign of Philip the Fair*, 288: "In the end the crown did make some profit from its administration of Temple possessions, but Philip did not live to enjoy it." Cf. J. Favier, *Philippe le Bel*, 409.

53. *Par.* XIX. 118–20: "There shall be seen the suffering imposed on the Seine by the one who falsifies his currency and who shall die attacked by a wild boar." See the chapter, "La Monnaie du Roi," in J. Favier, *Philippe le Bel*, 137–52. For some pertinent observations on the fact that Dante is "concerned with financial activities throughout his poem," see chapter 6 of J. Ferrante's *The Political Vision*, 311–79, with the interesting suggestion that in Dante's description of the Old Man of Crete (*Inf.* XIV. 94–120), "the statue of human and national corruption can also be read as an allegory of debased currency" (342).

54. See the decretal *Per venerabilem* of 1202 (in B. Tierney, *The Crisis of Church and State*, 136). Cf. W. Ullmann, *Medieval Political Thought*, 196: "Throughout the latter part of the thirteenth century the principle was voiced in France that 'the king was emperor in his realm' "; also, K. Pennington, "Law, Legislative Authority and Theories of Government, 1150–1300," *Cambridge History of Medieval Political Thought*, 433. It is possible that the contradiction in terms (for Dante) of the adage *rex in regno suo imperator est* prompted the statement in *Conv.* IV. iv. 7: "And this office is called empire *without any qualification*, since it is superior to every other office of government" (emphasis mine).

55. J. R. Strayer, *The Reign of Philip the Fair*, 423 (also, xii–xiii).

56. W. Bowsky, *Henry VII in Italy*, 124–25.

57. A. Pézard, "La politica antifrancese di Dante. I regalisti francesi dell'epoca di Filippo il Bello e l'idea imperiale," in *Il processo di Dante*, ed. D. Ricci (Florence, 1967), 57, quotes an anonymous treatise, *Imperii preeminentia in rebus terrenis*, which has many aspects in common with Dante's mature political thought; in particular, the same diagnosis of and solution for the world's ills, namely, that discord, violence, plunder, and wars will continue as long as there is no one greater than everyone else (*maior omnibus*), the Emperor, who can put an end to strife by the rule of law (*iuris ordine litibus possit imponere modum*).

Chapter 10. The Apocalypse

1. G. Padoan, *Il pio Enea, l'empio Ulisse*, 142. See, however, the objections expressed by A. Ronconi, "L'incontro di Stazio e Virgilio," in *Dante nella critica d'oggi*, ed. U. Bosco (Florence, 1965), 566–67.

2. See E. Paratore, *Tradizione e struttura in Dante* (Florence, 1968), 72–73, and chapter 3 above.

3. J. Ferrante, *The Political Vision*, 135 (cf. 194–95, "Dante has also created such a city, modeled on his own city, Florence, which, like Thebes, is destroying itself by its selfishness and total lack of moral order").

4. C. Kleinhenz, "Virgil, Statius, and Dante: An Unusual Trinity," in P. Cherchi and A. C. Mastrobuono (eds), *Lectura Dantis Newberryana* (Evanston, 1988), 1: 45.

5. E. Paratore, *ED* V, 420. For a brilliant analysis of Statius' discourse, see V. Russo, *Esperienze e/di letture dantesche, tra il 1966 e il 1970* (Naples, 1971), 103–58.

6. For a thoroughgoing analysis of these poets and their role in the poem, see T. Barolini, *Dante's Poets*, passim.

7. *Purg.* XXVII. 131–42: "Henceforth, take your pleasure to be your guide. . . . Do not expect any word or sign from me; your will is free, upright and whole, and it would be sinful not to follow its promptings: therefore I crown and miter you over yourself."

8. D. Consoli, *ED* 3, 979. Both Quondam and Consoli in fact echo Sapegno, (708), whose suggestion that Virgil's words are "to be taken as a fixed formula with a generic meaning" is virtually repeated by Quondam.

9. *Mon.* III. iv. 14: "if man had remained in the state of innocence in which God made him, he would have had no need of such guides" (*si homo stetisset in statu innocentie in quo a Deo factus est, talibus directivis non indiguisset*).

10. As C. S. Singleton points out, "Virgil's words 'crowning' and 'mitering' Dante over himself complete his declaration to his charge that he has been brought to justice, inner justice," although he goes on to claim that "the fact that this is *that* kind of justice, and not *iustitia infusa* . . . requires that the crown and miter . . . be the crown and miter which were used in the crowning of an emperor, and it should not be construed as pointing to *two* powers, empire and church respectively" (*The Divine Comedy* [Princeton, N.J., 1973], 2: 665). On the concept of individual, personal justice attainable in this life (as distinct from the Justice given to human nature in Adam), see C. S. Singleton, *Dante Studies 2: Journey to Beatrice* (Cambridge, Mass., 1958), 64–69. On the imperial symbolism of both crown and miter, see P. Armour, *Dante's Griffin and the History of the World: A Study of the Earthly Paradise* ("Purgatorio," Cantos xxix–xxxiii) (Oxford, 1989), 143–48. Be that as it may, I believe that it is essential to see in Virgil's words a reference to both Empire *and* Church, since it is Dante's intention to show us the Pilgrim in a truly edenic state.

11. J. Ferrante, *The Political Vision*, 233 (cf. 244). For the sacramental symbolism in Virgil's action, see P. Armour, *The Door of Purgatory*, 7.

12. E. H. Kantorowicz, *The King's Two Bodies*, 491–92.

13. See A. Momigliano's commentary, as given in: Dante Alighieri, *La Divina Commedia: Purgatorio, con i commenti di T. Casini/S.A. Barbi A. Momigliano*, ed. F. Mazzoni (Florence, 1973), 645. C. S. Singleton, *The Divine Comedy: Commentary*, 2: 678–79, points to a passage written over a century before Dante, where Peter Abelard quotes the Psalmist's words *Delectasti me* in order to illustrate the joy humanity should take in God's works; thus, "Matelda, by her allusion to the psalm, is telling us that . . . her song . . . is a love song in praise of the Lord who made these things."

14. See the entry "Matelda" by F. Forti in *ED* III, 854–60. The bibliography listed there should be supplemented by P. Armour's "Matelda in Eden: The Teacher and the Apple," *Italian Studies* 34 (1979), 2–27 and C. S. Del Popolo, "Matelda," *Letture Classensi* 8 (1979), 121–34.

15. Buti, 2: 674–75, not only identifies Matelda with "Countess Matelda who was the daughter of Countess Beatrice, daughter of the emperor in Constantinople"—although he hedges his bets by adding "but I do not affirm that this was the author's intention or that it can be proved textually." Buti even goes so far as to claim that the origin of the Guelf-Ghibelline conflict ("those two accursed parties") lay in her unconsummated marriage to a certain "Gulfo, or Guelfo," whose impotence was due to a spell cast on him by a close relative, Gebel (who went on to poison him). As a result of these two crimes, "the nobles of Germany and Italy all rushed to either avenge or defend . . . And since this most noble lady was exemplary in the active life . . . the author imagines that she is placed in the earthly paradise, as its custodian, together with those figures from the Old Testament: Enoch and Elijah . . ."

16. J. Ferrante, *The Political Vision*, 206.

17. See B. Nardi, *Nel mondo di Dante*, 275–84 (quotations: 277–78, 283). Nardi answers in characteristic fashion the objection based on Beatrice's words in *Purg.* XXXIII. 127–29: "If Matelda is the Countess of Canossa, who exercised before her the office which she now carries out? The problem is worthy of the shrewdness displayed by Dante scholars, which may well surpass that of Dante, who was a poet" (284).

18. P. Armour, "Matelda in Eden," 8. Cf. F. Masciandaro, *Dante as Dramatist*, 196: "Dante is thus invited by Matelda to see in her both the innocence and joy preceding the Fall and the innocence and joy that despite the Fall still exist in virtue of what can be termed the ontological good inherent in all creation"; also, the acute observation that "in the scene evoked by Matelda the fact of evil is represented as existing not outside but within man himself" (199).

19. P. Armour, "Matelda in Eden," 26–27.

20. *Purg.* XXVIII. 139–44: "Those who in ancient times sang of the golden age and its happy state, perhaps dreamed of this place in Parnassus. Here, humanity's root was innocent; here is everlasting spring and every fruit; this is the nectar of which each poet sings."

21. The image of the riderless horse is found in both the *Comedy* and the *Convivio*, where it first appeared c. 1307 in *Conv.* IV. ix. 10: "it is possible to say of the Emperor, if one wishes to convey his office through figurative language, that he is the rider of the human will. How this horse, when without its rider, careers about the field is all too obvious, especially in wretched Italy, which has been left without any means of government!" As we have seen, the image of the rider and the horse returns for a third time in *Mon.* III. xv. 9.

22. It is worth noting that biblical allusions are more prevalent in the *Purgatorio* than in the other two *cantiche*. For the influence of the Book of Revelation in this final section of the *Purgatorio*, see R. Manselli's entry "Apocalisse" in *ED* I, 315–17; the bibliography given in A. Ciotti's entry "Processione mistica" in *ED* IV, 689; P. Dronke, *Dante and Medieval Latin Traditions*, 55–81, also his "*Purgatorio* XXIX: The Procession," in *Cambridge Readings in Dante's "Comedy,"* ed. K. Foster and P. Boyde (Cambridge, 1981), 114–37; S. Cristaldi, "Dalle beatitudini all'*Apocalisse*. Il Nuovo Testamento nella *Commedia*," *Letture Classensi* 17 (1988), 45–67.

23. C. S. Singleton, *The Divine Comedy: Commentary*, 2: 706. For a fine study

of the scene described in *Purg.* XXIX and its significance within the economy of the poem, see the same scholar's *Dante Studies 1: "Commedia" (Elements of Structure)* (Cambridge, Mass., 1954), 45–60.

24. For a more detailed analysis, see below as well as J. A. Scott, "Dante's Admiral," *Italian Studies* 27 (1972), 28–40.

25. As so often in allegorical exegesis, there are problems although the identification seems correct. "The idea of associating the twenty-four Books of the Old Testament with 'the twenty-four elders' was probably derived by Dante from St. Jerome's 'Prologus Galeatus' to the LXX" (E. Moore, *Studies in Dante: Third Series*, 182, n. 2). However, "St. Jerome's computation of the books of the Old Testament as twenty-four in number does not correspond to the accepted biblical canon" (P. Armour, *Dante's Griffin*, 5 and n. 8); cf. the same scholar's "L'Apocalisse nel canto XXIX del *Purgatorio*," 145. Professor Ferrante has kindly brought to my notice the parallel that exists between Dante's procession and the procession in the Grail castle in Wolfram's *Parzival* (cf. also the Grail procession in Chrétien de Troyes' *Conte del Graal*).

26. *Purg.* XXIX. 106–14: "The space between the four of them contained a triumphant chariot on two wheels, which came drawn at the neck of a griffin. He stretched upward both wings, framing the middle band with three bands on each side, so that he harmed not one of them by cleaving. His wings rose up so high that they were lost to sight; his limbs were gold where he was a bird, and the rest was white mixed with bright red."

27. Sapegno, 729. Cf. the densely argued pages in E. Moore, *Studies in Dante: Third Series*, 190–99.

28. See F. Mazzoni, "Canto XXXI" (a *lectura* given in December 1963) in *Lectura Dantis Scaligera* (Florence, 1967), 2: 1164–67, who equates the griffin with Christ, while rejecting Isidore as a source "certainly, Isidore cannot as formerly be considered the source of the image" (1166); C. Hardie, "The Symbol of the Gryphon in *Purgatorio* XXIX, 108 and Following Cantos," in *Centenary Essays on Dante*, ed. C. Grayson (Oxford, 1965), 103–31, who points out: "The sarcophagus to the west of the south door of the Baptistery in Florence has a gryphon on its east end" (131); P. Dronke, "*Purgatorio* XXIX," 120–21, 131–3; D. Oldroyd, "Hunting the Griffin in Dante's *Purgatorio*," *Spunti e ricerche* 2 (1986), 46–65; P. Armour, *Dante's Griffin*, passim, as well as his "La spuria fonte isidoriana per l'interpretazione del grifone dantesco," *Deutsches Dante Jahrbuch* 67 (1992), 163–68.

29. P. Camporesi, "Grifone," *ED* III, 287 (my emphasis).

30. P. Dronke, "*Purgatorio* XXIX," 120.

31. As P. Dronke observes "*Purgatorio* XXIX," (134), the usual idea that this praise is addressed to the behavior of the Christian God is "senseless . . . it can only be meaningfully said of a being who has the power and impulse to do wrong, yet does not do so . . ."

32. The reference to Albertus Magnus is given in C. Hardie, "The Symbol of the Gryphon," 109.

33. P. Armour, *Dante's Griffin*, 24, 44.

34. P. Armour, *Dante's Griffin*, 52, 59. Other objections are that the griffin performs a menial task in drawing the chariot, and that, after Beatrice's appearance

as *figura Christi*, for a canto and a half the griffin "continues to be ignored by everyone": the griffin must therefore "represent someone or something preceding and inferior to Christ" (58).

35. P. Armour, *Dante's Griffin*, 45.

36. P. Armour, *Dante's Griffin*, 113: "The griffin is Rome perfected as never before or since, God's idea of Rome."

37. E. H. Kantorowicz, *The King's Two Bodies*, 87.

38. F. Mazzoni, "Il canto VI del *Paradiso*," 192–93.

39. P. Armour, *Dante's Griffin*, 154. Cf. page 138: "the griffin is the Roman Monarchy as a historical entity and as a political, juridical, and ultimately moral *exemplum* for the restoration of happiness to fourteenth-century mankind, for the re-creation of a Paradise on earth."

40. Cf. the image contained in Epistle XI. iv. 5, often quoted as proof of the identification of the chariot with the Church: "you, who are as it were the centurions of the vanguard of the Church militant, neglecting to guide the chariot of the Spouse (*currum Sponse*) along the track laid down by the Crucified One." R. Stefanini specifies ("I tre sogni del *Purgatorio*," 56): "In the chariot we must see . . . the projection and fulfillment of the ideal Church in society and in history. And . . . as a result of men's perfidious imperfections, anything can happen (the transformations of the chariot) . . ."

41. E. Auerbach, "Figurative Texts Illustrating Certain Passages of Dante's *Commedia*," *Speculum* 221 (1946), 478; J. Ferrante, *The Political Vision*, 52–53. It should be noted that *benedictus qui venit* ["blessed is he who comes"] "are the last words sung by the assistants before the Canon of the Mass, expressing the expectation of the bodily coming of Christ" (C. S. Singleton, *The Divine Comedy: Commentary*, 2: 734). F. Masciandaro, *Dante as Dramatist*, 214, describes the scene as "a hierophany."

42. *Purg.* XXX. 31–33: "olive-crowned above a white veil, a lady appeared to me, clothed under a green mantle in color of living flame."

43. To my study "Dante's Admiral," I should like to add the following quotation from Cardinal Matteo d'Acquasparta's *Votum*: "So, in the Church, which is the ship of Christ and Peter, there is said to be only one leader" (*Sic in Ecclesia, quae est navis Christi et Petri, dicitur esse unicus rector*). See P. Dupuy, *Histoire du différend d'entre le pape Boniface VIII et Philippe le Bel Roy de France*, 76, as well as the image of the Christian fleet contained in Beatrice's prophecy: *Par.* XXVII. 142–48.

44. The reader is referred to the comprehensive analysis in E. Moore, *Studies in Dante: Third Series*, 221–52.

45. *Purg.* XXXI. 34–36: "The things of this world turned away my steps with their false pleasures, as soon as your face was hidden from me." Cf. the Siren's song in *Purg.* XIX. 22–24, in which the same verb *volgere* ("to turn") is used to signify moral deviation: "Io volsi Ullisse del suo cammin vago / al canto mio; e qual meco s'ausa, / rado sen parte; sí tutto l'appago!"

46. M. Barbi, *Problemi di critica dantesca: seconda serie* (Florence, 1941), 37. Cf. J. A. Scott, "Beatrice's Reproaches in Eden: Which 'School' Had Dante Followed?" *Dante Studies* 109 (1991), 8–9.

47. Guido Cavalcanti, *Rime (con le rime di Iacopo Cavalcanti)*, ed. D. De Rober-

tis (Turin, 1986), 160 (ll. 5–11 of *I' vegno 'l giorno a te 'nfinite volte'*: "You used to dislike the crowd; you would constantly avoid the stupid rabble. . . . Now, your vulgar ways prevent me from showing that I like your poems and from coming to see you openly."

48. C. Calenda, *Per altezza d'ingegno / Saggio su Guido Cavalcanti* (Naples, 1976), 112. Cf. M. Marti, *Realismo dantesco e altri studi* (Milan-Naples, 1961), 23.

49. See, e.g., D. Ricci, ed., *Il processo di Dante*, 35: "Passerini claims that, at the time of his exile, Dante's debts amounted to . . . exactly 1,108 gold florins." For the period leading up to Forese Donati's death in July 1296, we have the evidence of the exchange of sonnets (*Rime* LXXIII–LXXVIII) with their scurrilous accusations of gluttony (Dante to Forese) and the unexpected portrait of Dante as a man possibly guilty of both cowardice and sycophancy. Whatever the reality behind the *tenzone*, its coarse, vulgar insults are proof of a phase in his life that the poet of the *Comedy* judged to be totally unworthy of Beatrice's lover—and from which Virgil saved him (*Purg.* XXIII. 118–20).

50. *Purg.* XXXI. 121–23: "Just like the sun in a mirror, so the dual-natured animal gleamed within, first with one and then the other regime." See P. Armour, *Dante's Griffin*, 173: "here Dante sees that the temporal regime, centred in Rome, is itself a compound of two 'regimes,' the imperial and the popular, the divine and the human, derived from heaven and realized on earth by a single, historical, political, and juridical entity and by the person who above all embodies it, the Prince."

51. P. Armour, *Dante's Griffin*, 66.

52. *Purg.* XXXI. 134–38 (emphasis mine): "toward your faithful lover who has come so far, *in order to see you! Out of your grace, do us this grace: unveil your mouth to him*, so that he may discern the second beauty you conceal."

53. F. Mazzoni, "Canto XXXI," 1178–80.

54. P. Armour, *Dante's Griffin*, 61–62, 72.

55. C. S. Singleton, *The Divine Comedy: Commentary*, 2: 780 (in which readers are urged to read "the fundamental essays" by E. Moore, "The Apocalyptic Vision" and "The DXV Prophecy," in the latter's *Studies in Dante: Third Series*, 178–220 and 253–83). Cf. K. Foster, *God's Tree* (London, 1957), 33–49, especially 44: "I take it [the tree] then as a symbol, primarily, of the moral order of the cosmos viewed in relation to man, and especially to the two chief and, so to say, typical sins of man: the sins of Adam and of Christendom, of man pre-Christian and post-Christian. The first sin is only recalled here as a memory; the second is enacted allegorically in the horrors of canto XXXII."

56. *Purg.* XXXII. 43–48: " 'Blessed are you, griffin, who do not lacerate with your beak this tree, which is sweet to the taste but then racks the belly.' So the others cried out around the sturdy tree; and the dual-natured animal: 'In this way is the seed of all justice preserved.' "

57. C. S. Singleton, *The Divine Comedy: Commentary*, 2: 787.

58. *Purg.* XXXII. 49–60: "And turning to the pole-shaft he had pulled, he drew it to the foot of the widowed trunk, and bound to it what had come from it . . . the plant was renewed, which before had had its branches so bare."

59. P. Armour, *Dante's Griffin*, 202; also K. Foster, "*Purgatorio* XXXII," in *Cambridge Readings in Dante's "Comedy"* (Cambridge, 1981), 148: "There is clearly,

I think, a parallel between the lines spoken here in praise of the Gryphon (43–48) and *Mon.* II. x–xi, where Dante insists that Christ lived and died an obedient subject of the Roman Empire . . ." Cf., however, R. Kaske, " 'Sì, si conserva il seme d'ogne giusto' (*Purgatorio* XXXII. 48)," *Dante Studies* 89 (1971), 49–54.

60. "si unus Imperator *aliquam particulam ab Imperii iurisdictione discindere* posset" (emphasis mine, "If any Emperor were able *to detach any part from the Empire's jurisdiction*"), cf. *Purg.* XXXII. 43–44: "non *discindi* col becco *d'esto legno.*"

61. E. Moore, *Studies in Dante: Third Series*, 219, in which the Oxford scholar points out that this legend "was very widely spread, and is found in France, Spain, Italy, Germany, &c. Thus the tradition, in one form or another, was so generally familiar that Dante would be safe in referring to it in this passing and allusive manner."

62. P. Armour, *Dante's Griffin*, 209 (quoting the Bosco-Reggio commentary in support of his rejection).

63. *Par.* VII. 97–100 (my emphasis): "Man, within his own limits, could never make reparation, since he could not descend *with humility to a degree of obedience* equal to that of his disobedience in aiming so high."

64. *Par.* VI. 82–90: "But all that the sign [the imperial eagle] which makes me speak had already accomplished and was yet to do . . . appears to be little and obscure, if one looks at what it did when in the hand of the third Caesar [Tiberius] . . . for the living Justice that inspires me granted it, in that third Caesar's hand, the glory of carrying out vengeance for Its own wrath."

65. K. Foster, "*Purgatorio* XXXII," 146.

66. *Purg.* XXXII. 103–5: "Therefore, for the sake of the world which lives badly, keep your eyes now fixed on the chariot, and write down what you see after your return there."

67. For a complex parallel with the seven successive conditions of the Church (suggested by the opening of the seven seals in Rev. 6–8), see R. Kaske, "The Seven *Status Ecclesiae* in *Purgatorio* XXXII and XXXIII", in *Dante, Petrarch, Boccaccio: Studies in the Italian Trecento in Honor of Charles S. Singleton*, ed. A. S. Bernardo and A. L. Pellegrini (Binghamton, New York, 1983), 89–113, who points out: "The second descent of the eagle (124–29) . . . corresponds to none of our *status ecclesiae,*" with the "tentative conclusion that it is an original adaptation by Dante" (96 and 106).

68. It is possible to catch in the phrase *riprendendo lei di laide colpe* (l. 121: "rebuking it for its foul offenses") an echo of *Inf.* XIX. 82 *di più laida opra* ("of fouler deed"), which refers to Clement V's simony, collusion with Philip IV, and the transfer of the papacy to Avignon—as though Dante were hinting that the Babylonian exile is itself a form of heresy in that it rejects God's choice of Rome as "the holy place where sits the successor of Great Peter" (*Inf.* I. 23–24). The fact that these two verses contain the only two occurrences in the *Comedy* of the epithet *laido* clearly strengthens the link.

69. Cf. E. Moore, *Studies in Dante: Third Series*, 203, n. 2: "It is possible that Dante may have had in mind a legend, mentioned by Pietro di Dante and others, that at the time when the Donation of Constantine was made a voice was heard from heaven, saying, 'Hodie diffusum est venenum in Ecclesia Dei' ['Today poison

has been spread through God's Church']." This legend is mentioned in Manfred's Manifesto to the Romans of 24 May 1265 (see E. Dupré Theseider, *L'idea imperiale di Roma nella tradizione del Medioevo* [Milan, 1942], 224), as well as by Remigio Dei Girolami, *Contra falsos Ecclesie professores*, ed. F. Tamburini (Rome, 1981), 58–59 (with the direct quotation "Hodie infusum est") and 237; the Dominican preacher says that the Church was planted in meager soil by poverty, but that it was poisoned by the riches granted it by Constantine, as a heavenly voice declared: "Sic ecclesia fuit plantata in terra macilenta per paupertatem et venenata fuit per divitias sibi concessas a Costantino, sicut dixit vox celica." For the Donation of Constantine, see chapter 2.

70. As is well known, Constantine is revealed to the Pilgrim in the Heaven of Jupiter (*Par.* XX. 55–60), where the celestial Eagle proclaims his salvation, since his "good act does not harm him, even though the world has been destroyed by it."

71. *Ottimo*, 2: 574, quotes the passage from Revelation cited above in order to bolster his assertion that "this was the greatest persecutor ever of the Church and of God's people"—which, in the context of the Apocalypse, would point to the Antichrist. The "Ottimo" commentary was the first to cover the whole poem, and was written in Florence during the third decade of the fourteenth century by Andrea Lancia, a Florentine notary who knew Dante and was even able to consult the poet on certain matters (e.g., on *Inferno* X. 85–87).

72. For example, Pézard, 1352: "Satan, spirit of pride and greed, who attacks the Church itself." R. Kaske points to the fact that the dragon appears as if from hell (l. 130 "the earth opened up") and claims that it represents "the devil inserting hypocrisy into the Church . . . the serpent is a natural and traditional symbol of hypocrisy" ("The Seven *Status Ecclesiae*," 97 and 99).

73. See also Rev. 17.3. The seven heads and ten horns are probably intended to reflect what we have already learned in Purgatory: that the three worst sins (pride, envy, anger) not only offend God's law but are also directed against one's neighbor; they are thus doubly harmful (*Purg.* XVII. 112–14).

74. P. Dronke, *Dante and Medieval Latin Traditions*, 39 (quoting Augustine on Nimrod as the giant responsible for the building of the Tower of Babel). Dronke further suggests (36) that "when Siena and Florence were allied in the Guelf resistance against the emperor, these towers [of Monteriggioni, *Inf.* XXXI. 40–44] may well in Dante's eyes have come to epitomise rebellion against empire . . ."

75. See Pézard, 1083–84, n. 7. In an earlier study, the French scholar had emphasized "the proximity of Roland and the giants, in other words the clear opposition between the Christian knight and the rebel powers," whereby the giants in the pit of Hell typify "the closest allies of the Roman curia, the Angevin kings of Naples, Charles of Valois lord of Florence, the Black Guelfs of Tuscany . . . the petty tyrants of Italy who waged war against Henry VII, God's envoy" ("Le Chant des Géants," *Bulletin de la Société d'Études Dantesques du Centre Universitaire Méditerranéen* 7 [1958], 55).

76. Mention should also be made of the sonnet (*Rime*, CV) *Se vedi li occhi miei di pianger vaghi*, in which the slayer of justice would appear to be Clement V, who seeks refuge with the great tyrant, Philip the Fair (ll. 6–7: "chi la giustizia uccide e poi rifugge / al gran tiranno"), even as he sucks "the poison which the tyrant

has already poured forth in the wish that it may flood the world" (translation in K. Foster and P. Boyde, *Dante's Lyric Poetry*, 1: 183). Dante's son Pietro, in an unpublished final version of his commentary on the *Comedy* "identified the Whore with the wicked prelates of the church and the giant with the king of France" (C. T. Davis, *Dante's Italy*, 62). Dante's anger surely knew no bounds, if he discovered that "the bull *Rex glorie* [27 April 1311] was capped by a sentence in which Clement declared that 'like the people of Israel . . . the kingdom of France, as a peculiar people chosen by God to carry out divine mandates, is distinguished by marks of special honor and grace'" (J. R. Strayer, *The Reign of Philip the Fair*, 295).

77. Quotations from R. Kaske, "The Seven *Status Ecclesiae*," 100. The most complex unravelling of the allegory at various levels is to be found in P. Armour, *Dante's Griffin*, 222ff. For a quite different reading of the episode, see P. Dronke, *Dante and Medieval Latin Traditions*, esp. 73: "The erotic dream of the canzone ["Cosí nel mio parlar," *Rime* CIII] here becomes a nightmare, the unyielding *petra* becomes the prostitute . . . the lover . . . becomes a monstrously large, sordid bully . . . revealing the desires in which he [Dante] had been disloyal to Beatrice's memory in a light very different from that in which they had previously appeared to him."

78. C. T. Davis, *Dante's Italy*, 62 (also, *Dante and the Idea of Rome*, 209ff.). Cf. R. Manselli, "Dante e l'*Ecclesia Spiritualis*," 125. P. Renucci, "Dante et les mythes du *Millenium*," *Revue des Études Italiennes* 11 (1965), 413, n. 2, sees "the sinister shadow of the Antichrist" even in the evocation of Philip the Fair in *Purg.* XX. 86–90. For the possible influence of Joachim Floris, see the entry "Gioacchino" by Arsenio Frugoni in *ED* III, 165–67, and M. Reeves, "Dante and the Prophetic View of History," in *The World of Dante*, ed. C. Grayson, 44–60.

79. J. Ferrante, *The Political Vision*, 251.

80. If the person responsible (*chi n'ha colpa*) is restricted to Philip the Fair, then G. Mazzoni's idea that the poet is referring to a quasi-sacrilegious rite performed by the French kings is highly pertinent. This rite consisted in making their vassals' oaths binding through a piece of bread dipped in wine (G. Mazzoni, *Almae luces malae cruces* [Bologna, 1941], 289–305). However, Beatrice's words can hardly be taken to imply that only the king of France will be responsible for the Church's corruption.

81. C. T. Davis, *Dante and the Idea of Rome*, 210.

82. *Purg.* XXXIII. 40–45: "for I see plainly and therefore I speak out, stars already close at hand, secure from all check and hindrance, shall bring a time for us when God's messenger, a Five Hundred and Ten and Five, shall slay the thievish whore together with that giant who sins with her."

83. P. Mazzamuto, "Cinquecento diece e cinque," *ED* II, 10–14. To Mazzamuto's list, I should like specifically to add R. Kay's fasinating study, "Dante's Razor and Gratian's D.XV," *Dante Studies* 97 (1979), 65–95. Professor Kay suggests that the DXV prophecy refers to *Distinctio* XV of Gratian's *Decretum*: "Gratian's D.XV provided Dante with a sovereign antidote to the extreme claims made for papal authority by both the Decretalists and the popes themselves since the time of Pope Innocent III" (77). Nevertheless, Kay (89, n. 16) does not exclude the possibility that "the DVX may also have a coordinate significance in numerology."

84. Ottimo, 2: 585: "l'Autore vuole dire d'alcuna grande rivoluzione del Cielo significatrice di alcuno giustissimo e santissimo principe, il quale reformerà lo stato della Chiesa, e de' fedeli Cristiani."

85. C. T. Davis, *Dante's Italy*, 66–67. Virgil, who had unconsciously prophesied the coming of the Redeemer under whose "sway any lingering traces of our guilt shall become void" in his Fourth Eclogue (cf. *Purg.* XXII. 66–73), is allotted the first prophecy in *Inf.* I. 100–111. For various interpretations, see C. T. Davis, "Veltro," *ED* V, 908–12; and A. K. Cassell, *Lectura Dantis Americana: Inferno I* (Philadelphia, 1989), 94–113, 175–81.

86. C. T. Davis, *Dante's Italy*, 38.

87. See M. Reeves, *The Influence of Prophecy in the Later Middle Ages* (Oxford, 1969), 309–14; P. Alexander, "The Medieval Legend of the Last Roman Emperor and its Messianic Origin," *Journal of the Warburg and Courtauld Institutes* 41 (1978), 1–15.

88. *Par.* XXVII. 140–41: "remember that no one governs on earth; so that the human family goes astray."

89. G. R. Sarolli, *Prolegomena alla "Divina Commedia"* (Florence, 1971), 266. In 1961, Professor Kaske had already focused on the initials of *Vere dignum* as they appear in medieval manuscripts, concluding that Beatrice's prophecy was intended to signify Christ's last advent; see R. Kaske, "Dante's 'DXV' and 'Veltro'," *Traditio* 17 (1961), 184–254.

90. It is clearly impossible to do justice to Sarolli's detailed and complex argument; the reader is therefore urged to turn to the section "Dante e la teologia politicia: simbolismo cristologico e cristomimetico," of the *Prolegomena alla "Divina Commedia,"* especially 247–82.

91. E. Moore, *Studies in Dante: Third Series*, 257.

92. E. Moore, *Studies*, 283.

93. For example, A. C. Mastrobuono in *Dante's Journey of Sanctification* (Washington, DC, 1990), 167–211. S. Pasquazi's identification of the "messenger from Heaven" with St. Michael the Archangel (in *Dall'eterno al tempo* [Florence, 1966], 61–159) has recently been upheld by G. Oliva, "Preludio al Paradiso," *Lectura Dantis Modenese: Purgatorio* (Modena, 1985), 225–27. It is obvious that the debate is far from over.

94. P. Renucci, "Dante et les mythes du *Millenium*," 418.

95. N. Cohn, *The Pursuit of the Millennium*, 108.

96. For this latter influence, see especially R. Manselli, "Dante e l'*Ecclesia Spiritualis*" and S. Cristaldi, "Dalle beatitudini all'*Apocalisse*." For the problem of Dante's knowledge of Joachim's writings, see the entry by A. Frugoni, "Gioachino (Giovacchino) da Fiore," *ED* III, 165–67—to which must be added M. Reeves, "Dante and the Prophetic View of History," with the conclusion (57): "All we can safely say is that a certain ambience of prophetic expectation within history had been created in the thirteen century by Joachim's disciples and was prevalent in Dante's lifetime. Dante's prophetic vision seems to belong to this mode of thought."

97. N. Cohn, *The Pursuit of the Millennium*, 110–12. Regarding Frederick II see page 111: "for the first time the image of the Emperor of the Last Days was

attached to the actual ruler of the territorial complex . . . which had come to be known in the West as the Roman [and latterly as the Holy Roman] Empire."

98. For the reader unacquainted with the labyrinth of numerological interpretations of Dante's work, G. R. Sarolli gives an excellent introduction in his entry "Numero" in *ED* IV, 87–96. For the importance of "numerical composition" in medieval thought, see "Excursus XV" in E. R. Curtius, *European Literature and the Latin Middle Ages* (New York, 1953), 501–9. See also M. Hardt, "Dante and Arithmetic," in *The Divine Comedy and the Encyclopedia of Arts and Sciences*, 81–94.

99. See the complex analysis given by G. R. Sarolli, *Prolegomena alla "Divina Commedia,"* especially 270 and 294–95.

100. I put forward the possibility that 151 may be taken to reflect the hypostatic union in Christ, since it displays 5, the number of human perfection, flanked on both sides by the 1 of divine unity in a three-in-one pattern not unlike that of one of Dante's *terzine* (a-b-a). The sum of its digits [7] "is the number of the Holy Spirit" (G. R. Sarolli, *Prolegomena alla "Divina Commedia"*, 230; but cf. C. S. Singleton, "The Poet's Number at the Center," *Modern Language Notes* 80 [1965], 1–10). It may be of interest to note that there are *three* cantos of 151 verses in the *Purgatorio*.

101. See the quotation from the pseudo-Joachite *Super Hieremiam*, in R. Manselli, "Dante e l'*Ecclesia spiritualis*," 131, n. 28. Cf. Benvenuto, 4: 272–73: "the poet tacitly signifies: just as one Roman Emperor gave the feathers, that is to say, the riches to the Church, from which sprang the insatiable avarice of churchmen, which has destroyed the world, so another Roman Emperor shall snatch away the feathers, that is, its temporal wealth and restore freedom to the Church." From this overview, I believe it is difficult to maintain (with Moore and so many others) that Beatrice's DXV prophecy refers specifically to Henry VII; with its reference to the killing of the whore and the giant, it seems likely that it was written after Clement V's treachery had been fully exposed.

102. *Conv.* II. xiv. 13: "and we are already in the world's last age, and we truly await the consummation of the movement of the heavens."

103. *Par.* XXVII. 61–63, and 145–48: [Peter] "But that high Providence which with Scipio preserved the glory of the world for Rome, will soon bring help, as I conceive"; [Beatrice] "the tempest so long awaited shall turn the sterns to where the prows are now, so that the fleet shall run straight on course; and good fruit shall come from the flower." It must be emphasized that it is no less an authority than St. Peter, the archetypal Pope and founder of the Church in Rome, who thus refers to the universal Empire as "la gloria del mondo" inherited by the heirs of Scipio (cf. *Mon.* II. ix. 18–19, which echoes "la gloria del mondo" in *coronam orbis totius* ["the crown of the whole world"] won for Rome by Scipio in his duel with Hannibal). From his quotation (*Conv.* IV. iv. 11) of Virgil's "prophecy" that God had given the Empire to Rome until the end of time, it would seem that—unlike Aquinas and many interpreters of St. Paul's Second Letter to the Thessalonians (2. 3–4)—Dante did not believe that the Empire would come to an end just before the reign of the Antichrist. Cf., however, the powerful arguments marshaled by Armour (*Dante's Griffin*, especially 250ff.) to show that the poet has in fact created "two millenarian scenes" in his Earthly Paradise, whereby "Dante is showing the entire history of mankind from Adam to its consummatin at the end" (257 and 265).

104. " 'So that you may know,' she said, '[the true worth of] that school which you followed, and see how its teachings can follow my words; and see your ways as distant from God's way as the highest and swiftest of the heavens is remote from the earth.' "

105. E. G. Parodi, *Poesia e storia nella "Divina Commedia"* (Vicenza, 1965), 136. However, as will be seen, I cannot accept Parodi's view that the way so distant from God's way is merely "that taken by the theorists of papal supremacy."

106. J. Ferrante, *The Political Vision*, 93–94: "the major lesson of the drama, the danger to the church when it takes on temporal power or possession or gives itself over to secular domination by the wrong leader, is the same for all of them [the early commentators]: when the church works with the empire, it serves the divine purpose." Cf. F. Mazzoni, "Il canto VI del Paradiso," passim.

107. *Purg.* XXXIII. 85–89: "So that you may know . . . that school *which you followed*, and see how its teachings can follow my words; and see *your ways* as distant from God's way" (my emphasis). The distinction between the singular form of the verb (*c'hai seguitata*) and the plural *vostra* is impossible to convey in English, unless recourse is had to the archaic "which thou hast followed."

108. John of Paris, Dante's contemporary, drives home the point when he writes that verses 3, 10, and 12 of the same Psalm have been misused by papal champions to "signify the church of recent times, when the pope, vicar of Christ, has power over the kings of the earth who are wholly subject to him although he did not have this power from the beginning" (John of Paris, *On Royal and Papal Power*, ed. with introduction by J. A. Watt [Toronto, 1971], 138–39).

109. *Mon.* II. i. 2–3. The political significance of the assertion that the Empire was founded on and extended through violence is clearly brought out in an anonymous tract during the dispute between Henry VII and Robert of Naples, in which it is claimed that, since the Romans obtained their empire through violence, it would be fitting for the empire to be dissolved by the same means, "since anything which is introduced by certain causes may be dissolved by those same causes" (the Latin original quoted in K. Pennington, *The Prince and the Law*, 176, n. 61).

110. *Purg.* XXXIII. 142–45: "I returned from the holy waters, renewed even as young trees are renewed with new foliage, pure and ready to ascend to the stars."

Conclusion

1. S. Battaglia, *Esemplarità e antagonismo nel pensiero di Dante* (Naples, 1967), 1: 40.

2. J. Ferrante, *The Political Vision*, 205.

Bibliography

Abulafia, David. *Frederick II: A Medieval Emperor*. Aldershot: Pimlico, 1988.

Alexander, Paul. "The Medieval Legend of the Last Roman Emperor and its Messianic Origin." *Journal of the Warburg and Courtauld Institutes* 41 (1978): 1–15.

Anderson, William. *Dante the Maker*. London: Routledge and Kegan Paul, 1980.

Aquinas, Thomas. *Aquinas: Selected Writings*. Edited and with an introduction by A. P. d'Entrèves. Oxford: Blackwell, 1959.

Armour, Peter. "Matelda in Eden: The Teacher and the Apple." *Italian Studies* 34 (1979), 2–27.

———. "Dante's Brunetto: The Paternal Paterine?" *Italian Studies* 38 (1983), 1–38.

———. *The Door of Purgatory: A Study of Multiple Symbolism in Dante's "Purgatorio."* Oxford: Oxford University Press, 1983.

———. "L'Apocalisse nel canto XXIX del Purgatorio." Giovanni Barblan, ed., *Dante e la Bibbia*. Florence: Olschki, 1988, 145–49.

———. *Dante's Griffin and the History of the World: A Study of the Earthly Paradise ("Purgatorio" cantos xxix–xxxiii)*. Oxford: Oxford University Press, 1989.

———. "La spuria fonte isidoriana per l'interpretazione del grifone dantesco," *Deutsches Dante Jahrbuch* 67 (1992), 163–68.

Auerbach, Erich. "Figurative Texts Illustrating Certain Passages of Dante's *Commedia*." *Speculum* 21 (1946): 474–89.

———. *Scenes from the Drama of European Literature: Six Essays*. New York: Meridian Books, 1959.

———. "Sacrae Scripturae sermo humilis." In D. Della Terza, ed., *Studi su Dante*. Milan: Feltrinelli, 1977, 165–73.

Aurigemma, Marcello. "Manfredi e il problema delle indulgenze." In Umberto Bosco, ed., *Dante nella critica d'oggi*. Florence: Le Monnier, 1965, 540–50.

Avalle, D'Arco Silvio. *Modelli semiologici nella Commedia di Dante*. Milan: Bompiani, 1975.

Baktin, Leonid Mikhailovitch. *Dante e la società italiana del Trecento*. Bari: Laterza, 1979.

Barański, Zygmunt G. "Dante's Three Reflective Dreams." *Quaderni d'italianistica* 10 (1989), 213–36.

———. "*Comedía*. Notes on Dante, the Epistle to Cangrande, and Medieval Comedy." *Lectura Dantis* 8 (1991), 26–55.

———. "*Sordellus . . . qui . . . patrium vulgare deseruit*: A Note on *De Vulgari Eloquentia*, I, 15, sections 2–6." In C. E. J. Griffiths and Robert Hastings, eds., *The Cultural Heritage of the Italian Renaissance (Essays in Honour of T. G. Griffith)*. Lewiston-Queenston-Lampeter: Edwin Mellen, 1993, 19–45.

———. "Canto VI." In Tibor Wlassics, ed., *Dante's "Divine Comedy." Introductory Readings, II: "Purgatorio."* Charlottesville: University of Virginia Press, 1993, 80–97.

Barasch, Moshe. *Giotto and the Language of Gesture*. Cambridge: Cambridge University Press, 1987.

Barbadoro, B. "La condanna di Dante e le fazioni politiche del suo tempo." *Studi Danteschi* 2 (1920), 5–74.

Bàrberi Squarotti, Giorgio. "Manfredi ('Purgatorio', III)." In Pasquale Sabbatino, ed., *L'uomo di Dante e Dante uomo: Lectura Dantis Pompeiana*. Naples: Pompei Biblioteca L. Pepe, 1985, 157–89.

Barbi, Michele. *Problemi di critica dantesca: prima serie*. Florence: Sansoni, 1934.

———. "L'ideale politico-religioso di Dante." *Studi Danteschi* 23 (1938), 46–77.

———. *Problemi di critica dantesca: seconda serie*. Florence: Sansoni, 1941.

———. *Problemi fondamentali per un nuovo commento della Divina Commedia*. Florence: Sansoni, 1956.

Barolini, Teodolinda. *Dante's Poets: Textuality and Truth in the "Comedy."* Princeton, N.J.: Princeton University Press, 1984.

———. *The Undivine "Comedy": Detheologizing Dante*. Princeton, N.J.: Princeton University Press, 1992.

Barraclough, Geoffrey. *The Medieval Papacy*. London: Thames and Hudson, 1968.

Battaglia, Salvatore. *La coscienza letteraria del Medioevo*. Naples: Liguori, 1965.

———. *Esemplarità e antagonismo nel pensiero di Dante*, 2 vols. Naples: Liguori, 1967.

Becker, Marvin V. "Dante and His Literary Contemporaries as Political Men." *Speculum* 41 (1966): 655–80.

Berretta, Giuseppe. "Il mal che tutto il mondo occúpa." *Filologia e Letteratura* 14 (1968), 163–91.

Billanovich, Giuseppe. *Prime ricerche dantesche*. Rome: Edizioni di Storia e Letteratura, 1947.

Binni, Walter. "Il canto III del *Purgatorio*." In Giovanni Getto, ed., *Letture dantesche*. Florence: Sansoni, 1964, 2, 725–45.

Boccaccio, Giovanni. *Trattatello in laude di Dante*. Pier Giorgio Ricci, ed. In *Tutte le opere*, V. Branca, ed. Milan: Mondadori, 1974, 3: 423–538.

Boethius. *The Theological Tractates and The Consolation of Philosophy*. Trans. H. F. Stewart and E. K. Rand. London: Heinemann; Cambridge, Mass.: Harvard University Press, 1953.

Bonora, Ettore. "Il canto XX del *Purgatorio*." In Giovanni Getto, ed., *Letture dantesche*. Florence: Sansoni, 1964, 2, 1071–91.

Bosco, Umberto. *Dante vicino*. Caltanissetta-Roma: S. Sciascia, 1966.

Bowra, C. M. "Dante and Sordello." *Comparative Literature* 5 (1953), 1–15.

Bowsky, William M. *Henry VII in Italy: The Conflict of Empire and City-State, 1310–1313*. Lincoln: University of Nebraska Press, 1960.

Boyde, Patrick. *Dante Philomythes and Philosopher: Man in the Cosmos*. Cambridge: Cambridge University Press, 1981.

———. *Perception and Passion in Dante's "Comedy."* Cambridge: Cambridge University Press, 1993.

Brandeis, Irma. *The Ladder of Vision: A Study of Dante's "Comedy."* New York: Anchor, 1962.

Brentano, Robert. *Rome Before Avignon: A Social History of Thirteenth Century Rome.* London: Longman, 1990.

Bueno de Mesquita, D. M. "The Place of Despotism in Italian Politics." In John Hale, Richard Highfield, and Beryl Smalley, eds., *Europe in the Late Middle Ages.* London: Faber, 1970, 301–31.

James H. Burns, ed. *The Cambridge History of Medieval Political Thought: c. 350–c. 1450.* Cambridge: Cambridge University Press, 1988.

Caccia, Ettore. *Il Canto III del Purgatorio.* Lectura Dantis Scaligera. Florence, Le Monnier, 1967, 2: 81–119.

Calenda, Corrado. *Per altezza d'ingegno/Saggio su Guido Cavalcanti.* Naples: Liguori, 1976.

Canning, J. P. "Introduction [to Chapter 5]: Politics, Institutions and Ideas." In James H. Burns, ed., *The Cambridge History of Medieval Political Thought: c. 350–c. 1450.* Cambridge: Cambridge University Press, 1991, 341–66.

Capitani, Ovidio. "*Monarchia*: il pensiero politico." In Umberto Bosco, ed., *Dante nella critica d'oggi.* Florence: Le Monnier, 1965, 733–36.

Caprettini, Gian Paolo. *San Francesco, il lupo, i segni.* Turin: Einaudi, 1974.

Cary, George. *The Medieval Alexander.* Cambridge: Cambridge University Press, 1956.

Cassell, Anthony K. *Lectura Dantis Americana: Inferno I.* Philadelphia: University of Pennsylvania Press, 1989.

Cavalcanti, Guido. *Rime (con le rime di Iacopo Cavalcanti),* ed. D. De Robertis. Turin: Einaudi, 1986.

Cervigni, Dino S. *Dante's Poetry of Dreams.* Florence: Olschki, 1986.

Charity, Alan Clifford. *Events and Their Afterlife: The Dialectics of Christian Typology in the Bible and Dante.* Cambridge: Cambridge University Press, 1966.

Chiavacci-Leonardi, Anna M. "La *Monarchia* di Dante alla luce della *Commedia.*" *Studi Medievali, Terza Serie* 18 (1977), 147–83.

Chydenius, Johan. *The Typological Problem in Dante: A Study in the History of Medieval Ideas.* Helsingfors: Centralryckeriet, 1958.

Cilento, Nicola. "La cultura di Manfredi nel ricordo di Dante." In *Dante e la cultura sveva: Atti del II Congresso Nazionale di Studi Danteschi (Caserta, 10–16 ottobre 1965).* Florence: Olschki, 1970.

Cipolla, Carlo M., ed. *The Fontana Economic History of Europe: The Middle Ages.* C. M. Cipolla, ed. London: Fontana, 1972.

Cognasso, Francesco. *Arrigo VII.* Milan: Dall'Oglio, 1973.

Cohn, Norman. *The Pursuit of the Millennium: Revolutionary Millenarians and Mystical Antichrists of the Middle Ages.* London: Temple Smith, 1970.

Comparetti, Domenico. *Virgilio nel Medio Evo.* Florence: La Nuova Italia, 1967. 2 vols.

Consoli, Domenico. *Significato del Virgilio dantesco.* Florence: Le Monnier, 1966.

Corti, Maria. *Dante a un nuovo crocevia.* Florence: Sansoni, 1981.

———. *La felicità mentale: nuove prospettive per Cavalcanti e Dante.* Turin: Einaudi, 1983.

Cosmo, Umberto. *Vita di Dante*. Bari: Laterza, 1949.

Cristaldi, Sergio. "Dalle beatitudini all' *Apocalisse*. Il Nuovo Testamento nella *Commedia*." *Letture Classensi* 17 (1988), 23–67.

Curtius, Ernst Robert. *European Literature and the Latin Middle Ages*. New York: Pantheon, 1953.

Davis, Charles Till. *Dante and the Idea of Rome*. Oxford: Oxford University Press, 1957.

———. "An Early Florentine Political Theorist: Fra Remigio de' Girolami." *Proceedings of the American Philosophical Society* 104, 6 (1960), 662–75.

———. "Rome and Babylon in Dante." In P. A. Ramsey, ed., *Rome in the Renaissance: The City and the Myth*, 19–40. Medieval and Renaissance Texts and Studies 21. Binghampton, N.Y.: Center for Medieval and Early Renaissance Studies, State University of New York at Binghampton, 1982.

———. *Dante's Italy and Other Essays*. Philadelphia: University of Pennsylvania Press, 1984.

———. "The Middle Ages." In Richard Jenkyns, ed., *The Legacy of Rome: A New Appraisal*. Oxford: Oxford University Press, 1992, 61–96.

De Rosa, Mario. "Prima che Federigo avesse briga." *Esperienze letterarie* 13 (1988): 79–88.

———. *Dante e il padre ideale*. Naples: Federigo and Ardia, 1990.

De' Girolami, Remigio. *Contra falsos Ecclesie professores*, ed. F. Tamburini. Rome: Pontificia Universitas Lateranense, 1981.

De' Negri, E. "Tema e iconografia del *Purgatorio*." *Romanic Review* 49 (1958), 81–104.

Del Popolo, Concetto S. "Matelda." *Letture Classensi* 8 (1979), 121–34.

Delcorno, Carlo. "Dante e l'*Exemplum* medievale." *Letture Classensi* 12 (1982), 113–38.

Della Vedova, Roberto and Maria T. Silvotti, eds. *Il "Commentarium" di Pietro Alighieri nelle redazioni asburnhamiana e ottoboniana*. Florence: Olschki, 1978.

Delmay, Bernard. *I personaggi della "Divina Commedia": classificazione e regesto*. Florence: Olschki, 1986.

Di Scipio, Giuseppe. "Dante and Politics." In Giuseppe Di Scipio and Aldo Scaglione, eds., *The "Divine Comedy" and the Encylopedia of Arts and Sciences*. Amsterdam-Philadelphia: J. Benjamins, 1988, 267–84.

Digard, Georges. *Les Registres de Boniface VIII*. Paris: E. de Boccard, 1921.

———. *Philippe le Bel et le Saint-Siège de 1285 à 1304*. Paris: Sirey, 1936. 2 vols.

Dronke, Peter. "*Purgatorio* XXIX: The Procession." In Kenelm Foster and Patrick Boyde, eds., *Cambridge Readings in Dante's "Comedy."* Cambridge: Cambridge University Press, 1981, 114–37.

———. *Dante and Medieval Latin Traditions*. Cambridge: Cambridge University Press, 1986.

Dupré Theseider, Eugenio. *L'idea imperiale di Roma nella tradizione del Medioevo*. Milan: Istituto per gli Studi di Politica Internazionale, 1942.

Dupuy, Pierre. *Histoire du différend d'entre le pape Boniface VIII et Philippe le Bel Roy de France*. Paris, 1655.

Ercole, Francesco. *Il pensiero politico di Dante*. Milan: Alpes, 1927–28. 2 vols.

Favati, Guido. "Sordello." In Umberto Bosco, ed., *Dante nella critica d'oggi*. Florence: Le Monnier, 1965, 551–65.

Jean Favier. *Philippe le Bel*. Paris: Fayard, 1988.

Fedele, Pietro. "Per la storia dell'attentato di Anagni." *Bullettino dell'Istituto Storico Italiano* 41 (1921): 210–11.

Ferrante, Joan M. *The Political Vision of the "Divine Comedy."* Princeton, N.J.: Princeton University Press, 1984.

Folz, Robert. *The Concept of Empire in Western Europe from the Fifth to the Fourteenth Century*. London: Edward Arnold, 1969.

Forti, Fiorenzo. *Fra le carte dei poeti*. Milan-Naples: R. Ricciardi, 1965.

———. *Magnanimitade: Studi su un tema dantesco*. Bologna: Pàtron, 1977.

Kenelm Foster. *God's Tree*. London: Blackfriars, 1957.

———. *The Two Dantes and Other Studies*. London: Darton, Longman and Todd, 1977.

———. "*Purgatorio* XXXII." In Kenelm Foster and Patrick Boyde, eds., *Cambridge Readings in Dante's "Comedy."* Cambridge: Cambridge University Press, 1981, 138–54.

Foster, Kenelm and Patrick Boyde, eds., *Dante's Lyric Poetry*. Oxford: Oxford University Press, 1967. 2 vols.

Frankel, Margherita. "Dante's Conception of the Ideology of the *Aeneid*." In *Proceedings of the Xth Congress of the International Comparative Literature Association*. New York and London: Garland, 1985, 406–41.

Freccero, John. *Dante: The Poetics of Conversion*, ed. Rachel Jacoff. Cambridge, Mass.: Harvard University Press, 1986.

Frugoni, Arsenio. "Il giubileo di Bonifacio VIII." In *Incontri nel Medio Evo*. Bologna: Il Mulino, 1979, 73–177.

Garin, Eugenio. "Il pensiero di Dante." In *Storia della filosofia italiana*. Turin: Einaudi, 1966, 1, 179–206.

Gauthier, R. A. *Magnanimité: l'idéal de la grandeur dans la philosophie païenne et dans la théologie chrétienne*. Paris: Vrin, 1951.

Gilson, Étienne. "Poésie et théologie dans la *Divine Comédie*." In *Atti del congresso internazionale di studi danteschi*. Florence: Sansoni, 1965, 1: 197–223.

———. *Dante the Philosopher*, trans. David Moore. London: Sheed and Ward, 1948.

Gimpel, Jean. *The Medieval Machine: The Industrial Revolution in the Middle Ages*. Aldershot: Pimlico, 1988.

Gmelin, Hans. "Il canto X del *Purgatorio*." In Giovanni Getto, ed., *Letture dantesche*. Florence: Sansoni, 1964, 2, 871–80.

Goudet, Jacques. *Dante et la politique*. Paris: Aubier-Montaigne, 1969.

———. *La politique de Dante*. Lyon: L'Hermès, 1981.

Graf, Arturo. *Miti, leggende e superstizioni del Medio Evo*. Milan: Mondadori, 1984.

———. *Roma nella memoria e nelle immaginazioni del Medio Evo*. Turin: Chiantore, 1923.

Grayson, Cecil. "*Nobilior est vulgaris*: Latin and Vernacular in Dante's Thought." In C. Grayson, ed., *Centenary Essays on Dante*. Oxford: Oxford University Press, 1965, 54–76.

———. *Cinque saggi su Dante*. Bologna: Pàtron, 1972.

Green, Vivian H. R. *Medieval Civilization in Western Europe*. London: Edward Arnold, 1971.

Grendler, Paul F. *Schooling in Renaissance Italy: Literacy and Learning, 1300–1600*. Baltimore: Johns Hopkins University Press, 1989.

René Guénon. *L'Esotérisme de Dante*. Paris: Ch. Bosse, 1925.

Hall, Ralph G. and Madison U. Sowell. "*Cursus* in the Can Grande Epistle: A Forger Shows His Hand?" *Lectura Dantis* 5 (1989), 89–104.

Hardie, Colin. "The Symbol of the Gryphon in *Purgatorio* XXIX, 108 and Following Cantos." In Cecil Grayson, ed., *Centenary Essays on Dante*. Oxford: Oxford University Press, 1965, 103–31.

Hardt, Manfred. "Dante and Arithmetic." In Giuseppe Di Scipio and Aldo Scaglione, eds., *The "Divine Comedy" and the Encyclopedia of Arts and Sciences*. Amsterdam-Philadelphia: J. Benjamins, 1988, 81–94.

Hazelton, Richard. "The Christianization of 'Cato': The *Disticha Catonis* in the Light of Late Mediaeval Commentaries." *Mediaeval Studies* 19 (1957), 157–73.

Herde, Peter. *Dante als Florentiner Politiker*. Wiesbaden: Steiner, 1976.

Hollander, Robert. *Allegory in Dante's "Commedia."* Princeton, N.J.: Princeton University Press, 1969.

——. *Studies in Dante*. Ravenna: Longo, 1980.

——. *Il Virgilio dantesco: tragedia nella "Commedia."* Florence: Olschki, 1983.

——. *Dante's Epistle to Cangrande*. Ann Arbor: University of Michigan Press, 1993.

Hollander, Robert and A. L. Rossi. "Dante's Republican Treasury." *Dante Studies* 104 (1986), 59–82.

Holmes, George. "Dante and the Popes." In Cecil Grayson, ed., *The World of Dante: Essays on Dante and His Times*. Oxford: Oxford University Press, 1980.

——. *Florence, Rome and the Origins of the Renaissance*. Oxford: Oxford University Press, 1988.

Huillard-Bréholles, Jean-Louis. *Historia diplomatica Friderici II*. Paris: Henricus, 1854.

Hyde, Kenneth. "The Social and Political Ideal of the *Comedy*." In Eric Haywood, ed., *Dante Readings*. Dublin: Irish Academic Press, 1987, 47–71.

Iliescu, Nicolae. "The Roman Emperors in the *Divine Comedy*." In Paolo Cherchi and Antonio C. Mastrobuono, eds., *Lectura Dantis Newberryana*. Evanston, Ill.: Northwestern University Press, 1988, 1: 3–18.

Jacoff, Rachel. "Dante, Geremia e la problematica profetica." In Giovanni Barblan, ed., *Dante e la Bibbia*. Florence: Olschki, 1988, 113–23.

Jacomuzzi, Angelo. "Il canto III del *Purgatorio*." *Letture Classensi* 5 (1976): 13–40.

Jacopone da Todi. *Laude*, ed. Franco Mancini. Bari: Laterza, 1974.

John, Robert. *Dante*. Vienna: Springer, 1946.

John of Paris. *On Royal and Papal Power*, ed. and with an introduction by J. A. Watt. Toronto: Pontifical Institute of Medieval Studies, 1971.

Jones, Philip J. "La storia economica: dalla caduta dell'Impero romano al secolo XIV." In *Storia d'Italia*. Turin: Einaudi, 1974, 2: 1469–1810.

Kantorowicz, Ernst H. *The King's Two Bodies: A Study in Medieval Political Theology*. Princeton, N.J.: Princeton University Press, 1957.

———. "Dante's Two Suns." In Ernst Hartwig Kantorowicz, ed., *Selected Studies*. Locust Valley, N.Y.: Augustin, 1965, 325–38.

Kaske, Robert E. "Dante's 'DXV' and 'Veltro'." *Traditio* 17 (1961), 184–254.

———. "'Sí, si conserva il seme d'ogne giusto' (*Purgatorio* XXXII, 48)." *Dante Studies* 89 (1971), 49–54.

———. "The Seven *Status Ecclesiae* in *Purgatorio* XXXII and XXXIII." In Aldo S. Bernardo and Anthony L. Pellegrini, eds., *Dante, Petrarch, Boccaccio: Studies in the Italian Trecento in Honor of Charles S. Singleton*. Medieval and Renaissance Texts and Studies 22. Binghampton: Center for Medieval and Early Renaissance Studies, State University of New York at Binghamton, 1983, 89–113.

Kay, Richard. *Dante's Swift and Strong: Essays on "Inferno" XV*. Lawrence, Kan.: Regents Press, 1978.

———. "Dante's Razor and Gratian's D.XV." *Dante Studies* 97 (1979), 65–95.

———. "Astrology and Astronomy." In Giuseppe Di Scipio and Aldo Scaglione, eds., *The "Divine Comedy" and the Encyclopedia of Arts and Sciences*. Amsterdam-Philadelphia: J. Benjamins, 1988, 147–62.

Kelly, Henry A. *Tragedy and Comedy from Dante to pseudo-Dante*. Berkeley-Los Angeles-London: University of California Press, 1989.

Kelsen, Hans. *La teoria dello stato in Dante*. Bologna: Boni, 1974.

Kleinhenz, Christopher. "Virgil, Status, and Dante: An Unusual Trinity." In Paolo Cherchi and Antonio C. Mastrobuono, eds., *Lectura Dantis Newberryana*. Evanston, Ill.: Northwestern University Press, 1988, 1: 37–55.

Lagarde, Georges de. *La Naissance de l'esprit laïque au déclin du Moyen Age*. 2 vols. Louvain-Paris: E. Nauwelaerts, 1958.

Lansing, Richard. "*Purgatorio* III." *Lectura Dantis* 9 (1991), 54–71.

Lanza, Franco. "Roma e l'emblema della lupa." In *Dante e Roma: Atti del convegno di studi (Roma, 8-10 aprile 1965)*. Florence: Le Monnier, 1965, 255–61.

Larner, John. *Italy in the Age of Dante and Petrarch: 1216–1380*. London-New York: Longman, 1980.

Latini, Brunetto. *Li Livres dou Tresor de Brunetto Latini*, ed. F. J. Carmody. Berkeley-Los Angeles: University of California Press, 1948.

Le Goff, Jacques. *Le Moyen Age*. Paris: Bordas, 1962.

———. *La Naissance du Purgatoire*. Paris: Gallimard, 1981.

———. *Medieval Civilization: 400–1500*. Oxford: Blackwell, 1988.

Leff, Gordon. *Heresy in the Later Middle Ages: The Relation of Heterodoxy to Dissent c. 1250–c. 1450*. Manchester-New York: Manchester University Press and Barnes and Noble, 1967. 2 vols.

Lenkeith, Nancy. *Dante and the Legend of Rome*. London: Warburg Institute, University of London, 1952.

Leo, Ulrich. *Sehen und Wirklichkeit bei Dante (mit einem Nachtrag über das Problem der Literaturgeshichte)*. Frankfurt-am-Main: Klostermann, 1957.

———. "Il canto XXVII del *Purgatorio*." In Giovanni Getto, ed., *Letture dantesche*. Florence: Sansoni, 1964, 2, 1215–1233.

Lévis-Mirepoix, Antoine de. *L'Attentat d'Agnani*. Paris: Gallimard, 1969.

Lumia, Giuseppe. *Aspetti del pensiero politico di Dante*. Milan: Giuffrè, 1965.

Maccarrone, Michele. "La teoria ierocratica e il canto XVI del *Purgatorio.*" *Rivista di storia della Chiesa in Italia* 4 (1950), 359–98.

———. *"Vicarius Christi": storia del titolo papale.* Rome: Facoltas Theologica Pontificii Athenei Lateranensis, 1952.

———. "Il terzo libro della *Monarchia.*" *Studi Danteschi* 33 (1955), 5–142.

———. "Papato e Impero nella *Monarchia.*" In *Nuove letture dantesche.* Florence: Le Monnier, 1976, 8: 259–322.

Maffei, Domenico. *La Donazione di Costantino nei giuristi medievali.* Milan: Giuffrè, 1964.

Mainoni, Patrizia. "L'orizzonte economico medievale nella *Divina Commedia* e nei principali commenti del Trecento." In Giuseppe Di Scipio & Aldo Scaglione, eds., *The "Divine Comedy" and the Encyclopedia of Arts and Sciences.* Amsterdam-Philadelphia: J. Benjamins, 1988, 315–38.

Malanima, Paolo. "La formazione di una regione economica: la Toscana nei secoli XIII–XV." *Società e Storia* 6 (1983), 229–70.

Malcovati, Enrica. *M. Anneo Lucano.* Milan: U. Hoepli, 1940.

Mancusi-Ungaro, Donna. *Dante and the Empire.* New York-Bern: P. Lang, 1987.

Manselli, Raoul. "Dante e l'*Ecclesia Spiritualis.*" In *Dante e Roma: Atti del convegno di studi (Roma, 8-10 aprile 1965).* Florence: Le Monnier, 1965, 115–35.

———. "Cangrande ed il mondo ghibellino nell'Italia settentrionale alla venuta di Arrigo VII." In Vittore Branca and Giorgio Padoan, eds., *Dante e la cultura veneta: atti del convegno di studi (30 marzo–5 aprile 1966).* Florence: Olschki, 1966, 39–49.

———. "Il canto XX del *Purgatorio.*" In *Nuove letture dantesche.* Florence: Le Monnier, 1970, 4, 307–25.

———. "Dante e gli Spirituali francescani." *Letture Classensi* 11 (1982), 47–61.

Marti, Mario. *Realismo dantesco e altri studi.* Milan-Naples: Ricciardi, 1961.

Martinelli, Bortolo. "Sul "Quodammodo" di *Monarchia,* III 15, 17." In *Miscellanea di studi in onore di Vittore Branca.* Florence: Olschki, 1983, 1: 193–214.

Masciandaro, Franco. *Dante as Dramatist: The Myth of the Earthly Paradise and Tragic Vision in the "Divine Comedy."* Philadelphia: University of Pennsylvania Press, 1991.

Mastrobuono, Antonio C. *Essays on Dante's Philosophy of History.* Florence: Olschki, 1977.

———. *Dante's Journey of Sanctification.* Washington, D.C.: Regnery, 1990.

Matthew, Donald. *Atlas of Medieval Europe.* Oxford: Phaidon, 1983.

Mazzeo, Joseph. *Structure and Thought in the "Paradiso."* Ithaca, N.Y.: Cornell University Press, 1958.

———. *Mediaeval Cultural Tradition in Dante's "Comedy."* Ithaca, N.Y.: Cornell University Press, 1968.

Mazzoni, Francesco. "L'Epistola a Cangrande." *Atti della Accademia Nazionale dei Lincei. Rendiconti. Classe di scienze morali, storiche e filologiche,* Series VIII (10: 1955), 157–98.

———. "Per l'Epistola a Cangrande." In *Studi in onore di A. Monteverdi.* Modena: Società Tipografica Editrice Modenese, 1959, 2: 498–516.

———. "Pietro Alighieri interprete di Dante." *Studi Danteschi* 40 (1963), 279–360.

———. "Teoresi e prassi in Dante politico." In *Dante Alighieri. Monarchia: epistole politiche*. Turin: Edizioni RAI, 1966, ix–cxi.

———. "Le *Epistole* di Dante." In *Conferenze Aretine*. Arezzo: Accademia Petrarca & Società Dantesca Casentinese, 1966, 47–100.

———. "Un incontro di Dante con l'esegesi biblica (a proposito di *Purg.* XXX, 85–89)." In Giovanni Barblan, ed., *Dante e la Bibbia*. Florence: Olschki, 1988, 173–212.

———. "Il canto VI del *Paradiso.*" In *"Paradiso": Letture degli anni 1979–81*. Rome: Bonacci, 1989, 167–82.

Mazzoni, Guido. *Almae luces malae cruces*. Bologna: Zanichelli, 1941.

Mazzotta, Giuseppe. *Dante, Poet of the Desert: History and Allegory in the "Divine Comedy."* Princeton, N.J.: Princeton University Press, 1979.

———. *Dante's Vision and the Circle of Knowledge*. Princeton, N.J.: Princeton University Press, 1993.

Melis, Fabrizio. "La vita economica di Firenze al tempo di Dante." In *Atti del Congresso Internazionale di studi danteschi*. Florence: Le Monnier, 1966, 2: 99–128.

Mineo, Niccolò. *Profetismo e apocalittica in Dante: strutture e temi profetico-apocalittici in Dante (dalla "Vita Nuova" alla "Commedia")*. Catonia: Edigraf, 1968.

Minio-Paluello, Lorenzo. "Tre note alla *Monarchia.*" In *Medioevo e Rinascimento: Studi in onore di Bruno Nardi*. Florence: Sansoni, 1955, 2: 503–24.

———. "Remigio Girolami's *De bono communi,*" *Italian Studies* 11 (1956), 56–71.

Mitchell, Charles. "The Lateran Fresco of Boniface VIII." *Journal of the Warburg and Courtauld Institutes* 14 (1951), 1–6.

Moleta, Vincent. *Guinizzelli in Dante*. Rome: Edizioni di Storia e Letteratura, 1980.

Mollat, Guillame. *The Popes at Avignon: 1305–1378*. New York: Harper and Row, 1965.

Momigliano, Attilio. *Dante Alighieri, La Divina Commedia: Purgatorio, con i commenti di T. Casini/S. A. Barbi A. Momigliano*. F. Mazzoni, ed. Florence: Sansoni, 1973.

Mommsen, Theodor E. and Karl F. Morrison. *Imperial Lives and Letters of the Eleventh Century*. New York: Columbia University Press, 1962.

Edward Moore. *Studies in Dante, Third Series: Miscellaneous Essays*. Oxford: Oxford University Press, 1903.

Morgan, Alison. *Dante and the Medieval Other World*. Cambridge: Cambridge University Press, 1990.

Morghen, Raffaello. *Medioevo cristiano*. Bari: Laterza, 1951.

———. *Dante profeta: tra la storia e l'eterno*. Milan: Jaca, 1983.

Morrall, John B. *Political Thought in Medieval Times*. London: Hutchinson University Library, 1971.

Morris, Colin. *The Papal Monarchy: The Western Church from 1050 to 1250*. Oxford: Oxford University Press, 1989.

Mundy, John. *Europe in the High Middle Ages: 1150–1309*. London: Longman, 1973.

Muresu, Gabriele. *Dante politico: individuo e istituzioni nell'autunno del Medioevo*. Turin: Paravia, 1979.

———. *I ladri di Malebolge: saggi di semantica dantesca*. Rome: Bulzoni, 1990.

Najemy, John. *Corporatism and Consensus in Florentine Electoral Politics, 280–1400*. Chapel Hill: University of North Carolina Press, 1982.

———. "Dante and Florence." In Rachel Jacoff, ed., *The Cambridge Companion to Dante*. Cambridge: Cambridge University Press, 1993, 80–99.

Nardi, Bruno. *Dante e la cultura medievale*. Bari: Laterza, 1942.

———. *Nel mondo di Dante*. Rome: Edizioni di Storia e Letteratura, 1944.

———. *Dal "Convivio" alla "Commedia": sei saggi danteschi*. Rome: Istituto Storico Italiano per il Medio Evo, 1960.

———. *Saggi di filosofia dantesca*. Florence: La Nuova Italia, 1967.

———. *"Lecturae" e altri studi danteschi*. Florence: Le Lettere, 1990.

Norton, Glyn P. "Retrospection and Prefiguration in the Dreams of *Purgatorio*." *Italica* 47 (1970): 351–65.

Novati, Francesco. *Indagini e postille dantesche*. Bologna: Zanichelli, 1899.

Offler, Hilary Seton. "Aspects of Government in the Late Medieval Empire." In John Hale, Richard Highfield, and Beryl Smalley, eds., *Europe in the Late Middle Ages*. London: Faber, 1965, 217–47.

Oldroyd, Drina. "Hunting the Griffin in Dante's *Purgatorio*." *Spunti e ricerche* 2 (1986): 46–65.

Oliva, Gianni. "Preludio al Paradiso." In *Lectura Dantis Modenese: Purgatorio*. Modena: Banca Popolare dell'Emilia, 1985, 211–27.

Ottokar, Nicola. *Il Comune di Firenze alla fine del Dugento*. Florence: Vallecchi, 1926.

Padoan, Giorgio. *Introduzione a Dante*. Florence: Sansoni, 1975.

———. "La 'mirabile visione' di Dante e l'Epistola a Cangrande." In Padoan, *Il pio Enea, l'empio Ulisse*. Ravenna: Longo, 1977, 30–63.

———. "Nelle cornici degli accidiosi degli avari." In *Lectura Dantis Modenese: Purgatorio*. Modena: Banca Popolare dell'Emilia, 1986, 83–99.

———. *Il lungo cammino del "poema sacro": studi danteschi*. Florence: Olschki, 1993.

Pagani, Ileana. *La teoria linguistica di Dante*. Naples: Liguori, 1982.

Pagliaro, Antonino. *Ulisse*. Messina-Florence: D'Anna, 1967. 2 vols.

Pampaloni, Guido. *Firenze al tempo di Dante: documenti sull'urbanistica fiorentina*. Rome: Ministero dell'Interno, Pubblicazioni degli Archivi di Stato, Fonti e Sussidi 4, 1973.

Paparelli, Gioacchino. "Il canto XV dell'*Inferno*." In *Nuove letture dantesche*. Florence: Le Monnier, 1970, 4: 267–306.

Paratore, Ettore. *Tradizione e struttura in Dante*. Florence: Sansoni, 1968.

Pardner, Peter. "Florence and the Papacy, 1300–1375." In John Hale, Richard Highfield, and Beryl Smalley, eds., *Europe in the Late Middle Ages*. London: Faber, 1970, 76–121.

Parodi, Ernesto G. "Il canto XV dell'*Inferno*." In Giovanni Getto, ed., *Letture dantesche: "Inferno."* Florence: Sansoni, 1964, 1, 269–90.

———. *Poesia e storia nella "Divina Commedia."* Vicenza: N. Pozza, 1965.

Pasquazi, Silvio. *All'eterno dal tempo*. Florence: Le Monnier, 1966.

Passerin d'Entrèves, Alessandro. *Dante as a Political Thinker*. Oxford: Oxford University Press, 1952.

———, ed. *Aquinas: Selected Political Writings*, Oxford: Blackwell, 1959.

Pennington, Kenneth. "Law, Legislative Authority and Theories of Government, 1150–1300." In John H. Burns, ed., *The Cambridge History of Medieval Political Thought: c. 350–c. 1450*. Cambridge: Cambridge University Press, 1991, 424–53.

———. *The Prince and the Law, 1200–1600: Sovereignty and Rights in the Western Legal Tradition*. Berkeley-Los Angeles-Oxford: University of California Press, 1993.

Pertile, Lino. "*Canto-cantica Comedía* e l'Epistola a Cangrande." *Lectura Dantis* 9 (1991), 105–23.

———. "*Cantica* nella tradizione medievale e Dante." *Rivista di Storia Letteratura Religiosa* 25 (1992), 389–412.

Perugi, Maurizio. "Il Sordello di Dante e la tradizione mediolatina dell'invettiva." *Studi Danteschi* 55 (1983), 23–135.

Peters, Edward. "I principi negligenti di Dante e le concezioni medievali del *rex inutilis*." *Rivista storica italiana* 80 (1968), 741–58.

———. "*Pars, Parte*: Dante and an Urban Contribution to Political Thought." In Harry A. Miskimin, David Herlihy, and A. Udovitch, eds., *The Medieval City*. New Haven, Conn.: Yale University Press, 1977, 113–40.

———. "The Frowning Pages: Scythians, Garamantes, Florentines, and the Two Laws." In Giuseppe Di Scipio and Aldo Scaglione, eds., *The "Divine Comedy" and the Encyclopedia of Arts and Sciences*. Amsterdam-Philadelphia: J. Benjamins, 1988, 285–314.

———. "Human Diversity and Civil Society in *Paradiso* VIII." *Dante Studies* 109 (1991), 51–70.

Petrocchi, Giorgio. *Itinerari danteschi*. Bari: Adriatica, 1969.

———. *Il Purgatorio di Dante*. Milan: Rizzoli, 1978.

———. "Autobiografia politica e religiosa nella *Commedia*." *Letture Classensi* 11 (1982), 81–96.

———. *Vita di Dante*. Bari: Laterza, 1983.

———. *La selva del protonotaro*. Naples: Morano, 1988.

Pézard, André. *Dante sous la pluie de feu*. Paris: J. Vrin, 1950.

———. "Le Chant des Géants." *Bulletin de la Société d'Études Dantesques du Centre Universitaire Méditteranéen* 7 (1958), 53–72.

———. "Le Chant premier du *Purgatoire*." In V. Vettori, ed., *Letture del "Purgatorio*." Milan: Marzorati, 1965, 7–35.

———. "La politica antifrancese di Dante. I regalisti francesi dell'epoca di Filippo il Bello e l'idea imperiale." In Dante Ricci, ed., *Il processo di Dante*. Florence: Arnaud, 1967, 53–8.

———, ed. *Dante Alighieri: Oeuvres complètes. Traduction et commentaires par André Pézard*. Paris: Gallimard, 1965.

Piattoli, Renato. *Codice diplomatico dantesco*. Florence: L. Gonnelli, 1950.

Pietropaolo, Domenico. "The Figural Context of Buonconte's Salvation." *Dante Studies* 102 (1984), 123–34.

Pounds, Norman J. G. *An Economic History of Medieval Europe*. London: Longman, 1974.

Proto, Enrico. "Nuove ricerche sul Catone dantesco." *Giornale Storico della Letteratura Italiana* 59 (1912), 193–248.

Raimondi, Ezio. *Metafora e storia: Studi su Dante e Petrarca*. Turin: Einaudi, 1970.

Raveggi, Sergio, Massimo Tarassi, Daniela Medici, and Patrizia Parenti. *Ghibellini, guelfi e popolo grasso: i detentori del potere politico a Firenze nella seconda metà del Dugento*. Florence: La Nuova Italia, 1978.

Reeves, Marjorie. *The Influence of Prophecy in the Later Middle Ages*. Oxford: Oxford University Press, 1969.

———. "Dante and the Prophetic View of History." In Cecil Grayson, ed., *The World of Dante: Essays on Dante and His Times*. Oxford: Oxford University Press, 1980, 44–60.

Renucci, Paul. *Dante disciple et juge du monde gréco-latin*. Paris: Les Belles Lettres, 1954.

———. *Dante*. Paris: Hatier, 1958.

———. "Dante et les mythes du *Millenium*." *Revue des Études Italiennes* 11 (1965), 393–421.

———. "Dante e gli Svevi: Alcune osservazioni e premesse." In *Dante e l'Italia meridionale: Atti del II Congresso Nazionale di Studi Danteschi (Caserta, 10–16 ottobre 1965)*. Florence: Olschki, 1966, 131–47.

Ricci, Corrado. *L'ultimo rifugio di Dante*. Ravenna: Longo, 1965.

Ricci, Dante, ed. *Il processo di Dante*. Florence: Arnaud, 1967.

Ricci, Pier Giorgio. "Dante e l'Impero di Roma." In *Dante e Roma: Atti del convegno di studi (Roma, 8–10 aprile 1965)*. Florence: Le Monnier, 1965, 137–149.

———. "L'ultima fase del pensiero politico di Dante e Cangrande vicario imperiale." In Vittore Branca and Giorgio Padoan, eds., *Dante e la cultura veneta*. Florence: Olschki, 1966, 367–71.

Rivière, Jean. *Le Problème de l'Église et de l'État au temps de Philippe le Bel*. Louvain-Paris: Champion, 1926.

Robinson, Ian Stuart. "Church and Papacy." In John H. Burns, ed., *The Cambridge History of Medieval Political Thought: c. 350–c. 1450*. Cambridge: Cambridge University Press, 1991, 252–305.

Ronconi, Alessandro. "L'incontro di Stazio e Virgilio." In Umberto Bosco, ed., *Dante nella critica d'oggi*. Florence: Le Monnier, 1965, 565–71.

Runciman, Steven. *The Sicilian Vespers: A History of the Mediterranean World in the Later Thirteenth Century*. Cambridge: Cambridge University Press, 1992.

Russo, Francesco. "Il Pastor di Cosenza." In *Dante e la cultura sveva. Atti del II Congresso Nazionale di Studi Danteschi (Caserta, 10–16 ottobre 1965)*. Florence: Olschki, 1970, 169–79.

Russo, Vittorio. *Esperienze e/di letture dantesche: tra 1966 e il 1970*. Naples: Liguori, 1971.

———. *Impero e stato di diritto: Studio su "Monarchia" ed "Epistole" politiche di Dante*. Naples: Bibliopolis, 1987.

Sanfilippo, Mario. "Guelfi e Ghibellini a Firenze: La 'Pace' del Cardinal Latino (1280)." *Nuova Rivista Storica* 64 (1980), 1–24.

Sansone, Mario. "Il canto I del *Purgatorio*." In *Nuova Lectura Dantis*. Rome: Signorelli, 1955, 1–32.

Sapegno, Natalino. *La Divina Commedia*. Milan-Naples: Ricciardi, 1957.

Sarolli, Gian Roberto. *Prolegomena alla "Divina Commedia."* Florence: Olschki, 1971.

Scholz, Richard. *Die Publistik zur Zeit Philipps des Schönen und Bonifaz VIII.* Stuttgart: Enke, 1903.

Scott, John A. "Politics and *Inferno X.*" *Italian Studies* 19 (1964), 1–13.

——. "Dante's Admiral." *Italian Studies* 27 (1972), 28–40.

——. *Dante magnanimo.* Florence: Olschki, 1977.

——. "Treachery in Dante." In Gian Paolo Biasin, Albert N. Mancini and Nicolas J. Perella, eds., *Studies in the Italian Renaissance: Essays in Memory of Arnolfo B. Ferruolo.* Naples: Società Editrice Napolitana, 1985, 27–42.

——. "Dante, Boezio e l'enigma di Rifeo (*Par.* XX)." *Studi Danteschi* 61 (1989), 187–92.

——. "Beatrice's Reproaches in Eden: Which 'School' Had Dante Followed?" *Dante Studies* 109 (1991), 1–23.

——. "Una contraddizione scientifica nell'opera dantesca: i due soli di *Purgatorio* XVI. 107." In Patrick Boyde and Vittorio Russo, eds., *Dante e la scienza.* Ravenna: Longo, 1995, 149–55.

Shapiro, Marianna. *De Vulgari Eloquentia: Dante's Book of Exile.* Lincoln and London: University of Nebraska Press, 1990.

Shaw, Prudence. "Sul testo della *Monarchia.*" *Studi Danteschi* 53 (1981), 187–217.

Silverstein, Theodore. "On the Genesis of *De Monarchia*, II, v." In A. Bartlett Giamatti, ed., *Dante in America: The First Two Centuries.* Medieval and Renaissance Texts and Studies 23. Binghampton: Center for Medieval and Early Renaissance Studies, State University of New York at Binghampton, 1983.

Simonelli, Maria Picchio. *Lectura Dantis Americana: Infero III.* Philadelphia: University of Pennsylvania Press, 1993.

Singleton, Charles S. *Dante Studies 1: "Commedia" (Elements of Structure).* Cambridge, Mass.: Harvard University Press, 1954.

——. *Dante Studies 2: Journey to Beatrice.* Cambridge, Mass.: Harvard University Press, 1958.

——. "In Exitu Israel de Aegypto." In John Freccero, ed., *Dante: A Collection of Critical Essays.* Englewood Cliffs, N.J.: Prentice-Hall, 1965, 102–21.

——. "The Vistas in Retrospect." In *Atti del congresso internazionale di studi danteschi.* Florence: Sansoni, 1965, 1: 279–303.

——. "The Poet's Number at the Center." *Modern Language Notes* 80 (1965), 1–10.

——. *The Divine Comedy.* Princeton, NJ: Princeton University Press, 1973. 3 vols.

Smalley, Beryl. "Church and State 1300–1377: Theory and Fact." In John Hale, Richard Highfield and Beryl Smalley, eds., *Europe in the Late Middle Ages.* London: Faber, 1970, 15–43.

Soave-Bowe, Clotilde. "*Purgatorio 19*: Adrian V." In Eric Haywood, ed., *Dante Readings.* Dublin: Irish Academic Press, 1987, 123–42.

Solerti, Angelo, ed., *Le vite di Dante, Petrarca e Boccaccio.* Milan: Vallardi, 1904.

Sordello. *Le poesie.* ed. Massimiliano Boni. Bologna: Libreria antiquaria Palmaverde, 1954.

Speroni, Charles. "Dante's Prophetic Morning Dreams." In Robert J. Clements, ed., *American Critical Essays on the "Divine Comedy."* New York: New York University Press, 1967, 182–92.

Spitzer, Leo. "Linguistics and Literary History." In Gregory T. Polletta, ed., *Issues in Contemporary Literary Criticism*. Boston: Little, Brown, 1973, 490–500.

Stambler, Bernard. *Dante's Other World: The "Purgatorio" as a Guide to the "Divine Comedy."* New York: New York University Press, 1957.

———. "Three Dreams." *Books Abroad* (1965), 81–93.

Stefanini, Ruggero. "I tre sogni del *Purgatorio*: struttura e allegoria." In Gian Paolo Biasin, Albert N. Mancini, and Nicolas J. Perella, eds., *Studies in the Italian Renaissance: Essays in Memory of Arnolfo B. Ferruolo*. Naples: Società Editrice Napoletana, 1985, 43–66.

———. "La visione politica della *Divina Commedia*: a proposito di un libro recente." *Aevum* 62 (1988), 259–85.

Stella, R. "L'Expression symbolique dans les trois rêves du *Purgatoire* de Dante." *Revue des Études Italiennes* 25 (1979), 124–44.

Stickler, Alfons M. "Concerning the Political Theories of the Medieval Canonists." *Traditio* 7 (1949–1951), 450–63.

Strayer, Joseph R. *The Reign of Philip the Fair*. Princeton, N.J.: Princeton University Press, 1980.

Sumner, B. H. "Dante and the *Regnum Italicum*." *Medium Aevum* 1 (1932), 2–23.

Tarugi, Giovannangiola. "Federico II e il suo umanesimo." In *Dante e la cutura sveva: Atti del II Congresso Nazionale di Studi Danteschi (Caserta, 10–16 ottobre 1965)*. Florence: Olschki, 1970, 207–30.

Thompson, David. "Dante's Virtuous Romans." *Dante Studies* 96 (1978), 145–62.

Tierney, Brian. *The Crisis of Church and State: 1050–1300*. Englewood Cliffs, N.J.: Prentice-Hall, 1980.

Toja, Gianluigi. "Buonconte da Montefeltro e l'epos dell'eroe morente," in *Studi in onore di Alberto Chiari*. Brescia: Paideia, 1973, 2: 1269–84.

Trovato, Mario. "Dante and the Tradition of the 'Two Beatitudes'." In Paolo Cherchi and Antonio C. Mastrobuono, eds., *Lectura Dantis Newberryana*. Evanston, Ill.: Northwestern University Press, 1988, 1, 19–36.

Ullmann, Walter. *Medieval Political Thought*. Harmondsworth: Penguin, 1975.

Valli, Luigi. *Il linguaggio segreto di Dante e dei fedeli d'amore*. Rome: Bertoni, 1928.

Vallone, Aldo. "La componente federiciana della cultura dantesca," in *Dante e Roma: Atti del convegno di studi (Roma, 8–10 aprile 1965)*. Florence: Le Monnier, 1965, 347–69.

Vasoli, Cesare. "La dottrina politica di Dante." In *La filosofia medievale*. Milan: Feltrinelli, 1961, 406–10.

———. "Filosofia e politica in Dante fra *Convivio e Monarchia*." *Letture Classensi* 9–10 (1982), 11–37.

Vinay, Gustavo. *Interpretazione della "Monarchia" di Dante*. Florence: Le Monnier, 1962.

Waley, Daniel. *Later Medieval Europe: From St. Louis to Luther*. London: Longman, 1975.

———. *The Italian City-Republics*. London: Longman, 1978.

Watt, John A. Introduction to: John of Paris (1240–1306), *On Royal and Papal Power*. Toronto: Pontifical Institute of Medieval Studies, 1971, 9–63.

———. "Spiritual and Temporal Power." In John H. Burns, ed., *The Cambridge History of Medieval Political Thought: c. 350–c. 1450*. Cambridge: Cambridge University Press, 1991, 367–423.

Whitfield, John H. "Dante and the Roman World." *Italian Studies* 33 (1978), 1–19.

Williamson, Edward. "De Beatitudinis Huius Vite." *Annual Report of the Dante Society* 76 (1958), 1–22.

Index

Abelard, Peter, 257
Abruzzi, 111
Abulafia, D., 218, 269
Acquasparta, Matteo di, 17, 19, 154, 260
Acre, 175
Adam, 66, 129, 181, 184, 186, 195, 197, 208, 257, 261, 266
Adolf of Nassau, 10, 34, 103, 124
Adrian I, 105, 238
Adrian IV, 161, 252
Adrian V, 63, 159ff., 177, 192, 252
Aeneas, x, 37, 39, 45, 64, 77, 81
Agapetus I, 156, 213, 250
Aglianò, S., 71
Aix-la-Chapelle, 55, 123, 243
Alagia Fieschi, 40, 177
Alberico da Romano, 111
Albert I of Habsburg, 25–26, 34, 40, 102–6, 124, 126, 138, 218, 238
Alberti di Mangona family, 98
Albertus Magnus (Albert the Great, St.), 188, 226, 259
Aldobrandeschi family, 106
Aldobrandeschi, Margherita, 19
Aldobrandeschi, Omberto, 144
Alessandria, 126
Alexander the Great, 167
Alexander IV, 85
Alexander, P., 265, 269
Alfonso the Wise, 216
Alighieri family, 29
Alighieri, Antonia, 58
Alighieri, Gemma, 15
Alighieri, Jacopo, 58, 215
Alighieri, Pietro, 11, 105, 120, 153, 200, 204, 215–16, 238, 242, 254, 262, 264
Alsace, 103
Amata, 45
Amidei family, 4

Anagni (Alagna), 20–21, 27–28, 46, 48, 172–73, 201, 212, 254–55
Anastasius, 219
Anchises, 39
Anderson, W., 255, 269
Anjou, 15–16, 170
Antepurgatory, 85, 89, 91, 96–97, 111, 116, 118, 120, 127, 129, 137, 185, 213
Antichrist, 86, 92, 200, 202, 204, 211, 218, 263, 264, 266
Aquinas, Thomas, St., 13, 31, 54, 70, 74, 76, 99, 112, 117–18, 125, 151, 153, 158–59, 167, 170, 184, 188, 225, 226, 227, 232, 253, 266, 269
Aragon, 98, 125
Aratus, 184
Archiano, River, 90
Arezzo, 6, 28, 34, 38, 42, 90–91, 97, 146, 220
Argenti, Filippo, 14
Ariosto, L., 147, 227
Aristotle, 7–8, 12–13, 99, 100, 102, 164, 206, 230, 236, 238, 253
Arles, 123
Armour, P., 81, 139, 183, 188, 193, 196, 217, 232, 246, 257, 258, 259, 260, 261, 262, 264, 266, 269
Arno, River, 55, 90, 145–46
Ascanius, 45
Assisi, 65
Astolfo, 227
Athens, 108
Auerbach, E., 73, 131, 190, 229, 237, 245, 260, 269
Augustine, St., 70, 82, 102, 159, 164, 167, 210, 221, 233, 251, 253, 263
Augustine of Dacia, 245
Augustus (Octavian), 100–101, 196, 204, 20, 235, 238, 239
Aurigemma, M., 236, 269

Austria, 103, 124
Avalle, D. S., 269
Avignon, 24, 36–37, 41, 65, 106, 143, 151,
    187, 201, 203, 209, 212, 251, 262
Azzo III, 113, 168, 172

Babel, 44, 126, 201, 263
Baktin, L. M., 240, 269
Baldwin of Luxembourg, 41
Baldwin II, 174
Bambaglioli, Graziolo dei, 215
Barański, Z. G., 225, 237, 241, 244, 269
Barasch, M., 251, 270
Barbadoro, B., 217, 270
Barbarossa, Frederick, 4
Bàrberi Squarotti, G., 89, 234–35, 270
Barbi, M., 191, 220, 260, 270
Bardi family, 108
Barolini, T., 96–97, 101, 110, 113–14, 119,
    237–39, 241–42, 257, 270
Barraclough, G., 216, 270
Battaglia, S., 267, 270
Battifolle, Guido di, 46
Beatrice, x, 7, 15, 53, 66–67, 72, 130, 136, 150,
    180, 184, 186, 187, 189ff., 224, 248, 258–59,
    260–61, 264–66
Beatrice, Countess, 184, 258
Beatrice d'Este, 172
Becker, M. V., 270
Belacqua, 90, 97, 128
Benedict XI, 28, 36, 46, 220, 255
Benevento, 5, 23, 86, 111
Benvenuto da Imola, vii, 97, 99, 109, 140,
    149, 153, 182, 199, 207, 237, 240, 245, 247,
    249–50, 266
Benincasa da Laterina, 97
Bérenger, Beatrice, 111
Bérenger, Raymond, 111
Bernard, J., 108, 239
Bernard of Clairvaux, St., 102, 120, 159, 175,
    251
Berretta, G., 238, 251, 270
Bigi, E., 232
Billanovich, G., 252, 270
Binni, W., 233, 270
Bithynia, 80
Blacatz, 110–12, 114, 123
Boase, T. S. R., 238
Boccaccio, Giovanni, 58, 227, 270

Boccasini, Niccolò. See Benedict XI
Boethius, 83, 145–46, 206, 233, 248, 270
Boethius of Dacia, 220
Bohemia, 124
Bolano, 40
Bologna, 20, 32, 38, 40, 58, 114, 123, 201, 221
Bonaccolsi, Passarino, 57
Bonagiunta da Lucca, 180
Bonaventure, St., 139
Bonconte da Montefeltro, 85, 90ff., 162, 233,
    235
Boniface VIII, 9–10, 16, 18–21, 24–28, 36–
    37, 41, 46, 48–49, 52, 54, 93, 95, 104, 108,
    121, 138–39, 153–54, 170–72, 176, 201,
    216–18, 221, 223, 233–34, 238, 246, 255
Bonn, 55
Bonora, E., 254, 255, 270
Bordeaux, 36–37
Born, Bertrand de, 114, 119
Bornelh, Giraut de, 113, 180
Bosco, U., vii, 10, 130, 135, 161, 232, 245,
    248, 252, 262, 270
Bostoli Family, 97
Bouvines, 254
Boyde, P., 235, 250, 253, 255, 264, 270, 273
Bowra, C. M., 112–13, 116, 241–42, 270
Bowsky, W., 50, 222–24, 226, 256, 270
Brandeis, I., 241, 271
Breakspear, Nicholas, 252
Brentano, R., 271
Brescia, 45–46, 114, 149, 177
Brosse, Pierre de la, 98
Brundisium, 236
Brunelleschi, Betto, 42
Bruni, L., 17, 47
Brutus, x, 69, 74, 81, 229
Brutus (Consul), 78
Bufano, A., 239
Bueno de Mesquita, D. M., 247, 248, 271
Buondelmonti, Buondelmonte dei, 4
Burgundy, 169
Burns, J. H., 216, 271
Buti, Francesco da, vii, 155, 182, 199, 227,
    239, 250, 258

Caccia, E., 233, 271
Cacciaguida, 28–29, 39, 222
Caesar, Julius, 69–70, 74–75, 78–82, 107,
    139, 219, 229, 23–32

Caetani, Benedetto. *See* Boniface VIII
Caetani, Francesco, 36
Cahors, 56
Calboli, Rinieri dei, 147
Calenda, C., 192, 261, 271
Caligula, 231
Caltabellotta, 26
Calvary, 27, 129
Camilla, Antonio da, 40
Camillus, 70, 231
Camino, Gherardo da, 38, 149
Campagnatico, 144, 247
Campaldino, 6, 15, 90, 235
Camporesi, P., 259
Cancellieri family, 16
Canning, J. P., 12, 216, 271
Canossa, 182, 258
Canterbury, 252
Capet, Hugh, 63, 113, 166, 168ff., 212,
    253–54
Capitani, O., 226, 271
Capitol, 133
Cappelletti Family, 105
Caprettini, G. P., 251, 271
Carpentras, 50, 106, 162
Carrara, 40
Cary, G., 271
Casentino, 46, 146
Cassell, A. K., 265, 271
Castel del Piano, 21
Castelnuovo di Magra, 40
Castile, III–II2
Cassius, x, 69, 81
Castelnau, Peire de, III
Catherine of Courtenay, 170
Catherine of Siena, St., 24
Catiline, 10, 16, 75
Cato of Utica, x, 63–64, 67, 69ff., 182–83,
    212, 228–32
Cavalcanti family, 15, 116
Cavalcanti, Cavalcante, 8, 16
Cavalcanti, Guido, 14, 16–17, 192, 260, 271
Celestine V, 8–9, 24, 215, 216
Cerchi Family, 14–16, 18, 20, 28, 217
Cerchi, Ricoverino de', 16
Cerchi, Vieri de', 15, 21
Cervigni, D. S., 244, 245, 251, 253, 271
Charity, A. C., 271
Charlemagne, 104–105, 156, 238

Charles I of Anjou, 5, 15, 86, 91, 97, III–II2,
    119, 123, 125, 162, 170, 201
Charles II of Anjou, 9, 18, 20, 23, 113, 125,
    149, 168, 170–72, 216, 254
Charles IV, 104, 226
Charles of Lorraine, 170
Charles of Valois, 18–21, 26, 40, 125, 170–71,
    176, 217, 254, 263
Charles Martel, 254
Chiavacci-Leonardi, A. M., 226, 271
Chrétien de Troyes, 259
Christ, 8–9, 13, 23–24, 42–45, 50–52, 56,
    64, 67, 76, 89, 94–96, 102, 104, 106, 118,
    121, 133–134, 140–143, 149, 153–55, 157,
    162, 164, 168, 172–75, 179, 181, 185–91,
    194, 196–200, 202, 205, 207, 209, 222–24,
    230, 233–36, 245, 247, 250–51, 255, 259,
    260–61, 265–67
Chydenius, J., 271
Ciacco, 236
Cicero, 8, 10, 70, 71, 75, 115, 177–78, 229
Cilento, N., 271
Cincinnatus, 70, 231
Cino da Pistoia, 40, 151, 183
Ciotti, A., 258
Cipolla, C. M., 271
Circe, 145
Clement IV, 86, 95, III, 201
Clement V, 36–37, 41–43, 46–48, 50–52, 54,
    56–57, 123, 153–54, 173, 176, 201, 221–22,
    224, 255, 262–63, 266
Cleopatra, 70
Cognasso, F., 271
Cohn, N., 205–206, 254, 265, 271
Coletti, F., 241
Colle Val d'Elsa, 145
Cologne, 55
Colonna family, 8, 24, 36–37, 93
Colonna, Iacopo, 24
Colonna, Pietro, 24
Colonna, Sciarra, 27
Colonna Stefano, 24
Commodus, 231
Compagni, Dino, vii, 4, 7, 14–16, 20, 28,
    41–42, 46, 108, 217, 222–23, 254
Comparetti, D., 271
Compiègne, 170
Comtat Venaissin, 37
Conrad III, 3

Conrad IV, 85–86, 170
Conradin. See Corradino
Consoli, D., 181, 257, 271
Constantine the Great, 22, 26, 49, 52, 84, 104, 123, 138, 156, 167, 183, 196, 199, 207, 209, 233, 262–63
Constantinople, 171
Corbinelli, Albizzo, 19
Corradino (Conradin), 85–86, 125, 170
Corrado da Palazzo, 149
Corti, M., 220–21, 242, 271
Cosenza, 88, 95
Cosmo, U., 51, 224, 272
Costanza of Aragon, 95, 125
Courtrai, 169
Cremona, 45, 105, 114
Crete, 82, 256
Cristaldi, S., 258, 265, 272
Cristoforo, Fra, 97
Croce, B., 99
Cunizza da Romano, 111, 116
Curio, 28, 219
Curtius, E. R., 266, 272

Daniel, Arnaut, 117–18, 180
Da Porto, L., 105
Davanzati, Chiaro, 134
David, 45, 65, 140–42, 160, 234
Davis, C. T., 10, 13, 65, 70, 204, 215–18, 220, 221, 228–29, 231, 239–40, 254, 264–65, 272
De Panna, L., 231, 272
De Rosa, M., 222, 250, 272
De' Girolami, Remigio, 12–13, 70, 74, 108, 216, 217, 229, 263, 272
De' Negri, E., 247
Delmay, B., 272
Del Popolo, C. S., 257, 272
Della Bella, Giano, 6–7, 14–16
Denmark, 26
Di Scipio, G., 226, 249–50, 272
Digard, G., 218, 272
Diodati, Gherardino, 19
Diodati, Neri, 19
Dido, 70
Diocletian, 199
Dis, 75
Domitian, 49
Donati family, 14–16
Donati, Corso, 7, 15–17, 19–20, 149, 217

Donati, Forese, 180, 217, 261
Donati, Piccarda, 217
Donati, Gemma. See Alighieri, Gemma
Dreux, 169
Dronke, P., 188, 225, 258, 259, 263–64, 272
Duèse, Jacques. See John XXII
Dupré Theseider, E., 263, 272
Dupuy, P., 218, 260, 272
Durant, Guillaume, 162
DXV, 204–7, 254, 264–66

Earthly Paradise. See Eden
Eden, 64, 66–67, 81, 85, 120, 122, 129, 132, 134, 136, 138, 166, 169, 179ff., 227, 240, 266
Edward I, 26, 126
Egypt, 132
Elijah, 227, 258
Elizabeth, 186
Elizabeth of Hungary, St., 236
Emilia, 41
England, 221
Enoch, 227, 258
Entrèves, A. P. d'. See Passerin d'Entrèves, A. P.
Epirus, 167
Ercole, F., 220, 272
Eunoë, 137, 178, 211
Eve, 66, 120, 186, 195
Ezechiel, 199
Ezzelino III, 111

Fabricius, Gaius Luscinua, 167, 230, 231, 234
Faenza, 147
Fabius Fulgentius Planciades. See Fulgentius
Faggiuola, Uguccione della, 16, 55
Favati, G., 239, 273
Favier, J., 218, 254, 255, 256, 273
Fedele, P., 255, 273
Federico Novello, 97
Ferrante, J., 65, 67, 157, 180–83, 190, 232, 240, 242, 250, 256–58, 260, 264, 26, 273
Ferrara, 114, 123, 201
Ficino, M., 51
Fieschi, Alagia, 40, 167
Fieschi, Luca, 177
Fieschi, Ottobono. See Adrian V
Fieschi, Sinibaldo. See Innocent IV
Filippeschi family, 105–6
Flanders, 169–70

Florence, x, 8, 13, 16–21, 28–29, 35, 41–42,
    44–48, 55, 58–59, 67, 70, 86, 97, 102, 107–
    9, 112–13, 116, 124, 146–47, 149, 154, 171,
    177, 202, 217, 219, 220, 222, 224, 226, 240,
    251–52, 254, 256, 259, 263–64
Foixà, Joifre de, 32
Folz, R., 273
Forlí, 21, 147
Forti, F., 120, 122–23, 228, 242–43, 257, 273
Fosco, Bernardin di, 147
Fossanuova, 170
Foster, K., 78, 231, 253, 261–62, 264, 273
France, 24–26, 41, 67, 86, 98, 104, 112, 125,
    169, 172–78, 198, 201, 211–12, 221, 254–56,
    262, 264
Francesca da Rimini, 58, 151
Francis, St., 14, 24, 65, 91, 93, 140, 168
Frankel, M., 222, 273
Frankfurt, 243
Freccero, J., 89, 234–35, 273
Frederick of Austria, 55, 57–58
Frederick II of Aragon, 26, 32, 47, 125, 171,
    243
Frederick II, Emperor, 4, 22–24, 30–32, 34,
    41, 49, 85–88, 92, 124, 147–48, 155–56,
    162, 173, 201, 206, 215, 218, 234, 236, 248,
    250, 252, 265
Frugoni, A., 240, 264–65, 273
Fulcieri da Calboli, 58, 147
Fulgentius, 179, 221
Furies, 75

Gabriel, Angel, 186
Gabrielli, Canto dei, 19–20
Ganymede, 130, 133–34, 244–45
Garibaldi, G., 92
Garin, E., 273
Gauthier, R. A., 241, 273
Gebel, 258
Gelasius I, 76, 219
Genoa, 47
Germany, 33–34, 42, 50, 121, 239, 258, 262
Geryon, 135, 157
Gherardo da Camino, 38, 149
Ghino di Tacco, 97
Giacalone, G., viii, 149
Giardini, Pietro, 58
Giordano, Fra, 81
Gilson, E., 114, 131, 225, 241, 246, 249, 273
Gimpel, J., 273

Giordano d'Anglona, 85
Giovagallo, 40
Giovanni del Virgilio, 38, 58, 133
Girolami, Remigio dei (see De' Giro-
    lami, R.)
Gmelin, H., 247, 273
Goito, 111
Got, Bertrand de (see Clement V)
Goudet, J., 273
Graf, A., 229, 247, 273
Gratian, 264
Grayson, C., 242–43, 273
Green, V. H. R., 221, 274
Gregory the Great, 83, 141, 247, 249
Gregory VII, 182
Grendler, P. F., 231, 274
Griffin, 65, 67, 81, 187–89, 193–98, 200, 208,
    211, 259–62
Grimaldo da Prato, 18
Guccio dei Tarlati, 97
Guelfo/Gulfo: 258
Guénon, R., 255, 274
Guicciardini, F., 215
Guidi, Counts of Romena, 15
Guido da Montefeltro, 87, 91–93, 147, 172
Guido da Pisa, 215
Guido del Duca, 145–47
Guido Novello di Bagno, 97
Guinizzelli, Guido, 7, 180
Guittone d'Arezzo, 101, 110, 180, 238–39
Guy of Dampierre, 169

Habsburg family, 41, 55
Hall, R. G., 225, 274
Halle, Adam de la, 233
Hannibal, 50, 106, 266
Hardie, C., 188, 259, 274
Hardt, M., 266, 274
Hazelton, R., 77, 231, 274
Hector, 81
Henry, Duke of Bavaria, 3
Henry, King of Navarre, 125
Henry III, 126, 252
Henry IV, 23, 121, 182
Henry V, 182
Henry VII, ix, 37, 40–50, 52, 54–55, 57–58,
    123, 133–34, 151, 154–55, 176–77, 205, 210,
    212, 219, 221, 223–24, 226, 237, 243, 263,
    266–67
Hercules, 76

Herde, P., 274
Hohenstaufen, 23, 25, 30, 32, 86, 90, 97, 112, 119, 162, 170
Holmes, G., 19, 217
Horace, 77
Hungary, 26
Hollander, R., 51, 76, 131, 133, 151, 221–22, 224–25, 230–32, 244–45, 248, 251, 274
Holmes, G., 221, 223, 240, 274
Hostiensis, 121, 155, 162
Hugh of St. Victor, 159, 251
Huilliard-Bréholles, J. L., 219, 274
Humbert, Cardinal, 249
Humbert of Romans, 103
Hyde, K., 248, 274

Ibn-al-Jazi, 236
Ida, 133–34
Iliescu, N., 146, 149, 248, 274
Imola, 114
Innocent III, 22, 25, 154, 177, 239, 264
Innocent IV, 4, 23, 85, 161–62, 252
Italy, 26, 28–29, 32, 34, 38, 42–44, 46, 49–50, 57, 96–97, 99, 100, 103–4, 106–7, 109, 110, 114, 117, 124, 126, 133–34, 148–49, 155, 167, 176–77, 180, 183, 204, 210, 212, 221, 223, 237, 239, 243, 248, 254, 262–63
Isaiah, 43–44, 141, 223
Isidore, St., 89, 229, 259
Israel, 45, 232, 246

Jacoff, R., 224, 274
Jacomuzzi, A., 274
Jacopo da Lentini, 180
Jacopo del Cassero, 172
Jacopone da Todi, 9, 216, 274
James I of Aragon, 241
James II, 125
Jason, 221
Jeremiah, 44, 50, 224
Jericho, 232
Jerome, St., 259
Jerusalem, 50, 65, 129, 142–43, 174, 186, 190–91, 202, 224, 255
Jesse, 45
Jesus, 45, 235. See also Christ
Joachim of Floris, 203, 206, 264–65
John, King of England, 22, 170
John, R., 255, 274
John XXII, 52, 56–57

John of Austria, 40
John of Gravina, 47
John I of Monferrato, 126, 219
John of Paris, 249, 267, 274
John of Salisbury, 161, 247
John the Baptist, 17, 45–46
John the Evangelist, St., 51–52, 133, 146, 153, 186, 202, 206, 227, 253
Jones, P. J., 240, 274
Joshua, 235
Jove, 77, 106–107, 131, 133, 172, 239, 263
Judas Iscariot, x, 69, 87, 171, 231, 234, 254
Jude, 91, 235
Julian the Apostate, 231
Jupiter. See Jove
Justinian I, 58, 84, 100–101, 108, 126, 152, 156, 165, 185, 189, 198, 213
Juvenal, 180

Kantorowicz, E. H., 11, 13, 74, 181, 207, 216, 222, 229–30, 233, 246, 250, 257, 260, 274
Kaske, R., 262–65, 275
Kay, R., 216, 264, 275
Kelly, H. A., 225, 275
Kelsen, H., 246, 275
Kleinhenz, C., 180, 257, 275
Kraus, C., 261

Labienus, 74
Lagarde, G. de, 275
Lana, Jacopo della, 149, 199, 215
Lancia, Bianca, 32, 88
Lancia, Andrea, 263
Landino, C., 250
Lansing, R., 235, 275
Lanza, F., 251, 275
Larner, J., 215, 218, 233–35, 240, 247, 275
Las Formiguas, 125
Lastra, La, 35
Lateran. See Saint John Lateran
Latini, Brunetto, 10–13, 35, 66, 71, 75, 86, 109, 116, 137, 216, 219, 227–28, 232–33, 237, 240, 242, 275
Lausanne, 42, 45, 123
Lavinia, 233
Le Goff, J., 129, 158, 231, 244–45, 251, 254, 275
Lebanon, 182, 190
Leff, G., 233, 275
Lenkeith, N., 275

Leo, U., 39, 222, 275
Lethe, 137, 185, 193, 211
Levi, 157
Lévis-Mirepoix, A. de, 254, 275
Lewis of Bavaria, 55, 57
Liguria, 41, 161
Limbo, 70, 97, 99, 128, 231
Loche, 173
Lombardy, 41, 57, 58, 105, 149, 226
Lorraine, 170
Louis IX, St., 86, 112, 170, 254
Lucan, viii, 71, 74–76, 219, 229, 232–33
Lucca, 17, 55, 112
Lucia, 130, 132–33, 135–37, 244, 245
Lucifer, 69, 139, 172, 174, 251. See also Satan
Lucretia, 70
Lucy, St. See Lucia
Luke, St., 23, 43, 45, 95, 101, 109, 121, 174–
    75, 186, 198
Lumia, G., 275
Luni, 40
Lunigiana, 40
Luxembourg, 41
Lyon, 23, 162, 170, 252
Lys, River, 169

Macaulay, T. B., 80, 229
Maccarrone, M., 218, 226, 246, 249–50, 276
Machiavelli, N., 3, 12, 57, 215
Maffei, D., 276
Mahomet, 199, 236
Maine, 170
Mainoni, P., 276
Mainz, 55
Malabranca, L., 5, 8
Malanima, P., 276
Malaspina family, 40
Malaspina, Corrado II, 40
Malaspina, Currado, 96
Malaspina, Francesco, 40
Malaspina, Moroello, 40, 177
Malcovati, E., 230, 276
Mancusi-Ungaro, D., 276
Manfred, 5, 23, 30–32, 63, 67, 85ff., 97, 111,
    118, 125, 155, 162, 171, 201, 233–35, 250, 263
Manselli, R., 56, 161–62, 236, 252, 258,
    264–66, 276
Mantua, 96, 99, 111, 114, 119
Manzoni, A., 97
Marca Trevigiana, 28

Marcellus, 107, 239
Marco Lombardo, 63, 149ff., 163, 248, 250
Maremma, 144
Marigo, A., 34, 220
Marittima, 19
Mark, St., 153, 174, 190, 253, 255
Mars, 4
Marti, M., 261, 276
Martin IV, 125
Martina, A., 231
Martinelli, B., 226, 246, 276
Mary, 65, 90, 94–95, 121, 130, 139–41, 143,
    166, 168, 186, 196, 202, 236, 245
Masciandaro, F., 240, 242, 258, 260, 276
Massa Trabaria, 16
Mastrobuono, A. C., 265, 276
Matelda, 182–85, 193, 195, 257–58
Matilda, Countess of Tuscany, 182
Matthew, D., 218, 276
Matthew, St., 8, 45, 95, 101, 142, 153, 156,
    174–75, 190, 196, 222, 228, 243, 255
Maximilian, 104
Mazzamuto, P., 264
Mazzeo, J. A., 238, 248, 276
Mazzoni, F., 51, 53–54, 132, 188, 194, 224–
    25, 238, 246, 250, 259–61, 267, 276–77
Mazzoni, G., 264, 277
Mazzotta, G., 81–82, 229, 233, 246, 251–52,
    277
Medici, D., 279
Melis, F., 240, 277
Menalippus, 180
Mengaldo, P. V., 31, 33, 114, 219, 241–42
Mercury, 129
Methodius, 204, 254
Michael, St., 91, 265
Micol, 137
Milan, 45, 57
Mineo, N., 222, 277
Minio-Paluello, L., 74, 216, 223, 226, 229,
    246, 277
Minos, 137
Mitchell, C., 138, 218, 246, 277
Modena, 114
Molay, Jacques de, 176
Moleta, V. B., 277
Mollat, G., 57, 221, 227, 277
Momigliano, A., 182, 257, 277
Mommsen, T. E., 277
Monaldi family, 105–6

Montano, R., 149
Montaperti, 5, 85–86, 144
Montecatini, 55–56
Montecchi family, 105
Monteriggioni, 263
Moon, 128
Moore, E., 197, 205–6, 225, 259–62, 265–66, 277
Morgan, A., 227, 277
Morghen, R., 51, 224, 234, 277
Morrall, J. B., 277
Morris, C., 218, 277
Morrison, K. F., 277
Moses, 42, 64, 91, 230, 235–36
Mucius Scaevola, 230
Mulazzo, 40
Mundy, J. H., 215, 238, 277
Muresu, G., 277
Myra, 167
Myrrha, 46

Najemy, J., 4, 215, 217, 219, 240, 278
Naples, 31, 37, 57, 86, 161, 171–72, 235, 263
Nardi, B., 45, 49, 65, 88–89, 183, 220, 222–26, 235, 238, 246, 250, 253, 258, 278
Nero, 49, 76, 79, 199, 231
Niccolò da Prato, 28, 40, 47
Nicholas III, 5, 37, 163–64, 201
Nicholas, St., 167–68, 254
Nimrod, 201, 263
Nogaret, Guillaume de, 27
Normandy, 170
Norton, G. P., 244, 278
Novello, Federico, 97
Novello di Bagno, Guido, 97
Novara, 111
Novati, F., 234, 278
Numa Pompilius, 31

Octavian. See Augustus
Oderisi da Gubbio, 144
Offler, H. S., 239, 248, 278
Oldroyd, D., 259, 278
Oliva, G., 265, 278
Olivi, Petrus Johannis, 14, 202, 218
Olympus, 201
Ordelaffi, Scarpetta degli, 21
Orestes, 141
Orfinus of Lodi, 250
Orleans, 169

Orosius, 231
Orsini family, 8
Orsini, Giovanni Caetani. See Nicholas III
Orsini, Matteo, 36
Orsini, Napoleone, 36, 40, 51
Orvieto, 16
Otta di Strasso, 111
Ottimo Commento, L', viii, 149, 182, 200, 204, 263, 265
Otto IV, 4, 22
Ottocar II, 124
Ottokar, N., 6, 278
Ovid, 77, 131, 184

Padoan, G., 179, 223, 225, 236–38, 252, 256, 278
Padua, 226
Pagani, I., 278
Pagliaro, A., 278
Palermo, 175
Palestine, 175
Pampaloni, G., 240, 278
Paparelli, G., 162, 252, 278
Paratore, E., 75, 180, 156–57, 278
Pardner, P., 278
Parenti, P., 279
Paris, 169, 174–75
Paris, Matthew, 234
Parnassus, 258
Parodi, E. G., 208, 254, 266, 278
Pasquazi, S., 118, 265, 278
Passerin d'Entrèves, A., 29–30, 219, 220, 222, 226, 278
Passerini, G. L., 261
Pastore Stocchi, M., 247
Paul, St., x, 43, 50–51, 56, 131, 138, 143, 184, 197, 227, 247, 250, 266
Pazzi, Carlino dei, 21
Péguilhan, Aimeric de, 233
Pennington, K., 224, 243, 256, 267, 279
Perini, Dino, 58
Persius, 160, 180
Pertile, L., 225, 237, 279
Perugi, M., 114, 237, 241, 279
Perugia, 36, 42, 51
Peruzzi family, 108
Peter, St., 23–24, 50, 56, 93, 100, 138–39, 143, 154, 160, 166, 169, 172, 199, 204, 207, 222, 227, 233, 246–47, 250, 253, 260, 262, 266
Peter III of Aragon, 125–26

Peters, E., 157, 219, 229, 242, 248–50, 252, 279
Petrarch, Francesco, 24, 71, 161, 220, 239
Petrocchi, G., 38, 51, 58, 217, 218, 220–21, 223–24, 227, 235, 237, 255, 279
Pézard, A., viii, 77, 116, 175, 216, 230, 239, 242, 249, 252, 255–56, 263, 279
Pharsalus, 79
Philip II (Augustus), 170, 254
Philip III, 98, 125
Philip IV (Philip the Fair), 18, 24–27, 37, 40, 46–49, 54, 98, 125, 154, 169–70, 173, 176–77, 201–2, 255–56, 262–64
Piattoli, R., vii, 279
Piedmont, 41, 111
Pietro da Morrone. See Celestine V
Pietro di Dante. See Alighieri, Pietro
Pietropaolo, D., 235, 279
Pignatelli, Bartolomeo, 88
Pilate, Pontius, 173, 255
Pisa, 6, 15, 41, 55, 101, 146, 179, 180, 248
Pistoia, 14, 16, 20, 40
Plato, 236
Po, River, 148
Poitou, 170
Polenta Family, 133
Polenta, Guido Novello da, 58
Polyphemus, 58
Pompey the Great, 79–80, 231–32
Portinari, Folco, 15
Porto, 56
Pothinus, 80
Potiphar, 98
Pounds, N. G., 215, 279
Proto, E., 73, 77, 228, 231, 279
Provence, 57, 111, 115, 125, 170, 241
Ptolemy of Egypt, 79, 231–32
Ptolemy, Governor of Jericho, 232
Pylades, 141
Pyrrhus, 167–68

Quondam, A., 181, 257

Raimondi, E., 279
Rajna, P., 253
Raspe, Henry, 162
Raveggi, S., 279
Ravenna, 56, 58, 59, 147
Reeves, M., 264–65, 280
Reggio, G., vii, 30, 232, 245, 248, 262

Regulus, 230
Reims, 169
Remus, 251
Renan, E., 221
Renucci, P., 38, 205, 208, 221, 231, 239, 253–54, 264–65, 280
Rhine, River, 103
Rhipeus, 77–78, 82–84, 88, 206, 234
Ricci, C., 280
Ricci, D., 261, 280
Ricci, P. G., 51, 224, 243, 280
Riccobaldo da Ferrara, 93
Rivière, J., 218, 250, 280
Rizzardo di San Bonifacio, 111
Robert of Anjou, King of Naples, 42, 46–50, 56–57, 224, 267
Robinson, I. S., 280
Roger, Archbishop, 100
Roland, 263
Romagna, 15, 17, 28, 43, 123, 147–48, 156, 201, 248
Rome, x, 13, 20, 33–34, 37–38, 44–47, 50, 64–67, 72, 77–83, 86–87, 97, 100, 102, 106, 115, 124, 129, 133–34, 138, 142–43, 154–55, 157, 163, 167, 184, 189, 194, 197–98, 210, 212, 217, 220–21, 223, 225, 230, 232, 238–39, 243, 247, 249–52, 255, 260–62, 266
Romulus, 251
Ronconi, A., 256, 280
Rossi, A. L., 51, 224, 231–32, 274
Roussillon, 111
Rubicon, River, 80–81
Rudolf, Count Palatine, 55
Rudolph of Habsburg, 34, 42, 96, 102–5, 118, 123–24, 126, 148, 201
Ruggiero di Loria, 172
Runciman, S., 254, 280
Russo, F., 280
Russo, V., 257, 280
Rutilius, 230

Saint Peter's (Church), 47
Saint John Lateran, 26, 47, 138
Saintonge, 170
Saladin, 99
Salerno, 172
Salsano, F., 134
Saltarelli, Lapo, 18, 217
Salvani, Provenzano, 144–45

Samson, 70
Samuel, 51, 234
San Gimignano, 17
San Giovanni (Baptistery), 55
San Godenzo, 21
San Miniato, 55
San Pier Maggiore, 58
Sanfilippo, M., 280
Sansone, M., 77, 231, 280
Santa Croce, 14, 97
Santafiora, 144
Santa Maria Novella, 13, 28
Santo Stefano, 40
Sapegno, N., viii, 173, 187, 245, 254–55, 257, 259, 280
Sarolli, G. R., 205, 222, 234, 265–66, 280
Sarzana, 17, 40
Satan, 201, 212, 252, 263. *See also* Lucifer
Scala, Alberto della, 32
Scala, Bartolomeo della, 21, 28
Scala, Cangrande della, 56–58, 131
Scala, Giuseppe della, 32
Scholz, R., 281
Sciarra, Iacopo, 24
Scipio Africanus, 207, 266
Scipios, The, 50
Scornigiani, Farinata/Gano degli, 97
Scornigiani, Marzucco, 97
Scott, J. A., 219, 225, 228–32, 239, 253, 259–60, 281
Seine, River, 256
Seneca, 31, 71–72, 74–76, 228–30, 232
Shakespeare, W., 105
Shapiro, M., 241–42, 281
Shaw, P., 51, 224, 281
Sicilian Vespers, 18, 171
Sicily, 18, 23, 26, 32, 42, 85–86, 112, 123, 125, 171, 173, 216
Siena, 42, 55, 85, 106, 144–45, 161, 247, 251, 263
Siger of Brabant, 208, 220
Silverstein, T., 70, 228, 281
Silvotti, M. T., 216
Simonelli, M. P., 215, 281
Singleton, C. S., 131–133, 140, 195, 242, 245, 248, 257–58, 260–61, 266, 281
Smalley, B., 281
Soave-Bowe, C., 281
Socrates, 230
Solerti, A., 281

Solomon, 77, 174, 186, 199, 206–7, 240
Sordello, 63, 67, 96, 98ff., 212, 241–42, 244, 281
Sowell, M. U., 225, 274
Spain, 176, 262
Sparta, 108
Speroni, C., 244, 281
Spini family, 15
Spini, Simone Gherardi degli, 18
Spitzer, L., 173, 255, 282
Stambler, B., 232, 244, 282
Statius, 175, 179–80, 182, 195, 255, 257
Stefanini, R., 130, 244, 260, 282
Stella, R., 244, 282
Stickler, A. M., 249, 282
Strayer, J. R., 255–56, 264, 282
Styria, 103
Sumner, B., 220, 282
Sun, 128
Susa, 155
Sybil, 39, 204
Sylvester I, 22, 26, 138
Syracuse, 107, 239
Switzerland, 103

Tarassi, M., 279
Tarugi, G., 218, 282
Temple of Solomon, 174, 202, 250, 255
Thebes, 179–80, 256
Theodoric, 22
Theseus, 179–80
Thompson, D., 282
Thuringia, 162
Thomas, St. (Apostle), 89
Thomas, St. *See* Aquinas
Thompson, D., 231
Tiber, River, 129
Tiberius, 262
Tideus, 180
Tierney, B., 27, 218, 236, 243, 249, 250, 252, 256, 282
Titan, 44
Titus, 198
Toja, G., 90–91, 235, 282
Totila, 171
Toulouse, 111, 241
Touraine, 170
Trajan, 49, 65, 78, 82–84, 140–41, 143, 247
Treviso, 38, 111, 149
Trier, 41, 124

Trivet, Nicholas, 70
Trovato, M., 226, 282
Troy, 83, 134, 180
Troyes, 175
Turnus, 45
Tuscany, 17, 20, 21, 25, 28, 41–42, 45–46, 55, 85, 145–46, 171, 184, 223, 226, 237, 263

Ubaldini family, 21
Uberti, Farinata degli, 8, 21, 29, 99, 114, 210
Uberti, Lapo degli, 21
Uberti, Schiattuzzo degli, 5
Uberti, Uberto degli, 5
Ubertino da Casale, 14, 202, 218
Uc de Saint Circ, 111
Ugolino della Gherardesca, 97, 100–101, 248
Uguccione, 232
Ullmann, W., 215, 218, 239, 243, 249, 256, 282
Ulysses, 66, 75–76, 219, 230
Urban IV, 23, 85, 201
Utica, 69, 228
Uzzah, 51, 142, 247

Valli, L., 282
Vallone, A., 218, 282
Vasina, A., 248
Vasoli, C., 115, 242
Val di Chiana, 21
Valla, L., 22
Valli, L., 255
Vasoli, C., 115, 242, 282
Vatican, 100
Veltro, 254, 265
Veneto, 41
Venice, 58, 149

Venus, 128
Vernon, W. W., 235
Verona, 15, 21, 28, 34, 56, 58, 105, 111, 114, 237
Vicenza, 58
Vienne, 37, 176, 221
Villani Giovanni, viii, 4–5, 8, 11, 15, 29, 45–48, 56, 65, 124, 145, 163, 169–71, 176, 220, 222–23, 243, 248
Villeneuve, Romée de, 111
Vinay, G., 226, 246, 282
Vincent of Beauvais, 102
Virgil, vii, x, 37–40, 43, 45, 53, 64, 66, 69, 72–73, 75, 77, 83, 94, 96, 98–99, 104, 109–111, 114, 119, 126–28, 130–31, 133, 135–36, 139–40, 145, 147, 150–51, 159, 167, 179, 180–82, 196, 204, 206, 221–22, 228, 235, 239, 243, 253, 256–57, 261, 265–66
Visconti, Matteo, 57
Visconti, Nino, 96–97, 101
Vulcan, 75

Waley, D., 215, 238, 247, 282
Watt, J. A., 243, 249, 252, 282–83
Wenceslaus IV, 124
Whitfield, J. H., 231, 283
Widdows, P. F., 229
William of Holland, 162
William III, Marquis of Monferrato, 126
Williamson, E., 226, 246, 283
Wittkower, R., 245
Wolfram von Eschenbach, 259
Worms, 121

Zingarelli, N., 174

University of Pennsylvania Press
MIDDLE AGES SERIES
Ruth Mazo Karras and Edward Peters,
General Editors

F. R. P. Akehurst, trans. *The* Coutumes de Beauvaisis *of Philippe de Beaumanoir*. 1992

Peter L. Allen. *The Art of Love: Amatory Fiction from Ovid to the* Romance of the Rose. 1992

David Anderson. *Before the Knight's Tale: Imitation of Classical Epic in Boccaccio's Te-seida*. 1988

Benjamin Arnold. *Count and Bishop in Medieval Germany: A Study of Regional Power, 1100–1350.* 1991

Mark C. Bartusis. *The Late Byzantine Army: Arms and Society, 1204–1453.* 1992

Thomas N. Bisson, ed. *Cultures of Power: Lordship, Status, and Process in Twelfth-Century Europe.* 1995

Uta-Renate Blumenthal. *The Investiture Controversy: Church and Monarchy from the Ninth to the Twelfth Century.* 1988

Gerald A. Bond. *The Loving Subject: Desire, Eloquence, and Power in Romanesque France.* 1995

Daniel Bornstein, trans. *Dino Compagni's* Chronicle *of Florence*. 1986

Maureen Boulton. *The Song in the Story: Lyric Insertions in French Narrative Fiction, 1200–1400.* 1993

Charles R. Bowlus. *Franks, Moravians, and Magyars: The Struggle for the Middle Danube, 788–907.* 1995

Kevin Brownlee and Sylvia Huot, eds. *Rethinking the* Romance of the Rose*: Text, Image, Reception.* 1992

Matilda Tomaryn Bruckner. *Shaping Romance: Interpretation, Truth, and Closure in Twelfth-Century French Fictions.* 1993

Otto Brunner (Howard Kaminsky and James Van Horn Melton, eds. and trans.). Land *and Lordship: Structures of Governance in Medieval Austria.* 1992

Robert I. Burns, S.J., ed. *Emperor of Culture: Alfonso X the Learned of Castile and His Thirteenth-Century Renaissance.* 1990

David Burr. *Olivi and Franciscan Poverty: The Origins of the* Usus Pauper *Controversy.* 1989

David Burr. *Olivi's Peaceable Kingdom: A Reading of the Apocalypse Commentary.* 1993

Thomas Cable. *The English Alliterative Tradition.* 1991

Anthony K. Cassell and Victoria Kirkham, eds. and trans. *Diana's Hunt/Caccia di Diana: Boccaccio's First Fiction.* 1991

John C. Cavadini. *The Last Christology of the West: Adoptionism in Spain and Gaul, 785–820.* 1993

Brigitte Cazelles. *The Lady as Saint: A Collection of French Hagiographic Romances of the Thirteenth Century.* 1991

Karen Cherewatuk and Ulrike Wiethaus, eds. *Dear Sister: Medieval Women and the Epistolary Genre.* 1993

Anne L. Clark. *Elisabeth of Schönau: A Twelfth-Century Visionary.* 1992

Willene B. Clark and Meradith T. McMunn, eds. *Beasts and Birds of the Middle Ages: The Bestiary and Its Legacy.* 1989

Richard C. Dales. *The Scientific Achievement of the Middle Ages.* 1973

Charles T. Davis. *Dante's Italy and Other Essays.* 1984

William J. Dohar. *The Black Death and Pastoral Leadership: The Diocese of Hereford in the Fourteenth Century.* 1994

Judith Ferster. *Fictions of Advice: The Literature and Politics of Counsel in Late Medieval England.* 1996

Katherine Fischer Drew, trans. *The Burgundian Code.* 1972

Katherine Fischer Drew, trans. *The Laws of the Salian Franks.* 1991

Katherine Fischer Drew, trans. *The Lombard Laws.* 1973

Nancy Edwards. *The Archaeology of Early Medieval Ireland.* 1990

Richard K. Emmerson and Ronald B. Herzman. *The Apocalyptic Imagination in Medieval Literature.* 1992

Theodore Evergates. *Feudal Society in Medieval France: Documents from the County of Champagne.* 1993

Felipe Fernández-Armesto. *Before Columbus: Exploration and Colonization from the Mediterranean to the Atlantic, 1229–1492.* 1987

Pier Massimo Forni. *Adventures in Speech: Rhetoric and Narration in Boccaccio's Decameron.* 1996

Jerold C. Frakes. *Brides and Doom: Gender, Property, and Power in Medieval Women's Epic.* 1994

R. D. Fulk. *A History of Old English Meter.* 1992

Peter Heath. *Allegory and Philosophy in Avicenna (Ibn Sînâ), with a Translation of the Book of the Prophet Muḥammad's Ascent to Heaven.* 1992

John Bell Henneman. *Olivier de Clisson and Political Society Under Charles V and Charles VI.* 1996

J. N. Hillgarth, ed. *Christianity and Paganism, 350–750: The Conversion of Western Europe.* 1986

Richard C. Hoffman. *Land, Liberties, and Lordship in a Late Medieval Countryside: Agrarian Structures and Change in the Duchy of Wrocław.* 1990

John Y. B. Hood. *Aquinas and the Jews.* 1995

Edward B. Irving, Jr. *Rereading* Beowulf. 1989

Richard A. Jackson, ed. Ordines Coronationis Franciae: *Texts and Ordines for the Coronation of Frankish and French Kings and Queens in the Middle Ages, Vol. I.* 1995

C. Stephen Jaeger. *The Envy of Angels: Cathedral Schools and Social Ideals in Medieval Europe, 950–1200.* 1994

C. Stephen Jaeger. *The Origins of Courtliness: Civilizing Trends and the Formation of Courtly Ideals, 939–1210.* 1985

Richard W. Kaeuper and Elspeth Kennedy, trans. *Geoffroi de Charny and his* Livre de Chevalerie: *Study, Text, and Translation*. 1996

Donald J. Kagay, trans. *The Usatges of Barcelona: The Fundamental Law of Catalonia*. 1994

Richard Kay. *Dante's Christian Astrology*. 1994

Ellen E. Kittell. *From* Ad Hoc *to Routine: A Case Study in Medieval Bureaucracy*. 1991

Alan C. Kors and Edward Peters, eds. *Witchcraft in Europe, 1100–1700: A Documentary History*. 1972

Barbara M. Kreutz. *Before the Normans: Southern Italy in the Ninth and Tenth Centuries*. 1992

Michael P. Kuczynski. *Prophetic Song: The Psalms as Moral Discourse in Late Medieval England*. 1995

E. Ann Matter. *The Voice of My Beloved: The Song of Songs in Western Medieval Christianity*. 1990

Shannon McSheffrey. *Gender and Heresy: Women and Men in Lollard Communities, 1420–1530*. 1995

A. J. Minnis. *Medieval Theory of Authorship*. 1988

Lawrence Nees. *A Tainted Mantle: Hercules and the Classical Tradition at the Carolingian Court*. 1991

Lynn H. Nelson, trans. *The Chronicle of San Juan de la Peña: A Fourteenth-Century Official History of the Crown of Aragon*. 1991

Barbara Newman. *From Virile Woman to WomanChrist: Studies in Medieval Religion and Literature*. 1995

Thomas F. X. Noble. *The Republic of St. Peter: The Birth of the Papal State, 680–825*. 1984

Joseph F. O'Callaghan. *The Learned King: The Reign of Alfonso X of Castile*. 1993

Odo of Tournai (Irven M. Resnick, trans.). *Two Theological Treatises:* On Original Sin *and* A Disputation with the Jew, Leo, Concerning the Advent of Christ, the Son of God. 1994

David M. Olster. *Roman Defeat, Christian Response, and the Literary Construction of the Jew*. 1994

William D. Paden, ed. *The Voice of the Trobairitz: Perspectives on the Women Troubadours*. 1989

Edward Peters. *The Magician, the Witch, and the Law*. 1982

Edward Peters, ed. *Christian Society and the Crusades, 1198–1229: Sources in Translation, including* The Capture of Damietta *by Oliver of Paderborn*. 1971

Edward Peters, ed. *The First Crusade: The* Chronicle of Fulcher of Chartres *and Other Source Materials*. 1971

Edward Peters, ed. *Heresy and Authority in Medieval Europe*. 1980

James M. Powell. *Albertanus of Brescia: The Pursuit of Happiness in the Early Thirteenth Century*. 1992

James M. Powell. *Anatomy of a Crusade, 1213–1221*. 1986

Susan A. Rabe. *Faith, Art, and Politics at Saint-Riquier: The Symbolic Vision of Angilbert*. 1995

Jean Renart (Patricia Terry and Nancy Vine Durling, trans.). *The Romance of the Rose or Guillaume de Dole*. 1993

Michael Resler, trans. Erec *by Hartmann von Aue*. 1987

Pierre Riché (Michael Idomir Allen, trans.). *The Carolingians: A Family Who Forged Europe*. 1993

Pierre Riché (Jo Ann McNamara, trans.). *Daily Life in the World of Charlemagne*. 1978

Jonathan Riley-Smith. *The First Crusade and the Idea of Crusading*. 1986

Joel T. Rosenthal. *Patriarchy and Families of Privilege in Fifteenth-Century England*. 1991

Teofilo F. Ruiz. *Crisis and Continuity: Land and Town in Late Medieval Castile*. 1994

James A. Rushing, Jr. *Images of Adventure: Ywain in the Visual Arts*. 1995

James A. Schultz. *The Knowledge of Childhood in the German Middle Ages, 1100–1350*. 1995

John A. Scott. *Dante's Political Purgatory*. 1996

Pamela Sheingorn, ed. and trans. *The Book of Sainte Foy*. 1995

Robin Chapman Stacey. *The Road to Judgment: From Custom to Court in Medieval Ireland and Wales*. 1994

Sarah Stanbury. *Seeing the* Gawain-*Poet: Description and the Act of Perception*. 1992

Robert D. Stevick. *The Earliest Irish and English Bookarts: Visual and Poetic Forms Before* A.D. *1000*. 1994

Thomas C. Stillinger. *The Song of Troilus: Lyric Authority in the Medieval Book*. 1992

Susan Mosher Stuard. *A State of Deference: Ragusa/Dubrovnik in the Medieval Centuries*. 1992

Susan Mosher Stuard, ed. *Women in Medieval History and Historiography*. 1987

Susan Mosher Stuard, ed. *Women in Medieval Society*. 1976

Jonathan Sumption. *The Hundred Years War: Trial by Battle*. 1992

Ronald E. Surtz. *The Mothers of Saint Teresa of Avila: Female Religious Voices from the Late Medieval to Early Modern Spain*. 1995

Del Sweeney, ed. *Agriculture in the Middle Ages: Technology, Practice, and Representation*. 1995

William H. TeBrake. *A Plague of Insurrection: Popular Politics and Peasant Revolt in Flanders, 1323–1328*. 1993

Patricia Terry, trans. *Poems of the Elder Edda*. 1990

Hugh M. Thomas. *Vassals, Heiresses, Crusaders, and Thugs: The Gentry of Angevin Yorkshire, 1154–1216*. 1993

Mary F. Wack. *Lovesickness in the Middle Ages: The* Viaticum *and Its Commentaries*. 1990

Benedicta Ward. *Miracles and the Medieval Mind: Theory, Record, and Event, 1000–1215*. 1982

Suzanne Fonay Wemple. *Women in Frankish Society: Marriage and the Cloister, 500–900*. 1981

Kenneth Baxter Wolf. *Making History: The Normans and Their Historians in Eleventh-Century Italy*. 1995

Jan M. Ziolkowski. *Talking Animals: Medieval Latin Beast Poetry, 750–1150*. 1993

This book has been set in Galliard. Galliard was designed for Mergenthaler in 1978 by Matthew Carter. Galliard retains many of the features of a sixteenth-century typeface cut by Robert Granjon but has some modifications that give it a more contemporary look.

Printed on acid-free paper.